LEGAL PROGRAMMING:
Designing Legally Compliant RFID and Software Agent Architectures for Retail Processes and Beyond

INTEGRATED SERIES IN INFORMATION SYSTEMS

Series Editors

Professor Ramesh Sharda
Oklahoma State University

Prof. Dr. Stefan Voß
Universität Hamburg

Other published titles in the series:

LEGAL PROGRAMMING:
Designing Legally Compliant RFID and Software Agent Architectures for Retail Processes and Beyond

Brian Subirana

Malcolm Bain

Brian Subirana
MIT, Cambridge, MA
USA

Malcolm Bain
IESE Business School
Barcelona, Spain

Library of Congress Cataloging-in-Publication Data
A C.I.P. Catalogue record for this book is available
from the Library of Congress.

ISBN 0-387-23414-4   e-ISBN 0-387-23415-2   Printed on acid-free paper.

Printed in the United States of America.

9 8 7 6 5 4 3 2 1   SPIN 11052852

springeronline.com

Dedication

This book is dedicated to:

B. Subirana to Mercedes Vilanova Ribas

M. Bain to Natacha Rodríguez Jorro

Contents

List of Figures

List of Tables

Contributing Authors

Brian Subirana, Associate Professor at IESE Business School

Visiting Associate Professor of RFID, Auto-ID Laboratory and MIT Department of Mechanical Engineering.

Visiting Associate Professor of Information Technologies at the Center for Coordination Science of the MIT Sloan School of Management.

Corresponding author:

subirana@iese.edu, subirana@mit.edu.

IESE Business School, Avda Pearson 21, 08034 Barcelona

MIT Auto-ID Laboratory, Building NE46-6th Floor, 400 Technology Square, Cambridge, MA 02139

Center for Coordination Science, Sloan School of Management, 3 Cambridge Center, MIT NE20-336, Cambridge, MA 02142, USA

Prof. B. Subirana holds a PhD in Computer Science from the AI Lab at MIT and an MBA from MIT Sloan where he has been Visiting Associate Professor in 2002, 2003 and 2004. Since 2004 he is also Visiting Associate Professor at the MIT Department of Mechanical Engineering. Prior to joining IESE, he was with The Boston Consulting Group. With over 200 publications, his research focuses on the computational modeling of firms including the MIT Process Handbook, Auto-ID/RFID, E-contracting; advanced learning technologies; and on the role of the CEO in Information Technology.

Malcolm Bain

M. Bain is an English solicitor, with a Masters Degree in International Studies (European Law specialty). His work experience includes 4 years in a City law firm in London and 3 years in an IT firm and recently as researcher for IESE Business School, working on ICT law and Information Society research projects, including ecommerce platforms, distributed systems and software agents. He has also taught English Legal System and Legal Translation at graduate level.

Preface

What would we show somebody who awoke from 500 years' sleep to illustrate life at the beginning of the 21st century?

One possibility would be to have her stand in the junction of Massachusetts Ave and Memorial Drive in Cambridge, MA. She would see vehicles of all types, including lorries carrying boxes, pallets, bottles or tin cans; tarmac streets and slim metal bridges; sailing, rowing or motor boats on the river; cables over and under the streets for electricity and telephones; and people in today's latest fashion, including fancy running shoes with lights on their heels and cell phone watches. Focusing in on nearby stores, she might see shoppers wandering around the shelves, listening to music on mp3 players through headphones, and the cashier running up the bill on the automatic till, complete with keyboard and computer screen.

The different details of this view would provide insights into society today, and recent and not so recent history in science and engineering, new businesses and lifestyles. From the motor engine to cars, planes and personal transport. From electricity to telephones to the Internet. From calculators to computers and PDAs. From local shops to large superstores – specialist or general purpose–, including cash and carry and home delivery. A similar view from Piazza San Marco in 15th century Venice or Leicester Square in the 19th century London would also have this special power to provide an understanding of society at that particular time.

What could we do if we wanted to understand how the world may be in the future? The store or shopping mall today is a meeting place and emblematic of our current lifestyle. Like the person at the crossroads looking at her close surroundings, we could sit in a future grocery store trolley and consider life within the shop. We could simply sit there and look at a few specific processes: advertising and making special offers, consulting product details, looking for complementary items, comparing brands. Just as the view on Harvard Bridge can reveal wider aspects of today's society, the store's processes are like a lens showing what the future will be like in a more general way.

Through this lens, we can see and try to understand a section of future lifestyles and of the world: new technologies, new processes, new attitudes.

This is what we have done in this work, focusing on a few select shopping processes, supported by emerging agent-based computing technologies linked to RFID-enhanced objects and environment, to act as our lens for the future.

As part of this quest for understanding, we have considered the alignment and compliance of these shopping processes with the current and emerging legal framework. The law, as the collection of normative precepts underlying the structure and interactions of society, not only establishes the regulatory framework of this future, but also creates a series of hurdles and challenges, risks and opportunities to get there. The law will directly affect the design and structure of this near future, both for the development and programming of hardware and software (in our case, for grocery shopping), and also for the business and social processes supported by these technologies.

We have considered four particular areas of law that define the behaviour of actors within this view "from-the-store-trolley": contract law covering buying and selling processes, intellectual property rights for the protection of digital materials and content, and consumer and privacy protections that regulate the interactions between businesses and individuals, and are fundamental for achieving trust in what has been called the Information Society.

These laws may determine certain constraints – and opportunities – for business and technical processes in the future. An easy example: many potential applications for agent technology will involve the identification of users and the use of their personal data by merchants or other organisations. We could cite payment authentication agents, or customisation agents for merchants to maintain details of customer purchases for targeted marketing and personalised assistance during the shopping experience. From a legal perspective the collection, storage and processing of this data, not to mention the transferring of the data to third parties for synergies with profiling and other marketing activities, raise serious issues as regards the privacy of individuals and the invasion of their private lives. They may also constitute breach of personal data protection rules under European and national legislation. The design of these processes and the development of supporting technologies (e.g. software agents) will have to take these rules into account.

In this research, we have learned a number of things. Among them, we have learned that while almost all on-line commercial activities and related processes may on the whole be illegal, agent-based transactions in RFID-augmented environments will expose businesses and individuals to higher levels of risk – while providing a glimpse of how certain obstacles created by the digitisation of society may be overcome. Our research has also shown that the hurdles towards regulatory compliance and trust in future and emerging technologies can be usefully analysed with a process view. This view provides a level of abstraction where the mismatch between law and technology may potentially be reconciled.

This work has not only led us to outline the legal risks for certain shopping processes in this not-too-distant future scenario, it has also enabled us to determine certain next steps for research in this area. On the one hand, the creation of a formal taxonomy of high level concepts that are legally and technically meaningful, together with the development of legal programming methodology and technologies. On the other, widening the sphere of interest, we believe that research should aim to develop unified view of the firm so that it can act as a lens not just for the legal aspects of society but also for understanding business and technological evolution.

Foreword

The ability to express and apply law to specific facts requires intelligence. This is true both of humans and computers. Though a challenging problem, there are computer systems today that show it can be done.

But it is genius to show with simplicity how people can structure their activities in light of the law to achieve their goals at work, home and in life generally. Such is the task Brian Subirana and Malcolm Bain have undertaken in this book, and they have succeeded in pointing the way for those that follow.

The approach to legal programming proposed in this book provides a workable, generic and reusable process. Subirana and Bain show how legal principles can be modeled and digitally codified in a standardized method. This process paints a picture of a future where the law can be directly supported and reflected in transactional systems, reducing the costs and delays of regulatory compliance, avoiding the harms these laws were created to combat, and enhancing the property protection, privacy and other freedoms and rights people expect. A vision of cross-border, efficient, real-time, interoperable systems of commerce, trade and business is made possible, with a sense of compelling nearness.

As nations teeter on the edge of the information age, it is becoming clear that as yet unimagined technologies, professions and entire economic sectors will soon emerge. Examples from the dawning of the industrial age illustrate this: electricity lead to mass production; the automobile lead to suburbia; the telephone lead to teleworking, etc In all these examples they entirely transformed industries and formed new economic, political, social and legal regimes that followed.

In previous global economic transformations, the law has kept pace by supporting and reflecting the underlying changes. The underlying principles of contract law have been applied by judges, attorneys and the parties to their newly emerging circumstances.

For example, several contract principles have been unchanged but applied in novel ways to novel facts from agrarian, to industrial scenarios, to pen and seal, to typed name, and now to any "symbol, sound or process".

Now, however, at the advent of the digital society, the law will not merely be applied to novel situations, it will itself be revolutionized by digital technology. MIT coined the view that computer code can itself be a form of law, by structuring the rights and responsibilities of users of systems.

In many ways directions markup languages in the legal arena, point out several ways in which computer code is in fact becoming de facto or de jure law. Now, it can also be said we are seeing the start of law addressing itself directly to computer systems and code. With RFID, Auto-ID, EPC and ubiquitous intelligence, there is an increasing opportunity for law makers to enact statutes and regulations that read like computer code. For example, one can point out the specific system requirements in various e-Banking regulations, eCommerce and digital signature statutes and extrapole a point of intersection where the law will be enacted as code or as models of code, perhaps according to the types of programming models and languages Subirana and Bain propose.

Daniel Greenwood, Esq
Lecturer, MIT
Director, MIT E-Commerce Architecture Program

Chapter 1

INTRODUCTION

Almost all on-line activities are illegal...

And so when men have both done and suffered injustice and have had experience of both, not being able to avoid the one and obtain the other, they think that they had better agree among themselves to have neither; hence there arise laws and mutual covenants.
Plato's Republic, Book 2. (Glaucon)

1. INTERNET TECHNOLOGIES AND THE LAW

1.1 Almost all online business activities are illegal

From many viewpoints, most commercial online transactions do not comply with the law and, even if they do, they generally fail to meet users' expectations in various ways. Recent examples of infringements include the invalidity of browser-wrap contracts in certain circumstances, multiple cases of breaches of European data protection requirements in relation to the collection and security of storage of personal data during the course of transactions, or the non-collection or payment of tax (VAT or Sales Tax) on cross border or interstate transactions.

These transactions are also carried out in a way which does not reflect the desires of the negotiating parties. For example, weaker or more technically lacking parties (usually buyers) generally have to accept the terms of the other party (seller). In Business to Consumer (B2C) ecommerce, this is in fact close to a real world store transaction, where shoppers are basically required to purchase goods subject to the store's terms and conditions. However in the real-world business to business (B2B) context most contracts are individually negotiated to achieve a balance of risk and allocation of liability. This is often not the case in B2B ecommerce.

In addition, online transactions rarely satisfy lower level non-binding but still valid standards of conduct, good faith and, in the consumer context, fair trading[1]. While some of these norms are indeed legislated in certain jurisdictions (for example, good faith obligations in negotiations in some European continental jurisdictions), they are often only contained in sector codes of conduct, like the direct marketing association's codes. Non-binding "norms" in the area of the marketing and sale of goods and services online (including spam emails - unsolicited commercial communications, in European legal language, which have now been regulated -, and banners, pop-ups, etc.), secondary actions involving the collection and use of personal data (the planting of cookies, web-bugs, etc.), and regarding the exclusion of liability and the provision of warranties or guarantees, are also widely flouted by online commerce platforms.

From a theoretical economic point of view, it can also be argued that these transactions lack efficiency due to the failure to fulfil participant expectations and demands. That is to say, parties have to accept what is technically feasible or technically required by online commerce platforms, but which is not necessarily the most economically efficient for them. This creates higher transaction costs than necessary.

Despite all its promises of efficiency and cost reduction, much of ecommerce seems therefore to break the laws of the market and society as well as the laws under the constitution.

In this, we are not just referring to the legal issues surrounding the technologies that underlie the Internet and World Wide Web (WWW) and create the network architecture and framework for ecommerce: these have their own separate legal issues. The Domain Name System is bedevilled with problems of cyber-squatting, typo-squatting, competing and non-competing uses of domain names, reverse hijacking and free speech, and overall governance issues. The patenting of technology and business methods, i.e. of protocols and standards, software applications and ecommerce models (e.g. "One click" shopping, information downloading, etc.), is still debated and is currently seen as an obstacle to technical and commercial development. The simple use of hyperlinks is considered a violation by some parties (especially deep-linking or in-lining links), an infringement of intellectual property rights, trademarks, database rights, trespass or unfair competition (see Table 1 below).

---

[1] What L Lessig might call market or social "norms" in *Code*, 1999. Some good faith and fair trading principles are indeed binding in certain European jurisdictions, but we refer here to the slightly greyer area of trading standards.

Table 1-1. Some legal issues relating to the Internet architecture

Linking: While no case seems to be definitive on the question, examples of hyperlink cases include the following[2]. In *Ticketmaster v. Tickets.com*, a California court decided that hyperlink from one website to another does not constitute copyright infringement: "deep linking by itself... does not necessarily involve unfair competition". It was argued that hypertext linking is not per se illegal if "consumers understand whose site they are on and that one company has not simply duplicated another's page", however when it is coupled with other business practices, it may be improper (e.g. anti-competitive practices). This was what happened in *E-bay v. Bidder's Edge*, where Bidder's Edge robots continuously searched and linked to E-bay's site to provide auction information to users and overloaded of E-bay site's servers

Deeplinking: In *Danske Dagblades Forening v. Newsbooster.com*, a Danish court declared that Newsbooster violated copyright laws by "deep linking" to newspaper articles of the Danish Newspaper Publishers´ Association and ordered Newsbooster to stop linking, bypassing the front page (with advertising revenue). Its service was competing directly with the newspapers and "eroded the value of banner advertising on their website", in breach of the Danish Copyright Act and the Danish Marketing Act. In December 2000, StepStone, an on-line recruitment company, obtained a court order in Germany under implementation of the EU copyright and database regulations preventing OFiR, a Danish rival from deep-linking to StepStone's job advertisements. StepStone argued this linking to be prejudicial to its brand position in the long term, and visitors were not taken to the home page and therefore did not see its banner advertising

Framing: In *Kelly v. Arriba*, in San Francisco in February 2002, the Court of Appeals held that a search engine that linked to copyrighted material by "framing" it in a new browser window (directly linked to the referring site) infringed the copyright owner's rights.

Exemptions: In August 2000, in *PCM v. Kranten.com*, an Amsterdam court ruled in support of deep linking in a case where one news site was linking to stories on other web sites of various newspapers. While the plaintiff argued that the links would bypass the branding and advertising on the home page of its web site, the court decided that deep linking to other sites is a widespread and commonly accepted practice on the Internet and that, under copyright law, there is an exception to copying for the reporting of current events, provided there is sufficient acknowledgement. In March 2003 a Spanish court denied penalties against *ajoderse.com* for linking to illegal content, as it could not be proved that the website had knowledge of the illegality of the linked page. While in Napster it was held that the system directly infringed copyright, providing and encouraging links to infringing materials (and indirectly facilitating individual file sharers' copyright infringement), recently (April 2003) *Grokster* and *Morpheus* – with a more decentralised system - were held exempt of liability for not contributing to or authorizing it.

---

[2] See for example: M Sableman: *Link Law Revisited: Internet Linking Law at Five Years*, 2001.

Database protection

In *Mainpost v Newsclub*, Munich's Upper Court held that using a search engine to locate stories on newspapers' sites violates European Union database protection law. NewsClub was accused of searching through and linking directly to Mainpost content which the court held was entitled to database protections. The actions of Newsclub led a systematic and repeated reproduction of immaterial parts of the database, an act which unreasonably violates the rights of the database producer.

Trademark protection

In *Shetland Times v. Wills*, it was held that trademarks use of third party trademarks to link to other sites could constitute a breach of the trademark protections. In *Playboy Enterprises Inc. v. Welles* Playboy objected to the use of its trademark in the webpage of one of its models, and there have been several cases of using competitors trademarks as website tags (metatags) or in invisible print, so they are picked up by search engines (*Road Tech Computer Systems v. Mandata (Management & Data Services) Limited*).

What we are discussing are simple commercial (and also non-commercial) activities carried out within this imperfect technological framework. Despite recent attempts to comply with relevant laws – enhanced privacy policies and statements, improved contracting processes, encryption and digital signatures for confidentiality and security, etc. – there are many specific instances of potential and real violations that occur during the course of any commercial transaction. These include accessing and extracting contents from online databases, the reproduction and distribution of protected or confidential materials, the conclusion of certain contracts where parties have not been informed of their rights, or attempts to remove or restrict rights that cannot be limited. This latter, for instance, is most evident in consumer transactions and is highlighted by the use of standard form "click-wrap" contracts.

Let us make a fairly extended example in the consumer context. Take a simple transaction such as an online purchase by a consumer of a book, CD, holiday or travel ticket. The following list sets out several different actions that could constitute a breach of regulation, market or social norms:

- The seller's platform[3] collects transmission related data ("traffic data": headers, clickstream data) that, if linked with personal data provided by the user, will start to create a user profile. Processing of such data may be restricted by data protection regulations.
- The seller's website plants a cookie on the user's equipment, allegedly for technical reasons. This cookie can send web-surfing (traffic) and other information back to the original website or to third party sites. The user is not informed of the reasons and processes of the cookie. The webpage

---

[3] We use the word "platform" for online commerce applications: this is principally a seller's web-site, but it is more than that, as it can include non-website based computing elements, such as the back-office components, where many transaction related processes are carried out.

may also contain web-bugs that can also be used for monitoring user data and activities

– The procedure for online contracting is not always clear though superficially obvious: "click here" to agree to a contract. In fact, consumers will probably find in the terms and conditions that the "I agree" or "I accept" button is only really an "I make an offer - and maybe the site will accept" button… in one jurisdiction (e.g. in the UK) while in another (e.g. Spain) sufficient description and clarity of terms may indicate that indeed the I Agree button is the final step for the conclusion of a contract.

– The seller's website collects personal data from the user (name, address, credit card numbers), over which the user has no further control. Most web site privacy statements relating to the use of this data are insufficient for the purposes of informing the data subject and obtaining properly informed consent. In addition, the consumer has little guarantee that the collecting enterprise will respect its own policy - or that parties to whom it transfers such data will also do so[4].

– The ISP may use the personal data in many ways that breach both the data protection regulation and the ISP's own privacy declaration: this includes automatic processing and transfers and sales of data to third parties or through jurisdictions which provide little or no personal data protection.

– The website does not contain a clear statement of the Information Society Service Provider (ISSP), its contact details, VAT registration number, etc. in accordance with the EC Ecommerce Directive.

– The website does not contain sufficient description of products and services offered, either to comply with consumer protection requirements or generally to give the consumers the information they want or need (misleading, insufficient, etc.). In addition, prices may not be what they seem to be, especially for mistaken special offers[5] and additional transaction costs (charges, transport, etc.)

– The user has to agree to unilateral (non-negotiated) contractual terms, that often include exemptions and restrictions that may be (a) invalid due to unfairness or (b) not acceptable to the user. Often such contractual terms are difficult to find and the user rarely reads them before entering into the online agreement.

– The transaction may not be recorded in such a way as to comply with legal requirements (e.g. set out in the EU Ecommerce Directive) or recommended information management procedures guaranteeing

---

[4] Despite efforts of trustmarks and other web quality seals for online trading.
[5] See for example, the problems of Argos when they advertised TVs at GBP 2.99, or Kodak commented in "Kodak snaps under customer pressure", ZDNet UK, 31.012002.

integrity and authenticity sufficient to satisfy legal requirements for evidence presented in court.

- The participants in the transaction may not be who they say they are, raising a problem of identification and authentication (that may partially be solved by digital signatures, which have not been taken up by the public in any degree). While the consumer may wish to maintain his or her anonymity (admittedly not possible in the purchase of a flight, where the passenger must be named, but in clear opposition to real world store sales where cash transactions guarantee anonymity), the website itself may be a "spoof", i.e. it is not who it says it is but some third party representing to be the airline / travel site in question, permitting various forms of Identity theft.
- The website may use images or text whose use may breach intellectual property rights of the original right holder, by copying, distributing, etc. The user may download such materials (content) and also copy, distribute and publish the data.
- The website's owner or Internet Service Provider may wish to apply the laws of its jurisdiction to the sale and have recourse to the courts of its country, whereas throughout Europe at least and in many other jurisdictions, the local courts will be competent and will apply local mandatory laws if they are more favourable[6].

This example is not aimed to scare the reader, as many of these problems are well known and have certain easy forms of redress; however it illustrates our argument that many online transactions, while seemingly acceptable, can and indeed do infringe a variety of applicable laws and other commercial and social norms – the Glaucon's *laws and mutual covenants* cited above.

Several recent and not so recent cases provide real examples of the above (see Table 1.2).

Table 1-2. Online commerce risks

Online Commerce risks
Cookie risks
While cookies are small files planted in your computer allegedly to assist browsing, they can collect, store and transmit considerable amounts of personal and confidential data to controllers. Another risk involves capturing a copy of the victim's browser cookies file, and reading cookies containing passwords to access web-mail files. - http://www.wired.com/news/technology/0,1282,52115,00.html
Procedure for online contracting, incorporation of terms and error correction It is still not clear whether a website will be construed as an advertisement (or invitation to treat, in English law) or a full offer, depending on the certainty of the terms and the jurisdiction and applicable law of the case. Mistakes in websites may bind ISSPs, debated (but not resolved as the case was settled) in the Argos case, when they advertised TVs at

---

[6] Under the Brussels Convention (now an EU Regulation, No 44/2001 of 22 December 2000.) and the Rome Convention 1980 on Applicable law.

Online Commerce risks

GBP 2.99. Kodak also offered cameras a low cost, and agreed to provide the cameras at ridiculously low prices[7]. In Germany, the Hamburg Regional Court (3 U 168/00 - 13/06/02) held that sending contractual and conditions via e-mail to a buyer cannot replace the seller adequately positioning those conditions terms on the website. The court held that terms and conditions must be present on a trader's website in such a way so that they are clearly visible to a website user, who could not be expected to search the website for such terms[8].

Collection and use of personal data

Amazon was to revise its privacy policy in response to concerns raised by customers, consumer groups and US regulators, clarifying the circumstances under which it might sell or share customer information. Under that policy, Amazon warned customers that it might transfer its personal data "in the unlikely event" that the company or its assets were acquired. Previously, the company said it would not "sell, trade or rent your personal information to others" and did not make an exception for the case of a transfer of business control. It is argued that this revision did not resolve the primary "inadequacies" of the policy: Amazon still holds the option of selling its customer database, refuses to give customers access to all the data it holds on them and refuses to delete their past purchase records.

In Spain, various Internet based companies have been forced to close due to the heavy fines – up to 300.000 Euros - levied by the Data Protection Agency, including for example Guía Empresas Internet SL for having sent advertising and publicity emails to individuals, and selling email addresses to third parties.

Unilateral (non-negotiated) contractual terms, incorporation and enforcement

In *Bruce G. Forrest v. Verizon Communications In*, a US court dismissed the action based on the a forum stipulation in the "click wrap" contract that required dismissal of claims in Virginia unless authorized by statute, upholding the online contract, while in Canada, in *Kanitz v. Rogers Cable Inc* the court found that website notices may result in the binding amendment of a services contract, if sufficient notice is given (e.g. clearly on the main page). The Court held that customers were obliged to check relevant portions of the website from time to time to determine if service agreement amendments had been made. On the other hand, other courts have denied the effect of web terms, as the consumer did not have to view and "click through" them to download them. In *Comb v. PayPal Inc.*, a U.S. court decided that an arbitration clause was procedurally unconscionable because it was a contract of adhesion, imposed and drafted by a party of superior bargaining strength; it therefore could not be enforced. In *Specht v. Netscape Communications Corp* the court ruled that an arbitration clause was unenforceable because Netscape failed to notify and properly obtain the users' assent to the terms (a "browse-wrap", where the user has to browse the site in order to know the agreement exists). More recently, in *DeJohn v. TV Corporation International* the U.S. District Court upheld a click-wrap agreement as the terms were not so unconscionable, and contained in a link directly above the Accept button.

Consumer protection rules

In the UK, in April 2003 Victoria Wines was obliged to change its online terms and conditions, when an Office of Fair Trading investigation claimed that it breached Distance Selling Regulations (implementation of the DSD and EU Ecommerce Directive) on delivery and cancellation rights and attempted to limit its liability to consumers in unfair and

---

[7] Commented in "Kodak snaps under customer pressure", ZDNet UK, 31.012002
[8] See at http://www.jurpc.de/rechtspr/20020288.htm.

Online Commerce risks
unlawful ways.

Website design: pop-ups and banners
America Online announced in October 2002 that it would stop accepting third-party pop-up ads on its internet service, following complaints from customers who find them an "annoying interference" with their on-line experience. Weight Watchers sued USA Prescriptions Inc. because pop-up ads for its diet drugs appeared on WeightWatchers.com if users have "ad-ware" (such as Save Now or Gator) loaded in their computers delivering adverts with the user's consent. In the lawsuit, filed in a federal court in New York, Weight Watchers alleged trade mark infringement and dilution, and "systematically and unlawfully trade" on its brand, while compromising Weight Watchers reputation and deceiving consumers. In Germany, a Düsseldorf court has recently held that exit pop-ups constitute unfair competition and are equivalent to spam – unsolicited commercial communications – which would require users' consent.

Identification
The FTC Report: "National and State Trends in ID theft, 2003" states that complaints of ID theft more than doubled to 85,820 in 2002 from 31,113 in 2000, accounting for 43% of total complaints made.

Jurisdiction and applicable law
While not specifically aimed at online commercial transactions, several cases illustrate the problem of determining the jurisdiction and applicable law to an Internet process or action. In *LICRA v. Yahoo! Inc.*, the French court held that content online published by a US site, Yahoo!, infringed French anti-racism laws as it was displayable in France. In *Gutnick v. Dow Jones*, an Australian court asserted jurisdiction over a defamation dispute relating to content published on the US-based Dow Jones website.

Paradoxically, these cases may seem to contribute gradually - in a "Common Law" type of manner - to the creation of a body of law applied to activities carried out on the Internet. However tempting this may seem, this body is not mature, homogeneous or coherent. The scope of issues at stake – both technically, functionally and geographically – preclude the creation of a stable legal environment for the near future.

The rapidly evolving technology is one of the main factors of instability. IPv6 is a case in point[9]. This proposed protocol would identify (with an IP address) all devices connected to the network, including mainframes, PCs, WAP enabled mobile phones, intelligent objects (items with an RFID or other active electronic tag that could be connected, such as the vision of an intelligent refrigerator or home), and even persons wearing electronic chips. There would be no longer any need for dynamic IP addresses, as each item would be identified. This provides greater levels of certainty through potentially better identification. However, this technology is raising serious privacy issues, as personal objects would be identifiable by third parties, and individuals would lose a high degree of anonymity in relation to networked interactions. A consequence of this is that the speed of technological change

---

[9] See the IPv6 website at http://www.ipv6tf.org/ and Table 1.3.

may prevent legal stability in this body of law relating to privacy, certainly in the short term.

Table 1-3. IPv6

IPv6
A new protocol for Internet addresses is being discussed – and gradually implemented -, to deal with the increased number of computers connected to the Internet: IPv6. This protocol will increase the number of bites from 4 to 16, with 6 of the 16 dedicated to a serial number of the Ethernet card on the computer or device, providing embedded digital identification of all devices connected to the net. Users will not be able to avoid this device identification (for all purposes: browsing, emails, SMS, chats, etc.), as with no number, there is no address and therefore no connection. Many new addresses are likely to be assigned to a new breed of internet-capable devices such as mobile phones, car navigation systems, home appliances, industrial equipment and other electronic instruments, some of them holding or revealing highly personal or sensitive information, such as location or device usage. This could enable the tracking of individual devices and thus potentially users, similar to a digital fingerprint. There have been initiatives to specify extensions to enhance privacy in IPv6 (RFC 3041, *Privacy Extensions for Stateless Address Autoconfiguration in IPv6*).

Another technology that may create a revolution in the way certain business are run – specifically logistics and supply chain management but potentially any business and the Internet itself – is Radio Frequency Identification (RFID). RFID tags are devices that may be added to certain goods or packaging (including transport pallets and cases) and provide a unique electronic identification (Electronic Product Code or EPC) of the item in question. These tags may transmit this identification (and other data, depending on the sophistication of the tag[10]) to readers installed at certain points, for example at the entrance and exits of warehouses or motorways, on the retail floor or at supermarket check-out areas, or even on a shopping trolley. It has been said that these identification systems will create an "Internet of things", as all tagged products may communicate with worldwide IT networks. This EPC network will allow computers to automatically recognise and identify any object, and then track, trace, monitor, and set off specific actions in relation to those objects. While potentially enabling a whole series of business innovations and efficiencies such as reducing shrinkage in supply chains, delivery tracking and customer personalisation, just like IPv6, RFID has set off a serious debate about the legality of emerging technologies, as it has the potential to be "privacy invasive" through tracking and tracing objects (and money[11]) in individuals'

---

[10] Tags come in different sizes of data and may be active or passive. Passive tags are smaller and may only be read, while active tags have an internal power supply (battery) and are usually "read/ write" – i.e. their data may be updated over time.

[11] The European Central Bank is said to be still studying the possibility of integrating RFID tags in bank-notes. Yunko Yoshida: *Euro bank notes to embed RFID chips by 2005*, 2001 and Andreas Krisch: *RFIDs in Euro banknotes*, 2003.

possession. Again, we find a technology that has profound social and legal implications.

Other factors than technological change also contribute to legal uncertainty. The cross border nature of the Internet is a major element, as participants act and websites have effects in several jurisdictions. On the one hand different countries have varying approaches both to the level of legislation and regulation of the net (privacy being the prime example, though there may be some movements towards "equivalency", as the USA seems to be moving towards legislated rather than self-regulated privacy protection[12]) and to the actual content of that regulation. Compliance with all jurisdictions is practically impossible (leading to the principle of regulation at origin embodied in the EU Ecommerce Directive – but hotly debated now in the ambit of VAT, as the EU tries to impose taxation at destination on non-EU sellers). Moreover, there are decisions from different jurisdictions leading to conflicting results, in a context where websites are accessible and transactions feasible in multiple jurisdictions. The *Licra v. Yahoo! Inc.* case commented above illustrates this: while the French court found that displaying and auctioning Nazi memorabilia violated France's anti-racism laws, the US courts, having been asked to declare on the matter, held that this decision would not be enforceable in the USA as it would breach the principles of freedom of expression guaranteed by the US constitution.

In addition, legislation is being enacted that has much wider cross-border effects than before, questioning the traditional and established principles of conflict of law which determine which courts can hear a case, and which law is applicable (private international law). Examples include the European Data Protection Directive, which indirectly forces other countries to establish equivalent levels of data protection, if they want to trade electronically with the EU. Personal data originating in the EU may only be transmitted to third countries that provide adequate protection. Non EU companies wishing to do business in EU now have to establish a data centre in the EU that complies with local laws or set up at home procedures for data protection that comply sufficiently with the EU regulations (e.g. under the Safe Harbour Agreement[13]). This has the effect of exporting EU levels of personal data protection to third countries. Another law with extra-territorial effect is the US Anti-cybersquatting Consumer Protection Act (ACPA), dealing with cases of domain name cybersquatting. The ACPA, by treating

---

[12] For example, see list of bills in congress at <http://www.cdt.org/legislation/107th/privacy/> (visited 05/04/2003).

[13] An agreement between the European Commission and the US Department of Commerce whereby US companies that agree to abide by the Safe Harbour international privacy principles, offer sufficient levels of privacy protection so that personal data could be transferred from the EU to them without further regulatory authorisation (e.g. from Member States). See US Department of Commerce: Safe Harbor Privacy Principles 21.7.2000.

dot-com, dot-net, and dot-org domain names as property that can be sued *in rem*,[14] allows all such cases to be taken in Virginia, USA, where the root-server is, no matter where the domain name holder resides (e.g. in the Barcelona.com case[15]).

This monograph does not aim to debate the cross-border nature of ecommerce and how to solve these problems through harmonisation or private conflict of law provisions, nor the politics of regulation and self-regulation. Our point is that while this *corpus juris* is being created, parties concerned may not (yet) count on it for the levels of consistency, legal certainty and protection that are afforded by national and international laws applied to offline transactions. Thankfully, this won't and hasn't stopped entrepreneurs setting up Internet oriented businesses and ecommerce websites, however the manager responsible for creating a web-based commerce platform, the developer in charge of designing and programming it and the lawyer hired to audit the legality of the site, its processes and the transactions carried by the platform find themselves confronted by a variety of laws, regulations, soft laws, codes of conduct and other "requirements" with which to conform... or not.

This uncertainty has led to serious fears about ecommerce, certainly on behalf of consumers, and possibly to a slowdown in the general progress of ecommerce – hidden, maybe by the bursting of the dot-com bubble and the current general economic slowdown. Major consumer concerns are raised by breaches of privacy and online fraud, and consumers tend to transact with sites in their own jurisdiction, feeling safer, perhaps correctly, in the belief that either that their own country laws will protect them more, or that redress - if needed - will be simpler or cheaper to obtain. Attempts have been made to facilitate cross-border dispute resolution for Internet related transactions, with a host of online dispute resolution services including BBB.Online, the Virtual Magistrate and others. In the EU through these are supported by the e-confidence initiative[16], a common package of measures which include the promotion of high standards of good business practices (e.g. codes of conduct, trust marks, complaint settlement procedures), and easy and affordable access to third-party alternative dispute resolution (ADR) systems, in particular for settling disputes arising from the expected increase in cross-border transactions over the Internet.

---

[14] In US law, an action *in rem* means that the plaintiff is taking proceedings against a "thing" as opposed to a "person" (*in personam*), which is the normal means of making a legal claim.

[15] *Barcelona.com Inc. v. Excelentisimo Ayuntamiento de Barcelona* – citations are in the reference section at the end of this work.

[16] Online at http://econfidence.jrc.it and http://www.eejnet.org/ (a network of contact points or "Clearing Houses" which provides consumers with information on available ADR schemes).

The EC reports that Europeans are far behind Americans in usage of the Internet for B2C shopping, with only 4.7% of European *Internauts* regularly shopping online compared to 30% of Americans[17]. The EU report "Trust barriers for B2B e-marketplaces" highlights the protection of confidentiality of sensitive data (59.4% of interviewees) and the security of information systems (57.8%) as the main barriers for the use of e-marketplaces, while other worries include a lack of clear information on the terms and conditions of contracts (such as applicable law and jurisdiction - 56,3%), lack of information on the different steps for the conclusion of a contract (42%) or about the identity of the companies (37%) and uncertainties related to the settlement of disputes and on-line payments (48-50%)[18]. Nearly all these issues are legal issues, and may be solved by technical-legal procedures.

1.2   Ecommerce technologies and models are also illegal

1.2.1   Ecommerce technologies

We consider that most of these problems come from both technical and business processes of online commerce: on the one hand, the technological infrastructure of the Internet environment, and on the other the participants in the transaction, their capacities, attitudes and policies.

Apart from the Internet infrastructure technologies mentioned above that cause legal uncertainty – links, domain names, caches, – other aspects of digital technologies contribute to legal uncertainty. First and foremost, *Digitisation* is the root of most Intellectual Property Rights problems, through the capacity to create infinite perfect copies of digital works and distribute, modify or publish them throughout the world. This also includes the availability of digitisation technologies (scanners, video capture) to create digital copies of non digital works. *Technology models* (client-server computing and distributed systems) cause other legal concerns: it is often unclear where data transfers are made (e.g. from, to, in or through a certain jurisdiction?) nor who is responsible. There are a series of intermediaries (application service providers, Internet website hosts, etc.) who are technically involved in online transactions and are being targeted in Internet related cases for primary or contributory infringements. *Internet languages,* mainly HTML – a language that only understands formats but not contents – is also problematic, as machines cannot yet automatically understand that a

---

[17] E. Likkannen Speech: *Going Digital: Meeting the E-Business Challenge for Europe in the New Economy*, European Days of Commerce Conference Brussels, 4 December 2000.
[18] EU Open Consultation Report, *Trust barriers for B2B e-marketplaces,* 2002.

document is a contract, or a paragraph is a contract term[19]. *Protocols* are also problematic, as they let Internet actors obtain hidden data from users (e.g. click stream data), in violation of the notification and consent obligations protecting personal privacy.

On a slightly less technical note, Internet related *standardisation* initiatives – W3C, IETF, etc – rarely take into account legal issues, while standard software development *design methodologies* don't take into account legal requirements unless users specify such a step.

Finally, and more generally, the *law follows technology:* hyperlinks, cookies and web-bugs, domain names, cache and mirroring, click-wrap contracts, click-stream data, pop-up ads, RFID tags, all predate regulation and rules. Regulators start applying "old law for new technologies", then have catch up with technology and its multiple implementations through new legislation, and then cope with the delay between legislation and implementation – while technology moves on. The law also has to deal with technological and geographic variation and evolution of such non-compliant technologies or processes. One such attempt has been made in the EU, aiming to reach a level of abstraction to achieve technical neutrality, with the phrase "unsolicited commercial communications" for various forms of email, SMS or other "spam" (potentially, for example, banners and pop-ups).

There is also a reverse problem, that technology platforms need to meet moving legal standards: while version "1.0" may comply with the law on a certain date, further releases may be required to bring the application up to date within a changing legal framework. This may cause substantial interoperability issues over several platforms that may or may not be updated to the latest legal change. One of the key issues for future technology development will be how to manage and integrate "legal release control" into standard release management.

On top of the opportunities for abuse and the deficiencies of the technical infrastructure, the very models chosen for online commerce have not favoured compliance with the regulatory framework… when it existed.

1.2.2   Ecommerce Models

We argue that ecommerce has gone through two phases with two predominant commerce models: electronic data interchange (EDI), and electronic marketplaces (EM). EDI involves the electronic exchange of purchase orders and payments within a closed computer network, replacing the paper medium on which trade data were traditionally communicated by structured computer-to-computer transfer. Processes were structured by

---

[19] This is being remedied by the semantic web efforts, whereby Internet content will be tagged for meaning and not just format. See www.semanticweb.org for more details on this, and our conclusions in Chapter 6.

trading partner agreements, which determined if not all, at least most aspects of data interchange and their legal validity between the parties. EMs establish an Internet based framework for connecting the many providers of a certain product with the many clients that want to purchase it. Products and prices may vary depending on each transaction, and often terms are dictated by either the seller website (seller-sponsored EM) or the EM's general terms of business.

Online commerce is now proceeding through a third: transaction streams, which may be defined as electronic markets in which more than one player are involved in the transaction process[20]. Transaction streams model how transactions on the Internet are actually being conducted – through a variety of intermediaries – and help explain the types of these new intermediaries that are appearing on the Internet.

Within these models, electronic commercial transactions are described as either hierarchical (within an established framework) or market-based (open participants, open parameters), and the appropriateness of one or other may depend on the products in question[21]. In hierarchical transactions, most technical and legal matters are determined beforehand, e.g. within a project specification and a framework contract. This would be the example of EDI and most B2B platforms for EMs today. These are usually product- or sector-specific (Airlines, Chemicals, etc.) with close and even "closed" business relationships. Markets, and most B2C websites, on the other hand, are open to all comers. They will require extra mechanisms for "creating a context", providing stability and trust through a variety of support services.

In the case of EDI, careful legal frameworks (including a UNCITRAL draft Model Law which became the Model Law on Ecommerce[22]) have been set up to deal with legal issues[23], including provisions for contractual validity and electronic consent, evidence and dispute resolution. Open online trading and EMs, on the other hand, have signalled a breakdown in legal compliance, involving some of the infringements and problems mentioned above. The move from closed-circuit EDI (with overall process standardisation and management of documents and risks) to open EM has therefore led to the boom in legal issues raised by electronic transactions.

Several characteristics of the open web models such as EMs and transaction streams create legal problems:

---

[20] B Subirana, *Transactions streams and value added: sustainable business models on the Internet*, 1998.

[21] T Malone et al, *Electronic markets and electronic hierarchies*, 1987; Dignum and C. Sierra (Eds.) *Agent-mediated Electronic commerce (The European AgentLink Perspective)*, 2000.

[22] United Nations Commission on International Trade Law, UN General Assembly Resolution 51/162 Of 16 December 1996.

[23] Georgios I Zekos, *EDI: Electronic Techniques of EDI, Legal Problems and European Union Law*, 1999.

- Underlying attitudes to enterprise: under a "do first, then sort out the legal issues" attitude, electronic processes acquired standards and protocols (for presentation of data exchange, for contractual processes) that are not necessarily legal, even in more flexible regimes such as in the USA and less so in more protective continental jurisdictions.
- The speed of web platforms design: in most online commerce platforms, priority is given to business functionalities. Legally important considerations such as consumer protection, applicable laws, privacy controls are not generally considered, or are included post facto.
- A philosophy of personalisation or customisation: one of the main business advantages and indeed revenue streams of online commerce has been based on obtaining personal data from clients to provide improved personalised services and products. This has led to the unnecessary collection of too much personal data, low security standards (cutting costs, not incorporating security processes in the initial designs) and temptation to abuse the processing and transfer use of the data, for instance through reselling to other Internet participants (advertisers, other companies).
- The non interactive nature of web platforms: Despite claims for personalisation and interactivity, websites establish commercial transactions on standard legal terms: this doesn't even involve the traditional "battle of the forms". The description of interactivity is misleading in a legal context: there is no interaction regarding contracting process or data collection: accept our cookie or do not enter the site. Accept our standard terms or do not contract with us or participate in our B2B platform are typical policies.
- Low revenue streams: as online traders realise that ecommerce provides low revenue streams, the income from indirect sources such as sale of personal data becomes highly relevant. In addition, there is the financial instability and fragility of ecommerce companies, whereby when they fail their client databases are transferred to third parties, against the consent of the data subjects.

Transaction streams multiply these difficulties, as direct contractual relationships are clouded, and responsibilities and chains of liability are difficult to determine. Within these models, transaction processes are more complex, they involve more players and more data is being transferred. This raises the quantity and quality of legal issues at stake, as these are linked to the number of parties involved and the data transferred.

1.2.3   Trading frameworks and Web-Service models

At an intermediate position between hierarchies and markets, we see the development of standardised trading frameworks (web-services, UDDI[24], ebXML[25], ICC, RosettaNet[26], e-Speak[27]). These involve industry supported frameworks for providing determined (commercial) services over the open network. Web services are business and consumer applications - that users can choose and combine to obtain a simple or more complex service. They use a set of common protocols and standards allowing different systems to automatically communicate with one another (to share data and services)[28]. This is envisaged to include commercial or technical services like processing power, storage space or goods delivery but could even include negotiation frameworks, contracting protocols, reputation systems and representation or online dispute resolution. EbXML, for example, establishes standard protocols for business relationships, with registries, protocol and contract templates.

It is still early to determine the extent to which such frameworks may comply with the law, and this has not been the focus of our work. Generally speaking, they are standardised and conceptually centralised systems (a contract template and repository imply that contracting is carried out on standard terms). This means that most legal issues should be elucidated and specified from the start, and that – unless a higher degree of flexibility is engaged than currently conceived – single jurisdiction (e.g. USA) law will apply to most commerce transactions carried out within these systems. This may eventually come into conflict with national laws in other countries. However most of these systems are aimed at business to business ecommerce, where the principle of party autonomy allows a high degree of flexibility and self-regulation.

We will see below that web services may be implemented through agent technologies, where applications and users can be represented by agents negotiating for services on the Internet[29]. We now briefly look at agent technologies, and then we shall introduce agent mediated electronic commerce.

---

[24] Universal Description, Discovery and Integration is a yellow pages service for web-services. Information available at http://uddi.org/pubs/UDDI-V3.00-Open-Draft-20020703.htm

[25] See description and specifications at www.ebxml.org

[26] See description and specifications at http://www.rosettanet.org

[27] Now called HP Web Services Platform 2.0 at www.hp.com/go/espeak

[28] See for example, at http://www.w3.org/TR/wsdl the WSDL (web-service description language) specification.

[29] See also J Hendler: *Agents and the Semantic Web* 2001.

2. AGENT TECHNOLOGIES APPLIED TO ONLINE TRANSACTIONS

The most advanced and ambitious view of ecommerce technology is currently through the use of agent-based computing, which we describe briefly in this section. In this monograph, we focus on agent technologies because they are one of the core elements of the Research Scenario that is the basis for our research. After reviewing here agent technologies and agent-based commerce, the next section provides the business use-cases that are studied in the Research Scenario, and the rational for using software agents

2.1 Agents: now and future

There are many visions of the nature, purpose, functionalities and properties of electronic agents and there is no "definitive definition"[30]. A generally agreed description would state that they are autonomous software entities that can react and interact with their environment on behalf of its user without (or with partial) review[31]. More advanced agents ("intelligent agents") are conceived as being adaptive, sociable, cooperative and mobile. This means respectively that not only can they evolve independently, based on their own experience, but they can also interact, cooperate or coordinate with other agents in multi-agent environments, and can move from one such environment to another[32]. For example, in the online shopping example described above, consumer shopping agents may verify the price and availability of products from an alternative supplier, personal assistant agents manage the customer's profile/preferences and timetable. While none of these have to be particularly intelligent or autonomous, designs could include versions that learn from customer behaviour, self determine their own state or status and take independent decisions for the user (store or consumer).

It is beyond the scope of this work to describe in detail the technologies researched and used by the agent computing community, although some references are made below. Agent technology is not a new, single technology but consists of an integrated (and rapidly evolving) use of multiple technologies: languages and protocols for logic programming,

---

[30] One thing that is important to note from the start is that there is a distinct difference between any technological definition of "agent" and the legal concept of "agency", without wanting to detract from the conceptual similarities regarding delegation and autonomy. This issue will be further developed below, and in the legal analysis chapters.

[31] See Wooldridge and Jennings: *Intelligent Agents: Theory and Practice*, 1995 or Object Management Group: *Agent Technology Green Paper*, 2000.

[32] Wooldridge and Jennings, op cit. We comment more on the attributes of agents below.

content definition and agent communication, transport mechanisms, etc.[33].
More importantly for our purposes, there are several agent theories and
models through which we may obtain an understanding of the possible legal
implications of agents and analyse them. These models underlie the
characteristics and functions of agents such as autonomy and proactivity that
have a series of legal implications, and are commented on below.

There are several formal theories supporting the development of
intelligent software agents, attempting to provide a representation of the
agent properties and thereby specifications for agent development[34]. One of
these considers an agent system as an intentional system or stance - i.e. an
entity that intends to do something. One model of active intelligence, the
BDI model, represents an agent by three structures: beliefs, desires and
intentions. The beliefs of an agent are its model of the domain (information
about the environment and cause/effect relationships), its desires provide a
list of goals, and its intentions are the things it has decided to do (chosen
goals). An additional list of representations would include perception
(representation of exterior information), situations (circumstances when to
(re)act), options (list of possible actions) and operational primitives
(available tools to implement the action).

Briefly, it is useful to look at the building blocks of these next generation
technologies for software agents and their environments, that may assist in
the "legal engineering" of agents. Our current interest lies in determining
how such tools allow agents to behave legally, for example as negotiation
and compliance tools, and what research work needs to be carried out to go
forward. Specific building blocks for agents can be grouped into two
categories: "internals", which consist of data and content elements (for the
definition and management of data and agent states) and logic machinery (its
reasoning capacity); and "externals", which mainly include communications
(access, interaction protocols, mobility and interoperability mechanisms)
but also comprise security layers, identification and permissions. Agents
exist within an environment, which will include an agent platform (host) and
agent management services (e.g. a directory or registry, security and
communication services, etc.). This environment may be enhanced by RFID
systems that can multiply the information inputs for agents, providing
detailed data about the real world items with which an agent may interact.

It is also important to consider elements of the agent life cycle: this
involves technologies for agent persistence, renewal, multiplicity and history
(evidence). These elements establish the requirements for ubiquitous
intelligence (see below): common vocabularies, languages and protocols;
and cooperation and coordination systems.

---

[33] Object Management Group, op cit., 2000.
[34] Wooldrigdge and Jennings , op cit., 1995.

The importance of understanding the nature and functionalities of electronic agents lies in the fact that only when one understands these different properties and functionalities can one carry out a proper analysis of the legal consequences. For example, in terms of Intellectual Property Right law (IPR), there is a difference between an agent that collects a list of URLs and presents them to the user (like a search engine), or an agent that collects, stores and presents items from online merchant catalogues with pictures, logotypes and text. In terms of contract law, there is a difference between an agent that transmits the actual consent to contract of a user (physical person) and one that independently enters into a contract on the basis of pre-programmed rules but without the actual knowledge of the user.

In the next section, we discuss the basic nature and properties of agents in order to determine some general legal issues that are raised.

2.2 Nature of agents, their properties

2.2.1 Agent properties

Although there may be no authoritative definition of electronic agents, certain key characteristics or properties have been determined and tend to be common to the technical and legal literature[35]. They are also properties which distinguish intelligent agents from other forms of software. The fundamental properties are autonomy, communication ability and reactivity[36], however a more complete list would be:

– Autonomy: agents possess a degree of independence and operate without direct intervention of humans. They have certain control over their actions and internal state and behaviour. This would imply that an agent must have the access to a network and possibly have the mobility to travel across it.

– Social ability / communication: agents interact with other agents (and possibly humans) via an agent communication language. This requires an ability to communicate with the repositories of this information – databases, web-sites and their dynamic elements such as web-forms, RFID tags, etc.. These may be other agents or gatekeepers of information stores. Communication is currently seen to be protocol-driven, statement exchanges ("does this site sell widgets?" – in XML or other Internet language). In the future, it could involve true dialog and negotiation of

---

[35] M. Wooldridge and Jennings, op cit., 1995; S.J. Russell & P. Norvig: *Artificial Intelligence: A modern approach,* 1995; B. Hermans: *Intelligent Software Agents On The Internet: An Inventory of Currently Offered Functionality in the Information Society and a Prediction of (Near) Future Developments,* 1997.

[36] See paper at http://www.mines.u-nancy.fr/~gueniffe/CoursEMN/I31/heilmann/heilmann.html

several different transaction parameters: agents disclose user objectives, eventually concluding a complex agreement or commercial contract.

- Reactivity: agents perceive their environment and respond in a timely and rational fashion to changes that occur in it. As we described above in relation to RFIDs, in an "Internet of things" where the environment is connected to the network through EPCs, this property may come to the fore;
- Pro-activeness: agents do not simply act in response to their environment, they are capable of taking the initiative (generate their own goals and act to achieve them).
- Temporal continuity: agents are continuously running processes (either running active in the foreground or sleeping/passive in the background), not once-only computations or scripts that map a single input to a single output and then terminate[37].

In addition, agents may have other properties (Wooldridge and Jennings' "strong notion of agents") tending towards a degree of humanisation: a more advanced form of agent. These may have "mental" properties, such as knowledge, belief, intention, obligation and visual representation. Finally, some other attributes may be associated with agents and are important from a legal point of view:

- Mobility: agents can move around from one machine to another and across different system architectures and platforms;
- Veracity: agents do not knowingly communicate false information;
- Rationality: agents will try to achieve their goals and not act in such a way to prevent their goals from being achieved.
- Collaboration: intelligent agents work together to perform mutually-beneficial but complex tasks.
- Adaptability: capacity to evaluate the current state of its external domain and incorporate this into its decisions about future actions. This requires the capacity to examine the external environment (i.e. the Web), remember the outcome of previous actions taken under similar conditions and adapt their actions to improve the chances of achieving their goals.

Table 1-4. Agents and traditional computing systems

What distinguishes a software agent from distributed computing and expert systems? Agents are different from distributed computing and expert systems, though they share some characteristics of distribution and expertise, as the latter generally lack the dimensions of intelligence and agency: ■ Intelligence: the degree of interpretation of knowledge and learning: user preferences, agent reasoning capacity (rule based and adaptive rule based) and agent learning

---

[37] Adapted from Wooldridge & Jennings, op cit. 1995.

capacity through the modification of rules, knowledge and beliefs.
- Agency: the perception of the environment, the degree of autonomy and delegation of responsibility from user (through user representation) and the level of interactivity with data, applications, services and other agents[38].

Traditional systems use low-level messaging rather than high level (declarative) communications used by agents, operating at the knowledge level[39]. In addition, it is argued that while such systems offer pre-ordained responses to determined input, agents can deal flexibly with more complex problems through context-dependant decisions in partially controlled environments (e.g. the Internet). Finally, agents may be mobile and may interface or cooperate with other (previously unidentified) computer systems, whether agents or not.

From a more technical - programming - point of view, agents have identification, behaviour, state and location:
- Identification: data about the agent and potentially user
- Behaviour: actions that the agent does / carries out
- State: current snapshot of agent contents (for example, list of links of a search engine)
- Location: where the agent is (has copied itself to) on the network

Each of these elements requires legal consideration and our work considers it important that legal prescriptions are defined in relation to each. For example, as regards identification, agents may need to communicate to hosts, other agents or enterprise systems certain data about itself (e.g. user name and residence and commercial/ private capacity). These data may determine such legal aspects of the processes, such as the nature of a transaction (interlocutors may wish to refuse to deal with consumers), relevant jurisdictions (only transactions with persons within the EU). However identification also raises issues of privacy, regarding personal data collected or processed by other agents or agent hosts.

In relation to state and/or behaviour, an agent may need to reveal its contents and/or nature (search agent, purchase agent), or hosts may want to screen the agent's contents for illicit or dangerous materials or executables before accepting transfer. On the other hand, hosts should reveal their behaviour about privacy invasive activities such as agent monitoring, recording behaviour or identity, or other behaviour that the agent may refuse or need to refer back to its user for consent before proceeding.

As regards location, although it is argued that server and data processing system location should not necessarily be relevant for determining the legal dimensions of certain online transactions (otherwise many servers would migrate to tax-havens, or low protection jurisdictions), agent location may be taken into account to determine the place of a transaction, which may then be relevant for determining jurisdiction or applicable law.

---

[38] Caglayan and Harrison: *Agent Sourcebook,* 1997.
[39] H. Nwana: *Perspective on Software Agents Research*, 1999; N Jennings: *Building Complex Software Systems*, 2001 (thereby potentially enhanced by the Semantic Web, see below).

2.2.2   Multi Agent Systems

One of the precepts of agent-based computing is the decomposition of complex problems into component parts, interests and control points (e.g. users, services), each of which will then be represented or handled by a separate agent. For example, in a communication service, one agent may be responsible for message handling, another for message encryption, another for virus checking, another for storage and audit trails, another for personal data monitoring and one each for sender and recipient. This means that most systems require or involve several agents interacting with one another within what has been called a multi-agent system or society or MAS[40], a group or *network of autonomous agents (problem solvers) acting and working independently from each other, each representing an independent locus of control of the whole system*[41]. For a MAS to solve a problem coherently the agents must communicate among themselves, coordinate their activities and negotiate when they find themselves in conflict or require third party services. These have legal dimensions that have yet to be explored.

Several approaches have been introduced to achieve co-ordination in multi-agent systems. Four (overlapping) categories can be identified: Organisational structuring, Contracting, Multi-agent planning and Negotiation. One main stream of research seems to move towards negotiation for managing inter-agent dependencies[42], within or without an agent supervisory institution, aiming to come to agreement on mutually acceptable terms. This leads to the formation of contract which will need to have external (real world) validity. The negotiation includes technical and commercial issues such as times, processing availability, access, and price, but could also include legal items such as the granting of consent for the collection and transmission of personal data or copyrighted materials, negotiation of contract fora and jurisdiction, determination of warranties and exclusions of liabilities, terms for guarantees, etc, i.e. any contract term that is normally negotiated between commercial parties.

MAS can be classified as open or closed[43]. In a closed environment (e.g. an intranet), agent communication protocols (languages, ontologies, norms), procedures and actions are decided at design time, and included into the (often proprietary) agent infrastructure. Rights and obligations can be determined beforehand, as could the contractual relationships between the parties. We could imagine, for example, the supermarket defining a closed agent environment restricted to its agents and those agents granted to

---

[40] Jennings et al.: *Automated negotiation: prospects, methods and challenges,* 2001; V
    Dignum et al.: *Agent Societies: towards framework-based design,* 2001.
[41] Zambonelli et al.: *Agent-oriented Software Engineering for Internet Applications,* 2001.
[42] N Jennings: *Automated negotiation*; Lomuscio et al: *Classification scheme, 2000.*
[43] C Dellarocas: *A contractual agent societies,* 2000; M Apistola et al, *Legal aspects of agent technologies,* 2002.

shoppers - or perhaps certified by the store. Such agents would only be usable within the store on the basis of a framework contract governing use of the agents, rights and obligations, personal data collection notifications and consents, etc. Open systems (e.g. based on the Internet) are open to new types of agents, from different contexts and different owners and do not have this level of determination and therefore regulation[44].

Apart from technical issues of language, ontologies and protocols, it is argued that such open models require some form of normative regulation system governing communication, coordination and negotiation between agents, creating a network model[45]. This has been another important area of research, including governance by communication of obligations / sanctions[46], agents that incorporate normative behaviour[47], Contractual Agent Societies[48] and Electronic Institutions[49]. Indeed, it has been postulated that such a society of agents can be governed completely by contract mechanisms[50].

This is one of the fundamental characteristics of agent technologies from a legal point of view: the interaction between agents will involve the modification of agents and agent states (contents, attitudes or beliefs, intentions), the granting or receiving of data, access rights and/or services from third parties, and accordingly the accrual of rights and obligations between them or, by attribution, their users. Each negotiation would lead to the formation of a contract, whose real world validity should be guaranteed and evidenced. This leads to issues of liability, responsibility, attribution of such rights and obligations to agent users or owners, and compliance with contractual and other procedures for commerce[51].

Agent research tends to look at normative behaviour and governance structures in general, from a theoretical perspective, as is witnessed by the

---

[44] This "openness" is also linked to hierarchical or market oriented agent-mediated electronic commerce, see below.

[45] See V Dignum et al: *Agent societies,* 2001. The author postulates an intermediate network framework where agents negotiate within society norms and rules.

[46] M Barbuceanu et al: *The role of Obligations in Multi-agent Coordination,* 1999.

[47] C Castelfranchi: *Deliberative Normative Agents,* 1999; M Boman: *Norms in Artificial Decision Making,* 1999; V Dignum et al.: *Agent Societies: Towards frameworks-based design,* 2001; R Conte et al: *Agents and Norms: How to fill the gap,* 1999.

[48] C Dellarocas, *Contractual Agent Societies,* 2000: "coordinated social activity emerges out of a set of negotiated social contracts (norms) enforced through mechanisms of social control (social institutions)". Agents incorporate degrees of flexibility in negotiating term, from rigid to flexible.

[49] M Esteva et al: *On the formal specifications of electronic institutions,* 2001.

[50] M Morciniec et al: *Towards regulating electronic communities with contracts,* 2001; C Dellarocas, *Contractual Agent Societies,* 2000.

[51] As we have seen, ecommerce and consumer protection laws require (technological) processes for order input correction, contract record storage, rights of withdrawal and cancellation, etc.

work referred to above. From a more specifically legal point of view, it seems important that existing legal rules be incorporated into such structures to create legally compliant agent systems and provide appropriate levels of trust. This has been the main objective of this work, as applied to the Research Scenario.

2.3 Electronic agents in online commerce

2.3.1 Agent applications

Agent uses have been classified into five areas: ecommerce, corporate intranets, personal assistants (schedule management, information retrieval, etc.), resource allocation and management, and middleware (interfacing between applications and network layers)[52]. Many of the current applications of agents are still purely technological, data traffic management, for example. Gradually agent technologies are entering the fields of enterprise applications (commercial and internal, such as ecommerce decision and logistic support), process control (network and system management, controlling product stocks, monitoring quantities, prices or the usage patterns of the products) and personalised user services (schedule management, information retrieval, etc.). These applications have mainly been internal to single enterprises and raise few legal problems as there are no interactions with third parties.

In Procter and Gamble's computer simulations, software agents represent the different elements of the supply network, such as transport vehicles, staff, warehouses, stores[53]. The behaviour of each agent is determined by rules that imitate actual behaviour, such as, "Dispatch this truck only when it is full" or "Make more shampoo when inventory falls to x days' demand." The simulations let P&G perform what-if analyses to test the impact of new logistics rules on three key metrics: inventory levels, transportation costs and in-store stock-outs. The models considered alternate rules on ordering and shipping frequencies, distribution centre product allocation policies, demand forecasting and so on. This scenario may now be realised through RFID technologies that identify the real-world items in the network, and link them with the corresponding agent processes and supply chain management software[54].

---

[52] H Nwana and D Ndumu: *Perspective on Software Agents Research,* 1999.

[53] Adapted from Gary H. Anthes: *Agents of Change - Software agents tame supply chain complexity and optimize performance,* Computerworld.com, January 27, 2003.

[54] Ephraim Schwartz: *RFID ripples through software industry,* 2003.

The following table from *CEO Guide to eCommerce Using Object-Oriented Intelligent Agent Technology*[55] highlights the opportunities and applications of intelligent agent technology in ecommerce as a whole. This list is wider than that envisaged in the Research Scenario, whose more consumer / supermarket oriented list is commented below

Table 1-5. Applications of intelligent agent technology in ecommerce

Data filtering and analysis.	Information brokering.
Condition monitoring and notification.	Workflow management.
Personal assistance / task delegation.	Collaborative application integration.
Collaborative systems integration.	Simulation and gaming.
Risk management.	Data mining.
Document management.	Knowledge sharing.
Real-time software configuration.	Distributed systems management.
Task automation.	Customisation.
Learning / performance improvement.	Tutoring.
Negotiation.	Product configuration.
Resource scheduling.	Optimisation.
Bandwidth management.	Collaborative filtering.
Communications.	Arbitration.
Production control.	Profiling.

As regards commerce, in a goods or service exchange transaction, it has been argued that (online) buying process can be broken down as follows in the Consumer Buying Behaviour model[56]:

1. Need identification
2. Product Brokering
3. Merchant Brokering
4. Negotiation
5. Purchase and Delivery
6. Personalisation
7. Services

Gradually agent technologies are entering ecommerce systems and processes areas at various stages of this model. As we will show below, this vastly increases the complexity of managing the legal issues surrounding computer applications. For example, the most significant steps in this process, the Product Brokering, Merchant Brokering and Negotiation stages, are described below (the actions in these "steps" can differentiate among the types of agents – as we comment later, they can be broken down into different processes):

---

[55] P Fingar: *CEO Guide to eCommerce Using Object-Oriented Intelligent Agent Technology*, 1998.

[56] P. Maes: *Agents as Mediators in Electronic Commerce*, 1998. See also P. Maes, R.H. Guttman, A.G. Moukas: *Agents that buy and sell, transforming commerce as we know it*, 1998.

Product Brokering (consumers determine what products to buy)

- <u>Filtering agents</u>: help consumers find products by filtering products based on features or by comparing the shopper's product ratings with those of other shoppers.
- <u>Find agents</u>: monitor the market for specific products, within customisable time span and price domains. These agents do not engage in negotiation processes; they only report to the user all the selling offers that satisfy specified requirements. (DealPilot, Acses)

Merchant Brokering (agent compares merchant alternatives)

- <u>Comparative shopping agents</u>: compare and rank products by evaluating personalised criteria, such as product features and merchant services. (ActiveBuyersGuide, Frictionless Value Comparison Engine)
- <u>Recommender agents</u>: track better deals for you as you shop. When you are at an e-merchant looking at products, it examines other sites to find better deals on the product you select. It then provides side by side comparisons that include not only price, but also factors such as shipping, handling and taxes. (iChoose Savings Alert)
- <u>Buying agents</u>: have a set of parameters that define and constrain their behaviour: minimum price, maximum price, description of the good to buy, time constraints, geography, agent strategy, etc. (mySimon)
- <u>Selling agents</u>: like buying agents, vendors create Selling agents by providing parameters like initial price, lowest acceptable price or negotiation strategy.

Negotiation (determination of the price or other terms of the transaction)

- <u>Matchmaking agents</u>: match buying agents with selling agents (Kasbah)
- <u>Auction agents</u>: create automated Internet auctions according to your specifications, or bid in existing AuctionBot auctions. A multi-auction search engine that provides real-time access to auction sites. This site helps you manage and monitor multiple auctions, including off-line auctions.

Table 1-6. Ecommerce oriented agent projects

Some initial consumer and business ecommerce agent initiatives and projects
BargainFinder[57] and **Jango**[58]: merchant brokering shopping agents
ShopBot: a domain independent comparison shopping agent
Metronaut[59]: a wearable computer that serves as a schedule negotiating and guidance system
AuctionBot[60]: a general purpose Internet auction server
Kasbah[61]: An agent marketplace for buying and selling goods.
Nectar[62]: a general model of a virtual shop for retail systems
InShop[63]: Item recommender, recipe recommender, and mapper (Impulse scenario, MIT)
Magnet[64]: A multi-agent contracting system for transaction execution.

---

[57] http://bf.cstar.ac.com
[58] http://www.jango.com

2.3.2   Agent-based electronic commerce

We have commented that electronic commerce is considered to have evolved through various stages, from EDI to electronic markets to transaction streams. It is argued that it is now on the way to a fourth phase, that of agent mediated electronic commerce (AMEC)[65]. In AMEC, agents can be used in several ways, for example representing buyers, sellers and intermediaries. They may participate in many EMs throughout the stages of need identification, matchmaking, negotiation, contracting, contract fulfilment and service provision.

There seems to be a close parallel between the conceptual ecommerce transaction models discussed above (hierarchies and markets) and agent systems. In hierarchical transactions, like closed MAS, most technical and legal matters are determined beforehand, e.g. within a project specification and a framework contract. This would be the example of most B2B platforms today, usually being product or sector specific (Airlines, Chemicals, etc.) with close business relationships. Markets, on the other hand, like open MAS, either require standardised interaction and are based on negotiation or need an extra mechanisms for "creating a context", providing stability and, as mentioned above, trust through a variety of support services.

This would mean that from a legal point of view, a significant parallelism could be drawn between closed and open agent platforms on the one hand, and hierarchies or markets on the other. This is a significant point that will be commented in each chapter as we review the legal issues raised by such agent systems.

Within these commerce models, in current electronic commerce software agents are used mainly as transaction mediators: intermediaries between the potential buyer and sellers[66]. Their functions extend from the simple (search engines share some aspects of agents) to the more complicated (including searching for, negotiating the price of and eventually effecting payment of goods). They are, however, more closely controlled by the user (initial parameterisation, monitoring and provision of consent). At the moment, some form of user involvement is usually required, for example for the final

---

[59] http://www-2.cs.cmu.edu/afs/cs.cmu.edu/project/vuman/www/metronaut.html

[60] http://auction.eecs.umich.edu/

[61] http:// kasbah.media.mit.edu/

[62] http://www.etnoteam.it/nectar/Default.htm

[63] http://agents.www.media.mit.edu/groups/agents/projects/impulse/inshop

[64] http://maya.cs.depaul.edu/~mobasher/Research-03.html

[65] C Priest: *Agent Mediated Electronic Commerce,* 2001.

[66] As F Dignum argues in *Agents, Markets, Institutions and Protocols,* 2000, this is in line with the hierarchical nature of most electronic commerce platforms and environments. As these move towards market oriented mechanisms, agents will evolve with more autonomy.

product selection, contract consent or payment instruction (password, etc.). In particular, shopping agents are used to help cope with the 'information overload', and to help them search for and select e-commerce products and suppliers. Agents are also used by enterprises and online merchants to improve marketing and targeting of their products to the online users (selling agents).

Current research on electronic agents has gone past the stage of aiming feasibility and simple functionalities for agents, as there are many simple versions already available online. Work now focuses on developing more intelligent forms of electronic agents for ecommerce known as "intelligent agents", which may be transaction initiators. These agents may have the ability to act independently and, once activated by the human user, may enter into legally binding transactions without any further involvement of the human user. I.e. they initiate and generate transactions without the individual being aware that any negotiation (e.g. for a contract) has been initiated, let alone concluded. They could also learn from experience and take more autonomous decisions without consulting the original programmer or user. These could be, for example, agents that control warehouse stocks and send purchase and payment orders to suppliers and banks as and when further supplies are needed, or shopping agents that have a weekly list of regular purchases for users and ensure that they are ordered, delivered and paid for with no further action taken by the human user. These services may be intensified in an RFID-enhanced world, where individual objects could provide input – temperature, status, expiry dates, etc. – to autonomous agent processes.

We consider the distinction between mediator and initiator as fundamental; for although mediator agents may already incur certain liabilities on the behalf of the user, it is still possible to view them as simple mechanical extensions of the will of the user (rather like a fax or a telephone). Initiator agents, on the other hand, raise some interesting and difficult legal questions of liability and autonomy, which we will discuss later. This classification is not definitive, however, more of a "sliding scale" and other roles and properties are used by researchers for analysis and design purposes and many agents may combine aspects of both classes.

In a not so far future new or more complex roles will be found for electronic agents, not just assisting users through the various stages of a transaction or even initiating and completing those transactions without user involvement at all, but providing complex additional functionalities, services and personalisation and the ability for adaptive reasoning. This involves not just issues, for example, of contract law and the attribution of transactions to users, but elements of autonomy and characterisation that go a distance beyond current agents working as "automation tools". For example, it is envisaged that in less than ten years' time, intelligent agents will be able not only to capture user's explicit or tacit preferences (people's subjectivity –

qualitative, emotional), but they will have developed a "virtual agent ecosystem" in which to inhabit. Projects such as the European AgentCities[67] work towards this end.

These new agents will be able to interconnect among themselves, to connect machines, human beings and businesses. Linked to RFID or similar identification systems, they will also interact with objects, places and other elements of the physical world. This "humanisation" is an aspect that may have to be dealt with by the legal framework in the future, for example maybe by establishing intelligent agent identity or registration similar to companies or even motorcars. This increases the complexity of legal analysis through concepts such as agent assets and liabilities (similar to corporations, for example), property transfers, decision recording, etc. Advanced computing could remove certain presumed features mentioned above, such as benevolence and veracity, to create agents that lie, misrepresent, breach contracts, circumvent technical protections, remove evidence and carry out other actions (illegitimate or not) while confusing or misleading interlocutors and even their own users.

2.4 An agent-based ecommerce scenario

Reviewing our online purchase example above, there are several potential agent applications or systems that could be introduced to improve the online transaction, and attempt to solve some of the legal issues at hand. On the one hand, one could consider agents implemented by the online store.

— Contracting agents could ensure that appropriate contracting procedures are followed. While proper website design should maximise "standard" compliance with applicable contracting laws (e.g. on the basis of the EU Ecommerce Directive, those applicable in the jurisdiction of the Internet Service Provider), the agent could monitor if the client checks or downloads the contract terms and conditions and record this event. More sophisticated contracting agents could enter into a negotiation with the client (or the client's agent), offering different personalised terms (e.g. differentiating between business and consumer clients, local and foreign clients) and negotiating the final applicable conditions, with regard to delivery terms, liability limitation and exclusions, dispute resolution, applicable law, etc. This would counter any claims that terms were unilateral and even unconscionable.

— Personal data processing interface agents, rather than simply notifying users of cookies as does P3P or declaring the privacy policy, could negotiate with the client the collection of certain personal data, the planting of cookies, the obtaining of explicit consent, and the restrictions

---

[67] See at www.agentcities.org

imposed by the client on processing this data. These could also remember client preferences.
- Personal profiling agents would keep track of client behaviour and purchases, an advanced version of today's cookie and client identification based systems for personalisation. These would interact with the previous agents, regarding personal data processing, and with the customer, to respect data protection regulations and record privacy preferences. Again, such agents would assist in the contracting and negotiation process, providing data about the client's nature (business, consumer, local, foreign), credit worthiness, past performance (for discounts, etc.)
- Data management agents could ensure that terms and conditions applicable to the specific contract are stored and accessible by the client, including encryption for proof of authenticity and integrity (even coordinating with a third party notary process for independent certification), enhanced by digital signatures if necessary.
- Transaction monitoring agents could combine both contracting and data management features, for full customer service, adding functionalities such as personalised after-sales service, connection with payment systems (credit card, electronic purses) or return and refund processes in line with distance selling requirements.
- Consumer Protection agents could review the website contents, to ensure that proper information is afforded to consumer clients, both as regards the store's identification and other EU Ecommerce Directive transparency requirements, but also in relation to specific products on offer (distance selling requirements). An agent-based site may be able to determine the origin of site users and automatically adapt the language, content and legal aspects (processes, contract terms, etc.) to the mandatory laws of the consumer's jurisdiction. This is a more sophisticated version of modern site's requests for user's country of residence.

On the other hand, one can envisage client controlled agents: These could include:
- Shopping agents, including comparison agents, models of which are already available[68]. Although these may raise more legal issues than solve them (problems of IPR in the collection of product data and comparison tables, of revealing personal data, etc.)
- Personal identification and privacy agents for storing and processing personal data (client side identification data, in contrast with the web-services vision of centralised identification, implemented for example by Microsoft in the much criticized Passport service). These agents could

---

[68] See above, Table 1-6 on current ecommerce agent applications and initiatives.

negotiate with the corresponding store systems (agents or not) regarding identification and data collection, consents and notifications.

– Personal profiling agents – similar to the store-based personalisation agents, these could track purchasing behaviour in various stores and carrying out various product and merchant brokering functions.

– Negotiation and contracting agents: agents specifically programmed to engage in auctions or single or multiple negotiations for products and services, with corresponding data management functionalities for contract storage, user consent and notification if necessary, etc. These agents could negotiate specific clauses (so the sellers can argue that key clauses such as liability limitation are expressly negotiated, and the contract is not one of adhesion).

– Payment agents that process client authorisation and communications with online or mobile payment systems, maintaining confidentiality, non collection of personal data and legally admissible records.

There is also potentially a series of "agent system services", consisting in agents without specific user-related goals, but programmed to provide "institutional" services: security wrappers, identification, data protection mechanisms, message transport, auditing and even potentially reputation control. Until such platforms are established on an open market or system basis, however, these services are likely to be provided only by the online or offline store.

These are just imagined agents that could encounter some of the legal issues outlined in the first section; two additional comments are required. First, many of the basic functionalities and processes of these "agents" can be and indeed are implemented through traditional – i.e. non agent-based – computing. Agent technology would add certain added features, mainly focussing on the independence of the systems from user control (autonomy) and the capacity to monitor independently outside events (purchases, changes in websites, etc.) and react accordingly (proactivity). In addition, especially in relation to profiling and negotiation agents, agent systems would have capacity to learn from previous events – negotiations, purchases, returns/refunds, errors – and gain a higher degree of intelligence. This can be used for user personalisation and adapting processes to user desires, negotiation techniques and strategies, and even anticipating user needs (e.g. in relation to programmed events such as birthdays, holidays, etc.).

Second, it is important to note how these software agents, while satisfying or aiding users to comply with certain obligations, both public (imposed by law) and private (contractually agreed), may raise further legal issues. This is the principal object of this monograph. As we will see, there are important questions of agent personality and the provision of contractual or personal data processing consent, IPR concerns regarding commercial data collection, storage and reproduction, privacy concerns relating to the security of agents and the data relating to individual users that they may contain.

2.5   Agent Legal issues

Now we have briefly presented software agents from a technical and business perspective, we need to determine and discuss in more detail what the legal framework within which they can be programmed today is, and – to the extent possible – what is coming in the future. This will determine, for example, what they may or may not do and the extent of their usefulness. A business or technical functionality may be regarded as highly desirable or useful, but not if it involves incurring liability or engaging into illicit actions (e.g. consumer behaviour monitoring, certain data storage or extracting product information from online catalogues). The amount of this liability, or extent of risk, should also be assessed.

From a legal point of view, the different agent properties each raise certain issues that may be considered as a starting point for legal analysis. Table 1.7 below provides a summary.

Table 1-7. Agent characteristics and legal issues

Feature	Short description	Potential legal issues
Autonomy	A degree of independence and operation without direct user intervention	Contract / Liabilities (IPR, Tort, etc): attribution to user? Contract, privacy: effective granting of user consent? Does the user know about it? Can you attribute the action to the user? Does the user give consent to a contract "concluded" by an autonomous agent?
Social ability / communication	Agents interact with other agents (and possibly humans)	Identification of counter-parts in transactions Attribution of statements to user? Privacy: monitoring of communications, identity, etc. IPR: effects of agent interaction (copying, storing data, etc.) Can an agent pose as a real person? Do interlocutors (humans, other agents, webpages) know who they are dealing with? Are certain communications illicit or prohibited?
Reactivity	Agents perceive their environment and respond	Liability for mistakes and errors: What if an agent makes a wrong reaction (refuses an order, mistakes an order for request for information, gives consent to collection of personal information, etc.)
Pro-activeness	Capable of taking the initiative	Liability for actions: (contract, IPR, Tort, Privacy, etc.) agent starts initiating or responded to actions without knowledge of the user
Mobility	Migration around environment	Jurisdiction: where is the agent based? – does its location determine jurisdiction or applicable law for action / transaction?

Feature	Short description	Potential legal issues
		Trespass: can agents copy themselves onto other servers – what if they cause damage?
Veracity	Agents do not knowingly communicate false information	Misrepresentation / presumption of good faith in civil law systems: protection of third parties in the event of misstatements – bad faith
Benevolence	No conflicting goals	As above
Rationality	Agents will try to achieve their goals	Contract / liability: what if agents are not rational, e.g. when a non-agent interlocutor would obviously see that the agent action is irrational (and e.g. would not conclude a contract with it) – how to determine real intent of user. Should agents be taken at face value?
Collaboration	Work in concert with other agents	Tort / liability for acts and mistakes in relation to other agents and other software.
Adaptability / inference	Capacity for abstraction and learning to infer methods and tasks	Risk of future undesired outcomes, as agents adapt in unforeseeable ways – acting in ways that engage user liability without his/her consent.

Taking the Consumer Buying Behaviour model outlined above, the following table creates a cross-section of issues that we can then regroup into different headings for presenting the legal framework. Later, when it comes to specifying each particular agent, their functionalities should be reviewed in the light of the relevant section.

Table 1-8. Legal issues of the Consumer Buying Behaviour model

Stage	General Process	Agents	Legal issues
A. Need Identification	Problem recognition	Reminder Filtering Shopping Recommender Advertising	Privacy IPR
B. Product Brokering	Information retrieval Filtering, recommendation Evaluation	Shopping Comparison Filtering	IPR data base issues
C. Merchant Brokering	Compare products, evaluate merchants Request for quotes Buy and sell agents	Shopping Comparison	Contract: authority to make an offer Competition / collusion Consumer protection / online transaction regulation
D. Negotiation	Determine terms of	Shopping	Contract: authority to

Stage	General Process	Agents	Legal issues
	transaction: choice and decision auction	Selling RFQ Auction Discount	negotiate: offer and accept
E. Purchase and Delivery	Payment Order control (client) Update (shop) Delivery	Shopping Auction Payment Discount	Contract: authority to order payment Security E-payments Consumer protection, Privacy and online transaction regulation
F. Personalisation	Filtering, recommending Geographic identification	Advertising Location services	Privacy
G. Services	Information provision: Navigation Location	Location services Payment	Privacy ISP liability

This summary Table 1-8 above shows that single agents may raise issues in several areas of law, while similar areas of legal issues are raised by different types of agents.

2.5.1 Legal definition of agents

In certain legislative documents, especially related to contracting (UETA, UCITA, UECA, UNCITRAL Model Law on Ecommerce[69]), efforts have been made to define agent based trading. However it might not be necessary with a stringent technical definition of electronic agents to discuss the legal aspects. The definitions given include those set out in Table 1.9 below.

Table 1-9. Legal definitions of agents

Law	Definition
UCITA	"Electronic agent" means a computer program, or electronic or other automated means, used by a person to initiate an action, or to respond to electronic messages or performances, on the person's behalf without review or action by an individual at the time of the action or response to the message or performance.
UETA	"Electronic agent" means a computer program or an electronic or other automated means used independently to initiate an action or respond to electronic records or performances in whole or in part, without review or

---

[69] UETA: Uniform Electronic Transactions Act (USA); UCITA: Uniform Computer Information Transactions Act (USA); UECA: Uniform Electronic Commerce Act (Canada). UNCITRAL Model Law on Contracting (UN). References at the end of the monograph.

Law	Definition
	action by an individual.
UECA	"Electronic agent" means a computer program or any electronic means used to initiate an action or to respond to electronic documents or actions in whole or in part without review by a natural person at the time of the response or action.
UNCITRAL (draft)	"Automated computer system" means a computer program or an electronic or other automated means used to initiate an action or respond to data messages or performances in whole or in part, without review or intervention by a natural person at each time an action is initiated or a response is generated by the system.

There will need to be careful reconsideration of this type of legal definition as electronic agents evolve over time and become more sophisticated, especially when the acquire learning and adaptation capabilities. These definitions may be more limiting than would be desired[70].

3. AN E-BUSINESS AGENT-BASED RESEARCH SCENARIO

We have now outlined in general terms some of the legal issues of online commerce and described agent technologies that, while they may help solve some of the legal problems caused by information technologies, they may also increase the difficulties for designing compliant commerce systems. In this section, we describe the Research Scenario considered as the basis for our analysis, setting its scope, context and limits.

First we define the scenario. Then we shall look at the agent technologies and functionalities to be implemented within it, before drawing up a general outline of the potential legal issues, in order to determine the scope of the legal research.

3.1 The Research Scenario: an augmented shopping experience

The research on which this work has been based aims to integrate the latest technologies into the common shopping experience, providing innovative services in the real-world retail store. This involves developing artefacts and the associated computer systems that will turn these retail

---

[70] For an interesting analysis of agent definitions, see I Kerr: *Providing for Autonomous Electronic Devices in the Uniform Electronic Commerce Act,* 2000.

stores, shopping malls, even sidewalks, streets, and public arenas into "the computer". A typical (idealised) scenario would be as follows.

As you approach the store, your mobile phone notifies you that the car park has bay G5 reserved for you. As you walk into the store and pick up a shopping cart, the onboard screen welcomes you and asks you to swipe your smart card and pin number. When you do, it welcomes you personally to the store and brings up your shopping list onto the screen. It also reminds you that you are short of kitchen roll at home that needs adding to the list. And that your wife likes some special (expensive!) moisturising cream for her birthday next week. John and Mary are coming on Tuesday, and John is vegetarian. Would you like a suggested menu and recipe for Tuesday dinner? Nappies (size and brand) are part of the standard shopping basket, although the screen reminds you that your second child is now ready for the larger size of nappies, which are by chance on offer that week at 10% discount. As you approach the vegetable section, the screen notes that you also want fresh cheese .... do you want a number for the queue now so that you don't have to wait? Yes thank you. You want to change the song on the PA system? Touch the right button on the screen, access the music selection and choose your song. Tinned tomatoes, by the way, are in the second isle on the left, and here is a plan of the store to show you how to get there from where you are. Oh, and as you go past the drinks stand, what do you think about two colas for the price of one today? You comparative shopping agent informs you that these are cheaper at another store (online) that will deliver them home at your convenience for no extra cost... Could we serve these biscuits to Gerald after dinner?... Hmmm, the ingredients list on the screen indicates that animal fat is used. How about some other brand of after-dinner chocolates that are fat-free? And finally, would you like four pints of milk, 12 pints of beer, 6 bottles of mineral water and the case of Bordeaux wine delivered to your car rather than picking them up in the store and hauling them downstairs? No problem. Confirm you credit card pin number here and "have a nice day!".

This scenario entails (1) redesigning physical environments and (2) redefining the consumer experience. To achieve the first aim, the technical focus of the research is on building technical products such as embedded location-based artefacts in real-world objects such as cereal boxes in grocery stores or similar stores in a shopping mall (these could be based on RFID tags or other form of electronic identification); and a wireless architecture and application server system integrating these artefacts with handheld devices and distributed software agents. The artefact and architecture development is oriented in three ways:

– Location: To develop specific location/identification-based artefacts that obtain processing power by communicating with agent processes via wireless technologies. Current technology solutions for this include embedding RFID tags in physical objects and shelves within the store.

Ultimately, the artefacts will communicate with humans via WAP-enabled phones, PDAs or notepads. The artefacts will be part of the complete redesign of the store including the physical appearance, layout, product placement, etc.

- Architecture: An artefact application development platform will be built that can be used as an environment to program artefact applications. The distributive agent based approach will ensure that the artefacts benefit from emerging functionalities.
- Human focus: It is important that humans engage with the artefacts and that we model artefact performance according to user preferences. XML-based object modelling and process definition will provide the basis for development. PML (Physical Markup Language) could be considered for processing information about the real world.

As regards the second aim, redefining the consumer experience, this will occur on the basis of consumer interaction with these novel artefacts and computer systems. This should include customers using handheld devices – PDAs, mobile phones, notepads – to communicate with RFID or Bluetooth-enabled artefacts embedded in products and product displays and the store's computer system, in a three-way conversation. The three sources (consumer, store and products) communicate using WAP or Wi-Fi technology transmitting data about price, ingredients, adverts, special offers and discounts, recipe suggestions, third party advice on diets, ecology or medical matters, anything. Any data may be included in this three-way conversation.

Over time, user profiles will be built on the basis of data collected relevant to shopping behaviour patterns, and consumers would be reminded of their regular monthly purchases or of recipe ingredients. Consumers will also be targeted based on their preferences for offers, coupons, and advertisements. For example, a chocolate biscuit lover might be offered special deals on milk; a dog food buyer would be courted by a competing brand. Eventually, products might compete for customers bargaining with one another through store-based agents, and final offers will be sent back to customers' handheld devices.

The research scenario shopping experience therefore combines database management and customer personalisation and profiling using agent technologies (as opposed to standard server-client distributed computing), linked to active tag identification (RFID), customer localisation and mobile devices.

This permits the store data systems to use the customer data, his/her generated profile, the store product/service databases and local communication networks (WLAN) for various "in-store" commerce applications:

- Customer personalisation (store welcome, shopping list management, customer preferences, advance knowledge of customer needs such as dinners, birthdays and child growing up)

- Location specific advertising (depending on customer location and cart contents identified by RFID tags) or cross-client rating and recommendations (e.g. on the amazon.com model).
- Product related advertising (depending on customer shopping list, electronically identified products and cart contents)
- Mobile payment systems (to avoid queues at the checkout point) potentially based on agent or store located personal identification and financial data.

3.2   Mobile commerce and ubiquitous computing

There are three basic technology areas that support the research, and indeed provide the foundations of a world were distributed eBusiness will thrive: mobile communications and devices, ubiquitous computing and object identification, and intelligent agent technologies. It is the combination of these three technologies that allows the research to integrate the electronic commerce experience into the real world itself. We have already commented on agent technologies, multi-agent software platforms and agent applications as a key implementation of the research. However, before describing in more detail the research, we must briefly introduce the two other areas of technology: mobile commerce and ubiquitous computing.

Although the promise of Third Generation (3G) or UMTS-based mobile communications has yet to be fulfilled[71], mobile and wireless technologies permitting data exchange (as opposed to voice telephony and Short Message Service - SMS) are slowly spreading in the commercial and private sectors. It is outside the scope of this monograph to present these technologies in detail[72], however particular communication technologies to mention are: 2.5 Generation mobile telephones, using GPRS; Bluetooth; and Wireless Local Area Networks (WLAN) or "Wi-Fi". A particular point to take into account when considering m-commerce capabilities is the processing and interface capacities of mobile devices: solution architectures contemplate both thin client systems (where the client devices have little if any processing capacities and most processing is carried out in the main server) and more developed clients with operating systems (e.g. Windows CE, Palm OS) and supporting software environments or platforms for simple applications to execute in the mobile devices (e.g. J2ME). Most PDAs currently provide for this, and some most advanced mobile phones.

The "first generation" of m-commerce excitement was about providing the ability to buy anything, anywhere, anytime. Applications currently

---

[71] European Commission: *Towards the Full Roll-Out of Third Generation Mobile Communications,* 2002.

[72] See for more details J L Mateo Hernández and Ma J Iglesias Portela: ***Mcommerce Contract Law, electronic Payment and consumer protection,*** 2001.

include basic mobile commerce services such as wireless alerts (prices, scores), mobile payment systems, local area sales and more commonly short range connectivity for data exchange between mobile devices (mainly portable computers) and corporate networks. More sophisticated applications will develop for the provision of services (marketing, data collection and other customer services), information and occasionally goods. It is judged that the fundamental m-commerce model will be to extend services now available on the Web to mobile devices. This is where the research aims as it proposes to use mobile technologies for enabling such online services in the (real) store environment rather than establish mobile commerce per se.

As regards ubiquitous or pervasive computing, according to the EU's Disappearing Computer Initiative, "*the vision of the future is one in which our world of everyday objects and places becomes infused and augmented with information processing and exchange. In this vision, the technology providing these capabilities is unobtrusively merged with real world objects and places, so that in a sense it disappears into the background, taking on a role more similar to electricity - an invisible pervasive medium*"[73]. The notion is to increase the properties (and processing power) of objects to enrich people's daily lifestyles. This vision is based on distributed computing models, using RFID tags or miniature devices inserted in objects - and eventually the components of the objects themselves - that allow these to communicate with hidden computing power and users' mobile or fixed devices. This vision is also funnelled by progress towards web-services using application environments including distributed computing standards such as J2EE and .NET.

A technology that is coming into prominence in the retail area which we have mentioned before is Radio Frequency Identification (RFID), which will replace existing Bar Code identification. RFID makes it possible to hold relatively large amounts of data (e.g. 1Kby) in small, lightweight electronic read/write storage devices called tags (or transponders). Data is accessible through handheld and fixed-mount readers in real time, using RF signals to transfer data to and from tags. This data is accessible through handheld and fixed-mount readers in real time, using RF signals to transfer data to and from tags[74].

The characteristics of ubiquitous computing include ubiquity (computing everywhere), invisibility, sensing (the ability to perceive the environment) and memory amplification (enabling the recording of actions and utterances)[75]. The ubiquitous or pervasive computing vision involves increasing the properties (and processing power) of objects to enrich people's daily lifestyles. While research projects focus on the positive and

---

[73] See information online at http://www.disappearing-computer.net
[74] See also the Auto-ID Center at MIT: http://www.autoidcenter.org/main.asp
[75] M. Langheinrich: *Privacy by design*, 2001.

practical applications of this vision, it is quite worrying from the user perspective, for example, with visions of Big Brother watching every step one takes and consumers being bombarded with commercial offers of all kinds. To counter this there is therefore an interest to ensure that individual and legal protections are established for data and consumer protection, security and trust, to provide the protection of basic human rights of privacy and autonomy.

3.3   Research Scenario Agent preview

The Research Scenario therefore envisages a personalised and information intensive shopping experience where
– Consumers interact with and purchase RFID-enhanced products via wireless devices and software agents,
– The store infrastructure is created so that merchants also use wireless applications, "active" products and software agents for better management of the store and selling processes.
The use of these agents is what we are concerned with here: it is in the interaction of the parties on the basis of agent-based computing that the legal issues arise. In order to carry out a contextualised legal analysis of the issues raised by the research, it is important to describe the agents envisaged within the Research Scenario. The following is a general list of potential agents that may be used in the implementation of this Scenario.
– Reminder agents: software agents can be installed to remind consumers of regularly but less frequently bought products, birthday gifts, recipe ingredients, etc.
– Filtering Agents: this agent filters out unwanted products within a domain specified by the consumer
– Recommending Agents: an agent to recommend products via 'Word-of-Mouth' system: it uses the opinions of like-minded consumers to offer recommendations. Other more commercial processes include sending advertisements suggesting alternative products
– Find Agents: Agents will monitor the market for specific products, within a customisable time span and price domains. The agent does not engage in negotiation but only reports the selling offers that satisfy the consumer's requirement
– Comparative Shopping Agents: these can compare and rank products by selecting individualised criteria, such as product features and merchant services
– RFQ Agents: to investigate the price of products and then decides between producers (Request for Quote)
– Buying Agents: agents that can purchase goods, according to a set of parameters define and constrain their behaviour, e.g. Minimum price, maximum price, locality, description of the product to be purchased, etc.

- Selling Agents: Similar as buying agents: vendors deploy selling agents, establishing parameters like initial price, lowest acceptable price, etc.
- Auction Agent: an agent that allows customers to negotiate the price they want to pay for certain products, e.g. produce. Agent will record and store consumer's preferences and limits, according to which it selects the optimal combination.
- Bulk Discount Agent: Upon buying products, this agent will alert customers of a bulk discount opportunity (e.g. If buy 20, 10% discount)
- Authorising agents: an agent that can authorise payment according to parameters set by consumer (certain budget, max. Price for products. Etc.)
- Prompt Payment agent: if product requires immediate payment (e.g. Coffee, candy, etc.), this agent will perform the payment according to pre-set instructions by the consumer
- Update Agent: Once products are purchased, an Update Agent will communicate with Inventory Agent of store to update inventory level. If necessary, replenishment will automatically be arranged.
- Delivery Agent: this contains details of delivery address which it will accordingly communicate with the store for delivery to be arranged
- Block Agent: an agent that remembers customers' feelings about a product and will act accordingly (e.g. If consumer was not satisfied with a certain brand, the agent will filter advertisements from that same brand.
- Geographic Agent: this agent can provide consumer with personalised information dependent on his/her geographic location.
- Information Agent: this agent will notify customer on parking availability upon approaching the shopping centre.
- Navigation Agent: An agent that can provide a map of the supermarket to find the location of a product. Based on consumer's shopping list, agent can provide consumer with an itinerary, e.g. the fastest route.
- Queue Management Agent: An agent that can take a number on behalf of the consumer and alert the consumer when it is about to be his/her turn.
- Recipe Agent: this agent can provide consumers with recipes refined to user profile. Recipes can be selected on type of cuisine, type of course, main ingredient, etc.
- Location Agent: an agent to determine the location of people, products or mobile devices in the store.

These are the agents whose principal characteristics and functions are analysed from a legal perspective in the following chapters. Now we have defined the agents under study, and before embarking on the detailed legal analysis, we outline in the final sections of this Introduction the scope of our research (section 3.4), and our methodology and analytical tools (section 4).

3.4   Research Scope

We have set out above the general business applications for the agents involved in online commerce, outlining the various types of agents that may be incorporated into the system for the Research Scenario. We saw a scenario for shopping in the future, using agent-based technologies and RFID systems. Let's imagine now what could happen if appropriate safeguards are not implemented in these agents and the consumer visits the store for a second or subsequent time.

As you approach the superstore, the competitor store over the road sends you an SMS suggesting its products are cheaper and you personally will get a special discount if you buy BBQ charcoal this weekend. You delete the message. Bay G5 has just been taken by another car.

As you enter the store, Cola brand A (not your favourite) sends a message to your mobile phone offering discount on the purchase of 6 litres and even more if you buy 4 frozen pizzas of Brand B. This can also be delivered straight to your home, and details added to your credit card bill. "Just push Accept on the phone". Having activated the shopping cart, another advert offers a holiday in Barbados, flights to Mallorca and special discounts in a hotel in Corfu ... again, "just press Accept and the holiday is yours with a 10% discount". Delete message!

A note flashes up on the screen saying your automatic shopping bot has purchased a super-pack of 20 kilos of cheap soap powder from another store, and you have to go and pick it up before 12.30 when the store shuts - or home delivery for an extra Euros 4.50 plus VAT. Cancel that... can't I? Who are these people anyway? Didn't you want only two kilos? What do you do about the mistake? Do you know the terms of the agreement and has the online store provided sufficient identification, etc.? The WAP-banner offer of chocolates for 15% discount looks good... but if you accept, will any more offers be made via mobile or email?

As your automatic shopping comparison agent (working down your shopping list) checks out the features and prices of competing store's nappies and wine, presenting you the results, the screen goes blank and a notice provides warning that you have violated the copyright, database rights and/or trade secrets of another store and proceedings will be taken against you and the shopping comparison bot developer....

Finally, when you confirm the current purchases, your authorisation is denied as you have reached your credit card limit. Checking the balance, you notice online purchases that you have never made. Someone has stolen your identity.

So, what went wrong? What are missing in this "nightmare" scenario are the legal protections that should be incorporated into the design, development and implementation of the system. It is fairly obvious that in the different elements of the nightmare scenario above various legal and regulatory infringements occurred: the store and shopping agents paid scant regard to (European) consumer and data protection laws and IPR protections; the consumer didn't read the privacy and other notices that were (or maybe were not) displayed to him/her - or in any event, if he/she wanted to receive a certain service, he/she had to accept them anyway; and weak, if any, security features were implemented in the store and mobile IT systems in play.

What is less obvious is that even in the "dream" scenario outlined first in section 3.1, while the same legal issues are at stake, various rules may have been breached - privacy protection or fair trading principles violated, security recommendations not implemented - that although superficially do not seem to harm the parties involved, from a purist point of view the systems, processes and transactions are not legally compliant.

Each of the agent applications within the Research Scenario, while enhancing the technical and commercial features of the implementation, raises several legal issues which should be carefully considered in order to determine the viability of the technical conceptions and the feasibility of and conditions for compliant implementation. If agents are to enter into the mainstream of computer engineering for ecommerce applications, they will have to be designed to embed compliance processes in relation to a wide array of legal issues. This means identifying any those legal issues and any legal modifications that should be envisaged for the optimum usage of products and systems resulting from the research.

The aim of the legal work is therefore to provide a legal analysis of these intelligent agents: what they are, what they may or may not do, what is the legal framework within which they can be programmed today, and – to the extent possible – what is coming in the future, in particular when the physical environment is enhanced by RFID or similar electronic identification systems that can interact with these agents. On this basis, we can then lay down some guidelines for more specific functionalities of agents (e.g. search and retrieve, negotiate, contract, privacy protection or payment functionalities) so that when it comes to implementing the Research Scenario, the parties involved are aware of the risks and potential liabilities, and are confident that legal risks have been minimised.

Finally, this research will assist the development work by defining the appropriate functionalities and information flows (agent dialogues, host permissions, RFID activation, etc.) for legally compliant agents, without detracting from the technical and commercial objectives and functionalities.

3.4.1 Preliminary determination of legal issues arising in this research

From a legal point of view, the steps of our analysis are as follows:
- Who are the actors in play (what parties, what roles)?

- What are the interactions between them (what processes)?
- What laws regulate the interactions and what difficulties arise because of them?

3.4.1.1   Actors

Apart from the principal actors (the consumer and the store), the Research Scenario envisages other services provided by different parties. Each party will have different type of relationship with the principal parties, with different obligations and responsibilities.

User oriented services and corresponding actors within the Research Scenario could include for example:
- Third party advisers: Medical advisers and dieticians, or ecology advisers. For example, an online medical advisory service could compare product ingredients with the consumer's medical profile and warn against using a certain product (e.g. for allergies, diabetics, cholesterol). A "green" association could provide immediate ecological information ("buy green") on products picked up from a shelf.
- General Services: recipe and cooking advisory services (menus, etc.). Relevant actors include the store itself, or an online recipe service provider.
- Personal information repositories. These could be service providers that maintain the consumer's personal data (identification, credit card details, health information) in a centralised data repository. Online versions of these already exist, such as Microsoft's Passport or Liberty Alliance initiatives.
- Product information suppliers: while the manufacturer and the store will provide basic (obligatory) information about products, third parties such as consumer associations could provide product comparisons, in depth research on a particular product, or market segment. These services could be activated by interaction with the EPC of the products in question.
- Comparison shopping service providers: online services providing real-time information about comparative products and alternative stores offering the same products, and/or additional services such as home delivery and credit.

Shop oriented services could include home delivery, credit checking and marketing services, among others. Actors here include credit card companies, logistics companies (transport), advertising agencies and other intermediaries that provide data mining or warehousing services, customer profiling, advertisement targeting, etc., similar to companies such as Overture that provide targeted banners and advertisements in search pages.

Another actor is the "Regulator", who may intervene directly in a commercial process (for example, providing a Robinson "Do-not-call" list) or indirectly ensuring consumer and personal data protection (privacy audits, unfair trading claims, etc.).

3.4.1.2 Interactions

The legal issues raised by the processes carried out in a traditional shopping scenario are fairly standard and are not relevant for the legal research in our work. This includes such items as occupier liability, offline advertising and payment processing, etc. The important issue for us is to determine the "extra elements" that exist in the Research Scenario due to agent processing and digital interactions. These include:

- New ways of carrying out traditional interactions and processes. These involve the provision of information between all parties involved through electronic and automated means, user profiling, third party or retail store provided services (from guides and real world advisors to shopping agents, online information providers mentioned above); and
- "New" m-commerce interactions, services and processes. These will comprise processes such as mobile advertising, mobile payments and mobile certifications. The aim in this work is to study these on the basis that they are innovative services generated through agent-based computing, and transmitted to clients through mobile communications (Wi-Fi, WAP, SMS, etc.) in an RFID enhanced environment.

While we aim to cover ecommerce oriented agents in general, we present four particular agents for implementing interactions between the parties:

a) Agent A is a store-based advertising agent, offering products to consumers in accordance with their shopping profile or other input such as consumer location in the store, the contents of shopping basket or an RFID activated by the client's actions (picking it up, putting it in the shopping trolley).

b) Agent B is a similar store-based selling agent, this time with added functionality of offering features such as contract conclusion and associated services: interconnection with payment systems and home delivery.

c) Agent C is a customer-oriented automatic shopping/buying agent. This agent is resident in a consumer controlled environment / host, searches for products in online sources (e.g. based on a current shopping list or activated product) and even suggests new products to the user and/or purchases them without review. It communicates both with the closed store systems (product and price databases, etc.) and with the open network (alternative shopping sites).

d) Agent D is an automated shopping assistant. A standard element of this agent is a process that collects relevant data from different sources (the retail store, online web stores, product catalogues and other online databases, even discussion lists for product ratings). It then filters, prioritises and organises the data, and creates a personal product list or database for the shopper to consider. This could include ecological or dietary information relating to the shopper's basket of goods or shopping list, for example.

These software agents are more particularly described in chapter 2 (Agents A, B and C) and chapter 3 (Agent D).

Figure 1-1 below summarises the agent-based interactions between the actors in the Research Scenario. The Store agent would include Agents A and B, carrying out advertising and contracting processes. The Consumer agent includes C and D, for comparative shopping and other processes related to shopping services. As we will see, we will need to study further processes or interactions between the actors, for example between the store and third party data services (via the Internet – for example web-based user profiling or ID management), and between the parties and the regulator, as regards auditing and oversight. These may also be agent-based, and in chapter 6 we outline a consumer protection oriented Process Monitoring Agent that could mediate between the principal actors (store and consumer) and regulators and other third parties.

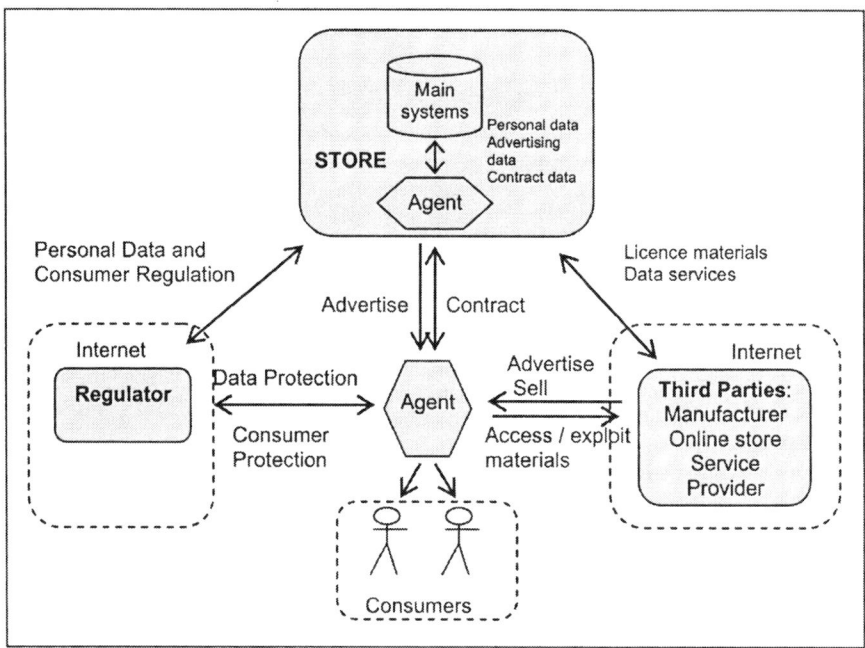

Figure 1-1. Research Scenario Interactions

The processes of these agents are more particularly discussed in the following chapters, but an overview table assists us in determining the particular areas of law that we need to study as a consequence of the interactions under consideration (Table 1-10).

Table 1-10. Potential Legal areas concerned by the research Agents' processes

Agent A	Agent B	Agent C	Agent D	Potential Legal Issues
Contains or accesses user profile	Contains or accesses user profile	Contains or accesses user profile	Contains or accesses user profile	Privacy
Obtains consumer location	Obtains consumer location			Privacy
Analyses shopping basket	Analyses shopping basket	May analyse shopping basket	May analyse shopping basket	Privacy
Sends advertisements	Sends advertisements			Privacy Consumer Protection and Contract Online regulation (Ecommerce
	Offers for sale			Contract Consumer Protection
	Provides accept function			Contract Online regulation and Privacy
	Provides payment data			Privacy (access to payment data)
		Searches online databases	Searches online databases	IPR / DB rights Access (contract / DRMS)
		Offers / accepts online purchase		Contract Consumer Protection Online regulation
			Filters and processes content	IPR / DB rights
Analyses consumer behaviour and updates profile	Analyses consumer behaviour and updates profile	Analyses consumer behaviour and updates profile	Analyses consumer behaviour and updates profile	Privacy

3.4.2   Relevant legal issues

On the basis of the preceding analysis, including both general issues of ecommerce oriented agents in the CCB model (Table 1.8 above) and those relating to agents specific to the Research Scenario (Figure 1.1 and Table 1.10 above), we have determined the most important legal issues related to the use of electronic agent technology in the Research Scenario that need to be examined. These issues are:

-   Contract formation: the formation of contract by automated means. This is the core element of agent-based transactions, as it involves the regulation of interaction between two or more agents and IT systems, and issues of intent and consent, liabilities and error handling. Contract aspects also arise in relation to IPR and privacy, for example as regards the automated granting of consent, DRMS licensing and correction of errors or violations. Agent-based digital signatures are also considered as these are considered a key element in trusted online commerce.
-   Intellectual property rights: due to the access to and processing of protected materials such as catalogues and other online content, copyright and trademark aspects need to be considered, as well as the non-creative database *sui generis* rights. These issues are important in relation to advanced shopping agents that can scan, copy and reproduce websites and product information.
-   Consumer Protection issues: as the agent system focuses on the interactions between store and consumers, the agent processes (advertising, product offering, delivery) will be heavily regulated by current consumer protection laws, both in standard legislation and in the ecommerce oriented EU Ecommerce Directive and Distance Selling Directive. Consideration must be made of how users of the system are protected as regards disclaimers, mistake, exclusions, purchasing processes and information.
-   Privacy: Privacy and the protection of personal data is the major debate in most countries undertaking advanced electronic commerce. Many, if not all, e/m-commerce transactions are based on data collected from consumers and ecommerce participants (identity details, email address, credit card details, delivery address, purchasing patterns, Internet surfing data) – data which is vital for the carrying out of online commerce, but also additional data that allows service providers to personalise and enhance their goods and services. The aggressiveness of the commercial actors and the potential for breaches of fundamental rights has induced governments (led by the European Union) to implement strict laws about the collection, storage, processing and transfer of personal data, for the greater protection of individuals. Accordingly any traditional or agent-

based e/m-commerce platform will have to take into account the principles and rules set out by the legislation. The research scenario model envisages very high levels of customisation, identification and location of users (personalised shopping bots and assistants, home deliveries, mobile payments, RFIDs), and the risk of infringing these laws is significant. Privacy threats in the scenario include uncontrolled profiling, data mining and consumer surveillance. On the other hand, our work also envisages considering how technology can be privacy enhancing, that is to say how it will not just improve commercial services for the merchant (supply-side benefits) but also provide technical means to protect users' privacy (user-side benefits).

In relation to this determination of the core subjects of study, three comments must be made. First, as mentioned above, there has been a substantial amount of legal research on the implications of new technologies, and of the Internet and ecommerce in particular. In our legal analysis of ecommerce oriented software agents, there is some overlap with these general Internet and ecommerce issues, as these are the media and the purpose of the electronic agents in question. We will be commenting some more general aspects of this "Internet law" insofar as it is relevant for a better understanding of the issues raised by the researched agents. However, the focus here is mainly on the additional aspects and issues raised by agent technology and automated processes within the RFID enhanced shopping scenario.

Second, as can been seen, we cannot and will not cover all legal aspects of agent programming. The legal issues raised by software agents are broader than those arising in the Research Scenario (e.g. cross-border agent transactions, which are not contemplated by the research). Even within the four chosen areas, we have decided to limit the work to the Research Scenario and the associated business and technical processes. An example of this limitation relates to consumer protection: most of the Scenario involves real-time shopping experience, with only occasional online purchases. Accordingly, many of the Distance Selling obligations may not apply and need not be included in the retail store's computer processes – while the consumer's purchasing agent may have to take this into account. Another area that we are not covering are any agent-based interactions between the store, its employees and electronically identified objects (for example, on the shop floor or in the warehouse), and between the store and its suppliers (agent-based supply chain management, as illustrated above in the Proctor and Gamble scenario).

Third, and in contrast to the above restriction, we will cover third party agents and open MAS when possible. We could have further restricted the legal issues by considering that the research's agent framework is "inside" or "closely related to" the supermarket, with agents doing various tasks between only the consumer, the products for sale, and the grocery store: parking agent, queue agent, auction agent (within the supermarket), payment agent, etc. This could generally be documented and framed by contractual relationship between supermarket and consumer and eventually e-payment parties. We could solve many of the legal problems of such "closed circuit" agents (or closed MAS) by creating a general legal (contractual) environment for using specific agents with specific parties, regulating privately most of the issues, such as consumer consent for data processing[76] or IPR exploitation rights. At the most, the system might consider a third party interaction with credit card systems such as Visa or MasterCard.

The difficulty – and legal interest – arises when we consider software agents that operate more independently on the Internet, for example going out and purchasing "alternative" cheaper products. So we also consider software agents that negotiate with third parties in open environments such as online grocers and other online suppliers: do they have capacity to negotiate with electronic agents? Can we tie them into the platform, or are there standard interfaces and protocols that we can use for (legally compliant) interoperability?

4.   RESEARCH METHODOLOGY AND TOOLS

4.1.1   Observers and actors

We have established a methodology and certain conceptual legal analysis tools, which has been useful for considering the functionalities or processes of specific software agents and delimiting (or expanding) capacities to maintain legal compliance. In analysing legal risks, apart from our initial classification of mediator / initiator (see above), it is also helpful to divide an agent's processes into two fundamental classes: observer and actor.

–   When an agent's objective involves only a desire to alter its own internal structure only (state), i.e., to receive information or create associations, the agent is an observer.
–   Anytime an agent's objective is to alter another's structure or state, i.e. to acquire or enforce any rights, the agent is an actor;

This is useful for legal analysis as actor agents raise many more issues than observer agents: each action will have a technical effect and therefore legal consequences in relation to third parties. For example, a search engine (in its classification / web crawler mode) is more of an observer, as the agent collects information about websites and classifies it in the search engine database. When a user inserts search criteria and searches the web or the engine's database to produce a list of URLs, the software is again acting as

---

[76] To the extent permitted by the regulatory framework.

observer. The same would be for a "privacy checking" agent programmed along the lines of P3P[77], which verifies website privacy statements and policies and reports back to the user. Initially it seems that the possibilities of legal risks are lower.

On the other hand, when an agent actually alters the state of another element of software (agent, website, database, RFID tag) by inserting a purchase order, concluding a contract, leaving a message, all of which would involve causing the interlocutor to add or modify a database or other software data repository or cause a program to execute (e-book delivery, software download, etc.), its role is that of an "actor", and the consequent liabilities are obviously greater, and the risks higher.

This Observer/Actor distinction is useful as it maps directly to the process orientation we have taken in our research, commented below: we while not necessarily sticking slavishly to this distinction, we can break down agent processes to determine their characteristics (observer processes, actor processes) and therefore evaluate the risk of the agent, and the need for legal caution. A comparative shopping agent for example may have some of both characteristics: initially it will only act as an observer, scanning websites for data matching its internal programming (product items, quantities, prices etc.). This initially raises no legal problems. However if it produces a comparative table to show to the user, it is likely that it will retrieve data from the website (images, text). Although it does not actually change the structure or state of the third party website and therefore cannot be qualified as an observer, it copies and presents contents from there and may deep-link directly to a webpage, raising certain IPR or fair trading issues. If it then goes on to actually purchase an item, it can be considered an Actor as it will negotiate with the website and modify the online store's databases.

4.1.2 Processes

We also want to introduce another useful analytical tool which will assist us in our task. We refer here to a process oriented approach to business transactions and online activities. Processes have been the focus of computer science for over a decade, and the gained knowledge is being applied in businesses[78]. It has been argued that companies can represent or conceptually "map" in graphical form their commercial activities and corporate knowledge. Well defined business and process models provide a complete end-to-end view of business activities, for example from purchasing through

---

[77] L Cranor, et al: *The platform for privacy preferences 1.0 (p3p1.0) specification*, 2002.

[78] Curtis et al: *Process Modelling*, 1992; Crowston: *A coordination theory approach to organizational process design*, 1997; Malone et al: *Tools for Inventing Organizations: Toward a Handbook of Organizational Processes*, 1999.

manufacturing to sales. Business Process Modelling (BPM) has been employed to encompass the knowledge of individual organisations into models that describe their processes and activities[79]. These are decomposed into transactions and processes to a varying degree of abstraction or simplification: e.g. from "invoice client" to "insert client VAT number in invoice file".

In the following chapters, we will try to define the commercial activities of the agents under study from a process view, breaking down each agent into a series of interdependent and coordinated steps (simpler processes). This focus describes the processes independently of their being carried out by humans or agents. It therefore integrates both human and automatic machine activities within a same framework. The analysis and understanding of the issues raised by the processes, their characteristics and procedures, should be valid for both forms of activities. We can then add in the agent dimension and analyse the differences.

We will see that, as the legal implications are discovered, further processes are required to provide compliance with the legal framework or for establishing higher levels of trust in the system. We argue that to minimise the risk, it will be important to establish a legal model that takes this into account, and adapt the business processes accordingly. We contend that the legal issues raised by agent technologies have implications for establishing organisational models and technical architectures for businesses that must respect what we call a legal architecture or legal process model, that is to say a model of legal entities, roles, concepts, data and processes established by the current legal framework. We will comment on this in more depth in our conclusions.

In Chapter 6, we discuss a conceptual model for business transactions using a new view of the firm and its processes (that we have called the MIT View of the firm). This provides a general framework for how organisations and their commercial processes may be considered and modelled, giving way to an easy means of process automation – by software agents as we consider here. We believe that this approach provides insights that assist in the analysis of these technical-legal issues, as a useful analytical tool and framework that will be used in the core chapters. It also illustrates why a conceptual and practical framework for legal architecture for e-business may be essential ingredients for a solution, together with new forms of laws and technical methodologies, languages, processes and platforms that are consistent with this legal architecture and laws.

---

[79] Giaglis: *A Taxonomy of Business Process Modelling and Information Systems Modelling Techniques,* 2001.

5. MONOGRAPH OVERVIEW

The rest of the book is organised as follows. First, in chapters 2-5, we shall review the legal issues raised by agent processing in the context of the research scenario, in relation to the four identified core areas: contract, intellectual property rights, consumer protection and privacy. Each chapter shall include the following sections:

1. A review of the relevant European legal framework (legislation and other regulation) setting out in general terms the laws applicable within the Research Scenario. This is used as reference for the legal analysis.
2. A process-based analysis of certain example agents, to define the challenges posed by these agents within the scenario (including Agents A-D outlined above). This defines the existence or occurrence of potential legal problems, and which processes and attributes may cause problems.
3. An examination of how the laws apply to the scenario, establishing the scope and particulars of the legal risks in the EU legal framework. This establishes the extent of the risks, and provides indications of how they may eventually be removed or minimised.
4. A review of some partial or potential technical and legal solutions for these issues. We examine what has been done to date, to remove or minimise the risks.
5. Each chapter will then conclude with some design recommendations for the agents under study.

This methodology allows us to gain an overall view of the legal background to agent transactions, and apply the relevant laws and regulations to specific agent processes. In each chapter some specific agent-based transactions and activities will be given as examples or illustrations, and commented on from a process-oriented perspective. We can also extrapolate from existing or proposed activities (for example, moving from an online commerce context to a mobile commerce context) to envisage future implementations in the context of the Research Scenario and legal problems that may arise from there. On the basis of the knowledge gained in the analysis, we can try to elucidate general rules underlying the problems (such as the questions of attribution, autonomy, trust), synthesise the issues and through abstraction look for a solution to the problems at a higher level (meta-models).

This procedure is illustrated below, in Figure 1-3. The "legal" Chapters 2-5 below concentrate on the middle and top half of the diagram, while Chapter 6 looks at the final part, outlining some design recommendations and arguing how a process view of online businesses and business models may help develop compatible legal and technical architectures. One of the fundamental objectives of this process-model based approach is to elucidate how to overcome the jurisdictional mismatch between laws and legal analysis (which are jurisdiction specific) and legal risks of the business and technical processes (which tend to be jurisdiction independent). We will discuss this in Chapter 6.

This diagram is repeated in each Chapter, providing a broad overview of the issues under study.

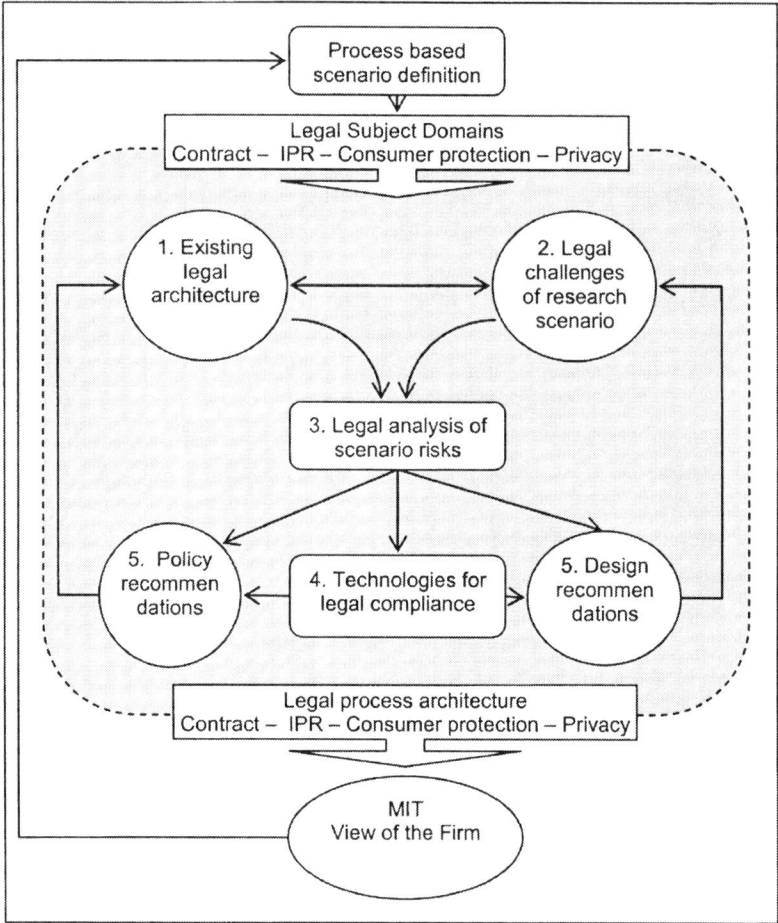

Figure 1-2. Research Process

This analytical work therefore leads us in Chapter 6 to draw some conclusions about the gap between law and technology, and how this may be bridged through a process-oriented approach that brings together both technical and legal processes within a same framework. This provides the basis for suggestions or general roadmap for future research in relation to both generic e-business processes and agent-based ecommerce.

Please note that our work mainly focuses on the European legal framework for the use of agents: the detailed analysis of each member state's national law is too great for the scope of this research. We include some comments and differences related to US law. National laws must be analysed in more detail when the research scenario is implemented in a specific jurisdiction, in conjunction with a store that can determine which is the most relevant applicable legal framework. For example we analyse the EU framework for consumer protection, looking at the directives and regulations, but when it comes to implementation, we will have to look at the national applicable laws. Please also note that where report refers to the application or effects of a Directive, reference is in fact made to national legislation implementing that Directive. This may have certain variations which will be studied when relevant. However there are certain important areas of law, notably contract law, where there is no European framework, in which case we will set out general principles applicable throughout the Union and comment on individual variations where relevant.

Chapter 2

CONTRACTS
Can agents do your grocery shopping...?

La gran corriente de voluntarismo jurídico que lleva a considerar que el origen de las obligaciones se encontraba en la expresión de la voluntad de las partes.
Luis Díaz Picazo, Fundamentos de derecho civil patrimonial, 1ª ed., 1970.[1]

Computers are no longer seen as simple communication tools for message transmission in ecommerce but, as we have discussed in the introduction, they are (becoming) capable of initiating transactions and entering into agreements with third parties. The Research Scenario envisages agents that are sufficiently independent to generate such agreements, and the principle issue we need to consider is whether communications by or with agents, i.e. agent based transactions, can form a valid and legally binding contract, and what conditions are required for more secure contracting.

We first set out in section 1 the basic general principles of contract law in Europe. In section 2, we consider certain agents that raise issues relating to contract law, and in section 3 discuss the most important of those issues. In section 4, we comment on certain legislated solutions and other measures that are being suggested for dealing with agent-based contracting, while finally looking in section 5 at recent developments in this area.

---

[1] *The significant current of legal voluntarism leads us to consider that the origin of obligations was found in the expression of the will of the parties.* Luis Díaz Picazo. Fundaments of civil property law, 1970, *(Authors' unofficial translation).*

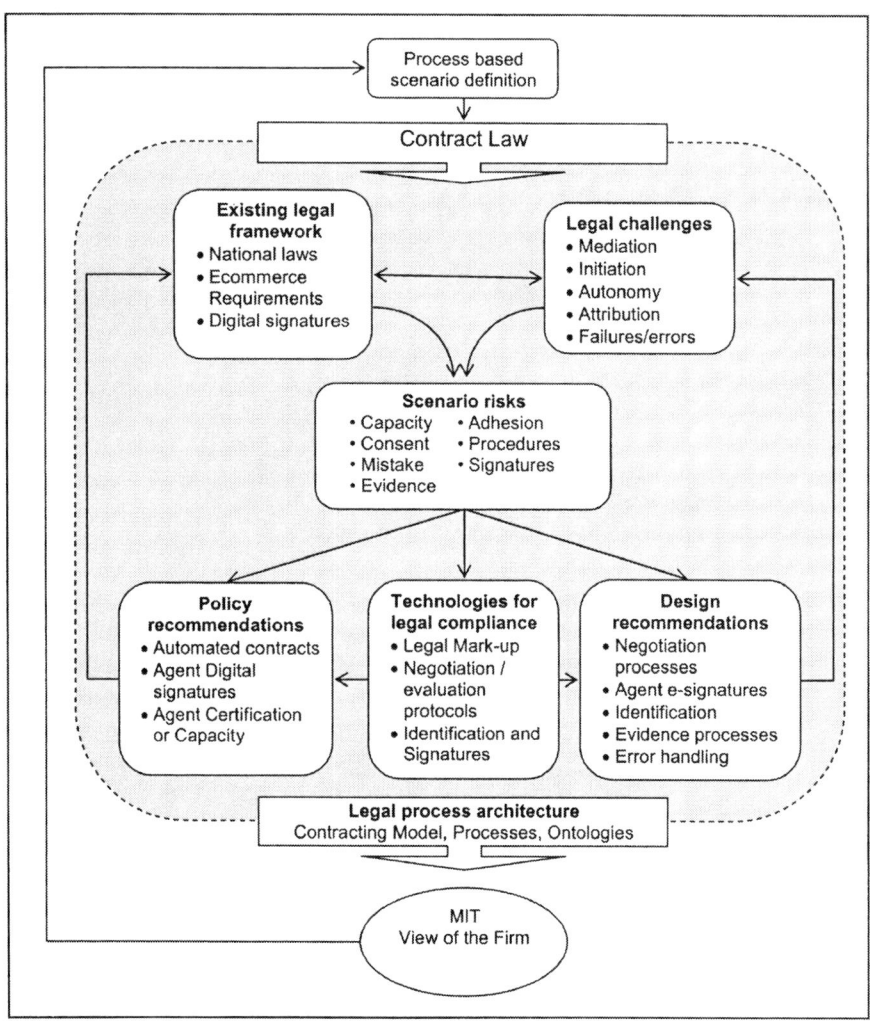

Figure 2-1. Contract Law Analysis

1. OUTLINE OF GENERAL PRINCIPLES OF CONTRACT LAW

1.1 Civil Law and Common Law systems

Contract law is a matter for national jurisdictions and has not (yet[2]) been harmonised at European level. Although the differences between Civil and Common Law systems are not substantial, some of them are relevant for our purposes in relation to agents (see specific sections below). The following is a brief outline of core contract principles applicable throughout Europe that are relevant for our study (mainly offer, acceptance and, consent (1.2), validity (1.3) and the incorporation of terms (1.4)). Our aim is not to discuss contract law, but to provide a general background showing the areas and concepts that will raise difficulties for the use of agents.

1.2 Formation

Consent: offer and acceptance – a meeting of minds. A contract is generally considered to be formed when all parties to the contract have consented to be bound by the contract: that is to say that there has been a suitably definite offer (not revoked) that has been validly accepted by the other parties. Offers may be made orally, in writing or even by conduct and accepted in any manner reasonable in the circumstances. Consent must be freely given, and may be affected by mistake (including lack of intent), misrepresentation or bad faith (see below). There is some divergence, however, as to what constitutes an offer, as some "offering declarations" may be considered an invitation to treat.

Intention. In Common Law systems, the parties must intend to be legally bound (i.e. not create a "gentlemen's' agreement"). This issue is incorporated in civil law systems into the validity of the consent. This is the presumption in normal commercial transactions.

Evidence in writing. Some European jurisdictions require contracts to be in writing and signed. In others, except for certain specific contracts specified in legislation (e.g. sale of land, securities, some consumer contracts[3]), there are no formal requirements for contracts to be in writing and signed by the parties: a verbal agreement is sufficient. The issue is one of evidence (acceptable in court or other dispute resolution procedure) to prove the existence and terms of the contract, for which written documentation signed by the parties is the strongest proof. For this reason,

---

[2] See CEC Communication on European Contract Law, 11 July 2001, COM(2001) 398 final http://europe.eu.int/comm/consumers/policy/developments/contract_law/index_en.html and
  Report of the Study Group on a European Civil Code at http://www.sgecc.net
[3] Also, in the USA, contracts above a certain sum - $500 – or for a certain period

contracts may be made over the telephone, by exchange of faxes, emails, website forms, and EDI (electronic document interchange) procedures, i.e. in electronic form.

Signatures. Again, apart from certain specific contracts such as the purchase and sale of land, there is no obligation for any written evidence to be signed by the parties. Signatures authenticate a document, as proof of consent and to prevent repudiation by a party who wishes to avoid being bound.

1.3   Validity and Enforceability

Capacity. To be valid and legally enforceable, all parties who enter into the contract must have legal capacity. This capacity is either an a priori condition for validity (Civil Law systems) or an a posteriori reason for invalidation (Common Law). Generally speaking, only natural or legal persons (organisations with legal identity: corporations, associations) have capacity to contract.

Object and cause. Some civil jurisdictions (e.g. France, Spain) require that a contract should have a definite object and a lawful cause. This is covered in Common Law systems by the concept of determination (the terms of the offer and resulting agreement must be sufficiently clear and determined) and frustration (illegality renders a contract non enforceable).

Consideration. Under Common Law, a party needs to provide "consideration" (a type of compensation to the other party, e.g. payment or a promise to pay) for it to be able to enforce the contract terms against the other party/ies.

Mistake. An error in the minds of the parties, i.e. a mistake as to the desires and intent of the parties (e.g. as to certain terms or the object of the contract in question), will render a contract wholly or partially invalid or voidable, as it vitiates the consent of the parties.

Misrepresentation and good faith. While in Civil Law systems there is often a duty of good faith imposed by law on the negotiators of an agreement, under English Law the principle of *caveat emptor* rules ("buyer beware!"): there is no such duty on the parties, for example to correct an erroneous belief of the other. On the other hand, if a party is intentionally misleading, the other may rescind the contract if it so wishes or maintain the contract and claim damages.

1.4   Incorporation of Terms

It is important for all terms to be known to the parties at the time of consenting (otherwise consent may be vitiated), and "incorporated" into the contract. A party may not, after agreement, add extra conditions that were not known or incorporated at the time consent was given[4].

1.5   Other contract issues

Invitations to treat. Common Law systems divide the contracting formation process into two stages: (1) pre-contractual negotiations and advertising, and (2) formal offer/acceptance. It is a question of fact as to what actually constitutes an offer (rather than an invitation to treat, such as an advertisement) - for example a website under English law would be considered an invitation, with the consumer making the offer that is accepted by the ISP. Other jurisdictions could consider the website the offer of the ISP (if the terms were sufficiently definite), with the consumer making the acceptance.

Time and place. For certain purposes, it is important to establish the time and place of formation. The place of formation may determine the competent courts or the law applicable to the contract, while the timing of the messages (offer, acceptance, or revocation or either) may determine whether there is a binding contract and the moment of passing of risk or title.

Absent parties. In distance contracts where the parties are not physically present, several provisions regarding consumer protection apply, legislated on the basis of European directives (see section on Consumer Protection). These provisions cover obligations on the part of suppliers that render a contract voidable if they are not fulfilled.

1.6   Harmonisation efforts

Ole Lando Commission and UNIDROIT Principles of European Contract Law. For the last 20 years of so, various academic projects have aimed to produce a set of contract principles or laws that are common to all European Jurisdictions. This may be the basis for future EC harmonisation, but for the moment these principles must be explicitly incorporated as the legal basis for contracting to have any effect.

UNCITRAL Model Laws. The Model Law on Ecommerce[5] was adopted in June 1996 – it was drafted by a special commission of the United Nations, to provide a common framework for nations to adopt and adapt their laws for ecommerce. The Model Law is not binding, but provides a model of internationally acceptable rules in order to remove legal obstacles to ecommerce. More specifically, it aims at the legal acceptance of

---

[4] Thus, for example in ecommerce, the importance in web pages of including any contracting conditions, either directly on the "Accept" page, or by a visible and easily accessible link.

[5] UN General Assembly Resolution 51/162 of 16 December 1996, online at http://www.uncitral.org/english/texts/electcom/ml-ecomm.htm

electronic messages and records. More recently, UNCITRAL adopted a Model Law on Digital Signatures[6], which establishes a common framework for implementing laws about these signatures in national law. Various countries have used these Model Laws for their ecommerce laws, including Brazil, Thailand, and UEA.

1.7   The legislative framework for electronic contracting

The following table presents a brief list of the major legislated sources of law governing electronic contracts.

Table 2-1. Laws on electronic contracting

Law	Brief summary
EC Directive on Electronic Commerce (Directive 2000/31/EC)	This Directive requires Member States to ensure that their legal systems allow contracts to be concluded by electronic means (Article 9).
EC Directive on a Framework for Digital Signatures (Directive 1999/93/EC)	This Directive establishes a liability, evidentiary and procedural framework for obtaining and using a digital signature.
EC Directive on Distance Contracts (Directive 97/7/EC)	This Directive establishes consumer protections for contracts where parties are not present.
National legislation	European member states are (slowly) incorporating the provisions of the EC Ecommerce Directive into national law.
Other jurisdictions	Many nations have established "Ecommerce laws" for the recognition of electronic contracting, including most specifically USA (UCITA, UETA and ESIGN) and Canada (UECA).

We will now proceed in section 2 to outline the legal issues raised by software agents within the Research Scenario regarding contract law, and then in section 3 discuss these issues in more detail.

---

[6] UN General Assembly Resolution 56/80 of 12 December 2001, online at http://www.uncitral.org/english/texts/electcom/ml-elecsig-e.pdf

2. CONTRACT ISSUES ARISING IN AGENT TECHNOLOGY WITHIN THE RESEARCH SCENARIO

In the first section, we have seen the main principles of contract law in Europe. In this next section, we will briefly establish the main issues that are raised by agent contracting, either between agent and humans, or between agents. We will consider these issues in relation to the degree of human involvement. At the one end of the spectrum, there are processes where there is human confirmation of a deal (this would include standard online contracting, where the person clicks "I accept"). At the other end, fully automated agent processes require no human involvement at all. If the agent is not a legal person, "on whom is such a contract binding, against whom is it enforceable, who is responsible for any mistakes or non-performance?" are questions that come to mind. These provoking issues are discussed more methodically below.

2.1 Contracting agents

Considering the Research Scenario, it is useful to set out the general processes of shopping agents that include contracting capabilities. We consider three different agents that intervene at different stages of the Consumer Model set out in Chapter 1: advertising, offering, and negotiation/contracting. These software agents are schematically described in the tables below, using the BDI model of agents[7] and a process description of tasks.

Agent A is a store-based advertising agent, offering products to consumers in accordance with their shopping profile or other input: e.g. the store's current list of offers, an electronically identified product picked up by the consumer, or external data such as time, weather or season. Processing and communications are internal to the store (i.e. closed agent network - e.g. provided by other store network agents) using a Wireless LAN to the customers mobile device[8]. Product identification is provided by RFID tags attached to the products or their packaging.

---

[7] The BDI model, represents an agent by three structures: beliefs, desires and intentions. The beliefs of an agent are its model of the domain (information about the environment and cause/effect relationships), its desires provide a list of goals, and its intentions are the things it has decided to do (chosen goals). Wooldridge and Jennings, *Agent Theory and Practice* (1995).

[8] The agent could also communicate by SMS through an external gateway to a telecom service provider. This raises additional issues of security and confidentiality (e.g. additional layers in the agent communication architecture), especially in relation to any transmitted personal data, although WLAN / Wi-Fi also has its own security problems. See Blanchard C W: *Wireless security*, (2001).

Table 2-2. Summary Description of Agent A

Agent A	Description
Beliefs	Knowledge or beliefs regarding the consumer (customer profile and preferences, current shopping list, past shopping behaviour, extrapolation / inferred rules from such behaviour and preferences), and of the environment: date, time, place, store-related data (stocks, prices, current offers).
Desire	To inform customers of current products, and (better) persuade them to purchase.
Intention	Associating a determined offer to a specific client.
Autonomy / Intelligence	Offers are made without the store's knowledge or review and the agent learns from experience how to best match offers and clients.
Steps	**Process**
1	Agent A becomes aware of customer within target area for its particular advert (outside store front, within the store, within an area of the store), through external sensors (e.g. a location service agent[9] or RFID activation).
2	Agent A considers rules for sending adverts and consults relevant data sources.
3	Agent A sends an advertisement to the customer device (WLAN or SMS), without review by store staff.
4	Agent A monitors and updates customer reaction to message and stores this for further processing in relation to this and other clients, and this and other products

Agent B is a similar store-based selling agent, this time with added functionality for offering features such as contract conclusion and associated services: interconnection with payment systems and fidelity programmes, and home delivery. A more evolved version may have an advertisement linked to a direct "on-click" purchasing process. This may seem not much more than existing online B2C ecommerce sites[10], however agent-based computing is considered for efficient interaction with external data and communication systems and added intelligence for determining the appropriateness of sending the offer, and learning from the acceptance and rejection of the goods or services.

Table 2-3. Summary Description of Agent B

Agent B	Description
Beliefs	The same information processes as Agent A as well as additional data relating to the customer, e.g. home address (probably in the customer profile anyway) and electronic payment details.
Desire	To inform customers of current products and sell them.

---

[9] Location issues are considered, but are not specifically relevant to agent transactions, more general issue of location based services and obligations to maintain confidentiality under the new Privacy and Electronic Communications Directive 2002/58/EC (when implemented).

[10] Ecommerce websites are already autonomous if one looks at them from the merchant side: often online sales occur without any review by the seller, and even performance is autonomous (but not necessarily intelligent) in the case of online delivery of digital content.

Agent B	Description
Intention	To sell a specific product to a determined customer, on the occurrence of a certain event.
Autonomy / Intelligence	Determining the appropriateness of sending the offer; making an offer without store review; learning from the acceptance and rejection of the goods or services.
Steps	**Process**
1-3	As for A
4	Agent B provides a means for accepting the offered product (accept button, voice acceptance, etc).
5A	Agent B records and processes sale: sends a delivery order to a delivery service agent and a payment process order to a payment agent.
5B	The payment agent contacts credit card or electronic payment service provider and processes payment according to relevant system (e.g. adds item to credit card account). This may require confirmation from user of PIN or other identification means. This agent reports successful payment back to Agent B.
6	As for Agent A, step 4: B monitors and updates customer reaction to message and stores this for further processing in relation to this and other clients and products

Agent C is a customer-oriented automatic shopping/buying agent. This agent is resident in a consumer controlled environment / host, searches for products (e.g. based on a current shopping list or an identified product picked up by the client) and even suggests new products to the user and/or purchases them without review. It communicates both with the closed store systems (product and price databases, etc.) and with the open network (alternative shopping sites). It has communication, information retrieval and assessment and negotiation functionalities added to those held by Agent B and (more or less) complete autonomy from the user as orders and purchases may be made without review.

Table 2-4. Summary Description of Agent C

Agent C	Description
Beliefs	The same information processes as Agents A and B as well as additional data relating to the customer: home contents (in a pervasive computing scenario, where the home inputs data to the agent through sensor devices, at the agent's request or on its own initiative); shopping list; user profile and preferences; rule inference from previous behaviour / standard shopping behaviour; other data (e.g. hot weather therefore search for sale and delivery of extra cold drinks)[11].
Desire	Maximising the customers purchasing potential and life-style.
Intention	Self-determined in relation to the general desire. Specifically, to purchase an item it considers the consumer wants or needs.
Autonomy / Intelligence	Determining the appropriateness of searching for and choosing an item; making a purchase without customer review; learning from the acceptance

---

[11] Each such input is envisaged eventually as the result of individual agent processes: the shopping list agent, the user self-profiling agent, the diary / agenda agent, etc.

Agent C	Description
	and rejection of the goods or services; anticipating future needs.
Steps	**Process**
1	Agent C determines a need to purchase a specific item through assessment of data inputs and beliefs (e.g. shopping list update, product RFID activation).
2	Agent C searches the network for various stores selling relevant products. This includes certain evaluation criteria (reputation evaluation, closeness to home, brand availability, etc.) and comparison functions, with e.g. the local store product catalogue.
3	Agent C negotiates with store(s) for the quantity, price and other terms of sale. This may involve negotiation with more than one store at the same time, or participating in an auction, in one of various agent systems[12].
4	Agent C concludes purchase agreement.
5	Agent C provides delivery and payment details (see Agent B above - the order of steps 4 and 5 may depend on online site / selling agent process).
6	Agent C records transaction and reports purchase (in due course) to customer. The item is removed from the customer's shopping list.

2.2   Contracting issues

It is important to note that we do not intent to deal with general issues of online or electronic contracting in B2B or B2C ecommerce. Most nations have now attempted – or are attempting – to regulate and promote ecommerce by adopting a clear legal framework to allow for online contracting[13]. The more general contract issues raised by online transactions are well researched and published[14], while our topic here is agent-based contracting. Accordingly, we will exclude the following topics:

- The formation and validity of online / electronic contracts - where physical users (persons) explicitly accept a transaction (click "I accept") and have direct access to contract terms. This topic has been widely discussed and debated.
- The recognition and use of digital signatures for identification, authentication and non-repudiation (generally speaking – we will consider the possibility of digital signatures being provided by agents): again, this has been the subject of wide discussion and research.

---

[12] Some of the implications of multi-agent systems are discussed in Chapter 6.

[13] Notably the UNCITRAL Model Law efforts, but also the US laws mentioned above (UCITA, UETA, E-SIGN), and the EC Ecommerce Directive 200/31/EC.

[14] See for example, IST Projects IMPRIMATUR at www.imprimatur.net, ECLIP at www.eclip.org, and more general books on ecommerce law: Electronic Commerce: Law and Practice (M. Chissik and A Kelman), Going Digital: Legal Issues for Electronic Commerce, Multimedia and the Internet, A. Fitzgerald, B. Fitzgerald, P. Cook & C. Cifuentes (eds); Butterworths e-Commerce and Information Technology Law Handbook - Jeremy Phillips (Ed); E-Commerce: A Guide to the Law of Electronic Business Second edition -Hammond Suddards Edge; Manual de Derecho Informático. 3ª edición, Aranzadi, etc. Also, R Juliá-Barceló, *Electronic contracts*, 15 CLSR 3 (1999).

Concentrating on agent issues, and looking at the general outline of contract law above, the following is a list of the most important topics which we will consider in this research. These will be considered in turn below.

a) Certain conceptual problems, most notably agent-based contract formation and validity:
   – Capacity: do agents have sufficient capacity to enter into a contract? (section 3.1)
   – Consent: can agents provide consent, either of themselves or of the agent user? (section 3.2)
   – Agent failures, errors and the legal apportionment of risk. For example, what happens when an agent purchases the wrong product, or the system crashes? (section 3.2.3)

b) More practical issues
   – Procedures: can agents distinguish invitations, offers and acceptances? (section 3.3.1)
   – Evidence: can / do the requirements for "in writing" be met? How does one obtain and maintain evidence of an agent-formed contract? (section 3.3.2)
   – Terms: can we ensure that all terms are properly incorporated into a contract? Can the user have or be deemed to have knowledge of the terms? Where is the line between advertising and contract terms? (section 3.3.3)
   – Signatures: can an agent provide a digital signature with binding effect? (section 3.3.4)
   – Consumer rights: how to comply with information, transparency and consent requirements when using agents? (section 3.3.5)

2.3   Secure contracting frameworks

The problem of establishing valid and secure automated electronic contracts is not new: the research on Electronic Data Interchange (EDI) looked into the legal issues raised be agent contracting within a closed messaging framework. This closed network, however, provided a framework contractual solution to most problems, because identified business parties could chose, through a "macro" EDI contract, to accept the validity of agent-based contracts. This made it difficult for transaction participants to repudiate any electronic contract. Open network contracting, where at least consumer parties are not necessarily identified, is another matter. Except perhaps in the context of a supplier-merchant relationship, there are no previous dealings or framework contract to provide easy such contract based solutions.

It is important to keep in mind why we need to consider the contracting capabilities of agents: to provide certainty and confidence for users (both merchants and consumers) so that agent based commerce - specifically transactions within the Research Scenario - may develop. Without any faith in the validity of agent contracts, and the application of legal protections granted to both merchants (e.g. non repudiation) and consumers (e.g. proper performance, consumer protections set out in national and EC legislation), the advanced agent based consumer model may not grow to maturity and achieve the promised ultimate efficiency.

From a practical point of view, the programming of each of the processes of the agent should be considered from a legal point of view. This should result in legal specifications that will cover the design of shopping agents (from basic to advanced), while in addition the specification will evolve as the project evolves: new agents, evolving electronic devices and capacities (currently for example, only UMTS allows sufficient speed and storage for secure mobile communication based agent contracting). Such a study should include an analysis of the stages of the contract formation process to determine:

– What is included / excluded from the terms
– Are there previous representations / "declarations" that are binding? And
– How do you provide evidence of the formation - do you need to email confirmation?

In the next section, we will review the issues outlined above in detail, and try to answer the questions asked. While sections 3.1 and 3.2 cover conceptual issues in relation to contracting regarding capacity and consent, section 3.3 deals with more practical problems such as evidence, procedural regularity and digital signatures.

3.   CURRENT LEGAL POSITION ON THESE ISSUES

3.1   Capacity: do agents have sufficient capacity to enter into a contract?

On the basis that only natural or legal persons have capacity to enter into a contract – i.e. not electronic agents – there are three ways to give an intelligent agent the appropriate capacity:

– Establish an independent legal personality for the agent.
– Establish that the electronic agent is an agent (in the legal meaning) of a person, i.e. is acting on behalf of the user.

– Determine that the agent is a communication tool for transmitting the user's consent.

These possibilities should all be considered in the light of the attributes of capacity: benefiting of rights, incurring obligations, having patrimony (assets and liabilities), identification and decision-making capacity – including making mistakes.

3.1.1 Legal personality

Capacity is not the same as legal personality: a minor or mentally "incapacitated" person both have legal personality but are not legally capable of entering into contracts. Traditionally, legal personality is conferred through moral entitlement (e.g. women in the 19th Century), social capacity (clubs, associations, etc.) and legal and business convenience - this last is already done in other fields than technology, such as for corporations or other business organisations. The first two justifications are not applicable as it would be difficult to argue for personality on moral grounds or on social grounds, at least until agents evolve to acquire social capacities (independent interaction with persons) – a scenario not to be discarded, though currently still part of science fiction.

The justification of legal expedience is very attractive: with such personality come assets and liabilities (patrimony) and forms of decision-taking as well as ownership and management and identity. These are concepts that are easily achieved in the world of business, with the different forms of incorporation and business organisation (limited liability companies, partnerships, "sociétés" or "sociedades" of different combinations of persons). As regards agents, it seems that:

– Concepts of ownership and management may also be applied. These issues could be determined in traditional ways such as public registers, recording of decision-taking and parameterisation[15].

– The possibilities of assets and liabilities are more difficult to conceive in relation to software agents. Unless or until agents evolve to the extent of being sentient of these elements, and able to defend (rights) or satisfy them (obligations) and even have a physical place to keep them, some mechanism of transparency (such as the legal construct of agency) would have to attribute any such rights and obligations to the user or definitive beneficiary of the agent actions. One could even go to the extent of conceiving default repositories similar to, in the UK today, the Crown in relation to certain incapable or dead persons (e.g. minors).

– Identification is another thorny problem as agents are not necessarily independent parts of code but may be part of or distributed over an environment / platform or several platforms, that could also include other

---

[15] C Karnow, *Liability for Distributed Artificial Intelligences* (1996).

elements both hardware and software. It would be hard to identify the extent of the entity. Again, registration of ownership (or user) could solve this problem, though raising questions of cost and ease of implementation.

Despite interesting arguments presented by E. Pelino[16] in favour of agent personality, there is also a problem of the question of "sliding scale" and mutual recognition. At what point or degree of autonomy and decision-making capacity would an agent acquire a separate legal identity? If one agrees that a registration and encryption procedure may be established, what criteria would be used by whom to analyse an agent to determine if it has sufficient attributes, autonomy or capacity for legal personality? How would users and/or registrars deal with the "identity key" which protects the agent from tampering and duplication? And would the personified agents of one jurisdiction be recognised in another, as companies generally are? While we believe that these are issues that are not impossible to solve with an appropriate registration system, this concept does not assist us currently in validating agent-based contracting.

All in all, it does not seem appropriate at the moment to go the extent of establishing legal personality to provide contracting capacity to electronic agents. As we will see below, and until agent technology progresses to such extent that agents acquire higher levels of autonomy and sentience when forms of registration may become desirable, there may be other ways of getting around the issue of contracting capacity of software.

3.1.2   Legal concept of agency

For the sake of clarity, in this section computer agents will be denominated with capital letters (Intelligent Agents) while legal agents will remain in lower case.

Under the law of agency in European countries (and in the US) an agent is a person who acts on behalf of another (called a "principal" or "*mandante*", etc.) and the agent's acts within the scope of its mandate binds that person. Any act outside that mandate is deemed an excess of authority and does not bind the principal unless he/she ratifies it[17].

It seems reasonable to think that a Software Agent could be considered the equivalent of a legal agent. A program given the capacity to sense its environment, deliver instructions to other parties (persons or computers), execute and perform agreements like downloading software or sending data without further input from the agent user, is acting in way very similar to

---

[16] E Pelino, *Autonomous Software Agents as Legal Persons*, Alfabiite (2002).

[17] See Van Haetjens, *Shopping Agents and Their legal Implications Regarding Austrian Law* (2002) and F. De Miglio et al. Electronic *Agents and the Law of Agency* (2002) for comments on representation rather than full agency

any human being doing the same things as a legal agent for another. Why should the law treat it any differently?

The advantages of this "legal agent" paradigm are several: under the principles of agency, the Software Agent's decisions and actions bind the principal, who engages his/her responsibility and would respond to any third party who had any claim. The obligations and rights under any contract formed by a Software Agent would be passed on to the principal. The agent itself does need not to have legal capacity to act (for example, a minor may act as agent for an adult) and the human or corporate principal can also ratify the (disclosed) agent's actions if necessary.

However there are currently several legal difficulties to this construct[18]:

a) Under the law of agency, principal and agent are separate persons[19]. A software program is not a person (yet – see section above on legal personality).

b) The agent has to consent to act as agent for the principal. For Software Agents, this becomes a circular argument: we are trying to solve the problem of agent consent by pretending it is acting on behalf of the principal. So in the end, it is the principal who is consenting to the agency relationship with itself. Neither does the idea of presumed consent from the Software Agent convince.

c) An agent may be liable for its actions when it acts outside the scope of its mandate – a possibility all the more likely as an agent such as Agent A gains independence, or when its principal is not disclosed to third parties. The principal may or may not ratify such act. We have seen that a Software Agent today has no legal capacity nor any assets or patrimony to respond to any liability.

d) The acts of an agent acting without disclosing its mandate may not be ratified by the principal.

e) How does one deal with any action undertaken by the Software Agent by mistake either through an error in programming, initial user parameterisation or subsequent malignant intervention or distortion?

f) Who is responsible in the case of viruses or errors in the operating system or agent host?

These objections could be solved if legal personality was conferred by law on Software Agents (a new legal fiction such as incorporated persons). It does not seem that legislation is pointing this way yet, as we will see below under the section on consent.

Interesting solutions have been offered to deal with the capacity of Software Agents in relation to agency law. We feel the most convincing has

---

[18] See also Allen and Widdison, *Can computers make contracts?* (1996).

[19] In most jurisdictions, and even under EC law for example Directive on Commercial Agents, 86/653/EC.

been offered by Kerr[20], who suggests that one should only consider the external aspects of legal agency, applied to the legal relationship between the principal and the third party (obligation, liability, ratification, etc) as any disputes would only arise between these persons. One would not apply the internal aspects (the relationship between the principal and the agent), as the conferring of authority on the agent could be deemed by the act of programming or parameterisation of the agent and initiating its activities. This has the advantage of:

– Using the concept of apparent authority[21]. This would apply when a person makes it clear that the Software Agent is acting on his/her behalf: the person is bound towards third parties by the agent's acts. In the context of the Research Scenario, we can consider if the Agent user, consumer or merchant, would make any Agent such as A, B or C appear expressly to act on their behalf. It will in fact be fairly obvious that A and B are performing on behalf of the Store. It may not be so clear who the user behind Agent C is. This apparent authority could be in the programming of the "identity" of the Software Agent, which could include identification or at least a declaration of the existence of the user/principal, as part of the user parameterisation. However, how this concept would apply in a relation between two Agents is unclear.
– Applying the concept of ratification. The user/principal could ratify any act outside the scope of the original mandate (especially with evolving agents that learn and adapt). This is only possible if the Agent discloses that it is acting on behalf of the principal, again something that could be included in the internal programming of the agent for greater certainty and contracting security.

This would deal with objections (a), (b) and part of (c) above, but does not help with problems of undisclosed excess authority, mistake and errors or bugs (objections (d), (e) or (f))[22]. In relation to autonomous and mobile Agents such as Agent C, the risks of excess authority and mistake grow with the advance of technology, as Software Agents become more functional and independent, carry out more complex transactions – including delegating to or collaborating with other Agents – with more parameters and "experience/learning" features, and as they acquire the capacity to migrate to less controlled environments. These issues are not resolved by the legal

---

[20] I Kerr: *Providing for Autonomous Electronic Devices* (2000), also discussed by E. Weitzenboeck, *Electronic Agents and the Formation of Contracts* (2001).

[21] This apparent authority is conceptually similar to the theory of "appearance" or "reliance" in some civil law countries – France, Spain, Germany, Netherlands -, where a third party is protected by their legitimate belief in an apparent situation – a sort of "constructive agency" or estoppel. There seem to be limits, to this, however, and the construct would not apply to more advanced software agents.

[22] These issues may have legislated solutions: see section 3.2.3 below under "mistake" and errors.

agency scenario and in the lack of any specific legislation[23] need to be dealt with in some other way.

This solution would also require legislation or judicial approval (and indeed, it seems that certain aspects of this theory are incorporated into the Canadian UECA). In Europe, however, the EC Ecommerce Directive has left it up to member states to "ensure their legal system allows contracts to be concluded by electronic means" and it remains to be seen what action will be taken in respect of Electronic Agents (see section 4.4 below – recent legislation).

3.1.3   Communication tools

The use and legal validity of technology to transmit the consent of a natural or legal person is already well established, since the days of the telephone, fax and even, more recently, Electronic Document Interchange (EDI). In these "low-tech" situations, technology does not have to have legal capacity as the person entering into any agreement is the user of the technology, usually a human being or corporation with full legal capacity. The technology is a communication tool.

In relation to software agents, this construct seems the most likely to achieve legal validity at present, even though it may be the most limiting paradigm from an artificial intelligence / independent agent point of view: it denies the autonomy of the technology. Insofar as agents are simple mediators of ecommerce, retrieving or supplying information, putting persons into contact with one another, transmitting the real consent ("I accept" click or statement) of the user, this construct will be the most appropriate. This is certainly the case for Agents A and B. As the word "mediator" implies, the software is only an assistant or tool of the user. This construct deals with all issues of rights, liabilities and obligations as these are attributed or accredited to the user.

The pros and cons of this are discussed below, under the section on attribution of consent. In addition, this view may encounter difficulties as agent technology evolves and it becomes no longer possible to consider the software as simple mediators but as initiators (Agent C), as we discussed in the introduction (Chapter 1).

Arguments have been made against this view on the basis that it may be unfair to automatically attribute to the user all acts of the agents, including mistakes, distortions and unexpected acts (all the more so as agents acquire autonomy) that may have serious legal and practical consequences (imagine Agent C hiring 10 motorcars instead of 1!). In some jurisdictions, as we noted above, there may be a duty of good faith on the counter-party to

---

[23] UCITA and UECA try to deal with mistake, etc. Failing legislation, it will be up to the courts to decide...

correct or at least question an unexpected request or act in the course of negotiations, a duty which puts them in a difficult situation regarding deciding what to do. It would also not be commercially reasonable to hold a person liable for such unexpected acts which would normally be corrected in non electronic/automated transactions.

Avenues should be explored to see how the excessive liability for unexpected acts could be restricted or minimised, for example:

– Technically: providing for some form of feedback or non-automated communication for counter-parties in doubt. Alternatively, programming for a time period for confirmation and/or rejection (similar to consumer protection laws in distance contracts – though this would cause problems in a supermarket scenario). Certain items that may cause mistake or distortion (identity, addresses, payments, etc.) could be dealt with by communications with trusted third parties. Regarding identity, for example, it has been suggested to create a registry of agents that could confirm original agent objectives for protection against intervening distortion of agent behaviour... This may have difficulties with evolving and learning agents, though limits could be described like in a companies "object" clause.

– Legally: providing some balanced system of liability limitation – similar to the application of the principles of mistake – so that on the one hand users can repudiate a contract that is not in accordance with its instructions, while on the other counterparties are protected from illegitimate repudiations. This could either be in the general law for agent contracting (see attribution of consent – liability limitation, below) or by establishing a framework for an organisation for the registration of agents similar to the one for digital signatures (see paragraph above, though there are doubts about the economic viability of this solution) which would show the contracting capabilities of the agents that have been registered.

3.2   Consent: can agents provide consent, either of themselves or of the agent user?

3.2.1   Subjective and objective consent

As we saw in the outline, a contract is formed when two or more parties agree upon a certain transaction, that is to say they consent to be bound by the terms. There is a slight difference in the content of such consent between Civil and Common Law: Civil Law will look for offer and acceptance while Common Law will also look for an intent to create a legal relationship (as opposed to a simply informal one). However, the greater issue among

European jurisdictions is the conceptual difference between the two legal systems as to intent:
- Civil law will base a contract on a subjective view of intent, the inner will: did the parties really intend to contract[24]?
- Common law looks only to the expression of such intent – an act –, in what is otherwise known as the objective view of consent: did the parties clearly express an intention to contract, from their words, writings and other circumstances.

Of course, there are several variations among legal systems, and these pure views are moderated by various additional concepts such as third party reliance or estoppel, good faith, misrepresentation and reasonableness. We will see the application of these below.

3.2.2 Application to agent-based provision of consent – the attribution of consent

The issue at hand is whether an electronic agent can intend or express intent. Taking the Civil Law view literally, it is obvious that an agent has no inner intent or state of mind (at the moment... again, one could argue that agents will evolve into devices that are self-determinate). The strictness of this view however is tempered at least in Germany, for example, where the objective view (based on the expression) will be taken to protect the recipient of any declaration of intent. This means that the party does not have to look behind the expression to determine whether the declarer actually intended the consent.

The objective view is of great assistance towards allowing software agents to contract: parties may rely on the outward expressions of the counterparties and do not have to look to their mental state. Electronic agents of course can express consent (offer or acceptance) by providing the appropriate electronic response to a request – e.g. the now traditional "I accept" message/click, but without the human action behind it. The validity of this consent is not determined on the basis of the inner mind, but determined on the basis of a test of reasonableness: would the reasonable counterparty believe that the declarer was giving his or her consent and intending to be bound. The consent only need be apparent, sufficient for the reasonable counterpart to base his response upon it (e.g. acceptance, performance or payment), so that the internal operation and programming of the electronic agent are irrelevant.

Problems may arise as to exactly whose consent is being expressed: the agent's or the user's? Insofar as the agent is merely a mediator like Agents A and B, and does not initiate a transaction without the intervention of the user,

---

[24] There are indications that this may be somewhat changing in France, for example. See E. Weitzenboeck, op cit.

then the consent in question must be considered to be that of the user. As we saw above, the agent can be considered a tool and the expression of consent is attributed to the user (either directly in relation to the transaction in question, or indirectly because the user knows that the agent is operating autonomously within certain parameters and entering into a series of transactions that tacitly the user agrees to). On the other hand, in relation to more advanced agents such as Agent C that can initiate a transaction without the knowledge of the user, the consent could seem to be technically that of the agent: the user is not aware of the transaction, so how can he/she give consent? In the end however, we contend that this consent will have to be deemed by the (reasonable) counterpart to be that of the user, unless certain circumstances indicate otherwise[25].

So it seems that this objective view, mainly prevalent in the Common Law jurisdictions, may assist courts in deciding affirmatively on the validity of an agent generated contract. The granting of this validity, attributing it to the user, would mean that contracts may be entered into by agents without the user(s) either knowing the terms of such agreements or even knowing that the agreement is taking place. Courts would have to rely on the initial parameterisation and operation of the devices to infer the general intent of the parties to enter into such agreements,

- either restrictively on the basis that the contract corresponds to the initial programming of the agent, and therefore the original intent of the user (closer to a subjective view of consent – the programming reflects the inner mind of the person); or
- more widely by enforcing contracts on the basis of the reliance of the counterpart upon the acts of the agent (pure objective view) – the user assenting to the means also assents to the consequences. Awareness of the time and terms are not relevant when considering the objective element of consent in the formation of contracts.

Again, it must be noted that the restrictive view may be difficult to use with more advanced agent technology. On the other hand, currently the more liberal interpretation may prove problematic even for common law courts and, until legislation is passed, require a fairly liberal interpretation of the law, as we discuss next.

---

[25] E.g. Trusted third party confirmation of limits of electronic agent's powers, or other intervening knowledge of the counterpart. If the consent could not be deemed to be that of the user, the answer to "whose consent is it?" is "no-one's": there is a mistake – somewhere along the line – that goes to the root of the contract and makes it void.

3.2.3 Certain problems with the objective view – liability limitation and mistakes

If we agree that the objective view of consent (and in the event of initiator agents, a liberal judge) will permit agent-based contracting, there will still be a fair amount of uncertainty and mistrust on the part of users if they know that they will be indiscriminately bound by any act of the agent. In relation to simple mediators, again we argue that there should be no problem for user confidence, except for problems of human or machine mistake or malignant intervention which would have to be dealt with. However autonomous and learning-functional agents may cause difficulties with unexpected acts and transactions that the user would not intend, foresee or authorise.

Accordingly, the following is a short list of reasons why persons (consumers especially but also merchants) may want to reject an agent-based contract, and without guarantees that this is possible, would hesitate to use these devices.

a) Mistakes: human mistakes – either in programming or parameterisation.
b) System failures: machine faults – power surges, etc., and external interference (viruses and other damaging acts).
c) Unexpected acts: through agent learning and autonomy and bad deals (potentially involving bad faith on the part of the user).

These issues may be resolved by the application of certain traditional or more modern concepts of contract law which are discussed below. Otherwise legislation will be required (see section 4.4 below on recent legislation).

a) Mistakes:

In any transaction there can be a mistake, and contractual frameworks include underlying principles about the effect of mistakes on a transaction. In the end, the question of mistake is one of apportionment of risk: what to do when one party alleges agent mistakes (either agent itself or site-related mistakes in relation to an online merchant, such as has happened to Argos in the UK, or Kodak in the USA[26]) in order to modify or annul a contract. There are three obvious parties to bear the risk:

– The innocent counterparty – seller or buyer – if the contract is cancelled.
– The mistaken user, if the contract is sustained with no modifications.
– The programmer/agent vendor in relation to defective agents (in relation to which, see also consumer protection issues below). In relation to programming errors, the user may have a remedy against the programmer or seller of the agent, whose liability may be limited, subject to mandatory law on exclusion of liability and consumer products.

---

[26] See "Kodak snaps under customer pressure", ZDNet UK, 31.01.2002.

The effect on the principal contract between user and counterpart (seller, etc.) will be determined by basic principles of contract law, modified by any legislation that considers machine and/or human mistakes.

Generally speaking:

– A mistake made by one party that is known to the other will cancel a contract (the other party may not take advantage of the mistake, both under Civil Law duties of good faith in negotiations, and under Common Law principles of mistake).

– A mistake made by one party that is not necessarily known by the other, but which affects the contract to the extent that a reasonable counterpart would suspect an error, would also cancel the validity of a contract.

– A mistake made by one party that looks reasonable (see above, on reasonable consent) will probably bind the parties. On this basis the risk of an agent mistake would fall on the user of the agent.

Recent legislative attempts to deal with human errors are commented below, in section 4.4. One issue that will have to be determined is the question of adaptive agents that "learn"... possibly mistakenly. They may then enter into contracts that would never have been contemplated by the agent user, who may wish to plead mistake to avoid the contract. It will be a question of fact if the parameterisation or the adaptive functionalities of the agent were incorrect (the latter being something which may be very difficult to judge). The former may be a technical issue, though some form of recording of initial parameterisation should be kept.

On top of these issues, courts may wish to apply what has been called the "external aspects" of agency, limiting users' liability to that which is reasonable – though this is yet to happen, and the effects fully understood.

b) System failures, exterior interference

We believe that the same principles should probably apply to system failures, certainly regarding mistakes that are so unreasonable as to affect the contract. An innocent party could also plead third party intervention (third party computer failures, power surges, etc.) to annul the contract. The same reasoning as above could be applied regarding the nature and extent of the mistaken terms in the eyes of the counterpart: if they are not unreasonable, the contract should be upheld and the user of the agent assumes the risk of using such technology.

Additionally there would be no recourse against the programmer, except if external interference such as interception or "spoofing" should have been foreseen and was not catered for (for which, the issue of agent security is essential using such technologies as encryption and digital signatures for secure contracting).

System failures and third party interventions such as denial of service attacks or viruses are a risk at all stages of online ecommerce, not just in agent based contracting. In section 4.4 below, we comment on how recent legislation in the USA and Canada attempts to deal with these problems, either by providing clear guidelines as to contract validity or by providing procedures for the elucidation of real intent.

c) Unexpected acts and bad faith

This question is raised by agents that learn and adapt their beliefs, desires and intentions (possibly mistakenly, thereby distorting the user's intentions). They could then initiate new processes and enter into contracts that would never have been contemplated by the user.

First, the fact that users cannot foresee the agent decisions may not mean that they cannot be bound by them. Courts may wish to apply the previously mentioned "external aspects" of agency, limiting but also enforcing users' liability to that which is reasonable in the circumstances. Sartor argues for an intentional stance: contractual validity is based on the agent declarations and any default or malfunction would be construed as default of will removing consent and therefore invalidating the contract[27]. In the event of any attempt to repudiate a deal on the basis of defects, it will be a question of fact if the initial parameterisation or the adaptive functionalities of the agent actually were incorrect, a technical issue which may be difficult to judge. Again, we argue that some form of record of initial parameterisation and user's intent could be kept. It must then be determined where the risk falls, in which case the rules of mistake should apply.

In addition, in some jurisdictions like Spain, for example, there may be a duty of good faith on the counter-party to correct or at least question an unexpected request or act in the course of negotiations, a duty which puts them in a difficult situation in deciding what to do. It may also not be commercially reasonable to hold an agent user liable for such unexpected acts which would normally be corrected in non-electronic or non-automated transactions. This issue is also complicated by consumer protections that allow consumers to cancel distance contracts within certain time periods, thus providing a consumer agent-user an advantage in relation to merchants.

3.3   Other issues

Now we have considered the fundamental or conceptual difficulties of agent-based contracting, we turn to some more practical or procedural problems that may be raised. This section looks in turn at the correct procedures for contracting (3.3.1), form and evidentiary requirements (3.3.2) the adequate incorporation of terms (3.3.3), whether software agents may provide legally binding or protected digital signatures (3.3.4) and the application of consumer rights in relation to contracts (3.3.5). After this, in

---

[27] G Sartor, *Agents in Cyberlaw* (2002).

Section 4 we turn to look at some legislative proposals that have been made (and some enacted) to deal with these issues.

3.3.1   Procedures – invitations and offers

The contracting framework regarding online contracting is still unclear within the European Union, especially as regards to the steps taken to form a contract (see above, general principles). The EC Ecommerce Directive left it up to Member States, in order to avoid upsetting national contract law frameworks.

As mentioned above, while a B2C site – and Agent A above, and maybe Agent B – may be considered by Common Law to be an invitation for a potential client to put in an offer for the goods on show which will then be accepted (or not) by the site, under Civil Law if the terms are sufficiently precise (they usually are, as they include description, price, delivery terms, etc. – and even more so if dialogues are standardised by the use of XML), the site will be considered an offer and the agent/user makes an acceptance – no further steps required. In practise, this is avoided by website terms of use that say that all consumer communications will be deemed offers, subject for example to availability and other criteria (payment authorisation, etc.).

When Agent B offers a special deal to the customer, is it really an offer, or would it be considered an invitation for the customer to make an offer to the store, and then store's systems decide whether there are sufficient units available to be able to accept it?

This means however that software agents may have to be programmed to take extra steps – more steps than may be really necessary – to comply with all national frameworks, which may vary from country to country. To add to this, the EC Ecommerce Directive requires electronic transactions to be acknowledged by Internet Service Providers (site owners). So this acknowledgement should also be incorporated into the programming, for compliance with procedural formation requirements. Extra processes will be required for Agent C, and maybe B, for them to satisfy these procedural requirements (please see the table at the end of this chapter, for a suggestion for Agent C).

The question is complicated however by the further requirement contained in the EC Ecommerce Directive regarding deemed reception: "when the data enter the recipient's information system"[28]. If it is the agent who is collecting the relevant information/confirmation such as Agent C, it may be difficult to argue that the relevant data has been received by the consumer until the agent "returns to the fold" or sends the data on (back) to the user. Static agents resident in a user's computer or linked to a mobile phone (with instant access to data) would not pose much difficulty (provided

---

[28] Article 11 EC Ecommerce Directive.

the user can access the "state" or data contained in the agent at all times), however mobile agents, especially if they are more autonomous and don't report back immediately after entering into an agreement, will cause serious difficulties with this. The transaction would not be deemed valid until the relevant acknowledgement was received, maybe days later, by the user. In fact, merchants may be disinclined to operate with agents as they will not be able to "presume" that the data is received by the user within a short period (like emails or SMSs). Programming specifications for agents could include a data field informing merchants when agents report back to Users ("immediate", "within X period", etc., or "by SMS", etc.). Merchants could then perform the contract (software download, home delivery, etc.) accordingly.

Finally, consumer protection law provides certain procedural safeguards for consumers. These are briefly commented in section 3.3.5 below, and developed in chapter 4.

3.3.2   Form and Evidence

We now comment on whether the requirements for contracts to be made "in writing" can or have to be met in agent contracting, and how one can obtain and maintain evidence of an agent-formed contract.

As to the former, the requirement for contracts to be "in writing" that is established in certain jurisdictions and in respect of certain contracts is to be dealt with by national implementation of the EC Ecommerce Directive. Article 9 requires that: "Member States shall in particular ensure that the legal requirements applicable to the contractual process neither create obstacles for the use of electronic contracts nor result in such contracts being deprived of legal effectiveness and validity on account of their having been made by electronic means"[29]. This has been understood to aim at allowing contracts to be made and evidenced in electronic form, with common exceptions for certain documents such as transfers of land. Most EU member states are adapting their legal frameworks to permit this[30].

The remaining question is a practical one of creating and storing evidence or proof of an agent-created contract, to provide higher levels of trust and certainty in agent based ecommerce. Similar to certain commercial sites that send email confirmations of sales (e.g. online air flight reservations or train bookings), software agents such as Agent C should be able to incorporate code to take advantage of these functionalities and even, for greater user comfort, refuse to deal with sites that don't provide this feature. Whether this should be obligatory in ecommerce is debatable, as some

---

[29] Art 9 of the EC Ecommerce Directive.
[30] E.g. see Ley 34/2002 de Servicios de la Sociedad de la Información y de Comercio Electrónico, for Spain.

offline transactions do not require documentary evidence, so why should online contracting be more burdensome? In the aim of providing certainty, transparency and predictability in ecommerce, some jurisdictions have required means to provide such documentary evidence. The EC Ecommerce Directive requires traders to provide recipients of a service a means for storing and reproduce contract terms, for example[31]. This may be all the more necessary – at least for the consumer – for agent contracting where the parties may not even be aware that such transactions are concluded.

This issue of form and evidence should also be linked to taxation requirements for invoicing, and electronic transaction record keeping. There does not seem to be any extra burden on companies in this area in relation to agent contracting. This issue should be dealt with by the internal programming of ecommerce merchant applications: appropriate invoices may be sent either by email or other communication system to purchasers. This issue is discussed further in section 3.3.5 below and Chapter 5 on Consumer Protection.

3.3.3   Terms

Agent contracting raises two questions regarding contract terms. Can we guarantee that all terms are properly incorporated into a contract? And, can the user have or be deemed to have knowledge of the terms?

One of the perennial problems of electronic contracting is the fact that contract law requires all terms applicable to the contract to be incorporated into the contract, otherwise they are not binding. Indeed, under consumer protection law the consumer must be notified of all these terms prior to conclusion of the deal (see below). In normal online contracting, the applicable terms are usually available to users and large notices (on good ecommerce sites) bring these terms to user attention. Ideally, the "I Accept" button presented by Agent B (which should often be "I Offer"!) is at the end of a scroll-down page that outlines all the applicable terms. Other now traditional procedures include adding the terms on a linked page (with the link next to the "I Accept" button). There are still debates about the validity of such links, but good website design should solve this issue. Additionally, if shoppers use agents to contract with the store that they are in, the log-on / registration system should provide an opportunity to give the general contracting terms to them.

As regards the question of attributing knowledge of the terms to the user, some questions that need to be considered are:
a) If the user is not aware of the existence of a contract, how will he/she be deemed to be aware of the terms? This issue may be solved by the application of the attribution theory: the knowledge of the agent is

---

[31] Art 10 of the EC Ecommerce Directive.

attributed to the user. As the user chooses to use an electronic agent, it is at the user's risk. This will have to be tempered by the application of mandatory consumer protection law (applicable according to the rules of Private International Law determined in the courts – usually – of the consumer's jurisdiction), for which, see below.

b) What terms will be considered incorporated into the contract, and how? Again, this may be solved by technical means – but subject to consumer protections: a dialogue should occur between the merchant site and software agent like Agent C so that the appropriate terms are notified to the agent (and even sent on immediately to users, in some conditions), stored and transmitted back to user for reference and reproduction. It will be a question of the programming of the agent as to how many of the contractual terms (product characteristics, sellers, privacy rules, payment procedures, guarantees, expiration dates, jurisdiction and applicable law, conflict resolution procedures, etc.) are considered "variable criteria" that can be parameterised by the user, and therefore expressly accepted. Other items that are not included in an agent/site dialogue may be deemed implicitly accepted by the user (on the basis set out above) once the express items are accepted.

3.3.4 Signatures: can an agent provide a digital signature with binding effect?

The provision of consent to an agreement need not always be in writing and signed by a party. Persons not requiring high levels of security for their online contracting – authenticity, integrity, confidentiality, non repudiation – will not have a problem to agent contracting (in this respect), even if they cannot prove that one party or the other signed an agreement. The very fact that electronic commerce has been so successful despite the lack of use of digital signatures is witness to this.

However, one of the concepts that have been developed for secure electronic transactions is the digital signature. This form of signature has been proposed as a solution to problems of identification, integrity and repudiation, i.e. that the parties know who they are contracting with, that the document has not been tampered with, and that the signatory cannot turn round after the transaction and say: "I didn't sign that" and try to avoid any binding obligations. A court will normally uphold the obligation. Table 2.5 provides a brief outline of the key points regarding electronic and digital signatures.

Table 2-5. Electronic and Digital Signatures in the EU Framework Directive[32]

---

[32] Directive 1999/93/EC of the European Parliament and of the Council of 13 December 1999 on a Community framework for electronic signatures.

Electronic signatures: A definition of Electronic Signatures is: "means data in electronic form which are attached to or logically associated with other electronic data and which serve as a method of authentication". This means data (signature) attached to other data (the document), that performs similar functions to a hand written signature. These can come in very many forms – e.g.: typed or scanned signature, electronic representation of a hand written signatures, a biological aspect, or a unique sequence of characters created by cryptographic means (providing better security).

Advanced electronic signatures: an "advanced signature" is one form of signature providing higher levels of security that has been given legal validity under the Digital Signature Framework Directive. It must be uniquely linked to the signatory and capable of identifying him/her, it is created using means that the signatory can maintain under his sole control and it enables data integrity. If it is backed by a "qualified certificate" (certificates that are produced (usually) by a trust service provider, whose obligations are outlined in the Directive) with a secure-signature creation device, like PKI software[33], it acquires legal validity as set out below. Only digital signatures using PKI currently fulfil the requirements.

Certificate providers: these constitute trusted third parties to ensure trust between trading parties, and are regulated by the EC Directive (and national implementation). They validate the linkage of the signature to its owner, issue certificates, generate keys or key pairs, and hold copies of keys.

The Digital Signatures Framework Directive: The Directive introduces a uniform standard for legal recognition of electronic signatures regardless of their origin in the EU, and facilitates the legal recognition of electronic writing. The legal effect of the Directive is that Member States must ensure that advanced electronic signatures satisfy the national legal requirements of a signature in relation to data in electronic form (in the same manner as a hand-written signature satisfies those requirements in relation to paper documents). Admissibility as evidence in legal proceedings can no longer be denied on the sole grounds that a signature is in electronic form, does not meet certain technical requirements or is not issued by an accredited issuer[34].

Advanced electronic signatures have not been taken up by the public, as they require obtaining a digital certificate from an authorised certificate authority and the process is cumbersome. As one may imagine, if these authorities are authenticating identity, they require proof of identity (ID cards, etc.) and other data from the user. This position may change, as governments promote the use of digital signatures for certainty and confidence in electronic commerce.

---

[33] There are some technical doubts about the strength of PKI, however this is the recognised standard, implemented in the original digital signature laws (Utah, Spain, etc.).

[34] National legislation is careful, however, not to provide definitive identification and admissibility through digital signatures, but aims to equate digital signatures and hand-written signatures in terms of evidence. There are times when a hand-written signature will not be admissible. Cf. for example, the UK Electronic Communications Act 2000 which will ensure that UK courts treat electronic signatures as producing the same evidential effects as physical signatures, but will not convert the document into a signed writing.

For our purposes it is relevant to see (1) if an electronic agent could incorporate digital signature technology (encryption and digital signature), which is a technical issue[35], and (2) if any digital signature issued by an agent would be a legally valid one.

The technical issue is not considered here – banks and other institutions are already incorporating digital signature technology in smart cards which can be inserted in computers or mobile phones, and we shall proceed on the basis that an electronic agent can technically issue a document with a digital signature attached.

What, then, are the legal effects? Are the conditions sufficient for the parties to benefit from the legal guarantees given by digital signatures? The construct relies on attribution. The basic assumption behind digital signatures is that if only one person has access to the private key and an encrypted document can only be decrypted using the corresponding public key then the encryption process must have occurred through the use of such private key, which means that it was the holder of the private key who encrypted the document. Consequently, the identity of the signatory of the electronic document has been revealed. But this does not mean that attribution has been achieved, because if the private key is stored in an electronic device such as an agent (or a smart card), then the agent can digitally sign a document. This means we are back in the situation where we have to see if a person can provide a signature through the mediation of an agent.

This question is similar to the debate on whether an agent may provide the relevant consent for a valid contract. We argue that there should be no problem with this, as owners of signatures have to use technological devices to insert a digital signature in a document anyway: why should the use of an agent prevent this?

There seems to be two basic issues, that of legal obligations and that of contractual obligations. First, does the law require that, assuming PKI technology is used for advanced digital signatures, a private key has to be used by a person (rather than a device)?

The UNCITRAL Model Law on Ecommerce allows data messages to be sent by an information system programmed by, or on behalf of, the originator to operate automatically (Article 13). However the Model Law on Digital Signatures adds some further requirements as to reliability (and therefore admissibility) of the signature:

---

[35] This involves an interface and communication with certification authorities, communications relating to private and public keys, storing private keys, etc. W3C is working on standards for XML solutions for Digital Signatures, which may be incorporated into agent technologies.

Article 6.b.3. "An electronic signature is considered to be reliable … if the means of creating the electronic signature was, at the time of signing, under the control of the signatory and of no other person;…"

This (among other requirements) is also contained in the EC E-Signatures Framework Directive:

Article 2.2: "… an advanced digital signature will be effective if it is created using means that the signatory can maintain under his sole control …"

The question therefore is whether the agent can be considered to be in the sole control of the signatory. This may be a question of technological fact that will be considered by the courts. The issue of who has the password or PIN required to activate the key would be considered. Storing this on the agent would be fairly risky (see below on user obligations), as the data is no longer "something that the user knows" but something that another person may acquire. This requirement, for example, would be even more problematic for mobile agents that can replicate themselves across the network in any hospitable server with the appropriate host environment. Are the keys then still in the control of the user? This issue may be solved by an agent that refers back to the mobile user (by SMS or other communication) for retrieval of the relevant data stored only in the user's memory / control.

The EC Directive also provides that an advanced digital signature is to be satisfactory and admissible if it is "created using a secure-signature-creation device" (Art. 5). These devices are subject to various requirements set out in Annex III to the Directive[36], including secrecy and protection against use by others. This looks much less promising, as agent technology aims to provide autonomous devices. If we are therefore considering agents that are initiators rather than simple mediators, this would require the private key details to be included in the programming. In addition, the more the agent is autonomous, the less the user is going to know that the security has been compromised (as even warning procedures could be compromised too).

---

[36] The Annex states:
1. Secure signature-creation devices must, by appropriate technical and procedural means, ensure at the least that:
   (a) the signature-creation-data used for signature generation can practically occur only once, and that their secrecy is reasonably assured;
   (b) the signature-creation-data used for signature generation cannot, with reasonable assurance, be derived and the signature is protected against forgery using currently available technology;
   (c) the signature-creation-data used for signature generation can be reliably protected by the legitimate signatory against the use of others.
2. Secure signature-creation devices must not alter the data to be signed or prevent such data from being presented to the signatory prior to the signature process.

The second question raised above is whether Certification Authorities, in their contractual rules with owners, require that owners have to keep the private key confidential and not record it in any way?

This will be a matter of contractual agreement (usually contained in a "Certification Authority Policy") between the Certification Authority and user. For example, Identrus, the largest international network recently established for providing certification services, requires as follows:

"The Subscribing Customer:

Is obliged to protect its Private Key at all times, against loss, disclosure to any other party, modification and unauthorised use, in accordance with the Identrus Operating Rules and relevant contractual agreements and this CP.

Is personally and solely responsible for the confidentiality and integrity of its Private Key.

Is obligated to never store the PIN (Personal Identity Number) or pass phrase, used to protect unauthorised use of the Private Key, in the same location as the Private Key itself or next to its storage media, or otherwise in an unprotected manner without sufficient protection."[37]

For an agent such as Agent C to sign a message autonomously, it would need to hold both the PIN and Private Key, unless a separate repository could be safely implemented which the agent could consult to obtain one or the other (something that is not inconceivable). Keeping the two separate would seem to preclude the use of fully autonomous agents for digital signatures, as they would have to report back to the user for digital signature approval or generation, as mentioned above. The question of "sufficient protection" would have to be considered, of course as it may be possible to program agents or design a more complex system in a manner to achieve this level of security. Again, this will be a question of technology.

3.3.5 Consumer rights

Agent based contracting in the Research Scenario, as conceived in Agents A, B and C, involve consumers. So we must also consider how parties comply with legally imposed information, transparency and consent requirements when using agents for contracting. These include rights set out in the Consumer Protection Directives and the Ecommerce Directive of

---

[37] Identrus Certification Policy, Operating Rules and System Documentation Release 1.7 available at http://www.identrus.com/knowledge_center/library/certpolicies.html (visited 02/0512003).

2000, and the main issues are considered in Chapter 4 on Consumer Protection issues.

One particular comment should be made here about consumer protection in relation to contracting. It is unlikely that everyday consumers are informed and knowledgeable users of agents. Holding them liable for unexpected acts of the agents (and even mistake, third party intervention, or unexpected evolution) may be harsh and unfair, resulting in mistrust and rejection by consumers. Consumer protection law may protect them to some extent, especially regarding exclusion of liability by programmers and resellers and online merchants (see below). However it may be very difficult to establish technical criteria for standards (e.g. standards of reasonableness regarding agent functionalities) for this type of product. Alternative solutions include

– agent labelling, with third party approval of legal compliance, security, privacy etc, elements of any given agent; this could "enforce" the inclusion of levels of consumer protection in the internal programming of the agent (see below, under consumer protection – technical solutions), allowing consumers to indicate their required level of protection.
– insurance policies for agent transactions; or
– imposing strict liability on users or sites that deal with consumer-controlled agents.

Please see Chapter 4 on consumer rights for more comments in relation to this.

So far in this chapter, we have outlined and discussed some legal issues raised by agent based contracting, considering certain processes carried out by Agents A, B and C in the Research Scenario. We have noted that there are both conceptual and practical problems with agent contracting that will have to be solved if agent-based electronic commerce is to spread. In the next Section 4, we turn to look at certain proposals that have been initiated and enacted to deal (partially) with automated commercial transactions. After that, in Section 5 we will consider some final developments in this area, focusing on current technical solutions that are being proposed.

4.   RECENT AND PROPOSED LEGISLATION AND DECISIONS

In this section, we well consider and comment certain legislative attempts have been made that may assist in overcoming some of the difficulties outlined above, and in promoting agent based contracting.

4.1 UNCITRAL Model Laws on Electronic Commerce and Digital Signatures

Although the UNCITRAL Model laws on Electronic Commerce[38] and Digital Signatures[39] is not applicable legislation, its provisions may be "applied" more and more through transposition into national laws (e.g. Brazil, Singapore, Thailand, etc.). This model law not only conceives of agent contracting, but also takes the approach of attributing the acts of an agent to the person that initiated the device: the "originator". The two relevant articles are:

"Art. 2(c): "Originator" of a data message means a person by whom, *or on whose behalf*, the data message purports to have been sent or generated prior to storage, if any, but it does not include a person acting as an intermediary with respect to that data message;" (*our emphasis*)

"Art. 13(2)(b): As between the originator and the addressee, a data message is deemed to be that of the originator if it was sent:

(a) by a person who had the authority to act on behalf of the originator in respect of that data message; or

(b) *by an information system programmed by, or on behalf of, the originator to operate automatically.*" (*our emphasis again*)

The Model Law Remarks explain: "Data messages that are generated automatically by computers without direct human intervention should be regarded as "originating" from the legal entity on behalf of which the computer is operated."[40]

Conceptually this should deal with the issues of capacity and consent for contracting, as automated processes (data messages) are attributed to the legal or human person on whose behalf the agents is acting. It does not, however, deal with problems of mistake (machine) and other unexpected acts to which the user would not have consented and which would be attributed directly to the user (see above). Neither does this require participants to establish any procedure for error handling.

---

[38] See note 4 above.

[39] See note 5 above.

[40] UNCITRAL Model Law on Ecommerce, Article by Article Remarks, para 35.

4.2   UNCITRAL draft Model Law on Electronic Contracts

UNCITRAL has issued a discussion draft Model Law on Electronic Contracts, which was presented in March 2002 but will take a fair time before approval[41].

The current draft directly considers agent contracting. The definition of "automated computer systems" involves a "computer program or an electronic or other automated means used to initiate an action or respond to data messages or performances in whole or in part, without review or intervention by a natural person at each time an action is initiated or a response is generated by the system" (Art. 5(e)).

As regards consent, the draft creates a presumption of the attribution of the action of the agent to the user of the software for the determination of the parties' intent:

> **"Art. 9.2:** In determining the intent of a party to be bound in case of acceptance, due consideration is to be given to all relevant circumstances of the case. Unless otherwise indicated by the offeror, the offer of goods or services through automated computer systems allowing the contract to be concluded automatically and without human intervention is presumed to indicate the intention of the offeror to be bound in case of acceptance."

Article 12. provides directly for automated transactions:

> **"Art.12:** 1. Unless otherwise agreed by the parties, a contract may be formed by the interaction of an automated computer system and a natural person or by the interaction of automated computer systems, even if no natural person reviewed each of the individual actions carried out by such systems or the resulting agreement.
>
> 2. Unless otherwise [expressly] agreed by the parties, a party offering goods or services through an automated computer system shall make available to the parties that use the system technical means allowing the parties to identify and correct errors prior to the conclusion of a contract. The technical means to be made available pursuant to this paragraph shall be appropriate, effective and accessible.
>
> [3. A contract concluded by a natural person that accesses an automated computer system of another person has no legal effect and is not enforceable if the natural person made a material error in a data message and

---

[41] A/CN.9/WG.IV/WP.95 - Electronic contracting: provisions for a draft convention at
http://www.uncitral.org/english/workinggroups/wg_ec/index.htm

(a) The automated computer system did not provide the natural person with an opportunity to prevent or correct the error;

(b) The natural person notifies the other person of the error as soon as practicable when the natural person learns of it and indicates that he or she made an error in the data message;

(c) The natural person takes reasonable steps, including steps that conform to the other person's instructions to return the goods or services received, if any, as a result of the error or, if instructed to do so, to destroy such goods or services; and

(d) The natural person has not used or received any material benefit or value from the goods or services, if any, received from the other person.]"

Paragraph 2 of this Article 12 attempts to deal with the issue of errors in automated transactions. Inspired in article 11 of EC Ecommerce Directive, it creates an obligation for persons offering goods or services through automated computer systems, to offer means for correcting input errors. It leaves open what happens if there is no such correction mechanism (except see para. 3 quoted above). While online commerce platforms are improving their processes, including confirmation pages and final acceptance mechanisms for human users, for automated contracting like that conceived in Agent C there will be little opportunity for correction prior to concluding the contract (the error will only really be noticed on delivery or when the Agent reports to the user).

Paragraph 3 covers situations of material errors made by a natural person communicating with an automated computer system (i.e. would not cover agent-agent contracts, unless it is read that this applies to natural persons who contract through the use of their agents). In addition, we believe that this provision will probably only really be applicable for consumers, as repudiation rights are not common in commercial contracts. Unfortunately, the draft law has not included any provision for machine-made mistakes, such as computer crashes but also programming mistakes, which will certainly continue to occur.

4.3 The EC Ecommerce Directive

Unfortunately the EC Ecommerce Directive is of no real help regarding the conceptual difficulties for agent-based contracting. The closest one gets is Article 9, which provides that:

> "Member States shall ensure that their legal system allows contracts to be concluded by electronic means. Member States shall in

particular ensure that the legal requirements applicable to the contractual process neither create obstacles for the use of electronic contracts nor result in such contracts being deprived of legal effectiveness and validity on account of their having been made by electronic means."

While this does not explicitly enable delegated or automated contracting, the preamble to the Directive includes agents as "electronic means"... which leaves the situation in the hands of national legislators and judges. National laws may indeed be more specific in implementation of the Directive, though this has yet to be seen. For example, this has not been the case of those countries who are writing new laws at the time of this work (UK, Germany, Spain), as we see next.

4.4   National legislation in the EU and third countries

So far, EU Member States are still discussing changes in national law required by this provision. Mainly governments are looking at issues of online contracting, i.e. without paper support or traditional signature. Several thoughts occur.

First, a variation among national regimes for electronic contracting will provide difficulties for the EU's goal of harmonisation and levelling of the playing field for ecommerce. What does an Irish shopper do if agent contracting is supported in Ireland but not in Portugal? Should Agent C be limited to "Irish sites" (if that can be determined)? And what of a Portuguese shopper in the same circumstances? The purchase possibly may not be enforced in the home jurisdiction.

In addition, an uneven legal framework for automated contracting may cause technical procedural problems for different websites from companies in different countries. They may have to program different processes for different visitors, multiplying the complexity of commercial websites. This solution may only be valid if they can determine the "origin" of the visitors, and such variations are not considered discriminatory or contrary to the rules of the internal market. This interoperability point may be solved by more complex agents with processes that can deal with several jurisdictions – but who will pay for such applications?

A few examples of national attitudes in Europe include:
–   **UK**: At the date of our research, the UK Government believes that no change is required to English contract law for valid electronic contracting. This would leave the question open until judicial comment or decision gave further precision[42].

---

[42] The Electronic Commerce (EC Directive) Regulations 2002 – and guidance: March 2002. At http://www.dti.gov.uk/cii/ecommerce/europeanpolicy/ecommerce_directive.shtml (visited 15/05/2002)

- **Spain**: The Spanish "Ley de los Servicios y Sociedad de la Información y Comercio Electrónico" (LEY 34/2002, of the 11th of July) reads

  "Art. 23(1): Contracts concluded by electronic means will produce all the effects established under the legal system, when all the requisites for consent and other requirements for validity are satisfied"[43].

This may be no advance on the current situation, as the Spanish code seems to take a more subjectivist view of consent.

In the USA, contract law is left up to the individual states, however there is a centralised "uniform code" system that proposes model laws in order to harmonise contract law, mostly to prevent differences from upsetting inter-state trade. The uniform laws then have to be enacted into law by the states (by adoption). Two relevant model laws for electronic contracting, either online or through agents, are UETA and UCITA.

- **UETA: Uniform Electronic Transactions Act:** This act contemplates person-agent and agent-agent contracts, and takes the approach of attributing the acts of an agent to the person that initiated the device (Section 9), even if the person had no knowledge of the agreement or of its terms (section 14). This strict liability could be problematic from the user's point of view, as he/she would not want to be bound by malfunctioning, unintended acts, errors or third party interventions, all the more so if the agent is intelligent and incorporates learning and adaptation. This act also deals with human mistake, providing for a correction mechanism, but not machine mistake (section 10).
- **UCITA: Uniform Computer Information Transaction Act:** This act recognises that contracts may be concluded by transmissions between agents and persons, "if the transaction demonstrates existence of an agreement between the parties using the agents" (section 202). In the USA the objective theory of consent would determine the validity of the transaction, subject to a reasonableness test which would temper the strict application of attributed liability. The Act aims to make clear the granting of assent, both by conduct and (somewhat unnecessarily) by electronic agents (section 112), applying the objective view (thereby allowing judges to take a more liberal view of consent mentioned above). What is more, the Act also indirectly provides for electronic mistakes, without specification, permitting courts to grant relief in certain cases (i.e. to annul the contract). This however applies only between agents and not between humans and agent: the latter would be left up to traditional concepts of mistake outlined above. To date, UCITA however is only

---

[43] Unofficial translation of the authors: *"Art. 23(1): Los contratos celebrados por vía electrónica producirán todos los efectos previstos por el ordenamiento jurídico, cuando concurran el consentimiento y los demás requisitos necesarios para su validez".*

enacted in two states. It has been rejected by most other States, as well as the American Bar Association, as unhelpful and unwieldy.

–   **US jurisprudence:** A recent decision in the USA, Specht v. Netscape Communications Corp[44], emphasises that traditional rules of contract law will apply to e-commerce transactions: a federal district court concluded that no contract had been formed when a user downloaded software without first having to click through a license. This focuses on the need to incorporate terms in the contract and bring certain key terms to the purchaser's attention (an arbitration clause restricting the consumer's rights). Such rules may be difficult to comply with, for example with Agent C, without further specific negotiating and notification processes being incorporated into the agent's programming.

Canada is an interesting study, having had the benefit of the US and preliminary European experiences: the Uniform Electronic Commerce Act (UECA) was adopted in 1999[45]. The act defines electronic agents, provides that contracts may be concluded by interaction between agents and humans and between such agents, and determines that persons are bound by the expression of consent by electronic means or by other electronic action (e.g. agent action) in a manner which is intended to express the consent, i.e. by conduct. Accordingly Canada would also apply an attribution rule and the objective test of consent, taking advantage of the reasonableness test to avoid excessive liability. There are rules for material errors made by persons when dealing with agents, but there is no rule for mistakes made by the agents themselves, through programming error or system failure for example.

5.   MATCHING LAW AND TECHNOLOGY WITH A PROCESS VIEW

To establish legal validity and efficacy of automated contracts, several technical approaches have been suggested.

First, recent work on intelligent agents, especially mobile agents, is focussing on policy expressions for security. This involves establishing a set of documented information system security decisions defining the rules needed to be enforced by security mechanisms and controls of the underlying hardware and software comprising the agent system (e.g.

---

[44] Specht v. Netscape Communications Corp., 150 F. Supp. 2d 585 (S.D.N.Y., July 5, 2001), aff'd. 306 F.3d 17 (2nd Cir. 2002).

[45] I Kerr, *Providing for Autonomous Electronic Devices in the Uniform Electronic Commerce Act* (2000).

privileges)[46]. Work suggests these policies could be included in an external object, an "attribution certificate" and "policy certificate" governing the agent's behaviour. This same principle can be extended to contracting (and consumer protection) issues, regarding definition of issuers and owners, authority, consent, definition of terms and conditions. Moreover, this trend towards expressing policies in objects can also be seen in relation to privacy, with the work on P3P dialogues. This is an issue which is commented on in Chapter 6, where we argue that one solution for incorporating these concepts of policies, rules and dependencies into the technical architecture is to use process modelling for higher level system design and interoperability.

Work is also being carried out in the area of commerce frameworks. As with EDI and B2B marketplace electronic commerce, electronic contracting (including agent contracting) would be more enforceable within a closed legal framework. Just as members of an EDI system or a B2B exchange agree to standard contract terms (including message validity and timing, jurisdiction, incorporation of certain terms – see UNCITRAL recommendation 31), agent users could agree to standard terms beforehand, through a registration mechanism, and then use the software agents for contracting within this framework. This may be applicable, for example, in the Research Scenario with agent contracting between the user and the store (Agents A and B), where there will be a registration / log-on process. This design precludes, however, open market contracting along the lines of Agent C (e.g. comparison shopping while the shopper is in the store)[47].

The question of open market trading raises the issue of the standardisation of shopping agents such as Agent C. This would entail agents being produced with a predetermined set of functionalities and processes recognised by merchants, who could agree to certain terms beforehand. This will subsequently provide more flexibility for agent contracting. The consequences of this include higher levels of consumer protection, the possibility of recourse to agreed dispute resolution mechanisms, and more certainty and trust in such dematerialised transactions. For example, standard processes for complying with the obligations of supplier information and error correction could be pre-established and incorporated into the technical architectures of affiliated merchants. This could also favour a standard for digital signatures among participants.

---

[46] See for example the National Institute for Standards and Technology Aroma project (www.itl.nist.gov/div897/ctg/aroma/home.html) and the IETF (http://www.ietf.org/html.charters/mobileip-charter.html) in the USA and in the EU, the PISA project (Privacy Incorporated Software Agent) online at http://www.tno.nl/instit/fel/pisa/ .

[47] Unless such competitors and other merchants also participate in a wider architecture such as ebXML or other trading framework.

On the other hand, this type of "bound" agents does not necessarily provide the full benefits of ecommerce – with the Internet as a virtually endless supply of alternative products, terms and suppliers. For example, while there are current proposals for XML digital certificate standards within the W3C, which may ensure wide adoption, this is not yet the case for other elements of contracts, especially taking into consideration the differing contract regimes.

In our Research Scenario, we have only considered the concepts of electronic contracting between natural persons and agents, and between agents under the direct control of single entities or persons (the store, a web-merchant). Further complications will arise with complex agent platforms, and even more so mobile agents, where there may be a multiplicity of owners and actors intervening in the transaction: consumer, merchant, site host, agent host, trusted third parties, payment intermediaries, etc. In such complex scenarios, it will be important to analyse process by process each transaction and the parties involved for a proper analysis of responsibilities and obligations, including consumer, data and IPR protection.

Another solution that has been put forward is the question of registration and/or certification of Intelligent Agents, in a process that would be similar to corporate registration. This would be akin to – or would allow - giving legal identity to Software agents[48]. It has been suggested that this would deal with some of the problems mentioned above: identification of the users, authority of the agent, mistake and proper functioning of the agents. Such a system, involving certification of the agents, including a security / authority classification which would determine what the limits of the agent's activities are, would allow counterparties to check up on the agent it is dealing with (similar to digital certificates for advanced electronic signatures). This would increase certainty and reduce the scope for mistake.

Less formal would be a private system of "trustmarks" or private certification, similar to a labelling system, providing a private framework for the operation of the agents. This would include determining minimum standards, including privacy issues, establishing dispute resolution procedures and jurisdictional issues, and is rather similar to the idea of using agents within a more "closed" framework commented above. Both merchants and users would subscribe to the minimum standards required by the certification system. This is also a selling point for merchants (as all trustmark schemes may be), enabling higher levels of confidence.

The problem with these formal proposals is that they reduce the scope for innovation and creativity in the development and use of agents. Understandably they would only apply to more advanced "actor" agents that can incur contractual liabilities on behalf of the user – both merchants and consumers (as opposed to more simple search and compare agents, which

---

[48] A Karnow, *Liability for Distributed Artificial Intelligences* (1996).

are "observers"). On the other hand, especially from the consumer's point of view, these schemes introduce an element of trust and confidence in agent trading. On the practical side, they would be fairly expensive to implement, involving registries, monitoring, standardising, verification processes which would incur a fair amount of time, effort and cost.

In the absence of immediate legal solutions to some of these problems facing agent contracting, we have argued that it may be possible to add certain technical features to software agents for enhancing the validity of any agent-based contract. The following list summarises suggestions made during the course of the analysis of Agents A, B and C in the previous sections.

- The identity of the user/principal (or at least, indicating that the software agent is a device and not a person) could be included in the coding, for the purpose of disclosing the existence of a principal and inferring apparent authority. This may run into problems of privacy (a user who doesn't want to disclose his/her identity) which may be solved by a neutral indication that the software agent is only an electronic device. For example, a tag would indicate "nature = software agent" while "Id = XXX".

- The nature of the user/principal could also be incorporated into the code: as business or consumer user ("nature of user = Consumer / Business"). This would provide the counterpart with some idea of its obligations, and the possibility or excluding certain consumer initialised agents if it only contracts (by law or by corporate policy) with businesses.

- Negotiation protocols should enable websites and agents to communicate regarding which party is making the offer, the acceptance and the acknowledgement required by the combination of national laws and the Ecommerce Directive.

- Run time errors and other unexpected events or state (e.g. after third party intervention) should be able to generate a "freeze/ refer or report back to user before proceeding" procedure – maybe with variable parameters to give the agent greater autonomy, parameters that could vary within even wider fixed limits as the agent learns, to reduce certain liabilities in the event of non-repudiatable mistakes.

- Communications could be confirmed by email or SMS to users, for providing greater evidence of transactions, either encrypted (for security) or not.

- Agents should include functionalities for creating, transmitting and storing electronic evidence of transactions (emails, SMS, invoices).

- For adaptive/advanced agents, initial parameterisation should be stored as evidence of user intent, especially in the case of mistake or unexpected learning processes.

– Security features should be incorporated to minimise the risk of contracting after third party intervention (viruses, etc.) or system failure (power surges, etc.).
– Agents should withhold from contracting when in doubt, especially regarding terms of sale (exclusions of liability, etc.): a fall back procedure should allow the agent to report back to the user.
– Agents should include programming to send an Acknowledgement of Receipt back to (consumer) users as soon as possible (email or other data transmission – SMS etc.).

Below in Table 2.6, by way of example we present a summary of these legal and technical issues for electronic contracting that are presented by Agents C, the most complex of those set out above. Taking a process view, we attempt to establish the legal risks for each of the agent's processes. This enables us to determine further processes that may be either necessary (for compliance) or recommended (good practice, for greater confidence).

Table 2-6. Legal risks of Agent C's contracting processes

Principal Process	Legal issue (contract related)	Additional processes for compliance and/or certainty
Agent C determines a need to purchase specific item	None (internal process)	Registration of original agent programming / parameters (trigger events, contract conditions)
Agent C searches the network for various stores selling relevant products	Pre-contract issues: web-pages as advertising or offer Information requirements (consumer contracting issue)	Identification of data messages as advertisements or offers Forwarding of obligatory information to users.
Agent C negotiates with store(s) for the quantity, price and other terms of sale	Identification of parties – agent user identified as consumer Capacity of agent to negotiate Good faith and withdrawing from negotiation	Registration of negotiation steps (assistance to determine true intent) Session control and processes for system failures Well defined negotiation protocols
Agent C concludes purchase agreement	Capacity and Consent Mistake Incorporation of all terms	Certification of agent's "authority to conclude contracts" Process for retrieving and storing terms Process for error correction and confirmation Process for acknowledgement of receipt
Agent C provides delivery and payment details	Identification of parties	Digital signatures for payments (e.g. SET protocol) Reference to User for PIN
Agent C records transaction	Storage of evidence	Register of processes (but security level? – e.g. Encryption for integrity and confidentiality)

We argue in Chapter 6 that if these technical advertising, negotiation and contracting processes can be completed and modelled so that they become "universal" for the majority of B2C or B2B contracting processes (rather like a process protocol), we maybe able to create a legal architecture that can be applied to the technical processes for agent contracting. This legal modelling in turn will enable ecommerce software developers to legalise their technical models – thus creating a framework for compliant "contracting agent" engineering. This approach is developed more in Chapter 6.

Chapter 3

INTELLECTUAL PROPERTY RIGHTS
Can agents create comparative shopping tables?

The Congress shall have power ... To promote the progress of science and useful arts, by securing for limited times to authors and inventors the exclusive right to their respective writings and discoveries.
US Constitution, Art.1, Section 8.

Con la denominación de propiedad intelectual se designa el conjunto de derechos que la ley reconoce al autor sobre las obras que ha producido con su inteligencia, en especial los de que su paternidad le sea reconocida y respetada, así como que se le permita difundir la obra, autorizando o negando, en su caso, la reproducción
José Puig Brutau, Fundamentos de derecho civil, tomo 3, vol. 2, 1979, ps. 210-211[1]

Software Agents may raise several concerns in relation to Intellectual Property Rights (IPR) due to the fact that they interact with materials and content available on the Internet that are protected by copyright or other rights. In fact, they may often exchange pieces of software, protected by IR as computer programs. The main issues in relation to IPR in the use of agents in our Research are related to copyright, database protection and licensing – specifically digital rights management systems (DRMS). Other areas of intellectual property right law (trademarks and patents), while important in the digital context, are not commented here because legal problems in these areas are unlikely to occur within the Research Scenario set out in Chapter 1.

---

[1] Intellectual property refers to the set of rights that the law grants to authors over works that they have produced with their intelligence, especially that their authorship be recognized and respected and that they have the right to publish the work, authorizing or prohibiting, as the case may be, any reproduction. (The authors' unofficial translation).

First in section 1, we provide a brief outline of the main principles of copyright and database law to describe the European legal framework. Then in section 2, we establish where problems with IPR may occur in relation to agent-based transactions, and in section 3 we discuss these issues to determine the level and scope of legal risks involved. IN section 4, we outline partial solutions to these IPR issues, and in the last section of this chapter we discuss a suggested approach for reducing these risks and raising IPR compliance in agent based transactions.

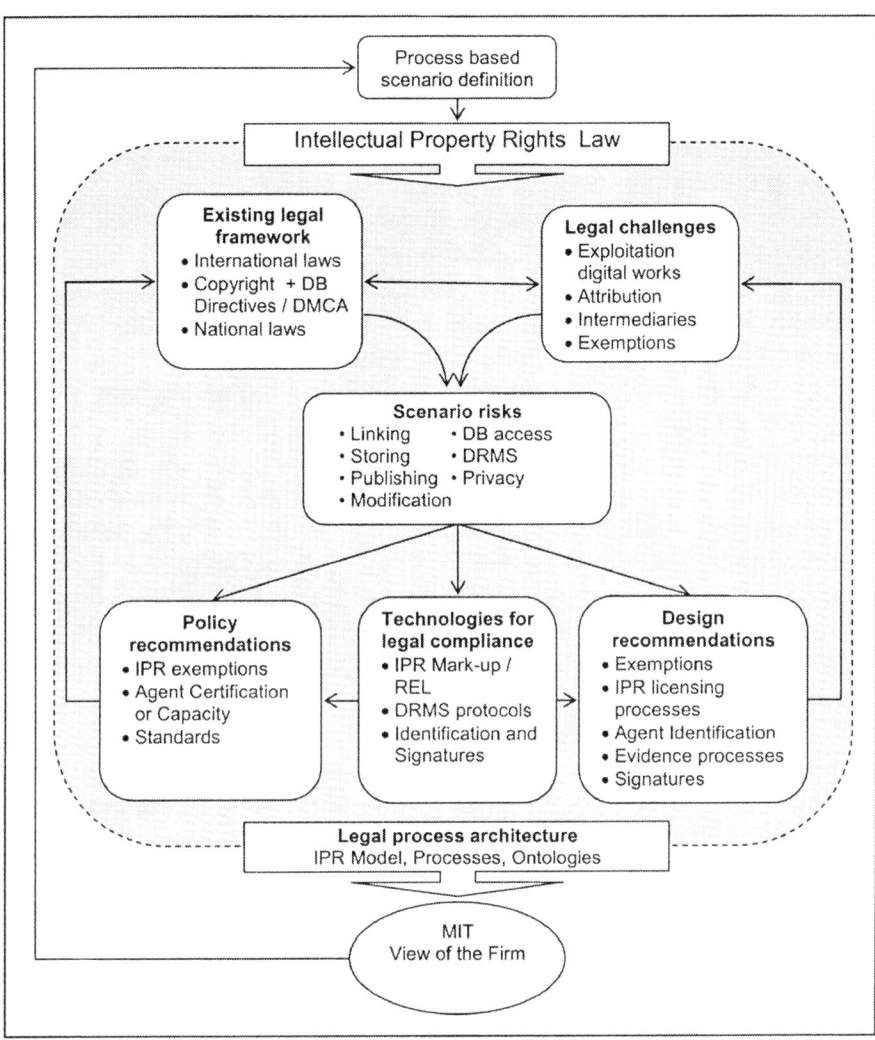

Figure 3-1. Intellectual Property Rights Analysis

1.   OUTLINE OF PRINCIPLES OF EUROPEAN COPYRIGHT AND DATABASE LAW

1.1   Applicable legal framework

There are certain international agreements that establish the framework of copyright law:
- The Berne Convention for the Protection of Literary and Artistic Works (1886) as modified by the Paris Act of 1971.
- The Rome Convention for the protection of performers, producers of phonograms and broadcasting organisations (Rome Convention, 1961).
- The Universal Copyright Convention (UCC, 1952).
- The Agreement on Trade-Related Aspects of Intellectual Property Rights (TRIPS, 1995).
- The World Intellectual Property Organisation Treaties: the WIPO Copyright Treaty (WCT, 1996) and the WIPO Performances and Phonograms Treaty (WPPT, 1996) which develop the TRIPS Agreement and reinforce both the Berne and the Rome Conventions.
- Various EC Directives, of which the most relevant are the Copyright Directive (93/98/EC), the Computer Program Directive (91/250/EC), the Databases Directive (96/9/EC) and the Copyright in the Information Society Directive (2001/29/EC)[2].

The TRIPS Agreement has the widest membership and is a comprehensive agreement between the members of the World Trade Organisation on IPR, setting out the minimum rights to be protected (and permissible restrictions), which are slightly wider than the Berne Convention, and enforcement and settlement procedures between participants. As part of the implementation of the WIPO Treaties, the European Community approved the EC Directive regarding Copyright and Neighbouring rights in the Information Society ("EC Copyright in the Information Society Directive").

Most of the international agreements require national implementation, so the directly applicable law is contained in country-specific legislation[3]. One difficulty that arises is the fact that different countries interpret and implement the treaties in different ways both as regards the scope of the rights and the accepted limitations and exceptions, a fact which counteracts the whole point of the "harmonisation" of these treaties. This monograph does not intend to cover detailed aspects of national copyright law, however

---

[2] All Directives and other laws are listed in the reference section at the end of this monograph.
[3] For example the US Digital Millennium Copyright Act, the EC Directive on Copyright and Neighbouring rights in the Information Society or the Australian Copyright Amendment (Digital Agenda) Act 2000.

it will include certain national rules that seem to be prevalent or of major relevance.

The Berne Convention, the UCC and the TRIPS Agreement establish the principle of national treatment, which means that protection under the national laws of copyright and the Treaties is granted by a member state to works of nationals of other countries that are parties to the international agreements.

1.2 Principles of Copyright law

There is a general agreement among participants in the international discussions about the Internet that there is a need to uphold the basic principles of copyright: to maintain the incentives to create and perform works, to recognise the importance of authors and allow them to profit from and have control over the exploitation of their works, balanced against the public interest (e.g. education), the development of culture, science and society generally[4]. However these principles should not extend any further than the existing protection that copyright law provides offline.

Copyright can be defined as the right of an author (or rightholder) to control the exploitation of his original work by way of the prohibition of certain uses by third parties without consent. This raises several questions which outline the nature of copyright: what work is copyright; who is the owner; what uses can constitute an infringement; the existence of any exemptions; and how authors can protect their works.

1.2.1 Nature of the protected work

Which works are protected differ according to national legislation, although as a general rule the Berne Convention applies copyright to "literary and artistic works"[5]. Most copyright laws include texts, pictures, photographs and graphics, speeches, musical works, artistic works in general, computer programs, etc. as protected works, all of which feature prominently in ecommerce oriented web-pages and websites. In most cases it does not matter what category a work falls into (artistic, literary or even scientific), as the scope of the protection is basically the same. There are, however, special provisions for computer programs and databases both internationally[6] and within the EU, which are mentioned next.

The fact that a work is in digital form will not affect the type of protection. Digitisation of existing works will not be considered a derived

---

[4] Recognised, for example, in Art.1 of the US Constitution cited above.
[5] Article 2 Berne Convention.
[6] Arts. 4 and 5 WIPO Treaties treat the first as literary creations, and the second as a separate form of intellectual creation.

work but generally will be considered a copy, and therefore a restricted use of the original, so the resulting digital file would not be protected as a separate work.

Collections of factual data are protected in so far as the data is selected and arranged in such way as to create an original work. Only the arrangement is protected, the underlying data is not protected and is available for others to use (see section 1.3 on databases).

Special provisions apply for composite works: technically, one needs to break down compositions into component parts, or look for main element. For "collections", copyright protection will be afforded both to separable individual parts (e.g. copyright for text and graphics, i.e. literary and artistic works, and separate copyright for HTML instructions or Java applets or programs) and to the collection as a whole. For example, a whole webpage could acquire protection as a collection, a database work or by a *sui generis* database right according to the level of originality and/or creativity. On the other hand, if no particular element is separable, the main composition (film, artistic work, text, etc.) will determine the nature of the work.

It is important to note that the international agreements concur in stating that only the expression of an idea (for example, a computer program or the text of a book) is protected by copyright and not the ideas and principles which underlie any element of a work (algorithms, or the plot of the book) which may have other forms of legal protection such as patents[7].

1.2.2   Minimum requirements for protection

The minimum requirements for a work to acquire copyright protection vary by country, but the fundamental conditions are that the work must be original and be recorded with some measure of permanence. Some jurisdictions require a level of creativity and/or that the work be personal (i.e. not automatically generated). In the EU, the European Commission is in the process of harmonising requirements, moving towards a civil law standard of minimum personal intellectual content (see EC Computer Program Directive and EC Database Directive, for example).

There are no formalities required to acquire copyright protection such as filing or registration in countries parties to the Berne Convention (which includes most developed countries). Some countries which are not members of the Berne convention require the © sign (with date and rightholder) on works published under the Universal Copyright Convention subject to certain conditions, and in Latin America the wording "All Rights Reserved" or equivalent may be required. Storage in physical form will be necessary, but saving to disk (hard or floppy) would satisfy this condition, and even

---

[7] The patenting of algorithms and software code is currently greatly debated, and we will not comment on it here.

RAM storage has been held to be sufficiently permanent. Greater protection may be obtained in certain jurisdictions by copyright registration (USA, Japan, Spain), especially for the purpose of establishing a date of creation.

1.2.3 Types of protection

Protection is territorial in nature, i.e. a work is protected where it originates (or is published[8]), however protection is extended by treaties on a reciprocal basis to other signatory territories under the law applicable there (which is not necessarily exactly the same as the original country).

The standard protection for a personal intellectual creation is literary or artistic copyright, however protection as a related right, or neighbouring rights, will be acquired for works which don't quite satisfy the levels of creativity required by national legislation. These neighbouring rights are also those to protect performers, producers of phonograms, film producers and broadcasting organisations. The time of protection is less for related rights (25 to 50 years instead of life plus 50 or 70 years). Additionally some jurisdictions allow authors rights over works derived from their copyright work.

The Berne Convention and certain national legislation recognise certain moral rights (*droits moraux*), which protect the connection between the author and its intellectual creation, and consist in the author's unalienable rights to control the integrity of work, to be recognised as author and to withdraw or disown the work after it has been published[9]. These rights are protected in jurisdictions that consider copyright to be a personal right (mainly continental Europe); as opposed to Anglo-Saxon traditions where copyrights are considered property rights that can be freely traded.[10]

Computer programs, considered in some jurisdictions as literary works, in others as a separate category of works, also acquire copyright protection in both machine-executable form and human-readable form. For example the WCT treaty recognises computer programs as literary works and EC Software Directive 91/250/EEC gives copyright protection to computer programs as literary works within the meaning of the Berne Convention. However the processes and algorithms that underlie a program are not protected, as only the "expression of the idea" is protected. In addition, other elements of expression (including the structure, sequence and organisation, and "look and feel" of a program) have sometimes been afforded protection under copyright law, especially in the USA.

---

[8] Art. 3 Berne Convention.

[9] Art. 6bis Berne Convention.

[10] For example in France, under Art. 121 of the Code de la Propriété Intellectuelle (1992). In the USA moral rights are recognised for limited editions of original paintings, drawing, sculptures and prints (Visual Rights Act 1990).

As a supplement to copyright protection, authors tend to enter into direct contractual relationships with users through licensing arrangements. This may provide rights above and beyond those restricted by copyright law (see section 3.4.1 Digital Rights Management).

1.2.4 Who is the rightholder?

Determining who the rightholder is varies according to national law. Generally speaking, on the European continent the only rightholder is the author of the work. National legislation then provides that only certain rights of exploitation can be transferred, by sale or by licence to another person or legal entity (e.g. employer), while other rights cannot be alienated (e.g. moral rights). In other jurisdictions, notably the UK, Ireland, Holland, Canada and the USA, a legal entity can be the original owner of copyright (as employer of the creator) and the whole copyright may be transferred to another person (except some moral rights in certain cases).

When there are several authors who have worked together to create a work, the result is a joint or collective work. Title in this work varies under the different national regimes, which provide for several forms of co-ownership, joint ownership or collective ownership when there are several authors or contributors[11].

As regards computer programs, copyrights are owned by the author of the program or, in certain jurisdictions where the authorship rights are transferable (e.g. UK or USA), by the company that arranges the creation of the program. This will often be the author's employer or contractor.

1.2.5 Exclusive exploitation rights

Copyright grants the rightholders certain exclusive rights of control and remuneration over the protected work. It is not necessary to have any contractual relationship between the parties to achieve protection. These rights include rights of reproduction and of certain acts of communication to the public. More specifically, these acts include the following[12]:
- **Reproduction**[13]: the making of a copy, in digital or physical form[14]. This does not necessarily have to be an exact copy, as the act of reproduction can also cover "substantial" copying (in terms of quality, not quantity).

---

[11] E.g. Section 10(1) of the UK Copyright, Designs and Patents Act, 1988, Sec. 8 and 9 of the German Copyright Act, Art. L 113 of the French Copyright Act; Arts. 7, 8 and 43 of the Spanish Texto Refundido de la Ley de la Propiedad Intelectual.

[12] This list is not exhaustive, and is only a summary of the internationally recognised restricted acts relevant for B2B and B2C E-commerce in the Research Scenario.

[13] Art. 9, Berne Convention, incorporated by Art. 1 of the WCT. Online at http://www.wipo.int/treaties/ip/wct/index.html (last visited 20.03.2003).

[14] WCT Agreed statement on Art. 9.

Source code and object code are protected against literal copying, with some exceptions (e.g. for executing the program, or for decompiling for bug correction).

– **Distribution**[15]**:** this usually is defined as the transfer of a tangible good (book, CD, etc) but it is arguable that is also includes transmission over the Internet of material in digital form (by analogy with the offline world, to produce a similar result).
– **Communication to the public**[16]**:** this covers broadcasting or communication to the public by wire or wireless means (wireless telegraphy, which may not yet be applicable to Internet). It is related in the US to rights of Public Performance and Public Display. The former, being communication of a performance to a public (including internet-type public), would cover streaming and live-casting, but not the transmission of a copy (music track or audio-visual), while the latter would include the presentation in the browser window both for open and restricted sites.
– **Making available to the public**[17]**:** under the WIPO treaties this is a new right (or broadening of the communication rights) that would include providing access to data and its transmission to the public over the Internet. The EC Information Society Copyright Directive also includes "communication and making available to the public" including by making them available 'on demand', i.e. from a place and at a time individually chosen by a member of the public.
– **Renting or lending**[18]**:** this applies to computer programs, films and phonograms, and consists in making available a protected good for a limited time.
– **Translation or modification**[19]**:** the making and authorising the translation, arrangements and other alterations of protected works.

1.2.6   Exceptions and limitations

Under the international treaties (Berne, TRIPS and WIPO Treaties) there are a few specific compulsory exemptions to the exclusive exploitation rights of copyright holders (news of the day, quotations), some optional exemptions for signatories to implement (e.g. for educational or information purposes) and a general clause that allows other exception for special non conflicting cases (a cumulative "three step test"[20]). The WIPO Treaties

---

[15] Art. 6 WCT.
[16] Art. 11bis, Berne Convention and Art. 8 WCT.
[17] Art. 8 WCT, WPPT.
[18] Art. 7 WCT.
[19] Arts. 8 and 12 Berne Convention.
[20] Article 10 WCT and accompanying Agreed Statement. The most important version of the test is that included in Article 13 of TRIPs. It reads: *Members shall confine limitations and*

together with the three step test are today the most relevant framework and the basis for exemptions set out in existing legislation[21]. There are exceptions to the exclusivity of related rights set out in the Rome Convention (private use, reporting, teaching and scientific, broadcasting purposes), though no general exemption provision similar to the Berne Convention.

In the Member States of the EU and other countries including the USA, there are several exemptions for copying for private use, educational and research purposes (fair dealing) and also an exemption for press compilations and criticism. These exemptions apply to the digital environment; however their scope varies from country to country[22]. There is also a generally accepted exception for copying of short quotations and extracts, with appropriate safeguards regarding citation, and other exemptions which are of limited economic significance in the internet context. These include reporting of current events and exemptions for the purpose of criticism and review, in favour of people with disabilities, for the purpose of public security, or for administrative or judicial procedures. Article 5 of the recent Copyright in the Information Society Directive sets out an exhaustive list of exemptions from which Member States may choose.

While the EC Computer Program Directive has exemptions for lawful users that have acquired a program[23], the EC Information Society Copyright Directive includes a mandatory exemption for acts of copying which are:
– either 'transient or incidental'; and
– 'integral and essential' to either (i) transmission of the relevant copyright work over a network, e.g. by an ISP; or (ii) some other technical process enabling legal use of the material (this would cover technical copies made by a browser accessing the Internet)[24].

Finally, there is also an exemption under the principle of "merger" which states that when there is only one means of expressing a concept, the expression and the idea merge and no copyright protection is available.

The principle of "exhaustion" is also another form of exception. The distribution right in IPR protected goods includes a theoretical right of the IPR owner to control the onward distribution of those goods. That right applies to tangible objects. It is "exhausted" once the owner has sold a

---

exceptions to exclusive rights to certain special cases which do not conflict with a normal exploitation of the work and do not unreasonably prejudice the legitimate interests of the rights holder (our underlining to highlight the 3 steps). It is taken up on Article 5.5 of the 2001EC Copyright in the Information Society Directive.

[21] US Digital Millennium Copyright Act; EC Copyright Directive and for example the Australian Copyright Amendment (Digital Agenda) Act 2000.

[22] Additionally, it is doubtful whether the press compilation exemption is applicable to online compilations, as the limitation includes a requirement for the compilation to be in print or broadcast.

[23] Art. 5 includes acts during the normal use of the program and for error correction, making back-ups, observing, studying or testing the functioning of a program.

[24] Art 5.1 EC Information Society Copyright Directive.

particular copy of it, and the buyer/buyers can resell the good without restriction. However, the resale can be restricted by licence and contract, such as in distribution contracts, subject to competition law. In the EU, the EC Information Society Copyright Directive and national legislation provide that such right is exhausted on first sale within the EU, "Community exhaustion" and in some countries on sale outside the EU, international exhaustion.

The European Commission currently considers that there is no particular application of this concept for online services (digital transmissions are generally considered services, and therefore cannot be exhausted), though it may apply to the resale of downloaded software legally copied onto disk or CD-ROM. In this case, the first sale of an object is the sale of the disk or CD-ROM. However the copier would need to have ownership of distribution right, not just a licence to use, which is what he would usually get, including a licence to make one copy for personal use. If the copier only acquires a use licence, any onward distribution would have to involve the user deleting his or her copy of the product, so that the same quantities of the product are in issue.

1.3   Database rights

While many of the principles of copyright may apply to databases, these acquire separate protection in the EU if, besides the requirement for personal intellectual creation, they consist in "independent works or materials arranged in a systematic or methodical way and are individually accessible by electronic or other means and whose making required the investment of substantial human, technical or financial resources"[25]. The Directive also provides for a weaker *sui generis* right for a database which shows that there has been "qualitatively and/or quantitatively a substantial investment in either the obtaining, verification or presentation of the contents to prevent extraction and/or re-utilisation of the whole or of a substantial part, evaluated qualitatively and/or quantitatively, of the contents of that database"[26]. This may apply for web pages (as a collection of graphic and textual items) and to contents available through web pages (e.g. commercial or scientific databases) and arguably is applicable to computer generated compilations.

Copyright only protects the arrangement of the data base and not the facts or data contained in it[27]. Only the creativity of the work is protected and

---

[25] Arts. 1 and 7 EC Databases Directive.

[26] Art. 7 EC Databases Directive.

[27] For protection in Europe, see above. In the USA, the collection is protected if it demonstrates "authorship", but not if they are just the product of compiling third party data ("sweat and brow").

only the use of qualitatively or quantitatively substantive part of the database would constitute an infringement[28]. The use of a small part would not constitute an infringement, although it may be difficult to determine what constitutes a substantial part. The new *sui generis* rights include the right to prevent the unauthorised extraction and/or re-utilisation of all or substantial part of the contents of the database, for 15 years. This threshold is also satisfied by the repeated use of insubstantial parts of those contents.

The EU Databases Directive provides for an exemption for reproduction or other acts necessary for the purposes of access to the contents of the databases and normal use of the contents by the lawful user, and allows Member States the possibility to provide exemptions for private use, teaching or scientific research and other general copyright exemptions.

2.   IPR ISSUES RAISED BY AGENT TECHNOLOGY WITHIN THE RESEARCH SCENARIO

Due to their interaction with materials that are likely to be protected by copyright or database rights – images of products, product descriptions, programs, etc., certain software agents within the Research Scenario may be considered to entail certain risks as regards IPR. Particular agents that raise concerns would include information retrieval agents, database creation agents and filtering agents. This is because among their processes the following actions – which we have seen are restricted or protected – may occur: copying (of a commercial site's pictures or other data), communicating (transmitting that data to the user), modifying (presenting the data in a new environment or format) and extracting (retrieving data from a site's database or catalogue). We shall study this in more detail below.

Note that these issues may not arise in relation to agents whose applications involve purely "internal" processes within the retail store's systems. Looking at the list of potential agents in the Research Scenario set out in the introduction, these are agents relating to the provision of information about the store (parking, store layout, queue management, etc.); internal management agents (monitoring, stocks, prices, risk or workflow management etc); document management; user profiling agents; real-time software configuration; task automation (within the store or in relation to the

---

[28] Database right holders control the rights of temporary or permanent reproduction, translation, adaptation, arrangement, any form of distribution to the public, communication, display or performance to the public, similar to normal copyright rights, subject to Art. 6 and 8 of the Directive which set out some exceptions and rights of lawful users.

user's tasks); communications between retail store and consumers); customisation and interface or communication optimisation agents.

In this section, we first describe a software agent that involves interaction with online content (section 2.1), and then outline the IPR related issues that are raised by its processes (sections 2.2 and 2.3). These issues will then be discussed in the next section.

2.1 Content processing agents

Agents that will be considered in this chapter include those that involve data collection and mining, product analysis, and external content sharing processes. These include filtering agents, find agents, comparative shopping agents and recommender agents. Typical examples are search engines and shopping bots but more sophisticated agents are conceived for the Project. Below, we describe the processes of one such agent, called Agent D. In fact Agent C, in the previous chapter, is already involved in content processing. Among its processes were: searching the web for alternative products, comparing products for example the local store product catalogue through a comparison table, and presenting data about products to the consumer. Let us consider a more specific shopping agent that has several risk bearing processes.

Agent D is an automated shopping assistant. A standard element of this agent is a process that collects relevant data from different sources (the retail store, online web stores, product catalogues and other online databases, even discussion lists for product ratings). It then filters, prioritises and organises the data, and creates a personal product list or database for the shopper to consider. An overview of Agent D, similar to that providing the details of Agents A, B and C, is set out below.

Table 3-1. Overview of Agent D

Agent D	Description
Beliefs	Agent D is based on the shopper's profile (shopping list, preferences, etc.), user home contents (in a pervasive computing scenario, where the home inputs data to the agent through sensor devices, at the agent's request or on its own initiative); data available from the store's information system and the Internet, and rules and policies (potentially inferred) about price, quality, timing, and relevance, etc. Rules may be inferred from previous behaviour / standard shopping behaviour; other data (e.g. hot weather therefore search for sale and delivery of extra cold drinks) and EPCs embedded in RFID tags. Each such belief is envisaged eventually as the result of other individual agent processes: the shopping list agent, the user self-profiling agent, the diary / agenda agent, etc
Desire	To provide the shopper with the best possible base from which to purchase relevant goods at the best price and right quality.
Intention	Its short term goals are to create a list of relevant products (maybe just links to catalogue descriptions,) for perusing and viewing, or an analysis of the

Agent D	Description
	goods in question with links to materials, product reviews and other third party comments (medical or ecological information, etc.).
Autonomy / Intelligence	Agent D may be different from current shopping agents (MySimon, Shopbot, etc.), because we consider it could progressively learn what type of goods (the local retail store's own brand, high quality goods, currently advertised products, etc.) and which retail sources the shopper prefers, as well as review new shopping suggestions from the store or a consumer association, inferring rules for prioritisation, filtering, etc. This adaptation or learning process could result, for example, in removing certain products from a list or web-page, or extracting only relevant parts of online content.
Steps	**Process**
1	Agent D determines a need to purchase a specific item through assessment of data inputs and beliefs, including activation through EPC identification (RFID tags).
2	Agent D searches the network for various stores selling relevant products. This includes certain evaluation criteria (reputation evaluation, closeness to home, brand availability, etc.) and comparison functions, with e.g. the local store product catalogue.
3	Agent D searches both the store database and the Internet for relevant information. This includes activating search engines, accessing online databases and websites,
4	Agent D retrieves the data, possibly downloading and storing it locally or in a host.
5	Agent D scans, filters, prioritises or provides a comparison table of the products or services
6	Agent D makes the result available to the shopper directly or via a list of links
7	Agent D adds associated comments, reviews, and other additional materials

Note that in fact, the services or processes carried out by Agent D may be broken down into several processes, each one completed by a different agent: product identification, messaging, security checks, data transfer, links or comparison table creation, etc. Note also that our discussion is limited to the issues raised by the use of agents and their interaction with protected works, not the protection by intellectual property rights of the computer code of the agents themselves.

2.2   IPR concerns in relation to online commerce

2.2.1   Traditional concerns

As our discussion focuses on Intelligent Agents, we shall not cover all the topics of IPR protection and infringement on the Internet. However it is relevant and useful to give a brief outline as background. We have already noted that several different processes related to the Internet and ecommerce raise legal issues in relation to copyright. This is due to the fact that most content available on the net is (or is potentially) protected by copyright: pictures, texts, and videos. In addition, the Internet itself (and each individual website) could be considered a database – which provides it with secondary protection under principles of neighbouring and database rights.

IPR concerns raised by online ecommerce activities and processes fall in two main areas:
– the protection of enterprises' material and information, and
– the commission of copyright infringements through the collection, presentation and communication of data and the commercialisation of protected material.

While we do not consider the former an area that is particularly relevant in the context of the Research Scenario (as regards the store's or any online commerce's website, for example), this protection is relevant for the protection of content generated by the shopping agent. In particular we need to consider if an automated process can have sufficient value (intellectual, creative) for copyright protection, or constitute sufficient efforts for Data Base protection. This is considered in section 3.2 below.

In relation to the second area, IPR infringements, the following processes have raised IPR concerns:

Processes that can constitute infringements in webpage/website creation and publishing:
– Linking in various forms: standard HREF links, deep-linking, framing and in-lining.
– Linking to illegal content.
– Modifying: different presentations of data.
– Commercialisation of third party materials / products such as software, images and music.

Processes that can constitute infringement by Internet use (users / consumers):
– Searching: creating new lists of links (through search engines – a form of agent).
– Extracting data, from web sites or ISP databases.
– Copying / downloading and local storage to User's equipment.
– Modifying, including making different presentations of data (through the use of agents).

These issues have been discussed in detail in various works, and we shall not comment on them further[29]. As we will see next, however, many of these concerns are also raised by agent processing.

---

[29] There are many works on IPR issues in the information society, for example Ian Lloyd: *Information Technology Law* (3rd ed.) Butterworths, 2000; Reed, Chris: *Copyright in www pages*, Computer Law and Security Report, 1997; A Strowel et al: *Le droit d'auteur, du logiciel au multimedia*, Cahiers du Crid, No. 11, Bruylant, 1997; Pamela Samuelson:

2.2.2   Software agent concerns

Information gathering and presentation agents such as Agent D have features that are similar to search engines, and raise similar issues. Indeed, search engines could be classified as intelligent agents, their degree of intelligence depending on the sophistication of the searching and classification process. Taking into account the description we have given of agents, and the preliminary taxonomy set out in the first chapter of this work (Information retrieval agents, Database creation agents, Filtering agents) illustrated by Agent D described above, the following processes carried out by such agents should be considered to raise IPR concerns. The table below summarises the potential issues, which are discussed in the next section.

Table 3-2. IPR concerns raised by Agent D processes

Principal Process	Legal issue (IPR related)
Agent D determines a need to purchase specific item	None (internal process)
Agent D searches the network for various stores selling relevant products	Browsing and caching
Applies evaluation criteria and comparison functions	None (IPR), but filtered or screened data may cause problems (see below, comparison table). There may be unfair competition problems if the evaluation criteria are supplied by a third party (similar problem to search engine sponsorships).
Accessing online databases and websites	Access rights to Databases Database extraction issues
Storage of information which is retrieved	Local reproduction of work
Scans, filters, prioritises or provides a comparison table	Presentation of work in modified for or new context Creation of a derivative work
Makes the result available to the shopper directly (links, full data transfer)	Linking issues - deep linking, framing and links to illegal materials Breach of exclusive display rights and "making available" rights Protection of "Agent work"? DB rights?
Associated comments, reviews,	Unfair competition (presenting data out of original

Principal Process	Legal issue (IPR related)
and additional materials	context)
	Modification of work
	Derivative work

In the next section, we will therefore consider the following issues in order:

— Agent browsing and caching, the retrieval of URLs and other materials (section 3.1.1)
— The creation of a list of links (section 3.1.2)
— Linking to illegal or IPR protected materials (section 3.1.3)
— The storage of third party data on the agent user's or another party's equipment (section 3.1.4)
— The modification of original environment and data (section 3.1.5)
— The creation of new materials, and databases in particular (e.g. a product comparison chart) (section 3.1.6)
— The transmission and presentation of protected data to software agent User (section 3.1.7)

In addition, infringements relating to *sui generis* database protection require us to consider the extraction and reuse of data (to present to IA User) (section 3.1.8), while the provision of agents as intermediaries could raise issues of contributory and intermediary liability. This liability of agent service providers and agent hosts (together, agent ISPs) who provide the equipment and services for online activities (and in the course of their business make available or transmit protected material) is complex, and is discussed in section 3.2.

Once we have commented on the potential issues, we will study any exemptions and exceptions that may be available, which reduce these previously outlined risks (section 3.3).

While in the area of the legal framework for IPR in relation to agents, we also need to contemplate what protection is provided by law for works that are produced by a software agent: this may be either potential copyright protection for agent produced works or as the creation of new database (e.g. Product comparison chart) and therefore potentially *sui generis* protection under the Database Directive (section 3.4).

After that, we proceed to consider partial approaches to compliance, with IPR licensing and Digital Rights Management Systems (section 4).

3.   IPR COMPLIANCE HURDLES FOR
ECOMMERCE SOFTWARE AGENTS

In this section, we aim to outline in more detail the particular IPR compliance problems raised by ecommerce oriented software agents, and discuss the legal implications (3.1). We also consider if agents may benefit from any exemptions, either acting on behalf of the users or as an intermediary (agents provided by a third party) (3.2 and 3.3). We also comment on the legal difficulties of protecting any results generated by an electronic agent (3.4). Then, in the next section we shall look at some recent approaches to solve some of these problems.

3.1   Principal infringement issues

We now comment in turn the issues raised above, in section 2.

3.1.1   Agent browsing and caching

Depending on the activities and processes of the agents in question, their applications may be considered equivalent to user browsing and then caching: the web-data is kept in the agent and/or transmitted by the agent to the user's cache. This has some legal consequences.

Due to the technical features of the internet, browsing can constitute a technical infringement of many IP rights, which would not occur in the offline world. Temporary storage in RAM or user cache could be technically (and in some jurisdictions such as the UK and the US, it is by law) considered a reproduction even though it is only temporary, but is currently being exempted, either under the exemption for private or fair dealing ("fair use" – the extent of this exemption depends on the specific jurisdiction) and now by the DMCA in the USA and forthcoming implementations of the EC Information Society Copyright Directive in Europe.[30] In addition, it has been argued that the reproduction is tacitly authorised by the rightholder by virtue of the mere posting of the material on the Internet: without such implicit consent, any browsing would potentially constitute an infringement. The fact that copyright consents usually need to be in writing argues against this claim. It is also questionable whether any express copyright notice on the web page against implied consent has any validity.

Viewing could also constitute a right of communication (public display and/or performance) in certain jurisdictions where the definition of "public" is wider and can catch Internet users.

---

[30] See Art. 5.1 set out above in section 1.2.6. Note that the Directive is yet to be implemented in many Member States, and has been delayed due to various disagreements about its scope.

As mentioned, the EC has now allowed a specific exemption for copies required technically for transmission and browsing in the EC Information Society Copyright Directive. On the other hand, the EC Database Directive specifically provides that this is a restricted use in respect of databases and although the Software Directive is not clear on this point, it appears that several national implementations of the Directive have specifically included temporary reproduction as a restricted act (subject to right to decompile and make temporary copies for operation). This would apply if the agent retrieved data from a protected database or the collected data itself was a software program, respectively.

Finally, note that certain forms of caching are not so temporary (browsers and presumable browsing agents can be configured in various ways) and can prejudice the information visualised by the user (i.e. it is no longer up-to-date).

3.1.2   Creation of list of links: direct infringement?

More problematic for copyright law is the question of presentation by the agent of the results of its operations in the form of a list of links, or as a set or texts and images (full size or thumbnail). This would happen in the case of shopping or comparison agents, and also filter agents that modify data present on the web.

In themselves, simple hyperlinks ("HREF") do not constitute any infringement of copyright as they are not an act of exploitation (reproduction, communication, etc) but an indication of the address of another webpage that the user himself activates. It has been argued that a link could constitute a secondary infringement as an invitation to make a copy of the linked page or a breach of the author of the linked page's exclusive right to distribution, or if the linked page contains infringing or defamatory material. In certain cases "consent to link" might be implied by the presence of the material on the Internet, taking into account the open nature of web pages and the structure of the Internet – but this would not be the case if there were an express notice or code (robot.txt) to the contrary on the linked webpage or site or if the site was "closed", i.e. of restricted access. Alternatively the linker could rely on principles of bona fide and appearance theory, invoking the behaviour of the right owner putting the materials on the web.

If the link pointer (wording or image) itself is copyright (or indeed trademarked), then the protections relating to items of the webpage design apply. Using a substantial part of the text (e.g. press article or product description) would also be considered an infringement, not subject to the implicit consent to link.

Linking could affect moral rights, through issues related to the connection of an author's name and keywords, other works or an environment considered undesirable or different from the original. This is probably the most dangerous aspects of simple links, though moral rights provide less protection and remedies.

However there are certain forms of links that could more seriously be argued to constitute an infringement (or contributory to an infringement). Deep links are links to pages that are not the home page of the linked site, possibly bypassing any disclaimers and copyright notices. This form of linking could constitute a contributory act to an infringement on the part of the user[5]. It has also been argued that this could constitute unfair competition, due to the importance of the home page (advertising, communications, and notices) to the owner of the linked site. Decisions in the US and Germany have, however, rejected IPR and unfair competition claims in the absence of confusion[31]. There may be some element of confusion in the minds of the users through an inferred association of the linked pages and infringe the moral rights of the authors of the linked page. There are, however, decisions going both for and against linking, so the question is unclear[32].

In all events, the links created by shopping agents are likely to be temporary, for the duration of the user's needs, not permanent ones such as on a website, though this does not affect the infringement. Even then, exemptions may be available (see section 3.3 below).

Presentation of the complete text or image will infringe copyright law: it is a reproduction of the materials. This issue involves two forms of "links" that have raised legal issues: framing and in-lining. The first, framing involves inserting directly the linked site in a larger frame (or border) of the original site, so that the former appears as part of the linking site. This would constitute a reproduction or derivative work of the original site. It also puts the linked site (or worse, only part of it, violating the integrity of the author's work) in a different context and could constitute an infringement of the moral rights of the authors and of the recognition of their authorship as well as raise questions of copying (by the linking site) in whole or in part. It has also been considered passing off or unfair competition.

The second, in-lining, involves inserting an item (e.g. picture) from another site directly into the original site. This is an indirect form of reproduction, as the item of the target page is "reproduced" in the linking page. The item is also communicated to the public (in the same way as any web-page). In both these cases there may be arguments to say that the author implicitly consented to any such act, but as the item is viewed out of context,

---

[31] See *Ticketmaster v. Tickets.com* (2000) in the USA, and Handelsblat and others v. Paperboy.de (ruling of July 17, 2003, Case No. I ZR 259/00)

[32] For example, *Ticketmaster v. Tickets.com* (2000) in the USA and *Verlagsruppe Holtzbrinck v. Paperboy*.de in Germany (2003). See also for example, *Stepstone v. OFir* or *Danske Dagblades Forening v. Newsbooster.com*. Interesting site at http://www.linksandlaw.com/. Case citations are in the reference section of this work.

it is unlikely. Finally, on the same basis as above, this could also be considered a breach of the author's moral rights (authorship and integrity) and unfair competition or passing off.

Both these cases could also be considered the creation of a derivative work, i.e. and adaptation of the original and therefore an infringement. This would be the case, for example, of a shopping agent that retrieved pictures of the items for sale and presented them to the user, together with pictures of competing products from other sites. Alternatively one could consider the situation where the agent presents just a picture, without the accompanying text (a form of filtering), or vice-versa, an agent that just presents the price and source, without the promotional picture or description.

In addition, the US courts have held that reproducing a photograph on a website (results of a search) did constitute a breach of the protected uses, however it was also held that showing a thumbnail image of the same picture (with an underlying link to the original site) did not, as it was similar to a simple link and was protected by fair use[33]. This may not be the case in the EU, however, where copyright is a bit stricter, and some countries such as the UK where such "fair use" does not exist. This should change with the implementation of the EC Information Society Copyright Directive (art. 5.1) which allows member states to create exemptions for necessary transient technical reproductions (i.e. presentation of the content) for lawful use (linking to the original site). It is arguable that such images are not necessary.

Finally, linked sites may object to links from sites they consider inappropriate (diminishing the value of its site) or to increases of unwanted traffic on the site and therefore claim for unfair competition or trading.

3.1.3 Links to illegal or IPR protected materials: contributory infringement

As stated above, these links might incur liability for contributory infringement: assisting in a breach – the most famous example being links to sites with DeCSS technology or MP3 files. This constitutes a tort in the USA, a concept that doesn't always exist in EU jurisdictions. In Holland, providing the software to swap mp3 files was not considered a violation in a case involving KaZaA[34]. In the USA, upon certain conditions (e.g. removing the links when notified of the infringement) intermediaries such as search engines and potentially shopping bots may benefit from the exemptions given in the DMCA for "information location tool providers", in the event of referring to websites containing illegal materials. There is no such equivalent

---

[33] *Kelly v. Arriba Soft Corp.* 77 F. Supp. 2d 1116 (C.D. Cal. 1999).
[34] *Buma and Stemra v. Kazaa BV,* Amsterdam Appeals Court (Netherlands, 28 March, 2002), zaaknr 1370/01SKG, LJN-nr: AE0805.

in the EU where, in those jurisdictions where the law provides for contributory or secondary infringement, intermediaries (including agent users) may have to rely on principles of bona fide and/or consent.

3.1.4   Storage of data on user's or third party equipment

Temporary storage or copying has been commented above, and often benefits from an exemption. Long term storage is another matter. Storage and copying on the user's computer (i.e. downloading to disk or other memory system) would constitute an act of reproduction which, we have seen, is a restricted act. Again, this reproduction may be exempted by virtue of the private use exception if the user is a private individual (which would be the case of the user of Agent D). It may also qualify for an exemption under the fair dealing rules, e.g. copying for educational or research purposes. An exhaustive list of these exemptions is now set out for European Member states to choose from, in Art. 5 of the EC Copyright in the Information Society Directive commented below. In addition, it is argued that this reproduction is not protected by the principle of implied consent discussed above in relation to browsing and caching, as that would only cover temporary copies.

On the other hand, there is the question of downloading copyright protected materials that are protected by a copyright notice, either contractually or as condition of a copyright authorisation. The principle is that the user is implicitly or expressly aware of the copyright restrictions contained in the notice before downloading and is therefore bound by them. This awareness would not arise on behalf of the agent user in the event of an agent retrieving such materials, unless the agent is also programmed to understand copyright notices. In addition, it has also been argued that a user would also notice if IPR protected material was being used by a site in obvious breach of the original copyright – many websites are made up of infringing materials. The user would have at least the option of deciding whether to view, copy, or download these materials whereas an agent may not. And when the material arrives in front of the user, the new infringement has already occurred and it is unlikely whether the user could rely on fair use or other exemption.

This liability may also be extended to the provider of the agent, for example if the agent is a third party service. In addition, agent providers or developers may not avail themselves of the "substantial non-infringing use" and "fair compensation" defences that traditional providers of copying systems use (videos, computers, arguable P2P services) as it could be argued that the main purpose of agents such as Agent D is to commit this form of infringement, namely copying and retrieving commercial third party materials from the Internet.

3.1.5 Modification of original environment and data

This potential infringement would arise with the use of filter agents, or agents that collected data and presented it in a new format, for example in a comparative table. If the contents of a website or database are copied or extracted from other sources (e.g. newspaper clippings, list of events for information, special offers or promotions, but also product catalogues and product information), there could be possible breaches of moral rights for the presentation of data out of context. This would only occur if the underlying data is copyrighted material: factual data, such as prices, or public domain data in databases is not protected.

3.1.6 Creation of a new set of data

In addition to the breach of moral rights for presenting protected content in a new environment – especially if there were competing products and photographs – an agent that creates a new work such as a comparison chart or product database could be considered the creating an adaptation or derivative work of the original author or authors (in the USA, defined as a "work based upon one or more pre-existing works"[35]). This is also an infringement of exclusive rights for which there is no exemption.

3.1.7 Transmission to the Agent's User

Copyright holders enjoy an exclusive right of distribution of their works. Agent D may be considered to transmit digital works to the user and would thus be infringing this right. It is more likely, however, that the agent will report the webpage where such product is available (i.e. provide a link) and the user personally connects to the site to download the material. On the other hand, subject the question of attribution discussed below (and also discussed in the chapter on contracts), the action of the agent could be considered the action of the user, in which case the agent is not distributing the work but collecting it on behalf of the user.

3.1.8 In relation to *sui generis* Database protection: extraction of actual data (to present to IA User)

We have noted that websites, and especially catalogues contained on websites, could acquire protection as databases. They are protected if they are deemed creative, by selection and arrangement of materials, or involve qualitatively and/or quantitatively substantial investment in the obtaining,

---

[35] Section 101 of the US Copyright Act

verification or presentation of the contents[36]. *Sui generis* rights provide data bases with some protection against extracting substantial amounts of information from a database or repeated extractions of insubstantial parts. There may also be full copyright protection for the actual contents of the database such as research papers, product studies and evaluations, etc. Note that facts like dates of an event or prices would not be protected, and names of products would only be protected by trademarks). The extraction by humans or electronic agents is not distinguished in the Directive.

We consider that it is unlikely that shopping agents such as Agent D would do such "substantial" extraction, within the Research Scenario: D is more likely to retrieve individual prices and quantities. However, if large amounts of data are retrieved, possibly whole pages of text such as product evaluation report, then it is possible that a breach occurs[37]. In the event of search-engine style agents that collect data to present to final end-users, it has been argued that such a breach is waived by the website owner due to the interest they have in being included in a web-search: they even include metatags or keywords to facilitate their finding. Owners can also include metatags and .txt files (robot exclusion protocols) on the sites to exclude such cataloguing. Their presence would remove any implied consent and increase the likelihood of breach, while their absence would reinforce a presumption of consent to retrieve at least certain amounts of data.

On the other hand, agents that retrieve commercial data for single users may not benefit from this "implied consent". There have been various cases regarding such extraction (newspapers items, ticketing data, auction items) and arguments as to whether a breach arises revolve over the two concepts of substantiality (in relation to the amount of data extracted) and repetition and/or reuses (in relation to the number of times the data is accessed and extracted).

– Substantiality: whether a certain amount of data is consider substantial seems to depend on the legitimate expectation of the database creator to receive a return: substantial would damage the investment (e.g. see recital 42 of the EC Database Directive);

– Repetition and/or reuse of any extracted data: the frequency of extraction from a database would be considered a breach if it conflicts with the normal exploitation of the database or unreasonably prejudices the legitimate economic interests of the creator (Art. 7 V).

---

[36] Art 3 and 7-11 EC Database Directive respectively.

[37] E.g. as in the E-bay v. Bider's Edge case (100 F. Supp. 2d 1058 (N.D. Cal. 2000)) in the USA, based on trespass and competition, and not tested under the EU *sui generis* rights, or German cases relating to classified ads: (e.g. *Stepstone v OFiR* (District Court (Landgericht) Cologne, 28 February 2001) and District Court (Landgericht) Munich, 18 September 2001). See also Grosse Ruse H: *Electronic Agents and the Legal Protection of Non-creative Databases*, 2001.

Until courts provide further precision on these terms, however, there is some ambiguity in the application of the directive and implementing laws. Any court interpretation would also have to take into account freedom of information and competition issues, thereby potentially restricting the protection afforded to certain collections of data (especially unique collections, and commercial data such as prices and quantities).

In the Research Scenario, it is unlikely that Agent D or other type of shopping agent (e.g. a comparison agent, or an agent monitoring special offers) would either extract large amounts of data or reuse the data to the economic prejudice of the creator. On the contrary, acting as a search engine, the agent is bringing the attention of the user to the products or services sold by the creator of the database. There may be some degree of prejudice, however, if the original creator relies on some form of banner or publicity advertisement, which Agent D may bypass by simply presenting the database results to the user.

Another risk may arise if Agent D performs a systematic and repeated search and retrieval of insubstantial data for users, which would not constitute a "normal use" of the data. It could be argued that as the items that are likely to be searched for by agents within the Research Scenario are items that are regularly purchased by shoppers on a weekly or daily basis, there is nothing abnormal about repeat searches and extractions. Again, this may prejudice any advertising revenue of the relevant web merchants, and make it difficult for advertisers to rely on "hit" numbers to determine revenues.

The risk is heightened by the commercial nature of any reuse: if the agent user is a consumer, it is arguable that there is no economic prejudice to the original owner/creator of the database. On the other hand, it is conceivable that the agent is used by a commercial intermediary: the retail store itself, or some third party service offering comparative shopping services. Such a third party will have some form of income stream from the use of the agent. In this case, the likelihood of breach is higher, subject to the need to prove prejudice to the original database owner.

3.2   Agents as intermediaries

It is possible that Agent D's services may be provided by a third party for the use of the retail store or consumer. In which case, the agent acts may be attributed to the third party, which may incur liability as an intermediary. This is similar to online search engine scenario, whereby services are provided by the search engine companies at the request of the users[38]. The liability and exemptions are similar to those listed above, except that one

---

[38] An interesting study of these issues is in A Cruquenaire: *Electronic Agents as Search Engines: Copyright related aspects,* 2001.

should consider the position of the intermediary in relation to the data and to the user.

Intermediaries are potentially liable for all infringements (primary or secondary) committed on their servers or with their tools. However they have successfully raised some defences against copyright infringement liability. They have argued that as mere conduits, they have no element of intention or volition, so they could only incur secondary liability as contributors (which is more difficult to prove). As common carriers, like the post office, they would incur no liability for acts committed by their customers. This defence, however, is not applicable to their own acts of breach of copyright such as copying. Finally, they have pleaded that they have no knowledge and nor technical ability to control the content of material that is transmitted over their networks or servers.

Case law in the USA has so far suggested that an element of knowledge and/or volition is required to incur liability for direct copyright infringement, and participation or direct involvement in the acts themselves (such as uploading), not just facilitating a service or space (BBS) or the act in question. The DMCA provides an explicit exemption from secondary liability.

As we will see next, the EC Ecommerce Directive excludes general liability for intermediary service providers in certain circumstances (conduits, caching and hosting), mainly when the ISP has no knowledge of the infringement, has no control over the information or promptly removes the violating information. This may be difficult to argue when they know what processes the agent may carry out (e.g. modifying the original data, extracting substantial parts or repeat extractions). In addition, the Copyright in the Information Society Directive provides for exemptions for temporary acts of reproduction in similar cases. These exemptions are discussed next.

3.3   Exemptions and exceptions

Before moving on to consider how technology may provide some solutions to the IPR problems discussed above, it is important to see whether any exemptions or exceptions may apply to the agent processes under discussion. In such a case, there will be no need to look for a technical solution.

We have mentioned certain exemptions in relation to each potential infringement above. Here we believe it is useful to outline in general certain exemptions that may be available for the use of agents, that can deem their behaviour legal despite possible connections with the issues commented above.

Under the EC Copyright in the Information Society Directive, there are some general exemptions set out in Article 5. These include many exemptions already available in national laws, and the aim of the directive is to harmonise these at European level[39].

Art 5.1 exempts temporary acts of reproduction which are transient or incidental acts of reproduction which are an integral and essential part of a technological process, including one which facilitates the effective functioning of transmission systems, or whose sole purpose is to enable use to be made of a work or other subject matter, and which have no independent economic significance. This may not cover ISPs and agents for non-ephemeral caching, which is arguably not an essential part of the process (e.g. mirroring) and is sometimes not transient[40]. An example of this could be when an Agent receives an advertisement and stores it for a while until it chooses to display to the user. Although at first glance, the storage (reproduction within the agent's system) is technically a breach of copyright, as part of technical process it may be covered by the exemption and therefore not involve any violation. On the other hand, if the storage is for a longer period of time, it could be considered non-transient, in which case the exemption does not apply.

Article 5.2 provides an exhaustive list of possible exemptions available to be selectively implemented by Member States. This list includes exemptions for private usage (subject to fair compensation to the author), and others that would not really apply in the context of the Research Scenario: illustration for education and scientific research, for people with disabilities for non commercial purposes, for libraries, public security and judicial and administrative functions, reporting of current events, and quotations for the purposes of criticism and review of legally available works.

In addition, although not a legislated exemption, ISP agent providers may find protection in Recital 27 of the Directive insofar as their activities consist in "the mere provision of physical facilities for enabling or making a communication" which does not in itself amount to an act of communication to the public in breach of a rightholder's exclusive rights. This may benefit agent platforms and ISPs that host potentially infringing agents provided by third parties.

Under the EC Database Directive, while certain exemptions are granted for certain categories that are not relevant for our purposes[41], there are lawful uses which are not to be prevented:

– Acts which do not conflict with normal exploitation of the database or unreasonably prejudice the legitimate interests of the maker of the database.

---

[39] Whether this harmonisation is achieved is another matter, especially seeing that the exemptions are not mandatory but "a la carte" for Member States to implement.

[40] Although copying itself is essential to caching.

[41] If the contents are from a non-electronic database; for the purposes of illustration for teaching or scientific research, and for the purposes of public security or an administrative or judicial procedure.

- Acts which do not cause prejudice to the holder of a copyright or related right in respect of the works or subject matter contained in the database.

Finally, under the EC Ecommerce Directive there are certain broad exemptions from liability (not specifically related to copyright or *sui generis* rights) for information society service providers. This may apply if the agent services are provided by a third party, for the user's or store's benefit (as commercial agent user). These agent ISPs could be exempted in relation to:

- the information transmitted in a transmission in a communication network of information provided by a recipient of the service, or the provision of access to a communication network" (**mere conduits**[42]), on condition that the provider (a) does not initiate the transmission; (b) does not select the receiver of the transmission (i.e. the agent user); and (c) does not select or modify the information contained in the transmission. This exception is of doubtful application as although the agent user may select the information to be retrieved and transmitted, the agent may modify the data collected. In addition, as Agent D gains autonomy, it will start to initiate transmissions on behalf of the user – again, we meet up with the issue of attribution.
- automatic, intermediate and temporary storage of information, (**caching**[43]) performed for the purpose of making more efficient the information's onward transmission to other recipients of the service (i.e. the agent user) upon their request, on condition that (a) the provider does not modify the information; (b) the provider complies with conditions on access to the information; (c) the provider complies with rules regarding the updating of the information, specified in a manner widely recognised and used by industry; (d) the provider does not interfere with the lawful use of technology, widely recognised and used by industry, to obtain data on the use of the information; and (e) the provider acts expeditiously to remove or to disable access to the information it has stored upon obtaining actual knowledge of the fact that the information at the initial source of the transmission has been removed from the network, or access to it has been disabled, or that a court or an administrative authority has ordered such removal or disablement. Again, the agent of the service provider may modify the data (point (a)), removing the availability of this protection.
- the information stored at the request of a recipient of the service (the agent user) (**Hosting**[44]), on condition that: (a) the provider does not have actual knowledge of illegal activity or information and, as regards claims for damages, is not aware of facts or circumstances from which the illegal activity or information is apparent; or (b) the provider, upon

---

[42] Art 12 EC Ecommerce Directive.

[43] Art 13 EC Ecommerce Directive.

[44] Art 14 EC Ecommerce Directive.

obtaining such knowledge or awareness, acts expeditiously to remove or to disable access to the information. This may be of use if the information collected by Agent D is stored (temporarily or permanently) by the agent service provider on behalf of the user.

Apart from these statutory (legislated) exemptions, agent users may try to rely on the doctrine of implied consent (which may be difficult, as copyright consents usually have to be in writing) or bona fide principles: the fact that the creators of the works make the information available on line precludes them from preventing the normal use of such information having regard to the usual actions possible on the Internet. Implied consents would not however extend to commercial use of the data by third parties (which would allow consumer controlled shopping bots, but not those operated by third party service providers).

3.4 Protection of agent created data and results

Finally, although this is not a key issue in the Research Scenario, for a more complete picture of IPR law as it applies to agents, we should contemplate what protection is provided by law for works that are produced by a software agent[45].

Generally speaking, digital content (a webpage or website as a whole) may acquire IPR protection in a variety of ways:

– As an artistic, literary or cinematographic work, for the originality or creativity in the design (or the text) of the whole webpage (not just the individual items), provided it satisfies certain the specific requirements for the work in question (e.g. the page itself as a moving image or literary text).

– as a database, if items are separable and methodically organised, e.g. a collection of pictures, a list of books or hyperlinks, (or for the website as a whole, a hierarchical set of web pages), provided there is an element of personal intellectual creativity in the choice and arrangement; or by *sui generis* database rights, if items are separable and methodically organised but lack an element of intellectual creativity and if involves substantial investment in obtaining, verification or presentation of data. This protection will only apply to a substantial part of the webpage (see above on the limitation of database protection).

– possibly as a software program, if the webpage or site design is programmed using specific programming language code (scripting languages, e.g. Java) and not just formatting or data definition language (HTML, XML), and satisfies the criteria for originality.

---

[45] For a more complete analysis of these issues, see H Grosse Ruse: *Electronic Agents and the Legal Protection of Non-creative Databases*, 2001

Separable items on a web page, when created by a company, are protected by copyright if they are artistically (semantically) and technically separable from the web page. This would include photographs, graphs, videos or "flash" sequences. This protection also applies to separate elements of software program that may be on the page (e.g. in Java, or other language). Graphic items could also be protected by registered design, as a logotype or trademark.

The protection of agent-created work is in fact likely to be a minor issue in the Research Scenario. The retail shopper is unlikely to wish to protect the results created by agents such as those we have described: shopping, comparing or filtering agents. However it is possible for the retail store, for example, to wish to create automatically a database of competitor prices and products (to present to consumers to prove that its prices are the lowest) and therefore want to protect these results.

The organisation and presentation of search results and data collected or created by agents usually lacks creative organisation to benefit from copyright under Art. 3 of the Database Directive (which requires the author's own intellectual creation). Even if there were such creativity, it is argued that to acquire copyright protection such originality must be created by a human, not a machine. Such work may, however, acquire *sui generis* protection under the EC Database directive, by involving substantial investment and resources, arranged systematically and methodically and individually accessible by electronic means (Arts. 1 and 7 of the Directive). In order to gain *sui generis* protection, the creator must show quantitative or qualitative investment in obtaining, verifying or presenting the data index. This could be shown in the time spent developing the agent (if it belongs to the creator of the potential database) or the efforts in executing the agent and maintaining the contents up-to-date. The complexity of the agent's user interfaces and indexation systems may also support the contention in favour of *sui generis* rights.

This question of database protection raises the issue of who is the author of the database: the user, the agent service provider, or the agent programmer? The agent is not a legal or natural person, and is therefore currently excluded[46]. Insofar as the user defines the parameters of the action of the agent, it could be argued that it is he/she who holds the rights in the produced materials. Otherwise the rights may be considered joint (Art 4.3), between the agent creator (who develops the program that creates the database) and the agent service provider and/or user (who establishes the criteria and launches the process).

We have now considered the application of copyright law to agent activities, focusing on potential acts undertaken by Agent D that may

---

[46] Art. 4.1 EC Database Directive.

infringe IPR of content owners. We note that there are several areas of risk, but also that it may benefit from some exemptions, all the more so if the agent is acting on behalf of a consumer rather than a commercial organisation (which is the case of Agent D). We now turn to comment on current attempts to solve the dilemmas of copyright in the digital environment – focusing on DRMS, and consider how they may be applied to agent transactions (section 4). Then, we shall conclude this chapter with a discussion on IPR infringing processes, and a commenting a means for analysing and possibly solving some of the issues through a process oriented approach.

4. PARTIAL SOLUTIONS FOR IPR COMPLIANCE

Although this chapter has focused up to now on the legal issues that are raised by agent transactions and actions, it is useful to anticipate and discuss some of the technical solutions that are being discussed to minimise legal risks.

The protection of content in the digital environment is probably the greatest debate currently being waged in ICT-law related legal circles (along with privacy). Issues extend from the number of years copyright protection is being afforded certain works (copyright being greatly extended from the 14 years or so that was originally granted to rightholders[47]), to the issue of copyleft and open source licences (to "free" programs and content from author's monopoly rights, and maintain that freedom[48]), to technical means for controlling the access and use of protected works – what have been called Digital Rights Management Systems (DRMS). This last is the main area where research efforts are being concentrated to try to ensure IPR compliance through technological solutions. It is one which may solve some of the issues outlined in section 3 in relation to agent-based processes and transactions, and one where agent-based computing may also possibly provide some form of answer to its own problems.

The principle areas where technical solutions have been sought are those of licensing and enforcement. While the first aims to verify how to achieve flexible automated online licensing of copyright protected materials, the second seeks to control unauthorised copying, communication and display of such materials and find means to sanction it. In this section, we consider how these partial solutions apply to agent transactions.

---

[47] See *Eldred v. Ashcroft*, 123 S.Ct. 769 (2003) in the USA, commented for example in P Samuelson: *The Constitutional Law of Intellectual Property After Eldred v. Ashcroft* (forthcoming 2003).

[48] See articles by Richard Stallman at www.fsf.org

4.1   "First generation" technological protections

We refer to these as "first generation", due to their simplicity and because they are mainly based on a netiquette system corresponding to the Internet's initial codes of conduct. These protections involve certain codes (protocols, tags) that may be added to web-pages to signal to certain automatic agents (robots, search engine spiders) that they should not access a website or index the site in some way or another. The agent first looks up the file *xxx.com/robot.txt* to verify the authorisation / exclusion.

These methods, however, are only as good as the code with which they are written (as the coding is open) and programming can override these restrictions fairly easily. Indeed, as they are based on an honour system, they can simply be ignored. Some people have argued that it is not legal to discriminate against search engines. Why, if any person is allowed to visit a site, shouldn't an automated process such as an agent representing such a person be allowed access[49]? The processing of these files could however evolve into a form of dialogue, similar to proposed licensing processes which are discussed next.

4.2   Automated licensing

Automated licensing schemes aim to prevent the extraction of music or materials from Databases without a licence being granted for access and use of the materials, and a payment or notification having been made to rightholders. An important dimension to legalising agent transactions may be the use of such automatic licensing systems for dealing with sales and other use of copyrighted materials. This aspect is relevant mainly for transactions whose object involves IPR materials of higher value, such as the purchase of music, software or other protected goods. This type of automatic processing should be considered in the event the consumer wishes to acquire valuable content online (as opposed to advertising or price data), e.g. music or videos from the store or other website. This process could, however, also be applied for the selection and extraction of content from commercial websites, including images, product description, catalogues, etc.

In the context of the European Research Frameworks, the project FILIGRANE among others focused on this sort of mechanism for software agents[50]. The project provides for a series of determined authorisations and steps, and predetermined licence agreements to obtain digital content legally on line.

---

[49] This topic is illustrated from a business and legal perspective in B Subirana: *J & J Internet Book Shopping Robot*, 1997.

[50] FILIGRANE: Flexible IPR for software agent reliance, ESPRIT 28423, documents available at <http://www.dice.ucl.ac.be/crypto/filigrane/> (visited 26/05/2003)

Licensing also leads us to consider the important question of agent-based IPR negotiation. In principle, should agents be able to do this, they would be able to read and "understand" copyright notices and potentially negotiate licences and exemptions, leading to seamless autonomous operations. Automated and protocol based negotiation may provide one means to achieve this, through rule-based contract templates, negotiation and monitoring capabilities. To operate widely on the Internet, this process requires a substantial standardisation effort, similar to P3P in relation to privacy, which may be difficult to implement in view of differing legal regimes regarding IPR. Some initiatives are attempting this, through the creation of an IPR ontology and negotiation languages and protocols, e.g. XRML, which aims to be a common language for IPR representation and negotiation on open networks[51].

One interesting licensing initiative in relation to standardisation of ontologies for online materials is the creation of the Creative Commons licence series[52]. This initiative uses mark-up and RDF to help tag and identify works with metadata, building up what could be called an open source re-usable digital objects repository (mainly aimed at learning materials). This metadata would allow documents to be marked up with relevant and computer-intelligible legal data about them, such as authors, licenses, access, etc., even bound onto the documents with digital signatures. Conceptually, we believe that this system could be linked with rule-based IPR licence, privacy consent or standard negotiation processes, for modular and specific contracting[53]. Standardisation of this type will assist enormously in developing interoperable information retrieval agents on the open network, such as Agent D commented here.

From a legal point of view, this raises certain conceptual legal issues of agent contracting that we have discussed in the previous chapter - a copyright licence being a form of contract. Technically speaking, whether appropriate levels of intention are identified and consent given (e.g. regarding IPR dispute resolution clauses), and how mistakes or errors are dealt with, may be a question of the granularity of user and consumer policies embedded into the agent processing. The higher the level, the greater the certainty. In addition, if online copyright licences are considered electronic contracts, it is yet to be seen whether software agents such as

---

[51] Garcia and Delgado: *Brokerage of Intellectual Property Rights in the Semantic Web*, 2001. Of interest is also the Dublin Core initiative, for metadata relating to publishing on the Internet, online at http://dublincore.org/.

[52] A form of OpenSource for online texts, see at http://creativecommons.org/. This initiative has been set up to expand the range of creative work available for others to build upon and share, as the licenses are mainly permissive. Authors can choose a variety of parameters regarding attribution, commercial use, modifying and sharing with others.

[53] E.g. see research projects such as SweetDeal (Grosof B and Poon, T: *Representing Agent Contracts with Exceptions using XML Rules, Ontologies and Process Description*, 2002).

those we are discussing will have to comply with procedural requirements under national implementations of the Ecommerce Directive, regarding access and storage of contract terms, opportunities for rectification, and the provision of information.

4.3   Enforcement through Digital Rights Management

The concept of automated licensing leads naturally to more advanced digital rights management systems, using rights management information (RMI) and technological measures to restrict non-authorised acts (anti-circumvention mechanisms). These systems are being developed to "secure" copyright in digital materials, i.e. to ensure through hardwiring digital content that it cannot be used without the appropriate authorisation and eventually payment for a license[54]. DRMS involve the use of various technological systems to facilitate and adapt rights management to the online environment. These include:

— Security mechanisms (against access or copying)
— Secure digital envelopes: encryption systems with trusted third parties who keep record of public keys, to be made available to users of the system.
— Trusted systems: prior authentication of users through trusted third parties (checking user name against a database).
— Embedded data in the protected material for identification of the rightholder (RMI).
— Intelligent DRMS (self contained encryption, with embedded RMI): in this, there is no need for third party involvement (useful for more simple transactions, though the software is more complex, less secure).
— Real time links to copyright licensing schemes.
— Trusted Computing platforms, where automatic processes are activated in computer equipment to verify rights and allow access on certain conditions being satisfied[55].

These mechanisms are protected by recent IPR legislation, originating in the 1996 WIPO treaties and implemented in the Digital Millennium copyright Act in the USA and EU Copyright in the Information Society Directive. In Europe, Arts. 6 and 7 of this Directive protect anti-circumvention mechanisms and RMI in most circumstances.

DRMS schemes could involve agents acting for both parties within a particular agreed framework (consumer shopping agents, and website protecting agents, that monitor user's behaviour on sites and report to

---

[54] There have been various European RTD projects relating to agent based services, including FILIGRANE; IMPRIMATUR; ECADEC, COPEARMS and TALISMAN (see at http://www.cordis.lu/ist/home.html for references).

[55] See online at www.trustedcomputing.org/

copyright holders). One solution therefore would be a standardised system of dialogue between the consumer agent and the website protection agents. User agents such as Agent D would have to negotiate with content owners and rightholders to have access and make any uses of the protected materials. While in the Research Scenario it is not considered very likely that web-sites will set up DRMS systems just to protect the commercial data contained on the site (photos, descriptions, catalogues, etc.), this may not be the case when such systems are more widespread or where the materials are more valuable.

Although this is not the place to discuss DRMS in depth, unfortunately proposed rights management schemes may have "overkill" effects, failing to account for rights of fair or private use and other exemptions[56]. A scenario for a shopper would depict a DRM service monitoring the shopper's agent activity and contacting the user, the person it deems ultimately responsible for the agent's actions, to recover compensation for infringing use of protected materials. This would become a nightmare for the shopper, if he or she were unaware of the potential for infringement through the automated processes of an agent such as Agent D, as discussed above. DRMS solutions currently proposed are not flexible enough to take into account the numerous exemptions and uses that are permitted to a variety of persons and for a variety of purposes, as set out above[57].

Another problem with DRMS is a lack of standardisation relating to technologies within this area (in software and hardware terms) and for rights management information. This lack will defeat the interoperability and openness of the Internet and the ease of e-commerce, including agent based trading. It is also likely that large players (content owners) will impose a quasi-standard of their own. Thus, to provide a platform for open trade with IPR protected materials, greater interoperability is required and "meta-standards" whereby different DRMS systems using different standards may communicate with each other.

Also, DRMS may considerably reduce the autonomy of information consumers, including their IT tools such as agents. Software agents will need to incorporate levels of complexity to take such technologies into account, for example by negotiating for access, if they want to achieve their status as autonomous and intelligent, and comply with laws regarding the protection of such technological measures and non removal of RMI.

Finally, another serious problem with DRMS is the issue of privacy, and how such systems depend on identification of users and controlling their use

---

[56] K Koelman: *The protection of technological measures vs. the copyright limitations*, 2001.

[57] For a recent comment, see P Samuelson, *Digital Rights Management {and, or, vs.} the Law*, 2003.

of protected content[58]. This question of the link between IPR and privacy law is discussed below, in section 5.

5.   DISCUSSION ON IPR INFRINGING AGENT PROCESSES

As we have now seen, Intelligent Shopping Agents create a potential for infringements in several areas of intellectual property rights law within the European Union[59]. Table 3.3 below adds a new column to the initial table describing Agent D, summarising the issues raised by the agent's different processes and providing some suggested additional measures to increase the legality and legal certainty or confidence in using such an agent.

---

[58] See for example, The Information and Privacy Commissioner, Ontario: *Privacy and Digital Rights Management (DRM): An Oxymoron*, 2002.
[59] See also, from a US perspective, H. Zhu: *The Interplay of Web Aggregation and Regulations,* 2002.

Table 3-3. Some suggested processes for legalising shopping Agent D's processes

Principal Process	Legal issue (IPR related)	Additiona processes for compliance and/or confidence
Agent D determines a need to purchase specific item	None (internal process)	Registration of original agent programming / parameters (trigger events, process conditions and rules)
Agent D searches the network for various stores selling relevant products	Browsing and caching	Ensure only temporary caching Program agent to fall within (DMCA-like) search engine criteria
Accesses online databases and websites	Access rights to DB DB Extraction issues	Program agent process to fall within exemption (non repetitive, non substantial extraction) or obtain agreement to retrieve data through negotiation (includes negotiation protocols such as DRMS, registration of negotiation steps) Session control and processes for system failures Identification process
Stores information which is retrieved	Local reproduction of work (potentially exempted)	Ensure temporary storage, to benefit from exemption Respect of "intelligent copyright notices" (e.g. temporary incorporation of copyright notice rules in agent processing, e.g. via XML and rule/workflow language)

Principal Process	Legal issue (IPR related)	Additiona processes for compliance and/or confidence
Applies evaluation criteria and comparison functions	None (IPR), but filtered or screened data may cause problems (see below, comparison table). There may be unfair competition problems if the evaluation criteria are supplied by a third party (smilar problem to search engine sponsorships)	
Scans, filters, prioritises or provides a comparison table	Presentation of work in modified or new context Creation of a derivative work Unfair competition regarding placing of data in the table Protection of "Agent work."	Obtain agreement to retrieve data (as above) Information processes to assure transparency of evaluation processing (sponsored products, etc.)
Makes the result available to the shopper: links, full data transfer	Linking issues - deep linking, framing and links to illegal materials Breach of exclusive display or "making available" rights	Obtain consent for agent action, through negotiation process (as above)

Thus there seem to be several concerns as well as obstacles to legally compliant automatic agent processing, such as that conceived for Agent D. First, the autonomy of the software agent raises concerns. Agent D may access and download copyright protected materials whose use is regulated by licence and/or contract (e.g. by a copyright notice). The general argument is that website visitors are implicitly or expressly aware of the copyright restrictions contained in the notice before making any action on the website (copying, downloading) and are therefore contractually bound by them. There would be no such awareness in the event of autonomous agent actions, unless Agent D was also programmed to pick up copyright notices – in line with automated DRM systems. In addition, human Internet users may also be aware if protected materials were being used by a site in breach of the original copyright (many websites are made up of infringing materials). They then have at least the option of deciding whether to view, copy, or download these materials. Agent D may not have this capacity.

There is also a question of the attribution of liability. Agent D has no legal personality, so from the copyright holder's point of view, actions should be attributed to its user. It will be important for the agent systems designers, and any agent service provider (such as the store in the Research Scenario), to determine who this user or "custodian" is: is it the store, who is offering a service to shoppers, or are the shoppers themselves using the agent? What are the criteria for deciding who is "in control", when both the agent provider and a shopper may determine different parts of the agent's processes and decision-taking? Could there be joint or severable liability? This distinction between third party agents and shopper controlled agents is also important with regard to available exemptions, as commented above.

Attribution may become tenuous when one considers Agent D's learning capacity and autonomy. Its actions and processes may no longer resemble its initial programming. In the previous chapter we saw that there were legislative proposals to deal with the attribution of consent in a contract context[60]. There does not seem to be any legal framework yet regarding this point in relation to IPR violations. Arguments arise as to the application of strict or vicarious liability regimes similar to juridical persons such as companies[61]. We argue that to minimise the risk, it will be important to establish a legal model that takes both the concept of control (e.g. specifying who is responsible for different agent processes) and that of agent evolution into account, and adapt the business processes accordingly.

Attribution will be difficult for third parties – thereby increasing mistrust in agent-based processing – unless agents and agent-users are identified. Content owners such as online stores will want to be able to determine when

---

[60] UNCITRAL Model Law on Ecommerce, UCITA, UETA and UECA. Please see Chapter 2 on contracts.
[61] G Sartor: *Agents in Cyberlaw*, 2002.

a breach has occurred (e.g. downloading a file or an image) and who did it. However, unless agents are identified by some third party trust scheme or directly in the agent coding, the dynamic IP of such devices and any mobile devices that supported the agents would not provide the content owner with sufficient information[62]. Content providers may turn to technical means to prevent agent technologies from accessing the site, or require agents to conform to trusted identity management systems.

User identification however, raises the issue of the relationship between IPR and Privacy: both areas of law establish rights to control the use of data, protected content and personal data respectively. DRMS, using identity linkage or user tracking, risk potential privacy violations[63]. Agents increase the complexity of this debate, as the needs for legal certainty and trust in IPR licence negotiation through identification or certification of agents mentioned above may conflict with privacy requirements. On the other hand, agent technologies may be appropriate technologies for achieving a balance between both as they could incorporate flexible policy-based mechanisms to heighten user trust[64]. This is discussed further in Chapter 5.

To take advantage of the current legal framework, any agent architecture needs to consider carefully any available exemptions. For example, agents acting for individuals could establish the non-commercial nature of their operations, and express a private usage or other exempted purpose. A complication is that different exploitation acts have different exemptions, which also vary from jurisdiction to jurisdiction. This constitutes a substantial barrier to developing seamless "DRM-enabled" transnational agents which may require significant tailoring to each act, content type, database and jurisdiction. This also complicates the modelling of any legal processes and architecture, as commented above, because the models and related automated processes may only be valid in specified jurisdictions.

There are also considerable risks for agent hosts, including liability as ISP or vicarious liability as agent provider. Even if the host is not the entity that is providing the agent services, it may incur liability as facilitator or contributory to an infringement. Third party hosts may be reluctant to receive in their server/environment any agent that could commit serious breaches of copyright (an example today being an agent-based file swapping service). To provide a more stable and trustworthy framework for agent

---

[62] This may change with IPv6, where it is conceived that each item connected or operating on the Internet will have its own IP number. See at <http://www.ipv6forum.com/index.html> or < http://www.ipv6tf.org/>.

[63] Ontario Privacy Commissioner: *Privacy and Digital Rights Management (DRM): An Oxymoron,* 2002; Korba and Kenny: *Applying Digital Rights Management Systems to Privacy Rights Management,* 2002.

[64] Xu and Korba: *A Trust Model for Distributed E-Learning Service Control,* 2002; Feigenbaum et al: *Privacy Engineering for Digital Rights Management Systems,* 2002; Korba and Kenny, op cit., 2002.

transactions, Multi-Agent Systems and agent hosts need to be supported by some form of trust system or mechanism – or even agent certification – so that they may overcome this reluctance to receive or offer processing services to third party agents. This is commented on next, and MAS is discussed in more detail in our conclusions in Chapter 6.

One of the principal issues raised by the use of agents in online commerce is how content owners will know that an infringement has occurred and who did it. From their own website registers, rightholders should be able to determine in certain cases when a breach has occurred (e.g. downloading a file, accessing a database or copying an image), although the extent of any subsequent breach will be unclear, if not impossible, to determine. As regards identification, unless agents are identified either directly in their programming (which may raise serious privacy issues, in any event) or indirectly by some trust scheme, the current structure of Internet addresses (IPv4) would not afford the owner the relevant information. Dynamic IPs, proxy servers and agent platforms, whereby the agent's "address" may only be the agent host's IP number, would give misleading identification information.

"Trust frameworks" for agent commerce are currently being seen as one of the best solutions to solve this issue among others. Such systems include privilege management systems, trusted third party certification, protected identification (i.e. released on certain conditions), etc. Although the main focus of these schemes is on security and certainty for online transactions, i.e. aiming at contract and contract performance issues, the management and protection of copyright and other IPR could also be dealt with in this way, combined with DMRS.

A first type of scheme could be some form of third party agent registry, approval or label, to certify the processes of an agent and allow traders a public means for determining if they want to exclude certain agents from their sites: i.e. because they may cause economic prejudice. Having such a seal, possibly combined with a dialogue process between websites and agents, would allow such sites to determine automatically the acceptability of the agent in question.

Another more open system would be to define a standard for IPR protection similar to the P3P initiative for privacy protection. This would not require third party approval but would involve determining a set of standards for IPR policy declarations and negotiations on the basis of Rights Expression Languages (REL). An automatic dialogue process would not verify the agent against a third party seal or registry but against corporate and private policies, on the basis of a technical negotiation standard accepted by the industry (e.g. within the W3C). This could also standardise the robot exclusions / acceptance system and provide more certain conditions for consent or withholding of the same. Users would no longer have to rely on statutory or implied consents, but could benefit from express website owner consent. Unfortunately there are several difficulties with this approach, not the least being that RELs may not incorporate ontologies for expressing fair usage and private or academic use exemptions. In addition, these forms of contractual consent may not be as wide in scope as the exemptions or implied consents set by law. In which case abiding by such a negotiation would lead to a certain form of restriction in agent's potential capability and scope.

From a commercial point of view, the infringements that have been discussed here in relation to the Research Scenario may appear fairly minor, compared to the possibilities of downloading software, music and video, currently the prime focus of attention of content providers and right holders. Setting up complex agent negotiation frameworks for access to commercial web sites or product catalogues may be too costly and heavy – i.e. disproportionate – for the objective, and would reduce the efficiency of the agents. In addition, such sites should in fact welcome shopping agents, as part of the marketing and selling process.

However, this does not remove the fact that IPR violations may occur. Retailers may put up with minor infringements, as occurs today in online commerce regarding search engines (thumbnails of online photographs, brief extracts of text associated to a link) and to a certain extent deep-linking and framing. It is when these breaches of copyright escalate to a degree where there may be unfair competition or abuse of trademarks and goodwill that right-holders have generally taken action[65].

In this chapter we have attempted to establish the IPR related risks for each of the processes of Agent D, a search and compare shopping agent within the Research Scenario. This has enabled us to determine further processes that may be either necessary for regulatory compliance or recommended for good practice and greater confidence in agent-based transactions.

We believe that these processes should be programmed into either the agent itself or the agent environment, embedding the legal rules. There are, however, two design constraints to implementing this approach. First, the agent's design may be proprietary but should be interoperable with other platforms, including interfaces coded in accordance with generally accepted Internet protocols, architectures and standards (FIPA-OS, CORBA, SOAP, etc.). This is important for example in relation to any DRMS negotiation and license process (as discussed above), whereby agents interact with online platforms and other third parties and, maybe, standardised DRMS systems. Second, if the business processes or the law changes, for example through new legislation or judicial interpretation, the agents will have to be reprogrammed to take into account the effects of these policy changes. This

---

[65] See *Kelly et al. vs. Arriba Soft Corp.*, or *Ticketmaster v. Tickets.com* (citations are in the reference section).

leads to requirements for interoperability, release control (i.e. processes certified "compliant" under the law of a certain country stated at a certain date) and persistence for any implementation of agents such as Agent D.

Our discussion, including the two constraints mentioned above, militate in favour of designing and modelling the processes of agents (and more generally the information systems in which the agents operate) at a higher conceptual level, taking into account the legal issues in the architectural and process models. This will embed compliance not just at code level, but higher up at business process level. If the legal obligations and constraints can also be modelled, with standardised ontologies and languages such as XRML or ODRL, a legal model may be applied to the business process model to determine the appropriate technical architecture and "legalise" it to comply with the relevant regulatory framework. Where the law gives parties freedom to negotiate permissions and private norms relating to online content (access consents, licences), this could result for example in standardised negotiation and licensing protocols and models for agent-platform interactions. Where the law mandates specific procedures, such as obtaining consent or a licence, then these could be included in the model as constraints or dependencies.

It is also easier at the modelling level to modify the business model (in both its business and technical dimensions) to adapt it to the changing legal, commercial or technological environment, adjusting to new legal or business constraints or rules. This in turn will enable ecommerce software developers to legalise their technical models – thus creating a standardised framework for IPR compliant software engineering. This approach is discussed further in the next Chapters.

Chapter 4

CONSUMER PROTECTION
Can agents be in charge of consumer protection?

El artículo 51 de la Constitución de 27 de diciembre de 1978 establece que los poderes públicos garantizarán la defensa de los consumidores y usuarios, protegiendo, mediante procedimientos eficaces, la seguridad, la salud y los legítimos intereses económicos de los mismos. Asimismo promoverán su información y educación, fomentarán sus organizaciones y las oirán en las cuestiones que puedan afectarles.
Preámbulo Ley 26/1984, de 19 de julio, General para la Defensa de los Consumidores y Usuarios (BOE 24 Julio)

Article 51 of the [Spanish] constitution of 27 December 1978 provides that the public powers will guarantee the protection of consumers and users, protecting by way of efficient procedures their safety, health and legitimate economic interests. They will also promote their education and information, stimulate their organizations, and hear them in questions that affect them.
Preamble to General Law 26/1984 of the 19th July, on the protection of Consumers and Users.[1]

One of the principal objectives of our research is to assist and improve the traditional retail shopping experience through enhanced electronic information services, available to consumers in the store through a mobile device such as a mobile phone, notepad or touch-screen portable computer and interacting with products through RFID systems. This means that the principal commercial transactions within the Research Scenario are between merchant and consumer. As described in the introduction, many of these interactions will supported or initiated by software agents, including profiling agents, information retrieval agents and consumer oriented shopping agents. These transactions raise certain issues relating to consumer protection, which are discussed here.

---

[1] Unofficial translation of the authors.

First, we set out the general framework of European consumer protection principles and law, including the main directives and regulations. It is important to note that each national jurisdiction has its own laws, often direct implementations of the directives, but that this is one area where substantial harmonisation efforts have taken place throughout the European Union. We then analyse the consumer protection issues raised by the software agents contemplated within the Research Scenario, and discuss the risks involved for both retailer and consumer. Finally, we look at both legal and technical means for reducing these risks and ensuring consumer confidence in these interactions through higher levels of compliance with the existing legal framework.

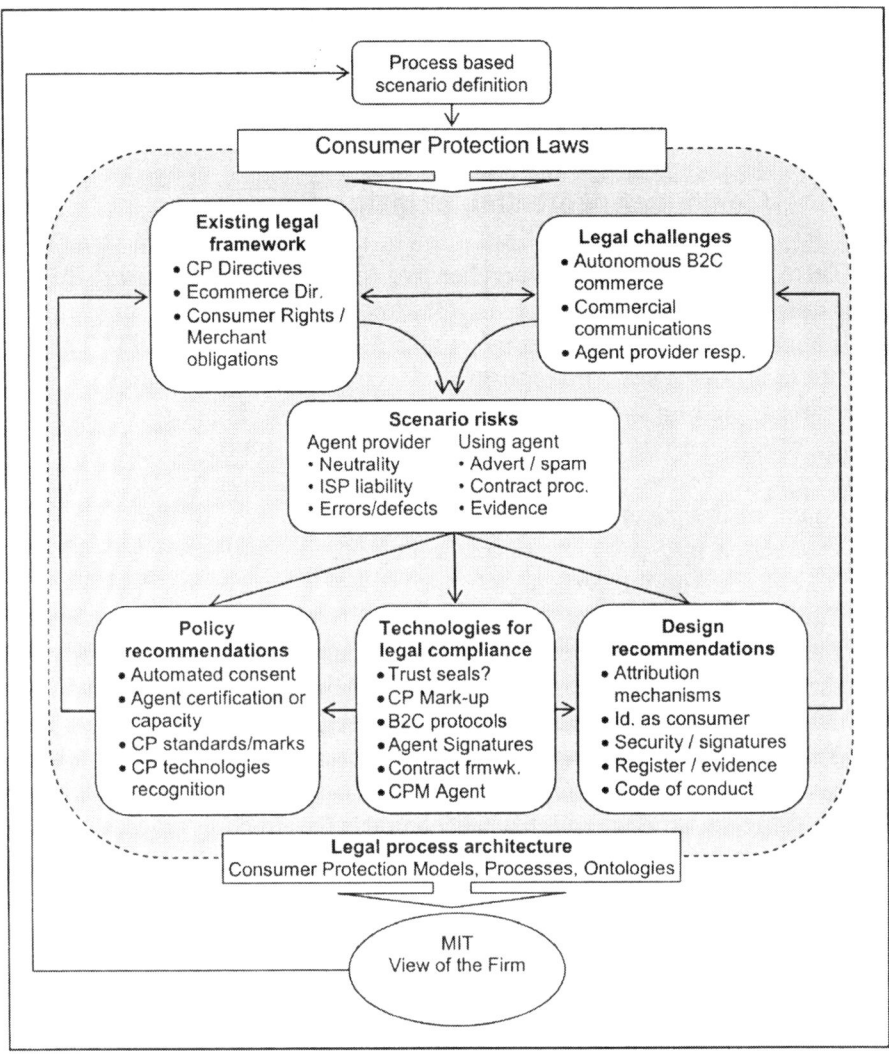

Figure 4-1. Consumer Protection Law Analysis

1. OUTLINE OF PRINCIPLES OF CONSUMER PROTECTION LAW

We use the term "consumer protection" to mean the regulation and protection of consumer economic interests in commercial situations where the negotiating position of parties is not necessarily balanced. This includes therefore the actions of government (laws, regulations, decisions, as established in Spain by the Constitution, cited above) but also public interest groups and businesses to protect the rights of persons buying products or services. In this section, we set out the general principles and main legislation protecting consumers within the European Union.

1.1   Consumer protection principles

There is no overall or comprehensive legal framework in the EU for consumer protection as there is for Intellectual Property or national legislation. While certain consumer rights are enshrined in the EC Treaties (rights to information, education and representation[2]), European level law is made up of a series of piecemeal legislation aiming at specific issues, from which certain general principles have been extracted.[3] The development of new commercial practices and technology has also tended to blur traditional distinctions made in EU rules between the different stages of the transaction (pre-contracting, contracting process, post-contract), thereby adding an element of uncertainty.

The main principles are:

– **Transparency:** this applies as to the business itself and the goods and services on offer (the provision of adequate information), a clear description of the contractual process and performance.
– **Fair business practices:** this involves appropriate safeguards in relation to advertising, commercial communications (which would include spam and SMS messaging) and distance contracts (contracting process).
– **Trust and Confidence:** this covers measures to build confidence in online commerce, including the provision of further commitments (e.g. guarantees, security, encryption, evidence and recording, dispute resolution facilities).

A further area where the EU has been focusing is enforcement: providing the appropriate fora and procedures for easy redress for consumers. Directives generally oblige Member States to take appropriate measures to ensure compliance either through national administrative authorities or through national courts at the request of consumer and/or trade organisations.

---

[2] Art. 153 of the EC Treaty.
[3] The EC is considering a Framework Directive on fair trading and consumer protection. See Green Paper on EU Consumer Protection, 2 October 2001, COM(2001)531 Final. This has now been presented, Proposal for a Directive of the European Parliament and of the Council concerning unfair business-to-consumer commercial practices in the Internal Market and amending directives 84/450/EEC, 97/7/EC and 98/27/EC (the Unfair Commercial Practices Directive), 18 June 2003, (2003) 356 final. Due to the timing of this proposal, it is not commented here.

The OECD set out in 1999 several guiding principles for consumer protection in electronic commerce similar to those delineated above: transparent and effective protection; fair business, advertising and marketing practices; online disclosures as to the merchant, the goods and the transaction, confirmation and payment; dispute resolution and redress; privacy[4]. These principles have (somewhat haphazardly) been implemented through EC Directives and national laws throughout the EU (see next section). One of the reasons for this is that member states have taken different approaches to consumer protection, the main difference being between the UK and Ireland on the one hand, which take a self-regulatory position (guided by government and the Office of Fair Trading, for example) while continental European countries tend to establish direct and explicit legislation.

1.2 Relevant EU Consumer Protection Framework

Below is a list of Directives and other regulatory documents which establish the European legal framework for consumer protection in relation to the Research Scenario and the agents contemplated by our research: agents assisting the purchase and transactions of consumers in a grocery store context. (Please see the reference section at the end of the monograph for references.) The next section details the key measures set out in the Directives.

a) General rules
- Directive on Misleading Advertising, as amended by Directive on comparative advertising (84/450/EC, 97/55/EC).
- Directives on Price Indications for foodstuffs and non-foodstuffs (79/581/EEC, 88/314/EEC and 95/58/EC).
- Directive on Unfair Terms in Consumer Contracts (93/13/EEC).
- Directive on the sale of consumer goods and associated guarantees (1999/44/EC).
- Directive on Liability for Defective Products (85/374/EEC).

b) Rules for different sectors
- Directives on foodstuffs, cosmetics, textile names, medicinal products for human use, package travel (76/768/EEC - 97/18/EC, 92/28/EEC, 96/74/EC, etc.).

c) Directives on selling methods
- Directive on Distance Contracts (97/7/EC).

---

[4] OECD Guidelines for Consumer Protection in the context of Electronic Commerce, OECD, 1999.

- Ecommerce Directive (2000/31/EC).
- EC Recommendation on Electronic Payments (97/489/EC).
- Directive on distance marketing of consumer financial services (2002/65/EC).

d) Enforcement
- Directive on Injunctions (98/27/EC).
- EC "Brussels" Regulation on jurisdiction and enforcement (44/2001/EC).

One should also include the Rome Convention on Applicable Law which is applicable throughout the EU (and EEA).

1.3   Key protections in relevant Directives

1.3.1   Misleading and Comparative Advertising

In order to control misleading advertising, the Member States must ensure that those persons or organisations with a legitimate interest may bring a court action against misleading advertising and/or bring the advertising before a competent administrative body to rule on the complaints or to institute the appropriate legal proceedings. That body can then order the withdrawal of misleading advertising or forbid misleading advertising whose publication is imminent (or institute the appropriate proceedings to those ends). "Misleading advertising" means any advertising which in any way, including its presentation, deceives or is likely to deceive the persons to whom it is addressed or whom it reaches and which, by reason of its deceptive nature, is likely to affect their economic behaviour or which, for those reasons, injures or is likely to injure a competitor

Comparative advertising, which is defined as "any advertising which explicitly or by implication identifies a competitor or goods or services offered by a competitor", is permitted if (among other items):
- it is not misleading and it compares goods or services meeting the same needs or intended for the same purpose;
- it objectively compares one or more material, relevant, verifiable and representative features of those goods or services, which may include price;
- it does not create confusion in the market place between the advertiser and a competitor;
- it does not take unfair advantage of the trade mark or other distinguishing sign of a competitor;
- it does not present goods or services as imitations or replicas of goods or services bearing a protected trade mark or trade name.

1.3.2 Price indications (general, food, non-food)

These Directives stipulate that traders must indicate the selling price and the price per unit of measurement of products offered to consumers, in order to improve consumer information and to facilitate comparison of prices. Generally speaking, the Directives determine that the selling price and the unit price must be indicated in an unambiguous, easily identifiable and clearly legible way for all products offered by traders to consumers. They also give details of which products must display unit prices and those which are exempt, in particular products pre-packed in pre-established quantities, while providing scope for exemptions for foodstuffs sold in bulk or pre-packaged where such indication would not have any meaning

1.3.3 Defective Products

This Directive aims to increase consumer protection against damage caused to health or property by a defective product. Directive applies to movables which have been industrially produced, whether or not incorporated into another movable or into an immovable. (This would not apply to software agents, but products purchased with or by the agent). The Directive establishes the principle of objective liability or liability without fault of the producer in cases of damage caused by a defective product. If more than one person is liable for the same damage, it is joint liability.

The injured person must prove actual damage, the defect in the product, and the causal relationship between damage and defect. The plaintiff does not have to prove negligence on part of the producer. There are exemptions for producers regarding liability in certain cases (e.g. state of the art, mandatory regulations)

1.3.4 Unfair Contract Terms

Generally speaking, this Directive provides that consumers are not to be bound by unfair terms in a contract signed with a professional. A term is unfair when it has not been negotiated and it establishes a significant imbalance, to the consumer's detriment, between the rights and obligations of the contracting parties. A list of terms which may be deemed unfair is annexed to the Directive. In assessing the unfair nature of a contractual term, the court should take into account (a) the nature of the goods or services covered by the contract; (b) the circumstances surrounding the drawing up of the contract; and (c) the other terms in the contract or in another contract to which it relates. This would also especially apply to unfair terms in non-negotiated contracts (click-wrap or WAP-style).

The Annex to the Directive contains a non-exhaustive list of terms that are likely to be regarded as unfair. They include excluding or limiting the liability of the seller or supplier in the event of the consumer's death, enabling the seller or supplier to alter the terms of the contract unilaterally, and excluding or hindering the consumer's right to take legal action or exercise other legal remedy.

1.3.5   Distance Contracts

This Directive covers contracts concerning goods or services concluded between a merchant and a consumer under an "organised distance sales or service provision scheme" (which includes web-pages) using one or more means of distance communication up to and including the moment of conclusion of the contract[5]. This Directive imposes obligations on merchants to provide:
- Prior provision of reliable clear and comprehensible information including description of merchant, the goods, price, delivery costs, rights to withdraw and special offers.
- Written confirmation of the contract.
- Proper performance of contract.
  It also sets out some consumer rights:
- A right to rescind / withdraw.
- Protection against credit card fraud.

Parts of the Directive do not apply to contracts for the supply of food, beverages or other goods intended for everyday consumption supplied to the consumer's residence or to his workplace by regular roundsmen; and also for auctions. The effect of these exceptions in the Research Scenario is discussed below.

The use by the supplier of automatic calling devices or faxes requires the prior consent of the consumer (Art. 10). Other distance communication techniques may be used only where there is no clear objection from the consumer. This has been affected by the proposed Directive on data protection and electronic communications, outlined in Section 1.3.7 below.

1.3.6   Electronic Payments

The Commission Recommendation mainly concerns the relationship between the issuer of electronic payment instruments and the user. It covers all types of payment, not just credit cards (like the Distance Contracts Directive). The main aim is to organise the responsibilities between the parties: purchase, merchant, banks and payment issuer.

It is possible that certain e-payment systems incorporate agent technology and, from a consumer perspective, there are certain safeguards that should be taken into account. Key protections in the Recommendation

---

[5] Art. 2.1 (Definition of distance contract).

include the provision of certain minimum information (in the terms that govern the use of the electronic payment instrument), obligations and liabilities of the parties at the time of payment and in relation to use of the payment instrument.

1.3.7 Data Protection in Telecommunication Services

Although the provisions of this Directive are mainly about privacy, they have consumer implications. Under Article 9 (Location data), traders that process data that relates to the location of customers, such as is conceived in the Research Scenario for sending location based advertising, must either do so anonymously, or obtain the informed consent of the person in question. More importantly, in accordance with Article 13 (Unsolicited communications), the use of automated calling systems, fax, or email for the purposes of direct marketing may only be allowed in respect of persons who have given their prior consent. This requirement is relaxed in the event that the original identifying data (such as a phone number) is obtained from the person in the context of prior dealings (sales or service), although customers must still be given the opportunity to object or reject the message each time.

1.3.8 The Ecommerce Directive

The Ecommerce Directive (2000/31/EC) sets out several legal obligations relating to the way marketing and sales are made by "service providers". A service provider is any natural or legal person "providing an information society service". This would cover the online grocery store services, and also the agent and agent provider (which may be the grocery store). It does not so much cover the goods (and off-line services) supplied by such persons as the way they are commercialised. Relevant articles include:
- Art 5: General information
- Arts. 6 and 7: commercial communications and unsolicited commercial communications
- Arts. 9, 10 and 11: contracting information and processes (see also the Chapter 2 on contracts where these are discussed)
- Arts. 12 - 15: liability exemptions for intermediaries

These are commented next.

1.3.8.1 Provision of Information

The Directive distinguishes between duties to supply information every service provider has to supply in general (Art. 5), information in commercial communications (Art. 6) and pre-contractual information (Art. 10). Art. 5 covers every action a service provider may perform, beginning with commercial communication and lasting at least until the contract is executed.

- Art. 5 information must be provided so that it is easily, directly and permanently accessible to the recipients of the service and competent authorities.
- Art. 6 information must clearly identify the nature of the communication
- Art. 10 information must be provided by the service provider clearly, comprehensibly, unambiguously, and prior to the order being placed by the recipient of the service. It must also be storable and reproducible.

Due to the importance of these provisions, we describe them in turn next:

a) Information to be supplied by every service provider
According to Art. 5, all service providers must provide certain information throughout the transaction. This includes:
- name and address of merchant
- details, including electronic mail address, which allow the supplier to be contacted, directly and effectively
- the trade register in which the service provider is entered and his registration number or equivalent
- relevant supervised activities and supervisory authority or relevant professional body or similar institution
- VAT identification number.

If prices are indicated, they are to be indicated clearly and unambiguously and, in particular, must indicate whether they are inclusive of tax and delivery costs or not. Note that Art. 5 applies to commercial communications as well, which affects advertising and marketing activities

b) Commercial communications
Commercial communications are subject to information rules for consumers and professionals (Art. 6). The information to be provided includes clear identification of :
- the commercial purpose, the person, on whose behalf the commercial communication is made;
- the fact, if applicable, that the recipient is facing a promotional offer (i.e. discounts, premiums and gifts, if permitted according to Member State legislation) and the conditions which are to be met in order to qualify;
- promotional competitions or games which are permitted according to Member State-legislation, together with the conditions for participation.

c) Pre-contractual Information
In addition to the information given under Art. 5, when the service provider executes Information Society services, Art. 10 obliges it to provide certain information prior to the order being placed by the recipient of the service:
- the different technical steps to follow to conclude the contract;

– whether or not the concluded contract will be filed by the service provider and whether it will be accessible;
– the technical means for identifying and correcting input errors prior to the placing of the order;
– languages offered for the conclusion of the contract;
– any codes of conduct to which the service provider subscribes and how these codes can be consulted electronically;

These are not necessary if the contract is exclusively concluded by exchange of electronic mail or by equivalent individual communication (Art. 10.4). This means, e.g. that if the consumer contacts the service provider directly without visiting the web-site, the service provider does not have to provide this information.

1.3.8.2 Contracting process

Under implementation of Art. 11. ISPs must provide the following, in cases where an order has been placed electronically (e.g. by or through an agent):
– Acknowledgement of receipt of an order without undue delay, by electronic means.
– Appropriate effective and accessible measures for correcting mistakes in orders prior to placing.

These issues have been discussed in more detail in Chapter 2, on agent contracting. Unless agents may be considered "individual communications" equivalent to email, which are exempt, this may have a serious effect on agent trading, due to the need to provide means for consumers to review an (agent-placed) order before confirming it.

1.3.8.3 Unsolicited Commercial Communications

The Directive provides rules for commercial communication, which is "any form of communication designed to promote, directly or indirectly, the goods, services or image of a company, organisation or person pursuing a commercial, industrial or craft activity or exercising a regulated profession". This includes discounts, promotional offers and promotional competitions or games. Unsolicited commercial communication by means of electronic mail is generally called "spamming" and the Directive leaves it to the Member States to decide whether or not unsolicited commercial communication is admissible. The Directive only requires that the unsolicited commercial communication is marked as such clearly and unambiguously as soon as the recipient has received it (Art. 7). The service providers undertaking unsolicited commercial communications by e-mail are obliged to consult regularly and respect the opt-out-registers (Art. 7.2).

These provisions should be read in the light of the distance selling obligations described above and in future in accordance with the Directive on Electronic Communications (see Section 4 below, and Chapter 5).

1.3.8.4   Liabilities of intermediaries (exemptions)

The Ecommerce Directive exempts certain activities from potential liability on the basis that the services provided by the "service provider" are those of online intermediaries for facilitating ecommerce. It is probable that these exemptions apply to online search engines, but it is not clear whether this would apply to agents operated by stores or third parties. They apply to the following online activities:

– mere conduits: data transmission and access services (Art. 12);
– caching: temporary recording of data for efficient communications (Art. 13); or
– hosting services: website hosting (Art. 14).

1.3.8.5   Codes of Conduct / Alternative Dispute Resolution

The Directive promotes the use of codes of conduct (including participation of associations such as consumer defence organisations) and alternative dispute resolution procedures, safeguarding however adequate procedural guarantees (Arts. 16 and 17). Although not directly linked to the Directive's provisions, this has been translated into reality in various public and private initiatives relating to online commerce:

– Marketing Association guidelines and codes of conduct, including for mobile commerce and SMS[6].
– Internet Service Provider codes of conduct[7].
– The EEJ: European network for online-ADR (ODR) under the auspices of the Joint Research Council (JRC)[8].
– General codes of conduct for ecommerce (e.g. the International Chamber of Commerce[9] or Better Business Online[10]).
– Trustmarks and other seals for consumer confidence (see below)[11].

[6] See for example the FEDMA code online at www.fedma.org
[7] There are various codes that have been published, for example in Canada by the Canadian Association of Internet Providers, online at http://www.media-awareness.ca/english/resources/codes_guidelines/internet/caip_code_of_conduct.cfm; or in the UK: ISPA Code of Practice, available online at http://www.ispa.org.uk/html/about_ispa/ispa_code.html
[8] See the e-confidence initiative site online at http://econfidence.jrc.it/
[9] See for example, the ICC International Code of Direct Marketing 2001, or the ICC Guidelines on Advertising and Marketing on the Internet, 1998, available online at http://www.iccwbo.org/home/menu_advert_marketing.asp (visited 05/07/2003)
[10] Examples include BBB Online's Code of Online Business Practices online at http://www.bbbonline.org/ or TrustUK; Whichwebtrader, etc. Many are listed under E-Commerce Codes of Conduct at the JRC e-confidence site.
[11] See also T Wagemans: *An introduction to the labelling of websites*, 2003.

1.3.9   The EU "Brussels" Regulation and Rome Convention and Consumers

In cases of a cross-border contractual dispute within the EU, the Brussels Convention 1968 (now an EU Regulation[12]) and the Rome Convention 1980 establish rules to determine which Member State Court should hear the case (jurisdiction) and which Member State's law will apply to the contract (applicable law).

The basic jurisdictional rule set out in the **Brussels Regulation** is that a defendant shall be sued in the state where he is domiciled. Exceptions to this rule include:

- Jurisdictional competence in the country where a contract is to be performed (e.g. delivery of goods) (Art. 5.1).
- Disputes arising out of the operation of a branch, agency or other establishment, in the courts for the place in which the branch, agency or other establishment is situated (Art. 5.5).
- In matters relating to tort, delict or quasi-delict, competence for the courts in the place where the harmful event occurred or may occur.
- When a trader concludes a contract with an EU consumer and the trader either pursues commercial activities in that consumer's country "or by any means directs such activities to that country," the consumer may sue the company in the courts of that country (Art. 15.1(c)). The Regulation does not define when the seller is deemed to "direct" its activities to an EU country, which will be determined by European courts on a case-by-case basis. The Council of the European Union declared that the mere fact that an Internet site is accessible in a given country, or that the site uses the language or currency of that country, does not trigger the application of Article 15.1(c).

The Regulation, however, only applies when the seller is domiciled (e.g., its jurisdiction of incorporation or its principal place of business) in the EU, or when the dispute arises from the operations of the seller's branch, agency or establishment in the EU. For other sellers, jurisdiction will not be determined by the Jurisdiction Regulation, but rather by the laws of the individual EU countries which have provisions allowing their residents to take legal action against non-EU defendants.

The **Rome Convention** determines that contracts shall be generally governed by the law chosen by the parties. If there is no choice of law agreement, the courts will look at the country most closely connected to the performing party. There are exceptions to this rule in relation to consumer contracts when a choice of law made by the parties shall not have the result of depriving the consumer of the protection afforded to him by the

---

[12] EU Council Regulation 44/2001, in force since 1 March 2002. It is not applicable in Denmark

mandatory rules of the law of the country in which he has his habitual residence (i.e. local mandatory rules apply) if a specific invitation or advertising has been directed to the consumer and he/she concluded the contract in his/her country, or the merchant received the order in the consumer's country. If no choice is made, the law of the consumer's country is applied (Art. 5) under the same conditions.

Exceptions to these governing law rules apply when there are questions of public order ("ordre public") and or where choice-of-law rules of European Community law apply.

The rules governing the choice of applicable law in relation to non contractual matters are not nearly so harmonised, even in the EU. There are discussions underway for a "Rome II" Convention applicable to such matters, but no progress has been made. It seems that the general rule is that the applicable law is the law of the country where the injured person or property was at the time (*lex locus delicti*). But it could also be the law of the country where the harmful act was committed. In cyberspace this is difficult to determine.

1.4   Other applicable laws

1.4.1   Tort laws

Tort laws will deal with the allocation of liability when there is no contractual relationship (e.g. with third parties), e.g. an agent that damages a webpage or a consumers mobile phone. This area of law, though fertile ground for analysing agent behaviour, is not covered in detail in this chapter which analyses merchant-consumer relations in the use of agents. We consider that this use between Store, Consumer and potentially an Agent Provider – the focus of the Research Scenario – will be governed by contract and pre-contractual obligations.

This does not mean that non-contractual conflicts may arise. Indeed many interactions on the web involve non-contractual liability, for example, defamation, trespass to property, negligence or even nuisance. In the USA, for instance, various cases have tried to establish trespass to property as a basis for action against several ecommerce abuses such as alleged "intrusion to computers"[13]. These have been successful when establishing intentional interference. In this case we meet up with the issue of agent intention, discussed in Chapter 2 on contracts. Does a consumer intend her agent to interfere with online commerce platforms? Can one analyse an agent in

---

[13] *eBay Inc. v. Builder's Edge* and Ticketmaster v. Tickets.com. See D Burk: *The Trouble With Trespass*, 1998

order to construe its intention, or should one just look to the effects of its actions (strict liability)[14]?

1.4.2 Unfair competition laws

Unfair competition may be claimed in respect of the provision of information, against unfair practices like selling information from another merchant's page, or monitoring a website of a competitor so that the trader can send alternative offer to prospective clients of that competitor. This applies between two businesses (e.g. web merchant and agent provider), while the consumer element of such unfair competition is regulated through consumer protection laws outlined above.

1.4.3 Trade description and trade practices laws

Each European member state has laws related to trade description and practices. This may be relevant to the provision of agent services, for example in giving a full description of the programming of an agent and its processes. In addition, these would cover website policies (such as privacy and consumer guarantees) as well as consumer interfaces.

2. CONSUMER PROTECTION ISSUES RAISED BY AGENT TECHNOLOGY

There seems to be a consensus among the different parties involved in ecommerce that there is still a certain reluctance on behalf of consumers to enter into electronic transactions. This is largely due to the lack of confidence consumers experience when confronted with Internet business. Several studies and reports have pointed out that there are sufficient grounds for the potential "e-consumer" to show caution before engaging in e-commerce transactions[15]. The legal framework set out above, complemented by the national laws, provides some basis for more confidence, however there are certain activities, especially related to the use of electronic agents, that raise concerns. For some of these concerns, there should be technical or commercial responses: the protection of private data, the provision of adequate information, the recording of evidence, etc. Other areas may remain "grey" until either more sophisticated agents are available, or on the contrary, further laws are enacted to deal with such advanced agents.

---

[14] See also, A Cruquenaire: Electronic Agents as Search Engines: Copyright related aspects, 2001, in relation to agents acting as search engines.
[15] See for example, PriceWaterhouseCoopers for the EC: *Study on Consumer Law and the Information Society*, 2000.

2.1   "Traditional" Internet features that raise Consumer Protection issues

Much has been written about consumer protection issues in electronic commerce[16]. Indeed one of the main aims of recent European and national legislation is to effect the protection of consumers in the online environment. Issues that have been raised and studied (and are undergoing discussion) include the transient nature of online communications, the lack of borders in Internet leading to an increase in cross-border consumer transactions, the relative weights of merchants and consumers online, the collection of data relating to consumers, spamming and other marketing techniques that may confuse or take advantage of a weaker party (the consumer), etc.

This has led to various discussions on the following topics:

− **Information and commercial communications online**: the provision of information on websites and email communications, misleading advertisements, spamming[17].
− **The conclusion of contracts online** (Contract formation and terms - procedures, incorporation of terms) and unfair contract terms: in access contracts and in online contracting (click-wrap contracts) - obligations, liability exclusions[18].
− **Contract performance online**, mainly for receiving digital products, i.e. downloading information, music, software, etc.
− **The determination of jurisdiction** in legal proceedings for cross-border transactions involving consumers[19].
− **Defects in products** that are bought online and merchant disclaimers and exclusions.

---

[16] See for example, the PriceWaterhouseCoopers report: *Final Report Study on Consumer Law and the Information Society* (2000); M de Cock Buning et al.: *Consumer@Protection.EU. An Analysis of European Consumer Legislation in the Information Society,* 2002; or Consumers International: *Consumers@shopping, An international comparative study of electronic commerce,* 1999. Also European Commission: *Green Paper on European Union Consumer Protection,* 2001. Also: Federal Trade Commission: *Consumer Protection in the Global Electronic Marketplace: Looking Ahead,* 2000.

[17] See for example, S Gauthronet et al: *Communications Commerciales Non-Sollicitées et Protection des Données,* 2001 or D Sorkin: *Technical and Legal Approaches to Unsolicited Electronic Mail,* 2001.

[18] Please see Section 2.2 of Chapter 2 for some works on contracting issues.

[19] Particular work is being carried out within the Hague Conference. See for example A Haines: *The Impact of the Internet on the Judgments Project: Thoughts for the Future,* 2002. Also see for example, J Zittrain *Be Careful What You Ask For: Reconciling a Global Internet and Local Law,* 2003; M Geist: *Is there a there, there?,* 2003, or L Gillies: *A Review of the New Jurisdiction Rules for Electronic Consumer Contracts within the European Union,* 2001.

- **Electronic Payment systems** in websites (mainly credit card, but also alternative online payment instruments like e-cash etc.): the provision of information and liabilities for fraud or loss[20].
- **Privacy protection** in online activities and transactions[21].

The last topic is commented in more detail in Chapter 5 on Agents and Privacy.

The importance of this topic for our research is due to the fact that while these issues are important in relation to general web-based online commerce, most of these issues are also applicable to automated agent-based transactions. Indeed, consumer concerns may be heightened by the added dematerialization and automation presented by the use of software agents.

2.2 Consumer protection concerns in relation to intelligent agents

2.2.1 Consumer oriented agents and agent services

The main aim of this chapter is to set out the consumer related legal implications of using electronic agents in the RFID-enhanced shopping scenario, taking into account the type and features of agents used in this scenario. Among those agents that may have consumer protection implications are the following:

- **Search / Observer Agents:** Information retrieval agents, Interface / interaction agents, Filtering agents (such as Agent D described in the previous chapter).
- **Interface agents**: agents which monitor the interaction of their users with information systems and regulate the interaction in ways that help the users (Profiling agents, Filter agents)
- **Decision/ Actor agents:** Auction agents, Broker agents, and especially contracting agents (buying or selling agents).

We have already described in more detail three such shopping agents in Chapter 2, which we summarise below:

a) Agent A is a store-based advertising agent, offering products to consumers in accordance with their shopping profile or other input such as consumer location in the store, electronic product identification, or the contents of shopping basket.

b) Agent B is a similar store-based selling agent, this time with added functionality of offering features such as contract conclusion and

---

[20] Various papers discuss these issues, including C Centeno: *Building Security and Consumer Trust in Internet Payments,* 2002 or European Commission: *A possible legal framework for the single payment area in the internal market,* 2002.

[21] See Chapter 5 below for works in this area.

associated services: interconnection with payment systems and home delivery.

c) Agent C is a customer-oriented automatic shopping/buying agent. This agent is resident in a consumer controlled environment / host, searches for products in online sources (e.g. based on a current shopping list) and even suggests new products to the user and/or purchases them without review. It communicates both with the closed store systems (product and price databases, etc.) and with the open network (alternative shopping sites).

These are agents that interact between the consumer and either the web merchant or the store's information systems (including the RFID-enhanced products), or the agent provider. We do not refer here to supply chain management agents that interact between merchants and their suppliers. Also, note that this chapter section looks at the process and means of using agents for store/third party/consumer interactions (communications, contracting - sales agents, purchase agents, search agents) and not at the laws applicable to the goods or services actually sold (defective products, guarantees).

Finally, also note that many agent-based transactions with consumers in the Research Scenario will not necessarily involve "electronic commerce" as such, i.e. purchasing goods or services online or through mobile communications. Generally speaking, consumers will purchase the products in the real world, in the store where they are shopping. The focus of this work is therefore on the provision of ancillary consumer-oriented services during the shopping process, particularly information and advertising services, and exceptionally the use of electronic devices to carry out an online purchase (e.g. purchase of certain elements of the consumer shopping list without picking it up in the store, for direct home delivery).

2.2.2   Perspectives

We believe that the legal implications should be looked at from the points of view of three different actors involved in the process:
- **The store** that offers or uses agents in its relations with third parties (suppliers or consumers), in particular how the store can satisfy the consumer protection regulations regarding the provision of information, rights of withdrawal, contracting procedures, etc.
- **Third party agent providers** that provide services for consumers or store (information providers such as search agents or comparative shopping agents, payment services and instruments, privacy management agents, etc.) and how they can also comply with relevant laws relating to offering both the use of agents as a service and the services provided through the agents.

- **Consumers** that use agents in their interactions with the store, its products and online merchants. Key issues for consumers will include controlling merchant advertising and communications through agents, the provision of reliable information (e.g. the availability of goods), procedures, terms and mistake in contracting, merchant product defects, disclaimers and exclusions, etc.

In the first two cases, we should look at the legal risks and difficulties of the commercial traders and other participants using agents when transacting with consumers and how those legal risks can be minimised. In the third case, we study how consumers interacting or using agents within the Research Scenario can not only be protected against unfair trading practices and deficient goods and services (such as agent defects) but also can gain confidence to participate in agent based commerce.

We therefore look at two relationships, which are illustrated in Figure 1.2 in Chapter 1. First, between the agent provider and the consumer in relation to the agents that are provided to the latter. This will mainly cover agent defects and behaviour - what happens if there are mistakes, invalid contracts, or torts committed by defective agents. Second, we will also consider the interactions between the store or other third party service providers and the consumer in relation to using agents for various transactions:

- **Advertising**; many merchant activities conceived in the scenario involve targeted advertising and providing commercial information for which there is a need to respect the consumer laws, for example if an electronic agent can be considered appropriate to receive information on the user's behalf.
- **Online Procedures**: as we have seen, consumer protection laws and the ecommerce Directive set out proper and fairly strict procedures for advertising and selling (notifications, confirmations, etc.).
- **Product defects**: this is fairly standard consumer protection issue – but how, for example, is the right to return goods affected by the use of agents?
- **Contract disclaimers etc**: these are usually too wide and often invalid under consumer protection laws.How are these affected by agents: does the consumer have notice of the terms when he/she uses an agent?

2.2.3 Issues raised by agents in relation to consumers

The tables below set out the main issues raised in this area:

Table 4-1. Issues between agent provider and consumer

Issue	Questions
The regulation of agents	Are the distribution and use of agents regulated by any applicable legislation?

Issue	Questions
The regulation of agents	Are the distribution and use of agents regulated by any applicable legislation?
Errors or defects in agent performance	What happens when a mistake is made or the user incurs liability due to the use of agents. This could happen in the area of Intellectual Property infringement, torts, errors as to the reliability and accuracy of information, incorrect responses to certain events, bias in the information retrieved by the agent (defect of neutrality[22]), etc.
Agent developer / supplier disclaimers and exclusions	What are the effects of these clauses on the consumer user?

Table 4-2. Issues between consumers and retail stores

Pre-contractual phase	
The provision of reliable information (general)	When the store contacts the consumer with an agent - e.g. the first log-on/in notice - , when the consumer approaches the store or when the store offers different services or products via a store-agent or in interaction with a consumer-agent, what information obligations bind the store, and what information should the store provide? Is such a service an "information society service" under the Ecommerce Directive, and is it covered by the Distance Selling rules? Would contacting without prior consent be considered cold calling or automatic communication? Can the store do anything to obtain the consumer's prior consent?
Commercial communications (Merchant advertising and communications)	When the store contacts the consumer in the context of the Research Scenario, with offers, promotions, or other information, is this covered by the requirements regarding commercial communications (Distance Selling or Ecommerce Directive, Data Protection). What rules apply to advertising? Are there codes of conduct should the store comply with? How much price information etc. should the store provide? If the services are offered by a third party, by what information and communication obligations is it bound? What if the agent removes or modifies data sent by the merchant (relevant to products on offer (price, size) or transaction process (e.g. level of privacy or security of communications)? What happens to the transaction (mistake, frustration)?
Contractual phase	
Information requirements in relation to the contract	What are the liabilities that arise in the provision of pre-contractual information offered through an agent: what obligations are applicable (e.g. transparency) and what are the liabilities for indexing etc.? Is it different if the agent is provided or controlled by the store, the consumer or a third party?
Process for the	Do agents have to follow a certain process when contracting with

---

[22] S Feliu: *Agents and Consumer Protection*, 2001

conclusion of contracts through agents	consumers (contracts at a distance, without consumer review)? What are the minimum requirements for compliant processes? Can stores or agent providers program the agents to minimise the negative effects of a weighty process (equivalent to lots of "clicks" on a website)?
Form requirements	How can a vendor comply with the contract form requirements set out in the consumer protection laws (on top of the contract law issue of incorporating terms into an agreement), e.g. by providing evidence on a durable medium, etc.?
General Terms and conditions	How can online merchants refer to and incorporate General Terms and Conditions? These are often only incorporated by reference (and registered in a central registry in many continental jurisdictions). What are the notice requirements for these general terms?
Payment	Apart from the consumer protection issues in relation to setting up a mobile payment system, are there any obligations that the provider or merchant have to comply with at the moment of sale/payment?
Post-contractual phase	
Liability for online performance	Can an agent perform a contract for a merchant or a user without the user's knowledge? Should the agent declare this beforehand?
Recording of transaction	There are certain important practical issues for recording evidence. Is there a need to program the agent for the secure recording of evidence in case of a dispute? How does one ensure that agent-created electronic records are admissible in dispute resolution?
Merchant disclaimers and exclusions	Are these affected by agent based transactions?
Dispute resolution and applicable law	What jurisdiction would be competent for an agent-based transaction? Which law would apply? Are there certain out-of-court procedures that could facilitate resolution in consumer matters when agents are used? Is there any advantage for consumers to choose these remedies?

2.3   Other areas relevant to consumers

As regards consumer protection, other issues are generally relevant, such as:

– Contract law: the most relevant issues, including certain consumer protection requirements, are discussed in Chapter 2 on agent contracting.
– Privacy issues relating to the collection of consumer personal data, which are discussed separately in Chapter 5.
– Private international law for cross border purchases. These are not considered here in the Research Scenario as our specifications do not include international consumer transactions. It would be beyond the scope of the research to treat this topic here, although we discuss it briefly below in section 3.2.6. Much work is needed to be able

incorporate various nations into the research scenario (e.g. using a personal agent in a foreign store, or purchasing an agent programmed to comply with the legal framework of another jurisdiction).

3.   THE CURRENT LEGAL POSITION ON THESE ISSUES

The aim of this section is to discuss the scope and sufficiency of current Consumer Protection laws in their application to agent-based transactions and the issues raised in the previous section. First in section 3.1 we shall review the rules applying to acquiring an agent, or the services of an agent, and those that apply to agent service providers. Then, in section 3.2 we shall review what rules apply to the actual use of an agent to interact with merchants in the Research Scenario (i.e. agent-based transactions). In section 3.3, we shall briefly discuss how the general European framework has been applied in the Member States, before moving on to current technical and self-regulatory solutions in this area.

3.1   Acquiring an agent or agent services

3.1.1   The possibility of direct regulation of agents under the Directives

The consumer protection directives in general, and the Ecommerce Directive in particular, regulate legal or natural persons. Software agents, however, are without legal identity and therefore cannot in themselves, for example, be "information society service providers" as set out in the Ecommerce Directive. This situation would change if ever a form of identity or personality was granted to agents, similar to that granted to corporations. Accordingly, for the moment one would have to look to the provider or the user of the agent to determine whether certain general regulation applies. Agents may be provided either online or sold (licensed) directly as software.

In relation to the provision of agent services over the Internet, certain information requirements and liabilities may be imposed by regulation to ensure consumer protection. This would be the case of third party or the retail store "web-service" style agents (search, filter, comparison or shopping agents, etc.) that may operate from the web. For example, online search engines provided by companies such as Google or Yahoo! may be considered simple software agents whose services are provided to consumers by those companies. The relevant obligations are similar to those applying to any service offered on the Internet, and we do not believe they are specific to agent-based services so they are not covered in detail here. Briefly, the consumer related requirements are as follows:

- Information requirements: The provider of the agent may be considered a service provider, especially if the consumer downloads all/part of the agent from Internet, in which case the provider is bound by the information requirements of the Ecommerce Directive[23] in relation to the service provided, and its procedural requirements for contracting a service on the Internet[24]. This is also a distance contract for the provision of services, and subject to the provider information obligations and certain consumer rights of withdrawal set out in national implementations of the Distance Sales Directive[25].

- Liability: The services provided will be subject to national consumer protection regimes, as well as tort and copyright laws. These include the regulation of exclusion of liability clauses in relation to services or implied guarantees of quality of performance of services. Depending on the activities of the agents, the liability of the agent provider towards third parties (consumer/users or merchant/content providers) as intermediaries may also be regulated by the Ecommerce Directive. There are exemptions for services that can be considered mere conduits, caching and hosting activities.[26] We believe that the main processes and services of search or shopping agents such as those described in this work (Agents A-D) do not fall within these categories, although they may undertake caching as part of the service[27].

In relation to the sale of agent software to consumers, ecommerce protections would only apply if the agent is sold over the Internet. The first question is the now traditional debate whether software is a good or a service. At least as far as the Consumer Goods and Guarantees Directive is concerned, agents would be excluded as they are not tangible. The sale of agent software over the Internet to the consumer would be covered by the contract requirements set out in Art 10 and 11 on top of the information requirements. This is also a distance contract, and subject to the provider information obligations and consumer rights of withdrawal and return set out in national implementations of the Distance Sales Directive. As regards, liability for use, the consumer would be deemed to operate it under his/her own liability, as owner.

---

[23] Arts. 5. and 10 EC Ecommerce Directive.

[24] Art. 11 EC Ecommerce Directive.

[25] E.g. UK consumer protection (Distance Selling) Regulations 2000; Spain: Ley General para la Defensa de los Consumidores y Usuarios (LGDC), Ordenaciòn del Comercio Minorista and Local Autonomous Community requirements; Germany: Fernabsatzgesetz, FernAbsG.

[26] Arts. 12-15 EC Ecommerce Directive.

[27] Note that the DMCA in the USA exempts such third party location tool providers under certain conditions.

If the agent establishes a payment method, such as Agent C, the relationship will also be covered by the recommendation on electronic payment instruments.[28]). There are no additional problems in relation to agent-based payments, however care should be taken regarding information requirements, recording and consumer rights of withdrawal. As regards making a payment, see next section 4.3.2.

A final important point in relation to consumer protection and agent regulation is that the country-of-origin principle (that service providers are regulated in the country they are set up in) is derogated in relation to consumer protection to the effect that its application cannot reduce the protection afforded by the national regime of the consumer's country. Even in the Research Scenario, where the store will be in the same jurisdiction as the consumer, it is possible for agents to be provided by a person in another country, programmed according to that country's laws (e.g. USA, Japan). Such third country agents, so to speak, would still have to comply with local rules.

3.1.2   Errors or defects in agent performance

In the event of a defect in the agent performance or process (e.g. when a mistake is made by the agent, or it does not live up to its description), the user may incur liability due to its use. This could happen in the area of Intellectual Property Rights infringement, torts, errors as to the reliability and accuracy of information, incorrect responses to certain events, or even bias in the information retrieved by the agent (defect of neutrality[29]). Such defects might affect an eventual transaction with a supplier: a wrong description or price, insufficient information for product warnings, etc.

Unfortunately the consumer may not have the benefit of some legislated remedies that are generally intended to provide protection against defective products and services.

−   The Consumer Goods and Guarantees Directive will probably not apply, as it only applies to tangible movable items. Software agents may not be considered tangible, especially if they are downloaded to the consumer's electronic device or operating as a web-based service.

−   Distance contracts: a right of withdrawal may not be available to consumers due to the exception for services commenced within the 7 day

---

[28] The recommendation is not binding law, but it has indirect binding effect. The Commission is studying the question of creating binding obligations (Directive or regulation) for e-payments. European Commission: *Study on the implementation of Recommendation 97/489/EC,* 2001 and *A possible legal framework for the single payment area in the internal market,* 2002.

[29] See S Feliu, op cit, note 6 supra.

period for withdrawal[30]. We conceive that the provider's service (provision of the agent) is likely to be immediate on contracting.

- The Defective Products Directive would also not apply. First, doubt is raised by the restriction of the application to "industrially produced movables". Second, it is difficult to consider that software agents such as Agents A-D could cause personal damages such as death or personal injuries or damage to property[31]. The one exception may be if the agent was considered movable and caused damage to the actual electronic device used by the consumer (e.g. with an effect similar to a virus) in which case the provider is subject to objective liability (or liability without fault) and the consumer does not have to prove any negligence on the agent provider's behalf (only damage).

Accordingly the consumer would have to rely on general principles of contract law to obtain compensation from the agent provider (either as a service or under a software license) in relation to any liability incurred by the user for actions committed through use of the defective agent. Such claims could be based on express and implied contractual guarantees[32], breach of good faith or misrepresentation, breach of contract for incorrect performance, etc. However, for those terms that imply a reasonableness test, such the obligation that services shall be supplied with "reasonable care", there is an. inherent uncertainty in what this level of care might mean in relation to agent computing.

At least the consumer will be protected from unreasonable exclusions of liability in these contracts, under implementation of the Unfair Contract Terms Directive, as we outline next.

3.1.3 Agent developer or supplier liability disclaimers and exclusions

The Research Scenario conceives that an agent or agent-based service can be supplied to the consumer under the conditions of a service contract or licence agreement, even if offered free of charge[33]. Often such agreements limit the liability of the goods/service provider, with clauses indicating goods or services being "*offered AS IS*", "*no warranty as to performance, merchantability or fitness for purpose of any kind*", "*no liability for accuracy, correctness, timeliness,...*" etc). These terms will be all the more

---

[30] Art. 6.3 EC Distance Contracts Directive.

[31] See S Feliu, op cit, note 6 supra.

[32] The UK legislation such as the Supply of Goods and Services Act 1982 provides for obligations of merchantable quality and fitness for purpose in relation to goods, and reasonable care in the supply of services, which cannot be excluded in consumer contracts.

[33] See for example the terms of service of the search engines and shopping bots available on line, e.g. Google at http://www.google.com/terms_of_service.html, or Alltheweb at http://www.alltheweb.com/info/about/terms_of_use.html

complicated for sophisticated transaction agents, autonomous "initiators" as opposed to mere "observers". There is a fair amount of doubt about the effectiveness of these disclaimers, especially with regard to consumer products and services but also, in fact, commercial contracts.[34] The consumer protection issues are however the same, as the agent provider will be provider the agent service in the course of its business.

The legislation implementing Unfair Contract Terms Directive (together with prior or subsequent national legislation[35]) will entitle the consumer to avoid terms in such agreements that "establish a significant imbalance, to the consumer's detriment, between the rights and obligations of the contracting parties" (Art.3)[36]. In the end, it will be a matter for the courts to determine what is considered unreasonable in the circumstances, especially given the nature of the agent in question, the nature of the consumer and the circumstances of the transaction.

3.2   Transactions through agents

In this section, we look at the issues raised by using an agent to carry out a transaction in the Research Scenario, for example the purchase of a good or service either from the store (Agent B) or from another web-merchant (Agent C). First we will study whether such transactions and agents are covered by current regulation, then we will consider different protections that are afforded consumers within the Research Scenario, and how agent-based trading is affected by these protections in the three identified phases of a transaction: pre-contract, contract conclusion, and contract performance.

3.2.1   General considerations

Some points are common to several of the issues outlined below, key among them being the application of the Directives.

The Distance Contracts Directive may not apply when the consumer is in the store (no distance) although it could be argued that any contract made by mobile device, even if the consumer is in the premises of the merchant, may fall under the definition of distance sale: "contract concerning goods or services concluded between a supplier and a consumer under an organized distance sales or service-provision scheme run by the supplier, who, for the purpose of the contract, makes exclusive use of one or more means of

---

[34] See for example, the English case of *St Albans City and District Council* v. *International Computers Limited* [1997] FSR 251.

[35] For example, implemented in the UK for example, through the Unfair Contract Terms Act (1977) and unfair Terms in Consumer Contracts Regulations (1994 and 1999).

[36] The Unfair Contract Terms Act 1977 s.3 also subjects exemption clauses to a reasonableness test where one party contracts on the other's 'written standard terms of business. See for example the English case of St Albans, cit. note 33.

distance communication up to and including the moment at which the contract is concluded" – distance communication meaning without the simultaneous physical presence of the merchant and consumer[37]. Mobile devices using WAP-mail, SMS or other online connection would fall within the categories of schemes listed in the annex and if the consumer concludes the contract for home delivery with the mobile device (rather than receive the information and then pick up the item in the store – the contract will not then be made at a distance), this may be a distance sale so long as the consumer is off the premises, or if the goods provider is not the store itself.

In addition, certain products are excepted from some information obligations the most relevant being contracts for the "supply of foodstuffs, beverages or other goods intended for everyday consumption supplied to the home of the consumer, to his residence or to his workplace by regular roundsmen"[38].

Accordingly the Directive will only apply if:
– The purchase contract is formed over the mobile device.
– The consumer is not in the store providing the goods (e.g. alternative store or web-merchant).
– The products are not everyday consumption items delivered home but special goods or services. Considering the extent of items now sold in stores, this could apply to furniture, outdoor goods, computers, etc.

Article 10 on restrictions on automatic calling systems with no human intervention, will apply in all events if the consumer is sent an SMS or other forms of message when outside the store (it has to involve a distance communication).

The Ecommerce Directive applies to the provision of "information society services", defined indirectly as services normally provided for remuneration, at a distance, by means of electronic equipment for the processing and storage of data and at the individual request of a recipient of a service[39]. This includes both business to business and business to consumer transactions (online shopping), services provided free of charge to the recipient (e.g. funded by advertising or sponsorship revenue) and services allowing for online electronic transactions (communication services).

First, if the services being considered are the actual use of agents (as opposed to the services offered by or through the agent), then the Directive will apply if such services were offered to consumers online (e.g. through the store website, or WAP-pages). This will probably be a single occasion when the consumer contracts or registers for such services, and has been discussed above in section 3.1.

---

[37] Art. 2(1) and (4) EC Distance Contracts Directive.
[38] Arts. 4 to 7(1) relating to prior information, written confirmation, withdrawal rights and due performance are excluded by Art 3.2.
[39] Art 1(2) EC Directive 98/34/EC, referred to in Art 2(a) of the Ecommerce Directive.

If the agents are already resident with the store network or Internet, then one needs to consider if offering goods or services through the agent is an information society service. On the one hand, it could be argued that the services are sometimes not rendered at the individual call of the recipient (like a click on a web-page) but on the contrary they are provided automatically by the store[40]. In addition, certainly in the case of Agent B, there is doubt whether the user within the store is "at a distance" from the store. On the other hand, the software agents in the Research Scenario are offering wireless transactions, and either they are installed by the consumer (in the mobile device or related computer system), or the consenting consumer will respond to a message offering such a service, or she will specifically request the service (e.g. a recipe recommendation) for example through a tablet PC or other device on the store trolley. All in all, we consider that the services provided through agents considered for the Research Scenario do fall within such the definition and therefore the store or trader providing a service through an agent would be subject to the obligations set out in the Directive.

Although WAP-based agents will be covered, there is some question whether the provisions of Art. 10 will apply in the event that SMS or agent communications are considered "emails or equivalent individual communications". This is discussed in section 3.2.5 below.

3.2.2   Agents as consumers

There is one major problem with agent-based communications and contracting, especially in relation to advanced agents that do not necessarily refer back to the users: the Directives (and implementing legislation) often determine that information must be provided to the consumer. This appears, for example, in Art. 4.1 of the Distance Contracts Directive: "the consumer shall be provided with" certain information[41]. It is arguable that an agent may not be considered the equivalent of the consumer for these purposes. The principle is one of transparency and information, and if an agent receives data without transferring it on to the consumer, the consumer is not aware of it. The consumer may therefore not receive relevant information or be aware of his/her rights in relation to transactions entered into by the agent. This foils the purposes of the consumer protection rules which are based on transparency and the provision of adequate information to the consumer. While national implementations have often transposed the wording directly into national law, it may be up to the national courts to determine what this entails in relation to agents.

---

[40] In which case the automatic calling rules will apply, in any event.
[41] Implemented in the UK as "supplier shall provide to the consumer" in the Consumer Protection (Distance Selling) Regulations 2000.

Insofar as the requirement is to make available, to the consumer (e.g. Arts. 5, 10, 11 Ecommerce Directive) or to make a communication identifiable (e.g. Art. 6 Ecommerce Directive) there may be a technical solution as it seems there is no requirement on the providers to ensure that consumers actually receive this data. It may be considered the consumers' risk if they do not avail themselves of information and technical processes properly provided by merchants in accordance with the legislation: identification and other general information, error correction, recording and reproducing the terms, etc.

3.2.3   Technical capacities

Another issue common to consumer protection obligations in the use of agents is the sheer quantity of information that is required to be provided to consumers. This is highly relevant for mobile transactions, for example in relation to short text messages (SMS) which have a standard 160 character limit, or the capacities of screens of mobile devices to present the full amount of information. This problem may be solved by the next generation of telephony (UMTS) or Wi-Fi transmissions, however, unless such higher bandwidth technologies are used, service providers may be in breach of these obligations because it is technically impossible to supply adequate information. To avoid these problems, among other reasons, the Research Scenario considers communications will be established with consumers on portable flat screen devices such as notepads or electronic PDAs, which have greater capacity. On the other hand, the UK government for example, has considered that so long as the information is available on a website (i.e. accessible via WAP) it would not have to be included in the messages subject to the availability of a link to the site. Generally speaking, though, this issue has led certain commentators to say that proper mobile consumer contracting will have to wait for the "next" generation telecommunications (perhaps UMTS and what has been called3G).

3.2.4   Pre-contractual phase

The pre-contractual phase has two relevant aspects: obligations to provide reliable information and those relating to advertising and "commercial communications".

As regards the provision of information, in accordance with national (and implemented European) legislation on consumer protection, some specific considerations may apply when such stores or other service providers contact the consumer via electronic agents. Here we may envisage the case where a store makes a special offer via a mobile device to a consumer when she approaches the store or a section of the store. This could include Agent A, providing additional information or other commercial services within the

Research Scenario (product information, prices and discounts, etc.). Another example is an outside service provider offering information, recipes, alternative products and services to the consumer within the store area.

Both the Distance Selling Directive and the Ecommerce Directive, as well as many national or sector codes of conduct, impose information obligations on service providers when they communicate with recipients of their services. The following information must be provided in the manner set out in section 1 of this Chapter above if the Directives apply:

– **Distance selling Directive**. In the event of the full application of the Directive the trader must supply its identity and address, description of the item, price, payment methods, the right to withdraw, cost of the distance sales technique, term of the offer/price. In the event of partial application, the consumer must be notified of the availability of the item in question (Art.7.2) This information may be provided at any time prior to the contract, in which case it could be supplied (in decreasing order of attraction for the store) either initially when the consumer subscribes to agent-style services within the Research Scenario, or each time when the consumer logs on, or at the time of the specific contract. Complications will occur when the consumer uses his/her own agent within the Research Scenario as the agent would have to read this information from the data provided by the store information system (web-site or specific agent-related platform). This could mean that merchants must make certain data fields automatically legible by automated agents (e.g. through standardised mark-up)

– **Ecommerce Directive**: as described in section 1, the Directive sets out several items of information that has to be available at all times: name, address, contact details, VAT registration, trade registration. Care should be taken in relation to the overlap of Distance Selling and Ecommerce requirements.

– **Price Indications Directive, etc.**: all agent communications regarding products offered by the store via the mobile device should contain the same details as the actual items in the store, and comply with the relevant indication rules (food, non-food) as to selling price and the unit price, etc.

For agents within the Research Scenario, and also in combination with the store's own information systems, specific standardised processes for providing this information may be required. This includes not only processes for the supply of information to the consumer at the relevant moment, but also programming interfaces to include options for consumer notification or storing such information. As we comment below, standardisation enables third party agents to interact with the trader's own systems. Another point certain shopping agents will have to be careful about is the screening and filtering of data: it is important for them not to filter out mandatory data (supplier identification, etc.) and other messages they may consider spam.

Specifications to achieve legally compliant agents should also take into account (non-binding) recommendations of the Convention on Provider identification in Electronic Commerce established by the Working Group of Consumer Protection Associations. This is a self-regulatory measure, designed to assist B2C ecommerce, and sets usability and content recommendations for websites and other electronic communications with consumers.

Finally, note that, under applicable laws of contract, agent providers may be liable for any misinformation and/or communications in bad faith (depending on the jurisdiction) in relation to the provision of pre-contractual information offered through an agent.

The second area where consumer related issues arise in relation to the commercial agents under study, is that of commercial communications, which covers merchant advertising and other directed communications.

Several agents considered by the Research Scenario may send messages to users (consumers) without solicitation, including Agents A and B described in Chapter 2. These messages may be activated by consumer interaction with RFID-enhanced products, e.g. by picking it up and putting it in the trolley. These will usually be advertisements, special offers, reminders, etc., and will constitute commercial communications to users either in or near the store, or even at home. Such communications are regulated by the Ecommerce Directive, and automatic calling (e.g. when a user is away from the store) is also covered by the Distance Contracts Directive. The implications are as follows:

− **Ecommerce Directive**: any messages that are of commercial nature should comply with the information requirements set out in Art. 6 (see outline above): identification, details, sender, etc. If they are unsolicited, this should be identified as soon as it is received by the recipient (allowing filter services, for example). The communication agent provider may also have to contact national "opt-out" register (Robinson lists) for consumers that do not wish to be contacted.

− **Distance Contracts Directive**: to the extent that the calling is automatic, the caller must obtain the consumer's consent (opt-in obligation). This should be expressly obtained when the consumer registers for the retail store or other agent service provider services or on log-in. Non-automatic calling should at least provide an opportunity for consumers to opt out.

These messages may also be considered advertising for the purposes of the misleading and comparative advertising rules (and under national obligations), whose requirements should be followed. These will change from country to country, and suppliers will already be aware of the requirements. The important point to note is that as the messages are sent at the point of sale (in the store), these are likely to be considered high pressure notices putting the consumer in an unusually weak position. However, except to the extent that agent processing permits them to be personalised, they are not really different from advertising messages commonly sent over a store's PA system.

Finally it is important to note that Data Protection issues require that calling originating on the basis of personal data stored by the system, or through belonging to a registry, is made according to the more general Data Protection requirements (e.g. no prejudicial automatic decisions under Art.15 of the Data Protection Directive). Art. 13 of the recent Privacy and Electronic Communications Directive regulates the use of automated calling systems for the purpose of direct marketing, which may only be allowed in respect to subscribers of telecommunications services who have given their prior consent (opt-in), or with whom there has been prior contractual dealings[42]. More details of this are set out in the chapter on Privacy.

3.2.5   Contractual phase

The agents considered here are those that offer goods or services for sale over mobile devices. Information, search or filter agents are not relevant because there are no consumer contracts involved. In particular, therefore, we refer to agents such as Agents B and C commented above and described in Chapter 2 on contracts. We consider the issues highlighted in Table 4.2 in turn. Please note that some of these issues have been discussed in chapter 2 relating to contracts, from the perspective of ensuring a valid contract. Here, we consider similar issues from the perspective of complying with consumer protection obligations.

The first issue is that of information requirements in relation to the contract. We have already considered the general information requirements for Information Society service providers set out by the Ecommerce Directive. In addition, this Directive requires the provision of other details when leading up to a contract. In the event of an agent sale that is not an "individual communication to the consumer" equivalent to emails (Art. 10.4), the service provider must inform the consumer of the steps to follow to conclude a contract, any codes of conduct, technical procedures for error correction and other information listed in Art. 10 (see the outline in section 1 above). It may be possible, however, to argue that the data message to the consumer is an individual communication equivalent to an email, on the basis that the offer may be personalised (i.e. in accordance with a user profile or other data stored on the trader's system) and that the same information is provided to the consumer on logging on or initial registration. The terms of the contract must also be accessible, storable and reproducible by the consumer (10.3). This is already rarely complied with in current merchant web-sites, and when dealing with agents this will require extra layers of interaction to ensure the agent can find, access and store the terms.

---

[42] This is further commented in Chapter 5 on Privacy and Data Protection.

The next issue relates to the proper process for the conclusion of contracts through agents. Apart from standard contact formation processes (offer, acceptance) agents dealing with consumers may have to follow certain extra steps. These include the following obligations imposed by the Ecommerce Directive: first, the supplier must acknowledge any order placed by the consumer (art. 11.1); also, the system must allow the consumer a means to verify and correct the order (input errors) prior to placing the order (11.2). Again, if the agent communications is considered equivalent to email (e.g. directed SMS could be so), these provisions do not apply.

A third issue is that of requirements of form: under national laws, certain contracts must be made in a certain form and manner[43]. Although in general the Ecommerce Directive requires member states to permit electronic contracts[44], i.e. allow them to be in digital form, certain additional form requirements may be applicable. In particular, under the Distance Contracts Directive (insofar as it is applicable), written confirmation of the contract on a durable medium should be provided[45]. Email confirmation would be sufficient, or even SMS if the storage and features of the mobile device allow it. This will include information on the right to withdraw, after-sales service and guarantees. These obligations may however be avoided if the contract is for a single performance (delivery) and the order is invoiced by the communication service provider (not the store). This may arise if the payment method chosen is for example, adding the amount to a telephone bill.

In any event, even though such rules may not apply, it would be good practice for the store and other agent providers to comply with these requirements, to avoid any doubt and in the interest of consumer confidence.

The latest VAT Directive[46] permits invoices to be sent by electronic means. This is only relevant for digital transfers, as home deliveries are usually accompanied by a paper invoice under VAT rules for offline transactions. However such electronic invoices must be accepted provided that the authenticity of the origin and integrity of the contents are guaranteed either by means of an advanced electronic signature (with an allowance for qualified certificates and created by a secure-signature-creation device) or by means of electronic data interchange (EDI). The Directive allows invoices to be sent by other electronic means subject to acceptance by the Member State(s) concerned, but it is yet to be seen how this is implemented. These

---

[43] We are not considering obvious examples such as contracts relating to land, which in many jurisdictions must be signed in writing and often before notary.

[44] Art. 9 EC Ecommerce Directive: "Member States shall ensure that their legal system allows contracts to be concluded by electronic means".

[45] Art. 5 EC Distance Contracts Directive.

[46] Directive 2001/115/EC of 20 December 2001 amending Directive 77/388/EEC with a view to simplifying, modernising and harmonising the conditions laid down for invoicing in respect of value added tax (full reference at end of monograph).

invoices must be stored so that the authenticity of the origin and integrity of the content of the invoices, as well as their readability, is guaranteed throughout the storage period. Certain member states such as Spain had already accepted the use of electronic invoices, under certain conditions, including the use of digital signatures.[47]

This may impose certain obligations on vendors using automatic agents for selling purposes, including those for "normal" ecommerce transactions (web-sales) and electronic storage of invoices within appropriate document management systems. It is more of a question of integrating commerce agents with back-office invoicing systems, and ensuring their capacity for digital signatures, with the added difficulty of sheer volumes of transactions and the need to effectively label each of them.

The next difficulty for agent based trading is the obligation to incorporate the contract's general terms and conditions into the contract (by reference or factually), and to taking steps to ensure that the consumer has had the opportunity to consider them. Considering this requirement it will be important to include a link or other technical means of retrieving or receiving such terms in the event of an agent-based contract. Often a store's general terms may be in a central registry (in many continental jurisdictions), and some form of standardised access could be provided. The question of whether the purchaser may be considered to have had the opportunity to review the terms before concluding the agreement is another hurdle for agent based trading, though we have commented on this in Chapter 2 (section 3.3.3).

The next concern involves payment issues: we are considering here the consumer protection related obligations in relation to the use of an online payment system with an agent (e.g. payment agent). There are certain consumer protections and other obligations for both payment providers and merchants dealing with the agent/consumer that have to be complied with. In accordance with the EC Payment Recommendation, subsequent to a transaction the consumer must be provided with the following information regarding electronic payment instruments other than electronic money instruments[48]:

– a reference enabling the holder to identify the transaction;
– the amount of the transaction debited to the holder in billing currency and, where applicable, the amount in foreign currency;
– the amount of any fees and charges applied for particular types of transactions;
– the exchange rate used for converting any foreign currency transactions.

---

[47] RD 1624/1992 and modified by RD 80/1996, and more recently Orden Ministerial de HAC/3134/2002, of 5 December 2002.
[48] Art. 4 EC Payment Recommendation 97/489/EC of the 30th July 1997.

Regarding electronic money instruments, the holder must have the possibility of verifying the last five transactions executed with the instrument and the outstanding value stored thereon.

Under the Distance Contracts Directive, Article 8 provides the right for the consumer to cancel a payment made with payment card if someone has used the payment card fraudulently. In case of such cancellation, the sums paid must be re-credited to the consumer. This means that an automated payment system should incorporate a means for re-crediting the consumer, something that is not allowed by all systems which often only permit payment from consumer to merchant. Note, however, that this right does only apply to payment cards, and so will not be applicable to payment systems based on other means, such as digital cash. The Directive is not applicable to contracts concluded by means of "automatic vending machines", so payments for articles in vending machines made with a smart card/mobile (which has been a popular trial for mobile payments) would not be covered by this cancellation right.

However we have already noted that it is doubtful whether the national implementations of these provisions will be fully applicable on transactions made within the Research Scenario context. Besides the possibility that a system based on other means than payment cards may be used, such as digital cash or charging the telephone operator, the conclusion of the contract is foreseen to be made in the store in the simultaneous presence of the consumer and the merchant. Therefore the purchase contract is not concluded by any means of distance communication as defined in the Distance Contracts Directive, and the transaction falls outside its scope.

3.2.6   Post-contractual phase

Four issues have been raised in relation to post-contractual obligations in consumer contracts. These are the liability for online performance, recording of a transaction, merchant disclaimers and application law and jurisdictional issues for dispute resolution. We consider these here.

So long as agent-based contracting is held valid, merchants will be bound be agent-formed contracts. This is in fact already the case for many semi-automatic operations on the Internet – air-flight or book sales for example, where consumers purchase items and agree to terms established by the merchant. The merchant then performs in accordance to the terms. The fact that this performance is carried out by software (e.g. a program download) does not vary this position, however it may be relevant that this fact is brought to the attention of the consumer. This may be taken into account in considering the reasonableness of any other term and the level of performance on the part of the merchant.

We also have considered the legal obligations for storing, accessing and reproducing a contract between an Information Society service provider and a consumer. Over and above the legal obligations, consumers will want to incorporate such processes into contracting agents, even if they are used for everyday grocery purchases. This builds consumer confidence and legal certainty. Such documentation will be required for all forms of dispute resolution, either in the courts or alternative fora.

Again here there are no extra rules for agent based transactions as there are for electronic commerce. As in the pre-contractual phase, in this phase appropriate processes should be programmed and established so that documentary evidence is kept of all transactions (both merchant-side and client-side) in such a way as to provide authenticity, integrity and non-repudiation. There are already certain standards relating to document management (BS7799 and ISO 17799, for example), although those are not guarantees of admissibility. These provide greater levels of protection than consumers usually have capacity for (home computers or portable devices do not usually provide such features). The issue will be more relevant for merchants, especially in relation to fraud, electronic payments and tax/invoicing requirements.

Merchant disclaimers and exclusions regarding products or services provided through an agent (as opposed to in relation to the agent itself) will be subject to the usual "unfair terms" tests set out in national and European legislation (see above, under "using agents" and the outline in section 1). In assessing the unfair nature of a contractual term, the courts should take into account:
- the nature of the goods or services covered by the contract;
- the circumstances surrounding the drawing up of the contract;
- the other terms in the contract or in another contract to which it relates.

The nature of the agent process will affect the context of the transaction and the application of the reasonableness tests. This will affect factors such as to what extent the terms were brought to the client's attention, whether the agent user should bear the risk of such use, etc.

The next issue concerns jurisdiction and applicable law. These are thorny issues, even without agent involvement. We comment on them in turn.

Jurisdiction: the position is fairly clear from most texts (international and European) that consumers are entitled to redress in their own jurisdiction, and the merchants are bound by the mandatory laws (consumer protection, data protection, product safety, etc.) of that country. Accordingly the situation for agent trading within the Research Scenario does not change this, as it is the consumer in the retail store which is the point of reference. If the consumer wants redress in the jurisdiction of the provider (where the laws may be more favourable to the consumer), this is no problem as this is always an option under principles of jurisdiction (jurisdiction of domicile of defendant). There are more difficulties where the consumer wishes to sue a third party agent provider or merchant in a jurisdiction where the agent may be understood to be "based" (e.g. the computer server where it is resident, if it is not a mobile agent). In general the position does not seem clear, as one would have to argue that the electronic agent is a branch, agent or other establishment of the service provider[49] or that there are special links with that particular jurisdiction[50].

Applicable law: we have noted in section 1 above that under the Rome Convention, contracts shall be generally governed by the law chosen by the parties. If there is no choice of law agreement, the courts will look at the country most closely connected to the performing party, which in the merchant / consumer scenario is the merchant. There are exceptions to this rule in relation to consumer contracts when a choice of law made by the parties shall not have the result of depriving the consumer of the protection afforded to him by the mandatory rules of the law of the country in which he has his habitual residence (i.e. local mandatory rules apply) if a specific invitation or advertising has been directed to the consumer and he/she concluded the contract in his/her country, or the merchant received the order in the consumer's country. If no choice is made, the law of the consumer's country is applied.[51]

Accordingly it is most likely that any contract made by a consumer when contracting with a merchant operated agent will be governed:
– By the laws of the consumer and merchant if they are in the same jurisdiction
– If the merchant is in another jurisdiction and agreement is made to apply the law of its own jurisdiction ("click-wrap" style), those laws will apply except to the extent that they reduce the consumer protection provided by the laws of the consumer's jurisdiction.
– If no choice is made, the laws of the consumer's jurisdiction will apply.
On the other hand, if it is a consumer controlled agent, we consider there are no particular marketing activities of the supplier towards the consumer (unless this is determined from other aspects of the supplier's activity), whereupon the supplier's laws will apply.

Finally, a note on dispute resolution processes. The digital and cross-border nature of online transactions creates several difficulties for normal judicial resolution of small or large claims. Although the Research Scenario does not contemplate cross-border transactions, several elements complicate the handling of consumer complaints relating to agent-based transactions, and the settlement of disputes in the e-commerce environment.

First of all, since the location of the establishment of either the consumer or the business is difficult to determine on the Internet, any dispute will raise jurisdictional issues concerning which court will be competent to decide the

---

[49] Art. 5 Brussels Regulation
[50] Art. 2 Brussels Regulation and also see J Olsen: *Agents and the notion of Establishment,* 2001.
[51] Art 5 Rome Convention on applicable law.

case and according to which law (see above). This kind of issues is not exclusive to e-commerce as they might occur in every cross-border dispute. Still, the advent of the Internet and e-commerce has considerably increased the (potential) number of non-professional individuals to be confronted with these difficulties. Moreover, even if the problems of jurisdiction could easily be overcome, the low value of many of the e-commerce transactions will rarely justify taking a dispute to court. These problems are increased by agent based trading, where it may be even more difficult to determine jurisdiction.

The cost of traditional courtroom dispute settlement (compared to the low value of the transaction) and the often long duration of the proceedings or the need for professional advice leaves the e-consumer in a rather precarious situation when a dispute arises. This insecurity does not really inspire confidence in the electronic marketplace. In fact, it may very well deter consumers from e-commerce altogether. For that reason, it is necessary to come up with a way of settling consumer disputes in a way that is more adapted to the e-commerce environment. On-line ADR (or "ODR") could offer this solution, and a large amount of work is being put into establishing codes of conduct for e-merchants and providing a consumer friendly framework for online alternative dispute resolution[52]. It is not, however, because a consumer uses an agent that he/she might want to use this form of ADR.

The Ecommerce Directive directs Member States to allow the effective use of ADR by electronic means. This solution is not affected by the use of agents, as any choice of such forum for dispute resolution is subject to the same requirements as any other electronic choice of forum. Indeed, in the case of advanced electronic contracting agents, the consumer may be in the position to argue that he/she is not bound by such a term as he/she was never aware of the ADR term in the contract. This would be countered in the event that an automated dialogue or negotiation process is established between merchant and consumer (via agents) providing for a choice of forum and law. In this case, any unusual term as to dispute resolution should automatically be brought to the consumer's attention. One of the principles of arbitration is the consent of the parties, and based on the Brussels Convention (now an EC Regulation) and other legal instruments, it seems that valid ADR agreements by consumers would have to be entered into after the dispute has arisen, and would have to give the consumer at least the same basic procedural rights as would the court system. Certain national laws may inhibit the conclusion of such arbitration agreements that exclude any resort to the consumer's courts. Such a term is also unfair under the Unfair Contract Terms Directive and therefore is not binding on the consumer.

---

[52] See for example the Joint Research Centre's E-confidence initiative, but also ICC, GBDe, the E-Commerce Group, EuroCommerce and the FEDMA.

Another difficulty arises in the form requirements for the effectiveness of arbitration agreements: they must be in writing and signed by the parties. It is very unlikely that an agent based transaction could currently comply with these requirements, until digital signature incorporating agents are created (with the associated problems commented in Chapter 2 on contracts).

Before offering such an ADR solution, the terms and procedures of the forum should be checked for consumer and merchant friendliness[53]. Certain principles are common to all these initiatives: free or low cost to the consumer, independence and impartiality of forum, transparency and speed of procedures, and accessibility to consumers. Two other aspects, which are closely connected to these five, still give rise to diverging opinions: the voluntary basis of process and the binding character of decision.

3.3   National laws and self regulation

Each Member State of the European Union has a relatively well developed regulatory environment aimed either specifically at consumer protection or which regulate business-consumer commercial practices for other reasons. However in addition to the kind of regulations that exist at EU level discussed here, many Member States have general legal principles, sometimes supported by specific laws, for regulating such business-consumer relations. These are often called principles of fair trading. While this research monograph does not focus on national regulation outside the framework established by the EU directives, the question of fair trading and local regulation will have to be looked at in each individual case on eventual implementation of the Research. The PriceWaterhouseCoopers report on consumer protection[54] commissioned by the EC highlights some of the difficulties with different levels of consumer protection throughout the Community. This has been commented on by the EC in its Green Paper on Consumer Protection[55], which is commented below in section 5.1.

The report also concluded that although self-regulation for consumer protection through codes of conduct is developing fast in many Member States, it is severely constrained at EU-level. Recent attempts that have been made to develop EU-level self-regulation have had only mixed results. Self-regulation has been shown to be a potentially useful complement to regulation that can reduce the need for very detailed legislation and provide benefits for consumers. Although codes of conduct are specifically referred

---

[53] See also T. Schultz, et al: *Online Dispute Resolution: The State of the Art and the Issues*, 2001 and also the Commission recommendation on ADR bodies (2001/310/EC), 4 April 2001, OJ L 109/56.

[54] PriceWaterhouseCoopers: *Final Report Study on Consumer Law and the Information Society*, 2000.

[55] European Commission: *Green Paper on European Union Consumer Protection*, 2001.

to in some EU legislation, they have been unable to fulfil their potential at EU level because of the degree of national legal diversity. Moreover, further problems stem from the uncertainty over the status of commitments made in codes and their enforceability.

These variations make it difficult to specify standard – Europe-wide – processes for consumer protection for agent based trading within the Research Scenario. In Chapter 6 we suggest a method for developing software systems so that local rules may be modelled and integrated into the systems at a high level, rather that within the nuts and bolts of agent programming. This should make the overall implementation more flexible and adaptable to local regulations.

In fact, there are many schemes that have been set up for consumer confidence in online trading[56], including a pan-European network for consumer assistance, EEJ-NET[57]. What it really lacks is a general framework establishing legal guarantees and overall enforcement. Commentaries have suggested that there should be a framework Directive of such codes, trustmarks and labelling schemes, in order to bring some order and transparency to the business. These are discussed in the next section.

4.   SOLUTIONS FOR CONSUMER PROTECTION

In this section we comment on certain commercial and technical solutions for the issues raised by agent-based trading in the consumer context. First, we look at codes and conduct and trust seals then insurance, while finally commenting on some technologies that may assist.

4.1   Trust seals and private codes of conduct

A trustmark or seal is a form of guarantee provided by an organisation that maintains a list of trustworthy companies that it claims it has supposedly audited and "certified". Examples include BBB (Better Business Bureau)[58], Webtrader[59], webtrust[60], Trusted-shops[61], Trust-UK[62], etc.[63] A company which wants to be approved has to comply with certain conditions, usually

---

[56] See examples cited in section 1.3.8.5 above, and in the next section 4.1 below.

[57] Online at http://www.eejnet.org.

[58] BBB Online at http://www.bbbonline.org/

[59] Which? Webtrader, online at http://www.which.net/webtrader/, which in fact has now closed down.

[60] Online at http://www.cpawebtrust.org/

[61] Trusted Shops online at http://www.trustedshops.de/en/index.html

[62] Online at www.trustuk.org.uk

[63] A more complete list is held by the E-confidence centre at http://econfidence.jrc.it/, under - Commerce Codes of Conduct / Trustmarks

compliance with a code of conduct consisting of different kinds of obligations. Once the conditions are met, traders are allowed to display the organisation's "seal of trust" logo or label on its website. It is assumed that the consumers will feel secure if they see this seal or label on a website.[64] This sense of security will hopefully result in the consumer engaging in e-commerce with the vendor. Often, the programme also includes some other function, such as a consumer insurance programme[65] or an on-line dispute resolution programme[66] that we have discussed above. Some even provide independent insurance and "money-back" guarantees.

The trustmark's code of conduct usually contains a series of legal and non-legal obligations. Among the usual obligations are those about the quality of the information given on the website, the ordering process, the protection of privacy and of minors, the withdrawal from a transaction, payments and deliveries, often in line with the obligations outlined above. Other items may refer to dispute resolution procedures, consumer support and claim mechanisms, and company behaviour monitoring.

To be of any validity, the trustmark provider should provide independent reviewing of the terms and conditions and processes of the site. It should also adopt security measures to avoid fraudulent use of the mark. However, there have been many questions about such trustmarks, often in the USA in relation to privacy, as there is no infallible enforcement mechanism to guarantee that companies comply with the trustmark's code of conduct or any decision by the trustmark provider.

Despite the drawbacks, this same procedure could be applied to electronic agents, having established a list of prerequisites for consumer and merchant protection. Such a list would include dialogue attributes and processes and minimum requirements relating to the issues discussed above: the provision of basic information, identification of parties and their nature, privacy guarantees for personal data, security measures and authorisations, contracting capacity, payment procedures, jurisdiction and dispute resolution, document retention or accessibility functions, etc. Taking a process modelling approach, this form of dialogue could be modelled and a "seal" or recognised standard given to it. Software agents and merchant platforms could then "advertise" that they are compatible with this standard, and therefore compliant with a set of consumer protection requirements at a certain date. Trader web-sites could then develop their systems to make them interoperable with these agents. Again, this provides support for taking a modelling approach to legal compliance...

---

[64] B Subirana and P Carvajal: *Transaction streams: theory and examples related to confidence in Internet-based electronic commerce,* 2000.

[65] Trusted Shops (note 60 above).

[66] Ex-Webtrader (note 58 above).

4.2   Insurance for e-consumers

Insurance is another form of indirect consumer confidence-builder: if the consumer knows that a transaction is guaranteed (money back features, anti-credit card fraud, or guaranteed performance), he/she is more likely to enter into such a transaction[67]. Current insurance schemes offer different features: cover for the hacking of the credit card details, for problems with the goods ordered (non delivery, delivery of a deteriorated or 'incomplete' product) and for problems with reimbursement after a return of the goods. Standard Visa credit card issuer insurance (full) covers only American e-customers, while in Europe this insurance is up to the bank issuing the credit card (and legislation that caps liability at 150 Euros) and Eurocard/Mastercard also left the matter up to the issuing banks. It is yet to be seen how such schemes may apply to agents and agent-based trading, however they may also assist merchants in accepting agent contracting as payment processes provide a form of identification and guarantee.

4.3   Technical proposals

Several technical solutions have been put forward for increased consumer confidence and transaction security: cryptography, labels, smart agents, physical devices / tokens, biometrics and watermarks.

One example is the protocol for securing on-line payments. Both technical and legal solutions have been implemented at a European level in attempts to reassure the e-consumer. Most websites now employ either the Secure Sockets Layer (SSL) and some the Secure Electronic Transaction (SET) protocol for payments. These protocols define the secure zones where the consumers can leave their credit card details in relative safety. The credit card issuing company Visa also offers the solution of the smart card reader, a small encryption device plugged into the computer. SET technology has been proposed by the issuers, in order to reduce the merchant's liabilities, but have not been much implemented due to technical difficulties.

Another example are smart cards, that are being sponsored by the EC for authentication and security purposes (digital signatures, and other issues[68]). These could be combined in portable devices for secure communications, identification and secure payments. They are part of the initiative for secure mobile payments set up by Visa and other payment providers[69].

---

[67] B Subirana and P Carvajal, op cit., 2000.

[68] See EC IST Smart Card initiative at www.cordis.lu/ist/ka2/smartcards.html and
   http://www.eeurope-smartcards.org/

[69] See for example, VISA's initiative of chip cards, at
   http://www.visaeu.com/iusevisa/whychip.html or the Mobile 3-D Secure specification at
   http://international.visa.com/fb/paytech/secure/main.jsp

While these technologies deal with certain consumer protection requirements, such as identification and data message integrity (records, communications), they do not help with the basic requirements for presenting and storing contract terms, guaranteeing performance, or respect for the online trading procedures.

A more interesting technological initiative is Legal-XML (within the XML standards organisation OASIS[70]). This technical standardisation proposal for a legal mark-up language is interesting, as it would allow automated processes such as agents and web-sites to "understand" legal text. Machines could recognise a web-trader's identification, terms of business, a dispute resolution clause, or a jurisdiction clause. On the basis of this understanding, it should be possible to establish true legally meaningful protocols for automated contract negotiation and conclusion. What is more, these protocols can incorporate the consumer protection requirements. Together with process modelling to define the processes for agent-based transactions (and the additional processes for legalising the same), this language technology should enable standardised models and architectures for agent based trading to be developed that incorporate consumer protection compliance.

5. DEVELOPMENTS AND INITIAL CONCLUSIONS

5.1 Regulatory Developments at EU level

On October 2, 2001, the EC Commission published a Green Paper on Consumer Protection issues[71]. This sets out a two-fold strategy to open and deepen consumer confidence in the single EC internal market. First, it suggested sustained efforts to eliminate legal barriers to the internal market through harmonisation. Second, it recommended the development of a platform for enforcement co-operation to ensure the effective and comparable enforcement of rules throughout the internal market. This was intended to initiate a wide debate on the future direction of consumer policy and all interested stakeholders were invited to actively contribute.

The Green Paper also suggested new ideas for the use of self-regulatory codes within a legislative framework. A framework Directive establishing EU-wide principles for fair trading practices would be adaptable and responsive to changes in market practices - allowing to tackle new unfair practices, such as those in the online world, quickly. It would however not include rules concerning health and safety (i.e. tobacco or alcohol advertising) or decency, or social policy issues such as shop opening hours.

---

[70] Online at www.legalxml.org/
[71] European Commission: *Green Paper on European Union Consumer Protection*, 2001

Although a framework could cover all commercial practices, specific legislation may still be needed to regulate specific practices or sectors in more detail. The main choice in the Green Paper is between further harmonisation (addressing specific issues) and setting out core principles of consumer protection (in a framework Directive to complement specific legislative measures) The proposal for a Regulation on Sales Promotion the Commission also adopted in October 2001 is an example for this[72].

The Green paper also developed concepts for improved enforcement of consumer rights in online consumer transactions. Currently there is no formal framework for co-operation between the bodies enforcing consumer rights in Member States and details are provided about establishing a system for co-operation between national consumer protection agencies and bodies to help consumers have their rights respected abroad. This may not be so relevant for the Research Scenario, as it is unlikely that there will be any cross-border transactions in a supermarket setting. However, outside the Scenario, it is likely that agent transactions occur across borders, as with any Internet based transaction.

On 17 June 2003, the European Commission adopted a proposal for a Directive on unfair business practices in sales to consumers[73]. The proposal prohibits practices like pyramid and inertia selling, and also forbids paid-for media coverage or "advertorials" unless it is made clear that the coverage is paid for. The proposed Directive provides a general test for unfair practices as well as defining two specific types of unfair commercial practice in more detail – classified as "misleading" and "aggressive" practices[74].

5.2   Initial conclusions

Having due regard to the legal requirements for consumer transactions – either active contracting or using agents as observers – any implementation that attempts to approach legal compliance will need to plan the business, technical and functional specifications carefully. Although the issues are fairly broad, both law and technology provide some answers.

---

[72] Proposal for a Regulation of the European Parliament and the Council concerning sales promotions in the Internal Market, COM(2001) 546 final, October 2, 2001, online at http://europa.eu.int/comm/internal_market/comcom/unfair/reg-en.pdf

[73] Available at http://europa.eu.int/comm/consumers/cons_int/safe_shop/fair_bus_pract/directive_proposal_en.pdf

[74] Due to the date of publication, this proposal has not been reviewed in detail in this work.

5.2.1 A legal framework for consumer relations within the Research Scenario

The legal framework for any implementation should aim to provide both compliance with legal standards and extra measures for consumer confidence, protection and beyond. This legal architecture should include:

- A contractual framework between merchants and users regarding use of agents including consents for messaging and communications, clear establishment of agent contracting process, proper and adequate information on supplier and general terms of contracting, indication of the proper use of agents (insofar as the user has access to control the agent).
- A binding trader code of conduct and supporting guarantees (maybe from third parties), together with dispute resolution procedures over and above national protections.
- A clear privacy policy for respecting legal requirements and user wishes, and express consents for automatic calling and other mobile communications with users.
- Document storage mechanisms for evidentiary and confidence building purposes.
- Declared levels of consumer protection and procedures for eventual acceptance of third party interoperable agents within the framework.

5.2.2 Technology solutions for consumer protection compliance: a process orientation

On the basis of the discussions set out in this Chapter, we argue that certain specific processes are necessary for consumer protection and confidence for agent-based trading within the Research Scenario. Any agent in the scenario should comply or fulfil the following needs:

- Respecting basic consumer protection principles: Transparency and fair trading.
- Supporting consumer requirements: authenticity, integrity, confidentiality and non-repudiation.
- Enabling secure supporting services: secure payments, privacy and protection against crime (e.g. fraud).

In previous chapters we have suggested certain additional processes for compliant agent programming in relation to contracting and respect for IPR. In a similar manner, in Table 4-3 we present a summary of issues for consumer protection that are presented by Agent B, one of the example agents under discussion, in circumstances where it is a store-based agent advertising certain goods to consumers, and enabling them to purchase directly through the electronic device. Considering the issues discussed above, we attempt to establish the consumer related legal risks for each of the agent's processes. This enables us to determine further processes that may be either necessary (for compliance) or recommended (good practice, for greater confidence).

We suggest that most of these issues can technically be dealt with by proper specification and programming of merchant sites and procedures, with supporting requirements dealt with by encryption and digital signature technology. Basic specifications for a use case in relation to Consumer Protection within the Research Scenario are outlined in Chapter 6. The disadvantage of direct programming of consumer requirements means that the resulting system is inflexible: it cannot be replicated in another jurisdiction without significant reengineering, and it cannot adapt to changes in consumer protection legislation and case-law. To overcome this problem, we suggest a modelling solution whereby consumer protection processes are incorporated within the higher level .

Table 4-3. Consumer Protection processes for advertising and selling agents

Principal Process	Legal issues (consumer related)	Additional processes: compliance / consumer confidence
Consumer registration for in-store agent-based services	Jurisdiction and applicable law, dispute resolution (acceptance of conditions)	Establish contract framework for notifications, consents, general terms of business, guarantees, codes of conduct,
Agent B becomes aware of customer within target area for its particular advert	Consumer Privacy issues	Transparency, consent and auditing mechanisms. Anonymisation of data when possible.
Agent B considers rules for sending adverts and consults relevant data sources	Rules for unsolicited commercial communications	Obtain prior consent for in-store advertising (e.g. at log-on)
Agent B sends an advertisement to the customer device, without review by staff	Unsolicited commercial communications Information requirements under Ecommerce and Distance Selling Dirs.	Identification of data messages as advertisements or offers
Agent B provides a means for accepting the offered product (accept button, voice acceptance, etc)	Information requirements (consumer contracting issue) Identification of parties Mistake and Incorporation of all terms Secure contracting	Full identity discloser processes Process for acceding to terms Process for error correction and confirmation Process for acknowledgement of receipt Security processes (SLL, SET, etc.)
Agent B records and processes sale	Recording and access requirements Electronic billing (VAT) requirements	Written evidence to be forwarded to consumer (through device, email, or on store exit)
A payment agent contacts credit card / electronic payment service provider and processes payment according to relevant system	Identification of parties Payment Recommendation obligations	Privacy processes re. transaction identification and details Digital signatures for payments (e.g. SET protocol) Reference to User for PIN
Agent B monitors and updates customer reaction to message and stores this for further processing	Privacy rules (e.g. retention of data files, anonymity) Evidence: Quality and storage for ODR/ADR	Register of processes (with appropriate security processes – e.g. Encryption for integrity, authenticity and confidentiality)

Chapter 5

PRIVACY
Do agents deserve privacy protection?

Privacy:
- *The right to be left alone* - **Supreme Court Justice Louis Brandeis, 1890**.
- *The individuals, groups or institutions' right to decide when, how and until which limit information about them can be disclosed to third parties.* **Westin: Privacy and Freedom. New York, NY, Atheneum (1967)**

Much has already been written about privacy and the digital world, and in relation to ecommerce in particular. Both academic and non-academic literature abounds about the various social, political and legal concerns raised by online practices such as cookies, spam, web-bugs, personal data-mining and profiling. This chapter will instead limit itself specifically to the legal implications of the Research Scenario for privacy and agent-based computing. The wider "social" or political privacy aspects have been considered elsewhere[1].

Following our methodology, we first set out the basic principles and rules for the protection of personal data in the European Union, established in the

---

[1] There is an extensive bibliography on privacy. Some articles and reports are: D Korff : *Study on the protection of the rights and interests of legal persons with regard to the processing of personal data relating to such persons,* 1998; J Reidenberg and P Schwarz: *Online Services and Data Protection Law: Regulatory Responses,* 1998; ARETE Study for DG XV: *On-line services and data protection and the protection of privacy*; Consumers International, *Privacy@net: an international comparative study of consumer privacy on the internet.* 2001; Federal Trade Commission: *Privacy online: fair information practices in the electronic marketplace:a Federal Trade Commission report to Congress,* 2001; Organization for Economic Cooperation and Development: *Report On The OECD Forum Session On Privacy-Enhancing Technologies (PETs),* 2001; E Bohlman: *Privacy in the Age of Information,* 2001. J Grijpink and J Prins: *New Rules for Anonymous Electronic Transactions? An Exploration of the Private Law Implications of Digital Anonymity,* 2001; E Lin: *Prioritizing Privacy: A Constitutional Response To The Internet,* 2003.

1995, 1997 and 2002 Directives. We will then determine the risks to privacy that are posed by the use of electronic agents for online commerce and within the Research Scenario, and discuss how the laws apply to those risks. After examining several self-regulatory and technical means for reducing these risks, attempting to comply with the regulatory framework, we conclude with some suggestions for how to develop the information systems to comply with privacy requirements.

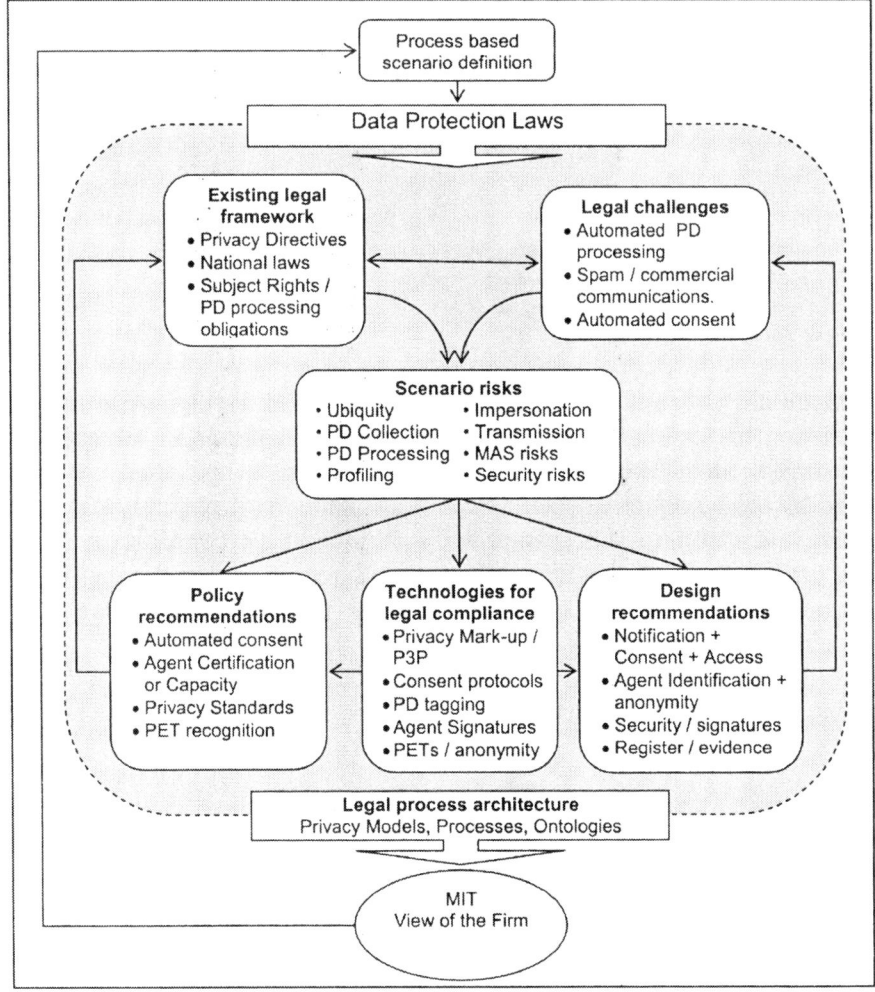

Figure 5-1. Personal Data Protection Analysis

1. AN OUTLINE OF PRIVACY LAW

Apart from the basic principle that privacy is a fundamental human right set out in the Universal Declaration of Human Rights, 1948[2] and the European Convention on Human Rights, 1970[3], the growth of potentially intrusive technologies has led various legal systems to legislate to protect individuals. These however vary throughout the world, as different systems incorporate different visions of the state and of privacy. While in the US most laws relating to privacy are sector specific, in the EU national laws and now the European Union laws provide a general protection and wide rights and obligations covering government and industry. Below, we look at the international and European framework.

The concept of privacy is commonly defined as the right to be let alone, as quoted by Justice Louis Brandeis above, or the ability to be secure in one's person, to be free from intrusion of others in one's person and in one's property. This concept is much broader than that of protection of personal data. Yet, with the increased intrusions of IT activities relating to Internet, and ecommerce and related activities such as data tracking and monitoring, it may be difficult to distinguish between personal data protection and privacy. In the European context, the 1995 Personal Data Directive described below is specific about its application to the protection of personal data. However a close reading of the document shows that its main objective seems to be the protection of privacy in a broader sense, with specific obligations reinforced by wide and general principles which must be respected.

1.1 The legal background

Data protection laws aim to strike a balance between the rights of individuals to privacy and the ability of organisations to use data for the purposes of their business. Several legal documents build up the legal framework for privacy protection. We now comment in turn the principal international documents and then the European Directives, whose rules will be developed below.

1.1.1 International instruments

The European Convention on Human Rights and Fundamental Freedoms[4] includes a right to respect for the private and family life of individuals, their

---

[2] Art. 12, Universal Declaration of Human Rights
[3] Art 8, European Convention on Human Rights
[4] Council of Europe Treaty 5, European Convention on Human Rights and Fundamental Freedoms, Rome, 4 November 1950 (ECHRFF).

home and correspondence[5]. Since then, IT developments over the last 20 years have led to increased public awareness of the issues in Europe (for example, the French privacy laws of 1978), and gave support for further guidelines and laws embodied in following two international documents.

In 1980 the Organisation for Economic Co-operation and Development adopted Guidelines Governing the Protection of Privacy and Transborder Flows of Personal Data[6]. These are: Collection limitation, Data quality, Purpose specification, Use limitation, Security safeguards, Openness, Individual participation, and Accountability. As we will see, these are reflected in the European Privacy Directives presented below.

In 1981 the Council of Europe opened the Convention for the Protection of Individuals with Regard to the Automatic Processing of Personal Data[7] () for signature by national governments. Those countries that wished to ratify Treaty 108 had to have in place national data protection legislation which met the standards of the Treaty. The treaty has been signed and ratified by 30 countries, including all the EU Member States It provides certain guarantees in relation to the collection and processing of personal data, and it outlaws the processing of "sensitive" data on a person's race, politics, health, religion, sexual life, criminal record, etc., in the absence of proper legal safeguards. The treaty establishes the individual's right to know what information is stored about him or her and, if necessary, to have it corrected, and also imposes certain restrictions on international flows of personal data to countries where legal regulation does not provide equivalent protection.

1.1.2 The European Directives

As opposed to the USA, where privacy protection is piecemeal (sector specific), the EU has established a broad framework for privacy protection in the 1995 European Directive on Data Protection (effective in October 1998), supplemented by the 1997 – 2002 Telecommunications and Data Protection Directives. European action was justified on the basis of the need to avoid barriers to the free movement of data.

Directive 95/46/EC[8] (the "Data Protection Directive") on the protection of individuals with regard to the processing of personal data and on the free

---

[5] Art. 8 ECHRFF.

[6] OECD Fair Information Principles: Recommendation of the Council Concerning Guidelines Governing the Protection of Privacy and Trans-border Flows of Personal Data (23rd September, 1980).

[7] Council of Europe Treaty 108, Convention for the Protection of Individuals with Regard to the Automatic Processing of Personal Data, Strasbourg, 28 January 1981.

[8] Directive 95/46/EC of the European parliament and of the council of 24 October 1995 on the protection of individuals with regard to the processing of personal data and on the free movement of such data.

movement of such data, is a more general directive covering all aspects of personal data processing.

Directive 97/66/EC[9] (The "Privacy in the Telecommunications Sector Directive") on the processing of personal data and the protection of privacy in the telecommunications sector, is sector specific. The adoption of the this Directive coincided with work that was proceeding at the GATT on the services chapter. It was a response to the opening of the telecommunications market and also the rapid deployment of new technologies such as caller line identification, which were raising significant public privacy issues. This Directive has been replaced by Directive 2002/58/EC on Privacy and Electronic Communications[10].

Member states were slow in implementing the 1995 and 1997 Directives. The Commission decided in December 1999 to take France, Germany, Ireland, Luxembourg and the Netherlands to the European Court of Justice. Since then, only France has now to implement the Directives, and has a bill before parliament[11]. Apart from late implementation, another problem is that the 1995 Directive allows Member States a degree of freedom as to how to implement some aspects of the law. In particular, it allows Member States to set varying levels for certain types of protection, such as security measures, offsetting the advantages of a unifying law. National laws implementing the Directive differ one from another in various ways, resulting in a lack of harmonisation which makes privacy compliance in trans-border electronic systems more difficult. For instance, some Member States have taken a more generous approach to the extent of manual data covered than others, some have tough rules for the submission of details of assessable processing requirements before permitting Data Controllers to appear on the public register. Variations also exist between the organisations that oversee data privacy and the ways they fine irregular behaviour.

1.2   European Data Protection Legislation

The 1995 Data Protection Directive provides a wide-ranging approach to data protection, whose effect is to limit the collection of data, control how it is used and requires comprehensive disclosure on the same. The European approach has also set up Privacy Commissions or Agencies for organising the protection of individual's rights, and carrying out monitoring activities of

---

[9] Directive 97/66/EC on the processing of personal data and the protection of privacy in the telecommunications sector (full reference at end of monograph).

[10] Directive 2002/58/EC on the processing of personal data and the protection of privacy in the electronic communications sector.

[11] European Commission: *First report on the implementation of the Data Protection Directive (95/46/EC)* (2003), and for France, *Projet de loi relatif à la protection des personnes physiques à l'égard des traitements de données à caractère personnel*, voted 30 January 2002.

corporate behaviour. In the following sections, we review the principle elements of the legal framework in turn:

- The data protection principles (section 1.2.1)
- A definition of privacy "actors" or roles (Data Subject, Data Controller, Data Processor (section 1.2.2)
- The concept and definition of Personal Data (section 1.2.3)
- An outline of the obligations and rights of the actors (section 1.2.4 and 1.2.5)
- Limitations on data uses (section 1.2.6)
- A prohibition on disclosures of data to third parties that do not provide adequate protection (section 1.2.7)

To complete the picture, we also briefly review the two Privacy in the Telecoms Sector Directives (1997-2002) in section 1.2.8.

1.2.1   European Data Protection Principles

The 1995 Personal Data Directive embodies fairly closely the general principles set out in the 1980 OECD Guidelines. These principles are:

1. Purpose Limitation (Art.6): Data should be processed for a fairly and specific purpose and subsequently used or further communicated only insofar as this is not incompatible with the purpose of the transfer[12].
2. Data quality and proportionality (Art.6): Data should be accurate and, where necessary, kept up to date. The data should be adequate, relevant and not excessive in relation to the purposes for which they are transferred or further processed.
3. Social justification (Art. 7): Personal data may only be processed if the Data Subject has given his unambiguous consent[13]; if processing is necessary for the performance of a contract or legal obligation; or if processing is necessary for purpose of legitimate interests pursued by a Controller or third party to whom data are disclosed, except when overridden by fundamental rights or interests of the Data Subject.
4. Transparency (Arts.10/11): Individuals should be provided with information as to the purpose of the processing and the identity of the

---

[12] The only exemptions to this rule would be those necessary in a democratic society on one of the grounds listed in Article 13 of the Directive.

[13] "freely given" means without pressure; "informed" means the Data Subject must be able to balance risks; "specific" means related to a particular purpose. This provision establishes the need to strike a reasonable balance, in practice, between the business interest of the Data Controllers and the privacy of Data Subjects. This balance is first evaluated by the Data Controllers under the supervision of the data protection authorities, although if required, the courts have the final decision.

Data Controller in the third country and other information insofar as this is necessary to ensure fairness[14].

5. The prohibition of processing of sensitive data (Art. 8): Sensitive data is Personal data revealing racial or ethnic origin, political opinions, religious or philosophical beliefs, trade-union membership, and the processing of data concerning health or sex life. If profile information reveals an individuals morals which fall within scope of Article 8, Data Processors must find grounds in Art.8.2 to be able to process such data (Data Subject's consent or if manifestly made public by Data Subject).

6. Security (Art.17): Technical and organisational security measures should be taken by the Data Controller that are appropriate to the risks presented by the processing. Any person acting under the authority of the Data Controller, including a processor, must not process data except on instructions from the Controller.

1.2.2   The actors involved

The 1995 Data Protection Directive divides the actors involved in a data related operation in four main categories:

- Data Subject: this is the person from whom or about whom data is collected and/or disclosed. Therefore anyone can be a Data Subject because nowadays virtually everybody discloses personal data on a daily basis.
- Data Controller (Art. 2d): this is the natural or legal person, public authority, agency or any other body which alone or jointly with others determines the purposes and means of the processing of personal data. In other words, a person is a Data Controller if the processing of personal data is undertaken for their benefit and they decide what personal data should be processed and why. A typical example of a Data Controller is an employer.
- Data Processor (Art. 2e): The natural or legal person, public authority, agency or any other body, which processes personal data on behalf of the Data Controller.
- Data Recipient (Art. 2g): The natural or legal person, public authority, agency or any other body to whom data are disclosed, whether a third party or not. However, authorities which may receive data in the framework of a particular inquiry shall not be regarded as recipients.

---

[14] The only exemptions permitted should be in line with Articles 11(2) and 13 of the Directive.

1.2.3   The concept of Personal Data

The 1995 Data Protection Directive defines Personal Data in Art.2a as "any information relating to an identified or identifiable natural person" (who becomes a "Data Subject"). An identifiable person is one who can be identifiable, directly or indirectly, in particular by reference to an identification number or to one or more factors specifics to his physical, physiological, mental, economic, cultural, or social identity.

This is fairly vague, and needs to be considered in each circumstance:
-   Data from an Identified Person: This is data linked to a natural person. But when is a person considered to be identified? When his name and national ID card number or address is provided seems to be the minimum. The Directive assists: "... in particular by reference to an identification number or to one or more factors specifics to his physical, physiological, mental, economic, cultural, or social identity".
-   Data from an Identifiable Person: This is data from a natural person who is not yet identified but who can be identifiable directly or indirectly, through one or various processes. The Directive gives some guidelines as to identification: to determine whether a person is identifiable, account should be taken of all the means likely reasonably to be used either by the Controller or by any other person to identify the said person.

Accordingly personal data means data which relates to a living individual who can be identified from that data or from that data and other information which is in the possession of, or is likely to come into the possession of, the Data Controller.

The Directive adds a sub-category of "Sensitive Data", which is data relating to racial or ethnic origin, political opinions, religious or philosophical beliefs, trade-union membership, data concerning health or sexual preference. Sensitive data should never be processed except in specific circumstances, set out below in section 1.2.6.

1.2.4   Data Subject Rights

One of the principle objectives of the Directive is to establish the rights of individuals in relation to data processing and which they can enforce against Data Controllers. These rights are the following.

a) Right to be informed of any data processing (Arts. 10 and 11)

Data Controllers are required to inform Data Subjects whenever they collect personal data concerning them, unless they have previously been informed. Data Subjects have the right to be informed of: the identity of the Controller, the purposes for the processing and any further information such as the recipients of the data and the specific rights that Data Subjects are entitled to. Data subjects also have the right to receive this information whether the data was obtained directly or indirectly from third parties.

Derogation may be allowed in the latter case if giving this information proves impossible or extremely difficult, or if the law requires it to, for example in the event of criminal investigations. Information must be given either at time of collection or when first recorded or disclosed. At least the identity of the Data Controller and the purpose of processing must be supplied. Further information is necessary to ensure "fair" processing of data.

b) Right to access the data (art. 12)

Data Subjects are entitled to contact any Data Controller to know whether or not any processing of their personal data is taking place, to receive a copy of the data in an intelligible form and to be given any available information about their sources. A reasonable fee for providing access may be charged in some cases.

c) Right to rectification (art. 12.2)

If the personal data are inaccurate or unlawfully processed, Data Subjects are entitled to ask for the correction, blocking or erasure of the data. In these cases, the Data Subject may also require the Data Controller to notify third parties who had previously seen the incorrect data, unless this proves impossible.

d) Right to object (art. 14)

A right to object is granted unconditionally as regards the processing of personal data for direct marketing purposes, and with certain conditions for public interest tasks carried out by official authorities or when the Controller or third party has a legitimate interest (see below in section 1.2.6).

e) Right not to be subject to a automatic decision which produces legal effects (art.15)

Decisions which significantly affect the Data Subject, such as the decision to grant a loan or issue insurance, might be taken on the sole basis of automated data processing. Therefore, the Data Controller must adopt suitable safeguards, such as giving the Data Subject the opportunity to discuss the rationale behind the data collected or to contest decisions based on inaccurate data. Exceptions include performance of a contract or legitimate interest (see section 1.2.6 below).

f) Exemptions and restrictions (Art. 13)

The right to privacy may sometimes conflict with freedom of expression and in particular, freedom of the press and media. National law might allow other exceptions to provisions of the Directive, including the obligation to inform the Data Subject; the publicising of data processing operations; the obligation to respect the basic principles of good data management practice. Such exceptions are permitted if, among other things, it is necessary on grounds of national security, defence, crime detection, enforcement of criminal law, or to protect Data Subjects or the rights and freedom of others. Additionally, derogation from the right to access data may be granted for data processed for scientific or statistical purposes.

g) Liability and Remedy (Arts. 22, 23)

Every person has the right to judicial remedy for any breach of the rights guaranteed by applicable national law. In addition, any person who has suffered damage as a result of unlawful processing or of any act incompatible with the national provisions is entitled to receive compensation from the Data Controller for the damage suffered.

1.2.5   Data Controller Obligations

a) Applicable law (Art.4)

Each Data Controller must comply with the data processing rules of the Member State where it is established even if the data processed belongs to an individual residing in another State. When the Data Controller is not established in the Community (e.g. a foreign company), it has to comply with the laws of the Member State(s) if the processing equipment is located within the European Community[15].

b) Respect of the Directive's general principles

The Data Controller must guarantee the respect of the principles set out above, in particular regarding data quality and technical security. It must also be responsible for the circumstances under which processing can be carried out. In particular, personal data must be:

– processed fairly and lawfully;
– collected for specified, explicit and legitimate purposes and not further processed in a way incompatible with those purposes. Further processing of data for historical, statistical or scientific purposes shall not be considered as incompatible so long as appropriate safeguards are maintained;
– adequate, relevant and not excessive in relation to the purposes for which they are collected and/or further processed;
– accurate and, where necessary, kept up to date; every reasonable step must be taken to ensure that data which are inaccurate or incomplete, having regard to the purposes for which they were collected or for which they are further processed, are erased or rectified;
– kept in a form which permits identification of Data Subjects for no longer than is necessary for the purposes for which the data were collected or for which they are further processed. Member States shall lay down

---

[15] For example, the Art. 5 of the UK Data Protection Act 1998 states that the Act governs Data Controllers established in the UK and the data are processed in the context of that establishment, or the Data Controller is established neither in the United Kingdom nor in any other EEA State but uses equipment in the UK for processing the data otherwise than for the purposes of transit through the UK.

appropriate safeguards for personal data stored for longer periods for historical, statistical or scientific use[16].

c) Security requirements (Arts. 16 and 17)

Data Controllers must set up adequate security measures to safeguard personal data which they are processing from destruction, loss, unauthorised access or disclosure. This would include, for example, security against hacking on any web site which collects visitors' e-mail addresses. The security measures adopted will also be dependent on the state of the art and the cost of their implementation. Furthermore, all Data Controllers must put in place processing contracts with their Data Processors. These contracts must be in writing and must set out what the Data Processor may or may not do with the personal data, including what security measures should be taken to safeguard the data.

d) Obligation to notify the supervisory authority (Arts. 18 and 19)

The Directive states that each Member State must provide one or more supervisory authorities to monitor the application of the Directive. One responsibility of the supervisory authority is to maintain an updated public register so that the general public has access to the names of all Data Controllers and the type of processing they do. In principle, all Data Controllers must notify supervisory authorities when they process data. Member States may require prior checking, to be carried out by the supervisory authority, before data processing operations that involve particular risks may be undertaken. Member States may provide for simplification or exemption from notification for specific types of processing which do not entail particular risks. Exception and simplification can also be granted when, in conformity with national law, an independent officer in charge of data protection has been appointed by the Controller.

Obviously, a computer agent will in general not be able to carry out most of these obligations, for example conclude an appropriate contract with a Data Processor. We assume readers may start to uncover by themselves some the daunting challenges that privacy obligations pose to legal compliance in the Research Scenario. Following our methodology, we postpone discussion of these issues until after we have covered the current legal architecture.

1.2.6 Data uses: What can be done with the Personal Data?

a) Defining Processing

The Data Protection Directive applies when personal data is processed or is to be processed by a computer or is recorded or to be recorded in a

---

[16] Art. 6 of the Data Protection Directive. Under this provision, for example Spain has allowed a period of one year from personal contact data.

structured manual filing system. Article 2.b defines processing as: "Any operation or set of operations which is performed upon personal data, whether or not by automatic means, such as collection, recording, organisation, storage, adaptation or alteration, retrieval, consultation, use, disclosure by transmission, dissemination or otherwise making available, alignment, or combination, blocking, erasure or destruction". This covers just about any action a software agent may take.

b) Sensitive data

Article 8 of the Data Protection Directive states very stringent rules to the processing of sensitive data. As a general rule, such data cannot be processed at all. Derogation is tolerated under very specific circumstances. These circumstances include the Data Subject's explicit consent to process sensitive data, the processing of data mandated by employment law, where it may be impossible for the Data Subject to consent (e.g. blood test to the victim of a road accident), processing of data has been publicly announced by the Data Subject or processing of data about members by trade unions, political parties or churches. Member states may provide for additional exceptions for reasons of substantial public interest.

c) Justifications

The approach laid down by the Directive is that at least one of a limited number of justifications must exist before processing of personal data is legitimate. Consent is one way to compliance, but other potential justifications for processing personal data are available. It is also critical to make sure that processing complies with the justification that has been given for that processing. For example, if consent is given for a particular form of processing, further or different processing would not comply with data privacy rules. Justification for processing sensitive data is more limited. The following Table 5-1 summarises available justifications.

Table 5-1. Justifications for personal data processing

Personal Data	Sensitive Personal Data:
Consent	Explicit consent
Contract conclusion or performance	Rights / obligations under employment law
Legal obligations	Deliberate publication by Data Subject
Vital interests of Data Subject	Vital interests of Data Subject
Legitimate interests of Data Controller (unless overridden by Data Subject's rights and freedoms)	Processing by non-profit-making political, philosophical, religious, or trade union bodies
Public function	

1.2.7   Transferring data

Under Art.25 further transfers of the personal data by the recipient of the original data transfer should be permitted only where the second recipient is also subject to rules affording an adequate level of protection. The only exceptions permitted should be in line with Article 26(1) of the Directive (consent, performance of contract, interests of Data Subject, public interest, etc.)

- To EU-countries: Member States shall neither restrict nor prohibit the free flow of personal data between Member States for reasons connected with the protection afforded.
- To non-EU countries: Art.25 establishes that personal data can only be transferred to countries outside the EU that guarantee an "adequate" level of protection. This level is considered by the Working Party on Data Protection (art. 29) which has issued some guidelines: privacy legislation of the third country should at least include some of the basic principles of the directive. Where a non-EU country does not ensure an adequate level of protection, the Directive requires the blocking of specific transfers. Protection can be provided by means of a contract between the company sending the data and the Non-EU Company receiving the data, to provide for adequate safeguards with respect to the protection of privacy and fundamental rights and freedoms of individuals and the exercise of the corresponding rights.

The determination of which countries provide an adequate level of data protection will become vital to some countries that want to maintain close economic relations with the European Union. For example, the lack of privacy regulation in the US caused US organisations to be required to respond to EU rules throughout the organisation. To avoid data blocking, the EU and the US Department of Commerce agreed on a set of "Safe harbour" principles in 2000[17]. Some countries (Argentina, Hungary, Switzerland and Canada) have been approved for data transfers[18].

---

[17] Safe Harbor Privacy Principles issued by the U.S. Department Of Commerce on July 24, 2000 and September 19, 2000 and EC Decisions 520/2000/EC and C(2000)2441 recognising the Safe Harbour international privacy principles issued by the US Department of Commerce. Documents available at http://www.export.gov/safeHarbor/sh_documents.html.

[18] A list of current approvals is available at http://europa.eu.int/comm/internal_market/privacy/adequacy_en.htm (last visited 20/09/2003).

1.2.8   The 1997 and 2002 Privacy Directives

The 1997 Privacy in the Telecoms Sector Directive[19] applies to processing of personal data in connection with the provision of publicly available telecommunications services in public telecommunications networks in the Community. Some of the most relevant provisions include the following:

- Member States must take the necessary measures in order to prohibit the listening, tapping, storage, or other kinds of interception or surveillance of communications
- The right to privacy of natural persons and the legitimate interest of legal persons require that subscribers are able to determine the extent to which their personal data are published in a directory.
- Unsolicited calls: "the use of automated calling systems for the purpose of direct marketing may only be allowed in respect to subscribers who have given their prior consent" (opt in system).

This Directive has been superseded in many relevant ways by the 2002 Privacy and Electronic Communications Directive[20], whose principal relevant provisions include:

- The use of location data (other than traffic data) must be anonymous or subject to the explicit informed consent of the individual phone user and users should have the possibility to temporarily block the processing of location data at any time (Art 9).
- The use of automated calling systems, fax, or email for the purposes of direct marketing may only be allowed in respect of persons who have given their prior consent. This requirement is relaxed in the event that the original identifying data (such as a phone number) is obtained from the person in the context of prior dealings (sales or service), and that the marketing is of the company's own similar products or services. Customers must still be given the opportunity to object or reject the message each time (Art 13.1 and 13.2).
- Member States may choose an opt-in or opt-out system for other forms of unsolicited commercial communications: "unsolicited communications for the purposes of direct marketing are not allowed either without the consent of the subscribers concerned or in respect of subscribers who do not wish to receive these communications, the choice between these options to be determined by national legislation" (Art 13.3).
- All communications must identify the sender and provide an address for cancelling the communications (Art 13.4).

---

[19] Reference in note 9 above.
[20] Reference in note 10 above.

1.3   A data protection summary

Before we proceed, we present here the following points that set out the main rules that should be applied to personal data processing within the Research Scenario:

1. Personal Data should be processed fairly and lawfully and may not be processed unless the Data Controller can satisfy one of the conditions for processing set out in the Act.
2. The principal means for authorising processing will be by obtaining the Data Subject's consent.
3. Data should be obtained only for specified and lawful purposes.
4. Data should be adequate, relevant and not excessive.
5. Data should be accurate and, where necessary, kept up to date.
6. Data should not be kept longer than is necessary for the purposes for which it is processed.
7. Data should be processed in accordance with the rights of the Data Subject under the Act. Sensitive data has a special treatment.
8. Appropriate technical and organisational measures should be taken against unauthorised or unlawful processing of personal data and against accidental loss or destruction of, or damage to, personal data.
9. Data should not be transferred to a person in a country or territory outside the European Economic Area unless that person, country or territory ensures an adequate level of protection for the rights and freedoms of Data Subjects in relation to the processing of personal data.

2.   PRIVACY ISSUES RAISED BY INTELLIGENT AGENTS

This section will look at privacy risks and threats arising through the use of software agents in our research scenario, due to processes such as profiling, marketing, data mining and covert actions and surveillance, including the use of RFID-enhanced products for interactions with clients and product tracking. First, to put these in context, we briefly review privacy issues raised by normal online commerce. Then, we shall review the threats specific to agent processing, including agent security and multi-agent system problems.

2.1   "Traditional" aspects of e-business that may cause privacy problems

In traditional online commerce, there are a multitude of different actions, processes and activities that can constitute privacy invasion. Intermediaries (e.g. Access Service Providers), online merchants and other sites, (non trusted third parties), Internet service providers (searches, payments, gateways) all collect and transmit data in ways which may infringe on a persons privacy (in principle) and violate privacy protection laws. Such activities include:

– browser chatter, the covert collection of data from browsing activities and server recordings (logfiles),
– the collection of personal data on/from Websites and planting and monitoring cookies and web-bugs,
– email address harvesting, commercial emails, spam and other direct marketing activities,
– the transfer or sale of files to third parties (advertisers, data aggregators, etc.) and countries where there is little or lower privacy protection
– the hidden downloading programs with privacy killing side-effects (spyware)
– breaches of privacy statements: when online traders do not respect the privacy policies published on their websites.

The main risks involve collecting, storing, processing and transmitting personal data. As we have seen above, these are the regulated activities under the data protection legislation enacted in Europe. Privacy issues of now traditional e-business processes have been addressed elsewhere[21], while we consider in this monograph those risks specific to agent processing in the Research Scenario.

2.2   Privacy risks in the Research Scenario

Over and above the traditional privacy invasive activities and processes in online commerce, software agents are recognised to present certain specific risks in relation to personal data processing[22]. This is all the more so in an area of ubiquitous computing, presented by the Research Scenario, where electronically identified objects may permit wider and more intense data collection. First, we comment on these risks (2.2.1), before considering the agents that may pose them (2.2.2) and which of their processes are problematic (2.2.3). Finally, given the importance of security, we will also consider the security issues posed by agent processing.

2.2.1   Overall risks

In the context of the Research Scenario there are certain aspects and processes of ubiquitous computing using software agents that pose problems over and above the normal Internet related privacy threats mentioned above.

---

[21] See references in note 1 above.
[22] JJ Borking et al: *Intelligent Software Agents and Privacy,* 1999.

While the risks posed by the autonomy of software agents and, more so, the capacity for multiplied interactions with IT systems through the "augmented reality" scenarios (the "Big Brother" accusations) have been overblown in the press, there are a number of legitimate concerns[23]. These include the following risks[24]:

- **Wide Coverage**: privacy threatening agents may be more present, through interacting with RFID-enhanced daily artefacts (cups, containers, packaging, etc.) and places (home, office, shops). This could lead to constant monitoring and data collection. This may lead to problems of data security (in transmissions) and breaches of principles of data quality and proportionality.
- **Loss of awareness**: individuals may be aware that data is collected when they use credit or store cards, however with "disappearing computers" lodged in everyday objects (e.g. using RDIF labels) they will be unaware that data (visual, tactile, audio) can be and is being collected. This goes against principles of transparency and notice.
- **More data collected**: as data is being collected from more sources, including greater details about 24 hour individual behaviour and preferences. In the Research Scenario, this would include shopping habits, preferred products, how much time is spent in front of one shelf or another inside the store.
- **New data types being collected**: new types of data can be collected, including seemingly minor details such as physical location, browsing or eating habits, health biorhythms, etc. This could conflict with the principles of proportionality.
- **More processing**: this greater amount of data of higher detail can be cross-related to other data for improved profiling and data mining, exposing more details about in the individual that is "more than the sum of the parts". This potentially infringes use limitation and purpose specification. One of the main purposes of the Research Scenario processes is to create detailed and incremental user profiles, to analyse and improve store services, products and advertising methods.

In summary, depending on the actual processes and programming of any agents linked to RFID artefacts, unprotected or uncontrolled agents may unlawfully prejudice the privacy of individuals, collecting and exchanging personal data of agent-users or interlocutors with other systems and data

---

[23] Commented, for example, in Auto-ID centre director Kevin Ashton's testimony to California Sate Senate Subcommittee on New Technologies, 18th August 2003. Both sides of the debate were heard at the MIT sponsored RFID Privacy Workshop on November 15, 2003. See in particular K Albrecht: *RFID: Privacy and Societal Implications* and R Kumar: *Interaction of RFID Technology and Public Policy. Online at http://www.rfidprivacy.org/agenda.php.*
[24] M Langheinrich: *Privacy by design,* 2000.

collection points. It is important to note that, just like CCTV or web-cookies, it is not the technologies in themselves that are threatening but the processes and applications to which they are put, the quality of the programming and the security levels incorporated in their design.

In this monograph, we focus on software agents in particular. One of the principles of their use is delegation: the user has to place a certain degree of confidence in the agent, as it carries out its operations. This confidence is mainly the belief that it will carry out these functions as programmed and that it will not be "tapped" for information. As an agent collects, processes, learns, stores and distributes data about its user and the user's activities, the agent will possess an increasingly wide variety and amount of information which should not always be divulged unless specifically required for a transaction. However, while operating autonomously, an agent may be required or be forced to reveal information about the agent-user that this person may not wish to be shared. The danger of this is heightened as agents gain more sophistication and evolve towards more autonomy.

There are many possible situations where the agent may reveal data about the agent-user that could be potentially significant and adversely affect the user and his/her privacy. One situation is when an agent "visits" a web-site, for example in the Research Scenario the store's own site. Logs record not only website traffic and movements, and store information transmitted to the site (passwords, customer addresses, credit card details, etc.) but also more detailed activity records: IP addresses, time and details of purchases or pages viewed.

These data can thereafter be used to profile a person for marketing or other reasons. Similar profiles may be made up on the basis of interaction with RFID tags, notably enabling the retail store to offer customised services to clients and improve its supply management. More dangerously, however, such accumulated information could be transmitted to other groups, often without the knowledge or consent of the subject, who is unaware of the extent of the agent's activities. While users normally have a certain amount of discretion about how much personal data to reveal, with the large amount of data mining capacity today there is a potential for even more significant data collection and exploitation about the most sensitive personal matters (finances, relationships, illnesses, insurance, employment, etc.) especially if this information was in the hands of an agent that is beyond the immediate control of the user.

2.2.2   Agents liable to privacy threats

The agents contemplated in the Research Scenario include various processes and services that are based on personal data. The agents or services in question are:
– Information retrieval agents

– Profiling and personalisation agents
– Interface / interaction agents
– Broker / contracting agents
– Reminder agents
– Filtering agents
– Geographic location agents

The software agents described in Chapters 2 and 3 (A, B, C and D) mainly determine their autonomous action on the basis of detailed information about the user that is stored within the agent or to which it has access. In addition, they may obtain input from RFID-enhanced products interacting with the store's systems. Using this data, the agents may accept or refuse advertised offers, make purchases without warning the user, or establish comparative shopping tables and product comparisons. It is this data, including preferences, habits, and financial situation, which could be considered personal data and which is likely to be collected and possibly stolen or interfered with. In the final section of this chapter, we analyse the specific processes of two of these agents, B and C, in relation to privacy threats and compliance processes.

2.2.3 Agent related privacy threatening processes

The principal processes of agents within the Research Scenario that create privacy risks are:
– The (automatic) data collection from users, from users' agents, from user's interaction with RFID-enhanced products, or from data bases of information about the individual (including personal or automatic profiles).
– The automatic processing of that data for profiling, direct marketing or decision making purposes (e.g. granting of credit): traffic flow, shopping or consumption patterns, daily habits, etc.
– The monitoring of user and agent operations, both openly and covertly.
– Processes for controlling the agent and agent data in relation to interactions with third parties: the risks of loss of control or security breaches (security threats are commented below).
– Notification, information and consent processes: whether agents can receive notifications from websites and other service providers and grant consent for processing.
– The exchange of personal data with the environment and with other systems.
– Processes for implementing the right of objection and the exercise of rights of access to data.

These threats include: collecting without consent, collecting too much data, revealing sensitive data, invading a person's area of autonomy (interference), automatic decision-making and data confusion.

The fact that agents can act for a multiplicity of parties brings a whole new set of problems. In a multi-agent infrastructure, other actors such as intermediary agents, including portals, information brokers, match makers, agent hosts, etc., act to put two agents in contact. Two examples of intermediary agents where privacy problems may arise are web proxies and mobile agents.

In summary, the two main categories of privacy risks posed by the use of agents are[25]:

1. Risks generated by agents acting on behalf of a user (user-agents) through the revealing of the personal data about the user, either to a person or agent it is interacting with or to a third party; and
2. Risks created by third party agents that act on behalf of others, such as traffic flow monitoring, geo-location, data mining and even attempts to obtain personal information directly from the user's agent.

2.2.4   Agent security problems

Network security is one of the major issues today. When consumer-merchant transactions are carried out by agents, new network security threats appear. Broadly speaking, there are two kinds of threats to agent transactions: external threats which involve third party action and internal threats where only the user / interlocutor are involved. We review these in turn, before commenting on additional problems arising due to multi-agent environments.

External network threats come from a third party which doesn't belong to the agent system. These include:

–   Physical attack: An attacker can physically access the end user's computer or device and obtain personal data (in a profile file), or modify it by adding or deleting elements without the user noticing. An intruder can also physically access the service provider system and read data stored there about different users.
–   Impersonation: An attacker can impersonate the service provider in order to capture user data. On the other, it can impersonate the user and access the service provider system on false pretences and initiate any transactions.
–   Network attacks. An attacker can monitor network activity to obtain end user data (such as credit card numbers, etc.). The personal data may be untouched or modified. In addition, the intruder can replay a profile request and receive profile data (packet replay).

Internal network threats are security threats which come from any party inside the system. Malicious usage occurs when someone within the agent network uses data for unauthorised activities, including selling data to third

---

[25] JJ Borking et al, op cit., 1999.

parties (advertising or direct marketing companies are prime buyers), profiling automatically the users, etc. In addition, ISPs with appropriate access can read, write or modify personal data in ways which are not authorised or are purposefully incorrect.

Agents can also operate in a multi-agent environment where many other actors are involved: portals, agent service providers, agent hosts, information brokers, etc... These put agents in contact with each other or with other network objects (sites, etc.). The most significant threats in a multi-agent environment are:

- Malicious usage. This occurs when the threatening agent is a simple active object on the network: a hidden link for example (or web-bugs, cookies) and carries out unauthorised or malicious activities. As agents multiply and carry out more and more transmissions and other actions, more data is shared and may be subject to eavesdropping, modification, storing or other unauthorised action by the active object.
- Impersonation. As above, this happens when the third party agent or environment is an intermediate service that poses as a legitimate object. This is a serious risk for mobile agents which move from host to host and may have delegated tasks to other agents.
- Network attacks. Serious security issues occur in relation to mobile agents which use the network to move and replicate from one host or agent server to another. This process will come under security threat if one of the hosts is malicious.

We have now set out the privacy risks that are posed by the processes of agents operating within the research scenario and also more generally within multi-agent environments. In the next section, we turn to analyse the scenario from a legal point of view and consider how privacy regulations apply to these processes.

3. LEGAL ANALYSIS OF AGENT-RELATED PRIVACY RISKS

We have seen that the activities of agents within the research scenario will lead to numerous ways of processing personal data, such as the data an agent provides to other agents during transactions, the data an agent collects for its user, and the data the agent-provider can extract from the agent. Generally speaking, to protect the privacy of the persons involved it is important that such personal data are properly collected, that they are necessary for legitimate purposes, that the data will not be disclosed to the wrong persons and that personal data are not processed without the knowledge of the persons concerned. These are principles that have been set out in the outline of European privacy laws in section 1 above. This section 3 aims to comment on how they apply to the agents contemplated in the Research Scenario.

In section 3.1 we comment on the application of data protection laws to the agents in question, while in section 3.2 we analyse more particularly certain privacy threatening aspects of multi-agent environments.

3.1   Privacy law applied to software agent processes

In relation to the different processes and actions of agents contemplated within the Research Scenario, the main issue is whether and if so how data protection laws are applicable to agents and to agent transactions. We will need to consider agents as Data Subject, Data Controller or Data Processor.

Before considering how data protection laws would apply to agents within the scenario, we need to consider if they will hold personal data (if not, there are no legal privacy risks). The answer is probably yes, especially if it stores delivery data such as name, address, or telephone, or financial details (payment agents) but also seemingly more innocuous data about purchasing habits and connectivity. Agents need to have specific personal data about agent-users so that they can achieve the results programmed into them. These data may be kept in a "user-profile" that may be automatically extended as the agent learns about its user's habits. This will constitute personal data as defined by the Data Protection Directive: information relating to an identified or identifiable natural person.

Although there may be means of reducing the risk by "pseudonymising" or completely anonymising the processing, the data may be related to the shopper within the general framework of the store's agent system. In addition, traffic information relating to itinerary (network location) and connection (communications between agent and resources) may also be considered personal in certain circumstances, such as fixed (static) IP addresses allocated to a client, user or personal mobile device.

3.1.1   Application of the data protection principles

If agents such as A, B, C or D described in chapters 2 and 3 "hold" or process personal data, the next question is whether software agents can themselves be subject to the data protection principles, and in what capacity: as Data Controller, Processor or Subject? We also need to consider the position of agent hosts who may control to a certain extent the processing of the agents in question.

Although these roles of Data Controller and Data Processor are primarily responsible for observing data privacy rules, they are limited under the Data

Protection Directive to natural or legal persons or other legal bodies[26]. The agent software could therefore not be considered the Data Controller or Processor, and the agent could not incur liabilities under the Data Protection Directive as such: it has no legal identity. It would, however, be considered equipment under the control of a person, i.e. the determined means for processing, and we contend that it is likely and logical that the principal obligations and liabilities for agent processing would attach to the "controller" of the agent.

In the Research Scenario, if the agent is supplied and controlled by the store, for example with the agent's user profile database within the store's information system, the store would be the Data Controller, and potentially the Data Processor. The same may apply to a third party agent provider.

The question is more difficult if the agent is either software or a service purchased by the user, and is under his or her control. If the agent is executed within the systems of the consumer (e.g. on a workstation at home), then it seems that the user could be considered the Data Controller of his or her own personal data. If however, the agent is run on third party systems or host, while the user is still the Data Controller (determining when and what processing is carried out), it is likely that that third party could be considered the Data Processor. In which case the obligations outlined above for Data Processors must be respected by that third party.

Another case is that of an agent operating on behalf of a company in a third country (non-EU/EEA). According to Art. 4 of the Directive, the EU Data Protection laws only apply if the processing can be considered to take place in the EU. This raises the question of deciding where the agent "is" or "executes". This will be a difficult question to answer, either if the agent executes in a variety of computers some of which may be outside the EU (distributed agent computing) or if the agent is mobile and can replicate itself in several hosts inside or outside the EU.

Turning to the Data Subject, this must be a natural person. Therefore the agent cannot be considered a Data Subject. However, the agent itself may constitute data of the agent-user, its parameters and programming representing facts, beliefs and other data that could be linked to the agent-user. Whether the data is in fact personal (i.e. of an identified or identifiable person) will depend on the strength of the link for identification, for example if the agent stores or processes identification data such as the name and address of the user. As we have seen, in the Research Scenario shopping or information agents are likely to store user profiles, so this is most likely.

---

[26] Art. 2 (d) and (e) of the Data Protection Directive.

In addition, agents in general might be considered automated decision making processes under Article 15 of the Data Protection Directive[27]. This article grants persons the right not to be subject to a decision that produces legal or otherwise significant effects on them (e.g. performance grading, credit rating) which is based solely on automated processing of certain data. The wording of this article suffers from ambiguity and complexity, referring to "certain personal aspects relating to data subject", and "suitable measures to safeguard legitimate interests". Although it may not be aimed at the kind of decision taken by shopping related software agents, they are potentially covered, for example in respect of any automated profiling (Agent A) or the sending of adverts (Agent B). The question of how legal or significant the effects of any agent decision within the Research Scenario are, is also open. Articles 15 and 12(a) also grant persons certain rights of access to the knowledge of the logic of such automatic processing, which will require advanced autonomous agents (that may redefine their own decision processes) to incorporate special registration processes[28].

As a consequence of this, if an agent under the control of a trader or merchant (or a third party on behalf of the merchant) does indeed process customer personal data and/or that agent itself represents personal data, care must be taken to ensure that all the procedures for consent and notification are given, and Data Subject's rights of access and modification are satisfied. The specific obligations will depend on the agent processes of any implementation of the Research Scenario.

The design of the agent processes should also incorporate adequate levels of protection in terms of security, confidentiality and data integrity[29]. This is all the more so if such data could be considered sensitive data (e.g. medical or religious data used to determine which products may safely be purchased by the consumer), whereupon additional obligations as to processing accrue to Data Controllers – namely obtaining explicit informed consent from the Data Subject on collection.

The question whether agent hosts, providing a processing environment for agents controlled by other parties, are covered by the Directive, is difficult to determine. To the extent that they process any personal data themselves e.g. through storage, transmission or reproduction of the data (this depends on the configuration of the services offered by the host, such as

---

[27] There is an argument that if "decision" is considered broadly as including the parameterisation of the agent, the actual decision-maker may be the person who establishes these parameters, who in certain cases may be the shopper.

[28] L Bygrave, *Minding the Machine: Article 15 of the EC Data Protection Directive*, 2000 and *Electronic Agents and Privacy - A Cyberspace Odyssey*, 2001.

[29] Under Art. 17, the Data Controller must implement technical and organisational measures for protecting against privacy breaches. Recommendations include especially minimising the amount of personal data that is processed outside the specific context of the student's profile, e.g. by making data anonymous or pseudonymous (J Borking, op cit., 1999)

database storage, cache, communications facilities), such hosts may be under Data Processor obligations. As such, they should enter into agreements with the Data Controller to determine the processing instructions and, for example, security levels[30]. To the extent they have any autonomy in relation to the processing, they would also be considered Data Controllers. Another scenario is if the host is considered a third party. In this case the Data Controller, on collecting the data, must inform the Data Subject of the recipients of the data[31].

3.1.2 Agents, user consent and privacy negotiations

The principal means enabling commercial parties to process personal data lawfully is to inform the Data Subjects and obtain their consent. In the event of agents that process personal data and operated and controlled by a commerce platform (e.g. profiling or personalisation agents), one means to achieve this is to design the trader's information system so that Data Subjects provide consent to any personal data processing when logging on or on initial registration. This is the now "traditional" means for lawful personal data processing in online commerce.

In the Research Scenario, apart from a general notification that certain data may be collected by the store in relation to interaction with RFID-enhanced products, Agents A and B could also include processes for specifically notifying the shopper when any personal data is being collected and processed. More practically, such consent can be obtained – with an opt-in process – when the user "logs on" to the system or registers the first time. In addition, the services of the Agents may be configured to be contracted by the user, in which case the store may have the benefit of the justification of "processing necessary for the performance of a contract"[32].

What happens, however, when the agent is operated by the Data Subject (e.g. a shopping agent such as Agent C operating on behalf of the consumer)? The merchant's information processing systems (such as a website) may interact not with the Data Subjects themselves, but with an agent acting on their behalf. In this case, an interesting question arises as to whether the Data Subject's agent could be considered to receive the notification and grant valid consent on behalf of the user.

Consent for personal data processing must be an unambiguous, freely given, specific and informed indication of subject's wishes[33]. There are two questions: one of information, one of consent. First, the merchant's systems may be programmed to provide user access to a privacy policy or maybe to a

---

[30] Arts. 16 and 17 EU Data Protection Directive.
[31] Art 10.
[32] Art. 7(b) EU Data Protection Directive.
[33] Article 7 EU Data Protection Directive.

more automated privacy declaration, as part of its notification obligations. Arguably, if it is an agent that is interacting with the platform, the human user does not actually receive information about the processing of the data by the merchant's systems. Accordingly the human user may not be considered informed, and any apparent agreement to personal data processing given in a data message sent by the agent may not be valid. Unfortunately also, many web platforms may like to use the uncertain concept of implied consent for any justification for processing, whereby the human user is deemed aware of privacy policies and notifications set out in a link on the web-page. Unless the agent was programmed to pick this up, and understand it (in the event that it is not in machine-readable language), this argument would no longer be valid, even if it were accepted for human users. On the other hand, it is not the fault or decision of the web-merchant that the "user" is an agent. It could be argued that users should be responsible for all aspects of the use of agent technologies, and assume the risk of using agents that do not have appropriate privacy protection processes built in.

Second, and this issue is related to the discussion on consent set out in Chapter 2 on contracts, it is questioned whether an agent can give consent on behalf of a human. We argued there that at least for the moment, the agent should be considered a means for transmitting the consent of the user. A person activating the agent could be deemed aware of and therefore responsible for all the processes undertaken by that agent, including the granting of any consent for purchasing a good or, the case in point, for personal data processing. In this, the agent is little different from another net-related application such as a browser, that the user can configure to accept or reject cookies automatically. If the agent processes are designed and programmed to transmit the user's consent in reaction to certain circumstances previously specified by the user (e.g. similar to a tailored version of P3P applications[34]), then we could argue that the Data Subject is aware of the circumstances and has given his or her informed consent. What's more, if the merchant's privacy policy is actually transmitted onwards from the agent to the shopper before any consent is given (which may have to be the case in the event of sensitive data), then any subsequent consent would be clearly valid. There may be a time lag problem, as the information must be provided when initiating processing, which may cause problems if agents only report back to users once every while.

This requirement for actual user notification and consent would seem to limit the autonomy of the user's agent. This is one area where systems such as the P3P model (discussed in section 4.3 below), including the automatic evaluation of merchant and shopper privacy policies and the subsequent

---

[34] This is discussed below, in section 4.3. See also, for example, L Cranor: *The P3P Protocol Standardizes Online Privacy Statements,* 2002.

granting of consent in the case of a match, may provide a solution. More advanced systems, still at the stage of research, contemplate rule-based negotiations of policies[35]. In theses models, the different circumstances and policies relating to personal data processing may be formalised in machine-readable declarations, which are compared and even negotiated. The agent is therefore "pre-programmed" to receive notifications and grant consent on certain conditions. In this case, while this does not ensure all aspects of privacy compliance, it is argued that adequate notification of the agent-using Data Subject may be inferred[36]. The granularity and specificity of this notification and negotiation process may, however, be adversely affected by agent learning processes. Any evolution of the agent's processes away from the initial programming may break any links of information, consent and causality. For example, if the consent of the Data Subject is granted in a series of situations, the agent may infer that consent is always to be granted in these situations. This may not necessarily be the case, as the Data Subject may be more wary of some web-sites or merchant platforms than others.

We suggest that a solution may be based on process modelling that might assist in technically specifying the issues and provide a high level design for building ecommerce applications, including agents, that respect privacy to a greater extent. If the processes and architecture of the interacting applications (web-based platform and shopping agent) can be modelled[37], then first of all the processes may be designed to take privacy into account, "legalising" the model and, second, such commerce platforms may become interoperable to carry out customised negotiation over personal data processing across the open network.

3.1.3   Privacy and autonomous agents in distributed computing

Several further points need be made about agent processing of personal data. The first point relates to control: who controls the agent, who controls what the agent does, and does physical possession (in computing terms, control of the machine where the agent runs) have implications for control of the agent? This question is important, as we believe that the agent can be considered a "means for processing" or processing equipment under the Personal Data Directive. Not only does this control indicate who the Data Controller may be, but also where the processing takes place. In a world of distributed computing, even more so maybe in the event of agent-based Web-services, this question may be very difficult to answer. Certain agent

---

[35] See for example the SweetDeal project, commented in Grosof and Poon, *Agent Contracts with Exceptions using XML Rules, Ontologies and Process Description*, 2002

[36] L Cranor et al: *The platform for privacy preferences 1.0 specification*, 2000.

[37] This modelling is all the better if it standardised, as this allows for interoperability and persistence.

models envisage agent providers who supply some essential services for agent processing to consumers (the computer code itself, or as services, the host environment, communications, security layers, etc.) but where the Data Subject controls this access through passwords and other security measures, inputs the processing parameters and loads the data. Just as we commented in chapter 3 on the difficulties of attribution of liability for IPR reasons, for legal certainty it is important to be able to attribute liability for personal data processing between Data Subjects, Controllers, Processors and Recipients.

The autonomy and learning capacities of a software agent also raise difficult questions as to how the Data Protection regulations apply once the agent has acquired more autonomy and new processing functions. First, from the Data Subject's point of view, while they may be adequately informed of the extent of the initial personal data processing by an agent (including communications with third parties and the provision of consent in certain circumstances), the evolution of the agent may extend this processing beyond that initially notified. Ideally, agents should be able to inform the Data Subject at any time of the extent of any processing, and maintain a record of relevant processing or transmissions. From a Data Controller's point of view (the retail store, or the agent service provider), it is conceivable that agents acquire sufficient autonomy to act in ways that are not taken into account by agent controllers, who could wish to disassociate themselves from their agent's acts.

As the agent controllers risk being held liable for these acts, they need to incorporate "agent data handling processes" to remain aware of the agent's evolution and anticipate any breach.

The introduction of mobile agents that move from platform to platform also poses a number of questions. In situations involving unknown third party agents or interlocutors (intermediaries), should an agent carry any personal information on the user at all? How can Data Subjects and Controllers determine the extent of the risks involved, in the absence of certain standardisation of agent platforms and hosts, or their certification for privacy compliance? Attacks from malicious hosts may be able to access any personal data, read, write or modify it. An important principle may be to minimise the amount of information carried by any mobile agent.

These questions about mobile agents lead us to another area of concern, which is the development of multi-agent environment where several agents may interact and share processes, tasks and resources on a same platform.

3.2   Multi-agent issues

Multi-agent systems involve various agents interacting within open or closed agent systems (hosts). The hosts themselves and the third party agents within them may be characterised under the European legislation as third parties and/or data recipients[38]. Because these roles are contemplated in the Data Protection Directive, it is easier to establish the corresponding obligations and rights in relation to interactions within such systems, and set up appropriate enforcement mechanisms.

Compliance within MAS with the rights of Data Subjects and corresponding obligations of Data Controllers and Processors may become very complicated. Some examples of difficulties in relation to the information, rectification and objection rights[39] include:

- The right to be informed. Data subjects must be informed of the identity of the recipients or categories of recipients of data, including third parties if deemed necessary in order to guarantee "fair processing" of the data. In closed MAS, the host will control the identity and processing that is carried out, and therefore the Data Controller, as host or participant in the system, may be able to comply with these requirements. In open MAS, this may be an unknown factor.
- The right of rectification. Data Controllers must notify to the third parties receiving personal data any rectification, erasure or blocking of the data, unless this proves impossible or involves a disproportionate effort. In the context of MAS, this notification obligation could become very burdensome as rectification data must be transmitted to all recipients of the data to maintain accurate records. Again, the MAS host may find it necessary to include a privacy compliance architecture on top it its own data architecture, ensuring the maintenance of updated records and register of communications.
- The right to object. Furthermore, when personal data are to be disclosed for the first time to third parties or used on their behalf for the purposes of direct marketing, the Data Subject must be informed of this before the data are disclosed and must be offered the right to object free of charge to such disclosures or uses. Accordingly data sharing between actors within MAS (for example sharing consumer profiles) requires the consent of the Data Subject prior to the disclosure of the information to new participants.

Again, we suggest building a model of MAS platforms and their processes (agent handshakes, resource allocation, security layers, transmissions and registers) that enables privacy to be built into the architecture. If this is standardised to a certain extent, agents conforming to the same standard can interact more easily with the platform, in the knowledge that personal data will be used in accordance with either pre-determined protocols or negotiated agreements.

---

[38] Art 2(f) and (g) EU Data Protection Directive.
[39] Arts. 10, 12 and 14 EU Data Protection Directive.

4.   PRIVACY COMPLIANCE

We have seen that agents pose several risks in relation to personal data processing, and that the current legal framework imposes various obligations and liabilities on the parties involved in agent-based transactions contemplated within the Research Scenario. We now turn to consider the various solutions that have been provided in the context of e-commerce, to consider whether they can be applied in relation to agent processing. We shall look at both self-regulatory measures such as commercial privacy policies and trustmarks (section 4.1), and also technical measures for protecting privacy, generally called PETs: Privacy Enhancing Technologies (4.2). As regards the latter, we shall focus on a W3C initiative called Platform for Privacy Preferences (P3P[40]) as it aims to introduce certain concepts present in agent computing – automation, policy declarations and evaluation, negotiation – into the privacy debate (4.3).

4.1   Self-regulation

Various measures have been set up to try to regulate data protection outside the legal regime, mainly in the USA, where there is no or few mandatory rules regarding data processing[41]. Attempts have included privacy statements, privacy seals, industry or sector codes of conduct, and technical privacy standardisation initiatives which we review in turn below. Within the EU, most of these measures attempt to bring commercial behaviour within the strict rules of the Data Protection laws.

4.1.1   Privacy statements

Policies let consumers know about a website's practices relating to data collected from users, who can then decide whether or not practices are acceptable, when to opt- in or opt- out, and ultimately who to do purchase from and on what basis[42]. Privacy statements aim therefore at providing the appropriate information (often now under the rules and according to good business practices and codes of conduct) at the appropriate time. Agents would have to be programmed to "read" such statements (see P3P below for automatic statements) and forward them if necessary to users for consent or express notification. However policies are often difficult to understand, hard

---

[40] L Cranor et al: The platform for privacy preferences 1.0 (p3p1.0) specification, 2000.
[41] See for example, Federal Trade Commission, *Privacy online: fair information practices in the electronic marketplace,* 2000; or E Lin: *Prioritizing Privacy: A Constitutional Response To The Internet,* 2003.
[42] Most commercial and non commercial sites now have a privacy statement. Whether the company follows it is another matter, one that privacy seals and other mechanisms are aimed to assist in enforcing.

to find, take a long time to read (usually several pages), may be modified with or without notice…and, for our purposes, difficult at best for agents to read intelligently. In addition, there is no guarantee that the company respects its policy. Privacy seals aim to solve this issue.

4.1.2   Privacy seals

Seals or trustmarks are means of providing rapidly recognisable levels of protection, by displaying the logo of a trusted third party. That third party supposedly monitors its affiliates for compliance. They usually assure that the site in question respects a certain level of data protection, but suffer some drawbacks: (1) not complying with European laws or granting an adequate level of protection (e.g. from the USA) and (2) not providing much in the way of enforcement or compliance mechanisms. Users then have to rely on statutory protection, always the final fallback position. There are discussions of providing a legal framework for these "trusted third parties", for privacy as for consumer protection. Some privacy seals include TRUSTe, BBBOnline, CPA WebTrust, Japanese Privacy Mark, and TrustUK.org.uk[43].

4.1.3   Industry or sector codes of conduct

Industries and certain sectors have established guidelines for respecting privacy in relation to the collection and use of data in that specific sector[44]. These are usually voluntary guidelines for members of the association in question (for example the Direct Marketing Association Privacy Promise[45]). More generally, privacy related organisations have set up some codes of conduct: examples include the Online Privacy Alliance[46]. Even more generally, the OECD established guidelines and a privacy statement generator to help industry provide some level of guarantees[47]. This establishes a certain standard (not necessarily complying with the European legal framework, but at least the beginnings of a privacy compliance process) so that if software agents are to be available for sale or licence to consumers, suppliers could guarantee that they comply with certain sector or industrial codes of conduct.

---

[43] Seal organisations are all online: www.truste.org, www.bbbonline.org/privacy/, www.cpawebtrust.org, www.jipdec.jp/kyotu_page/outline.htm, www.trustuk.org.uk, etc.

[44] See for example FEDMA Code of conduct available at www.fedma.org

[45] See at www.the-dma.org/consumers/privacy.html. There are many examples, including the Biometrics Institute in Australia at www.biometricsinstitute.org/bi/codeofconduct.htm, or the UK Internet Services Providers Association at www.ispa.org.uk/html/about_ispa/ispa_code.html, or the Internet Advertising Bureau at www.iabuk.net/files/551.doc

[46] Online at http://www.privacyalliance.org

[47] Online at http://cs3-hq.oecd.org/scripts/pwv3/pwhome.htm

4.2   Privacy Enhancing Technologies

Regulation and self-regulation provide a framework for potentially privacy-threatening activities. From a technological point of view, the question is whether the tools and processes of digital processing can be turned to reduce or remove the threats rather than cause them[48]. This is all the more so in the area of agent computing, which aims to provide intelligent automated processes to facilitate commerce. It is therefore natural to think that agent-based technology should assist in protecting personal data. However, certain questions have been raised about the technological feasibility of privacy protection, its convenience for both Data Subject and data collectors/processors, and community and commercial considerations, balancing the needs of each against the other[49].

Certain agent applications (programmed within the commerce platforms, or as more independent agents) can be conceived in the Research Scenario as directly protecting the consumer's privacy. Interface or interaction agents, that monitor communications and interactions with third parties, should be able to recognise when personal data is being collected or transmitted (this would require personal data items to be tagged or marked-up in some form). Filter agents could control the data transmitted to and from third parties, while personalisation agents may have layers of security to protect the personal data included in the agent system, including access control mechanisms and encryption protection.

Generally speaking, various technologies have been suggested and can potentially be combined to enhance privacy in a digital context. These include the following:
– Appropriate system design that is compliant with the personal data protection rules (section 4.2.1)
– Security measures for protecting personal data (encryption, authentication, access control, etc) (section 4.2.2)
– Using anonymisers and other data stripping applications (section 4.2.3)
– Interfacing with Trusted Third Parties (e.g. for secure data storage) (section 4.2.4)
Let us now review these in turn.

---

[48] See generally, for example, J Borking: *On PET and other privacy supporting technologies*, 1999; or P Hustinx and A Cavoukian: *Intelligent Software Agents: Turning a Privacy Threat into a Privacy Protector*, 1999.
[49] L Bygrave: *Privacy-Enhancing Technologies – Caught between a Rock and a Hard Place*, 2002

4.2.1   Privacy enhancements through system design

To prevent information systems that record, store and process online data from accessing too much data, or sensitive information, and to provide a safeguard for a user's autonomy, integrity and dignity, the first requirement is that information systems need to be properly designed to minimise data protection risks. There are various options to carry out this design in relation to privacy:

— Avoid generating or recording data at all.
— Avoid recording data that is unique to an individual (identifying data). Without such data it is almost impossible to link existing data to a private individual (anonymising).
— Combine the first two options: recording only strictly necessary identifying data, together with the non-identifying data.

This requires not only an awareness of data protection issues on the part of the IT system's project owners and technical leaders, but also a new methodology for a privacy compliant architecture and approach to computing[50]. One of the key elements to this design is the identification of what data are personal, and tagging this data so that it can be "tracked" either within the system design or ultimately in the code. So that privacy compliance can be incorporated at design time into information systems, it is also suggested that the privacy regulations and constraints be modelled and transformed into rules and process diagrams. Ideally, these models could be standardised throughout a specific jurisdiction (Member State, EU) for interoperable applications between platforms and companies.

4.2.2   Technological security measures

Agents communicate, transmit data and eventually move about over networks and within third party hosts. These transmissions should maintain confidentiality and integrity and there are several tools that have been developed for this. The principal means today is symmetric and asymmetric cryptography. Public Key Infrastructure (PKI[51]) allows (fairly!) secure key exchange over insecure channels. Applications and protocols that are used include:

— IPSec (Secure IP[52]): an Internet Protocol for secure transmissions
— SSH (Secure Shell[53]): a method of connecting two computers together such that the data sent between them is encrypted to prevent eavesdropping.

---

[50] Kenny and Borking, *The Value of Privacy Engineering*, 2002
[51] See information provided at the OASIS standardisation site at http://www.pkiforum.org/ or the NIST site: http://csrc.nist.gov/pki/
[52] Details at www.ietf.org/html.charters/ipsec-charter.html (last visited 20/09/2003)

- SSL (Secure Socket Layer[54]). This is used to encrypt the data transmitted between a browser and web server (and vice versa). It is of general use for more secure communications, as this stops snooping. However, in general it does not guarantee identity of sender or recipient.
- SET (Secure Electronic Transactions[55]). This is promoted by Visa for payment instructions, as this would guarantee identity of sender or recipient using PKI.
- PGP (Pretty Good Privacy[56]). This is used mainly for email communications.
- WEP (Wired Equivalent Privacy[57]): security protocol for wireless communications. This is to be replaced by WPA (Wi-Fi Protected Access[58]), approved by the Wi-Fi Alliance in early 2003, stated to be a temporary fix until standard 802.11i for wireless security is approved.

Some forms of encryption may, however breach export control laws (which, generally speaking, have been liberalised in the EU[59]). Anonymizer software usually provides that their use is legal if the user or customer is careful to obey the intellectual property and export rules, as well as any local rules that may apply in the nation they are in.

One of the main problems of privacy is not just the collection and transmission of the data, but their storage. To solve this problem (and required in legislation as minimum standards, e.g. Art 17 of the Data Protection Directive), technical security measures are required, to provide access control and user authentication, log auditing and data integrity. BS ISO/IEC 17799[60] provides an internationally standard for data management, though it does not guarantee freedom from liability should any problem arise.

4.2.3   Anonymisation / pseudonymisation (for data stripping)

One way to reduce the amount of information collected is to reduce the amount given or transmitted. To do this, users can set up forged or incorrect accounts with service providers and provide incorrect data. This does not help convenience, trust and electronic payments. There are various technical

---

[53] Details online at www.ssh.com or http://www.openssh.org/
[54] Details at http://wp.netscape.com/eng/ssl3/
[55] Details online at http://www.setco.org/set_specifications.html
[56] Details online at http://www.pgpi.org/
[57] Part of the IEEE 802.11b wireless standard, at www.ieee.org. See also Wireless Ethernet Compatibility Alliance: *WEP Security Statement*, September 7, 2001.
[58] Details at http://www.wifialliance.org/opensection/protected_access.asp
[59] For the USA and Canada, E Gratton: *The legality of online Privacy-Enhancing Technologies*, 2002.
[60] Details online at http://www.bsi-global.com

tools to increase anonymity, mainly called anonymisers. These are set out in Table 5-2 below.

Table 5-2. Anonymiser technologies

Anonymiser technologies
Anonymiser programs act as proxies for users, hiding information from end servers (commercial sites). They monitor the web traffic and take out revealing data. Rewebber.com, for example, provides both client and server anonymity as it hides the commercial site data too: in the outbound flow, it decodes target URL checks (internal), anonymises transport protocol information (i.e. headers), while on the return flow it anonymises headers again, checks contents and encrypts all embedded items. Proxymate (Lucent Personal Web Assistant (LPWA) - now defunct) automatically generated user names, passwords and email addresses unique to each web site so that the user remained "multiple" rather than "individual" and allowed selective blocking of email aliases.
Mix programs send route message randomly through network of "Mixes" or rerouting servers, using layered public- key encryption. Examples include Freedom (Zero- Knowledge Systems) http://www.zeroknowledge.com and Java Anon Proxy (JAP from TU Dresden) http://anon.inf.tu-dresden.de.
Crowds help users join a crowd of other users so that web requests from the crowd cannot be linked to any one individual. This protects the users, the end servers, other crowd members and system administrators from eavesdroppers and data collectors, as the data is not personal. This is an interesting concept, as it is the first system to hide "data shadow" on the web without trusting a central party (the anonymiser or mix program).
Filters: these applications filter out unwanted data, mainly flowing to the user to monitor its activities, such as cookies and web-bugs. "Cookie Cutters" block cookie and allow for more fine-tuned cookie monitoring, while other filter advertisements and banners, cut out referrer headers and other browser chatter. Examples include http://www.webwasher.com/ and http://www.junkbusters.com/ijb.html

Anonymity has its drawbacks, as anonymity on the Internet can be viewed as threatening especially given the surge of near anonymous spam email[61]. A Study on Legal Aspects of Computer-Related Crime in the Information Society[62] stated that technical solutions and measures against the abuse of anonymity on the Internet should be taken. Another perceived problem is when services based on certified pseudonyms and the certification authority (for non-repudiation) can and may be obliged to

---

[61] There many reports on spam activities: recently, the Australian National office for the Information Economy released: Final Report of the Noie Review of the Spam Problem and How It Can Be Countered, online at www.privacy.gov.au. Other reports include ARETE Report: *Communications Commerciales Non-Sollicitées et Protection des Données*, 2001.

[62] COMCRIME-Study, prepared for the European Commission by Prof. Dr. Ulrich Sieber, University of Würzburg Version 1.0 of 1st January 1998.

provide the user's name and address, however this is usually under clearly defined circumstances.

4.2.4   Trusted third parties (for storing and providing access to personal data)

Certain intermediary services, often called "infomediaries" or "trusted third parties"[63] aim to provide data privacy by supplying services and tools for transaction streams that help people manage their online identities and enable users to know that assurances about information practices are trust worthy[64]. Some also claim to monitor sites behaviour, such as the trustmarks mentioned above under self-regulation, on the basis that privacy compliance is part of many codes of conduct. Mainly these intermediaries provide datasets with different degrees of security, for the use of personal data online. Examples of informediaries that include certain identity protection include[65]:
- Digitalme - http://www.digitalme.com
- Lumeria - http://www.lumeria.com
- Microsoft Passport - http://www.passport.net/[66]
- Liberty Alliance - http://www.projectliberty.org/[67]

The disadvantage of these proposals is that users have to trust the third party to deal with the data in a privacy respectful manner, and although the technologies themselves may be safe (which is also uncertain[68]), ultimately there is little guarantee that these third parties comply with their own policies.

While these designs or technologies may make useful contributions for trusted computing, they are only components of an overall architecture that should aim to achieve privacy compliance. In addition, they do not contribute much to solving the privacy related issues of autonomy and adaptation of software agents that we outlined above. We now turn to consider an initiative that may contribute more directly to this objective,

---

[63] These TTPs should not be confused with those organisations established for certifying Digital Signatures, (for example, see Istituto per lo Studio della Vulnerabilità delle Società Tecnologicamente Evolute: *Legal Issues of Evidence and Liability in the Provision of Trusted Services, Final Report*, 1998), although many of the issues are the same (PKI for protected communications, access control and passwords, etc.).

[64] B Subirana and P Carvajal: *Transaction streams: theory and examples related to confidence in Internet-based electronic commerce*, 2000.

[65] For a technical work on Trusted services for privacy management see for example Sameer Ajmani et al: *A Trusted Third-Party Computation Service*, 2001.

[66] Commented in *Working Document on on-line authentication services*, Working Paper 68 of the EC Art 29 Data Protection Working Party.

[67] Also commented in Working Paper 68 of the Art 29 Data Protection Working Party.

[68] See for example, N. Szabo *Trusted Third Parties Are Security Holes*, 2001.

through the standardisation of software architectures to enable automated notification and negotiation of privacy preferences.

4.3   Standardisation and P3P

Standardisation is not really a technology but a result of a consensus building process of a community, aimed to determine a mutually accepted technical process. In this section, we comment on certain technology standardisation initiatives in the area of privacy, with a focus on P3P.

4.3.1   Standardisation for interoperable privacy compliant processes

The aim of standardisation in the area of privacy is to establish common privacy related vocabulary, processes and protocols so that different software applications can automatically reach agreements on when and how to process certain personal data. The most advanced example is the Platform for Privacy (P3P) initiative of the W3C, which, due to its conceptual affinity with agent technology, is discussed in more detail below.

The Liberty Alliance mentioned above also attempts to establish standards for privacy processes, for federated or distributed network identity management and identity-based services[69]. It aims to specify an architecture, security and privacy guidelines and practices for discovering, sharing and authenticating personal information and attributes, in a permissions-based manner, over any platform or network device. This should enable applications sharing the standard to use personal data (passwords, credit card numbers, etc.) in a manner specified by the Data Subject in an online repository. This architecture is generally modelled on the concept of web-services, with identity management being one-such service. At the date of this work, it is yet to be seen how this may be fully specified and how it may inter-relate with agent-based computing.

4.3.2   Platform for Privacy Preferences P3P

P3P, while not a privacy solution in itself, calls itself a "user empowerment tool"[70]. It is a standardised means of informing users about a web site's privacy practices so as to assist consumer interpretation of sometimes complicated privacy policies.[71] It creates an automated "privacy handshake" between websites and browsers or online proxies. These

---

[69] Online at http://www.projectliberty.org/

[70] W3C standard published and commented at http://www.w3.org/P3P/. See also, L Cranor et al: *APPEL: A P3P Preference Exchange Language*, 2002.

[71] L Cranor et al, *The P3P Protocol Standardizes Online Privacy Statements*, 2002

automated dialogues attempt to match website and user's privacy policies, for example regarding cookies.

It provides a basic vocabulary and base data set for websites to express privacy practices (for example with respect to privacy threatening items such as cookies) and a protocol for publishing them. These policies can be automatically retrieved and interpreted by P3P-enabled web browsers and other user agents. P3P readers (browsers, agents) can be configured to compare P3P policies with privacy preferences established by the user and take certain actions based on such comparisons. The most widely publicised example to date is Microsoft's partial implementation of a P3P-based cookie filtering mechanism in Internet Explorer 6, but there are now other applications such as the ATT PrivacyBird[72] and the EU JRC privacy proxy[73]. Future versions of P3P may incorporate additional functionality, such as a mechanism that allows web sites to offer users a choice of P3P policies (it currently only provides a take-it-or-leave-it mechanism). Table 5-3 below provides a more technical description of the P3P standard.

Table 5-3. Elements of P3P

P3P Element	Description
P3P Policies	These are machine- readable (XML) versions of web site privacy policies, using P3P Vocabulary to express data practices and P3P Base Data Set to express type of data collected. This language may capture common elements of privacy policies but may not express everything (sites may provide further explanation in human- readable policies).
P3P Clients	These can be implemented as browsers, proxies, plug-ins, java applets, JavaScripts, etc. and they can be entirely server side or part of an infomediary service, shopping tool bar, automatic form filler, etc. They act by looking for link to P3P policy and fetching the policy with HTTP GET request. They then check the policy and take appropriate action which can include displaying a symbol, playing a sound, prompting user action (accept, reject), etc. The action can optionally be based on user preferences or allow data to be automatically filled into form or transferred from electronic wallet.
User Privacy Preferences	P3P interlocutors (browsers, agents) may also take action based on user preferences (users should not trust privacy defaults set by software vendors). In addition, user agents that can read APPEL (A P3P Preference Exchange Language) files can offer users a number of preset choices developed by trusted organisations (TTPs). Also, preference editors allow users to adapt existing preferences to suit own tastes, or create new ones
The P3P Vocabulary	This covers concepts such as: Who is collecting data? What data is collected? For what purpose will data be used? Is there an ability to change preferences about (opt- in or opt- out) of some data uses? Who are the data recipients (anyone beyond the data collector)? To what information does the data collector provide access? What is the data

[72] Online at http://privacybird.com/
[73] Online at http://p3p.jrc.it/

P3P Element	Description
	retention policy? How will disputes about the policy be resolved? Where is the human-readable privacy policy?
P3P Base Data Schema	This includes a set of common data elements that all P3P implementations should know about. It includes user, third-party, and business elements such as name, address, phone number, etc. It also includes "dynamic" elements such as indicators that a site collects click-stream, uses cookies, collects info of a certain category, etc. they are extensible using custom data schemas.

There have been a number of comments on P3P throughout its different stages. We find it useful to highlight some benefits and criticisms that have been made[74].

The principal benefit of P3P is that it provides information to the Data Subject in a machine readable manner. Internet users can a priori decide what kind of purpose are legitimate for them, and if they are knowledgeable enough and the policies clear enough, they will be able to determine the purposes of the Web site's privacy invasive practices such as planting cookies. Such automated declarations in machine-readable language are a first step for enabling agents to interact autonomously with commerce platforms[75].

There have been many criticisms on both sides of the Atlantic, from advocates of both legislated and self-regulated privacy protection. On the client side (i.e. website users), the first problem with P3P is that it doesn't really make user's data more private or secure[76]. It's mainly an information medium, meant to make website privacy standards more transparent to users. P3P does not offer any guarantee for the legitimacy of the processing, adequacy of data collection, right of access to the data, and adequate level of protection for data transferred outside of the EU[77]. This is due to the fact that P3P does not create or operate within an existing privacy framework, although it could be adapted to comply more fully with the EU framework. More importantly, there are no enforcement procedures: there is no guarantee that websites comply with the internal parts of the policy (i.e. data use, transfer and automatic processing). P3P may also effectively exclude automated client applications from interacting with "good" web sites that lack P3P code, even though the privacy practices of these sites may far

---

[74] For more details on P3P, see for example: L Cranor: op cit., 2002; J Harvey and KM Sanzaro: *P3P and IE 6: Raising More Privacy Issues Than They Resolve?*, 2002; G. Hogben: *Technical analysis of problems with P3P v1.0 and possible solutions*, 2002; Clarke, R: *Platform for privacy preferences: A critique*, 1998; D Mulligan et al: *P3P and Privacy: An Update for the Privacy Community*, 2000.

[75] L Cranor: *The P3P Protocol Standardizes Online Privacy Statements*, 2002.

[76] J-M Dinant: *Platform for Privacy Preferences (P3P): How Far can P3P Guarantee the Respect of the Data Protection Directive Requirements?*, 1999.

[77] G Hogben: *Technical analysis of problems with P3P v1.0 and possible solutions*, 2002.

exceed those that are "P3P compliant." In addition, if a site isn't designed for P3P properly, consumers could get a message stating they can't trust the site, regardless of whether or not the site matches their preferences. There is also scope for confusion: consumers may be unwilling to take the initiative to learn about P3P and set their preferences accordingly[78]. Conversely, consumers not fully versed in P3P's limitations may confuse privacy with security. For example, they may see a privacy icon and think it is an indication that a site is secure. P3P does not require sites to implement security measures and is not a guarantee of "safe" interactions.

On the server-side (website), there are several criticisms. First, P3P cannot replace compliance with the legal framework, nor is it a means to enforce it[79]. In particular, the choice of a P3P compliant server will not be sufficient to guarantee compliance with the EU privacy rules for a particular Web site[80]. It therefore does not free the data collectors from fulfilling their legal obligations of legitimacy, adequacy, right of access to the data, opt-out / opt-in opportunity and protection for international data flow. P3P is also currently expensive to implement and maintain[81]. Creating policies in a well-reasoned manner is likely to be a costly and time-consuming task (though worth it if it makes companies think about privacy). Developing a privacy policy and accurately documenting that policy, even in the traditional "human-readable" form, is difficult. There are P3P policy generators[82], but they need to be used carefully. In addition, even with careful review, P3P 1.0 may not adequately describe complex and subtle web site information management practices[83]. The W3C has noted that there is concern that the current P3P specification may not be "rich" or vetted enough to accurately characterise a web site's plain language privacy policy[84]. Later versions should become richer and more expressive[85].

P3P may also lead to unclear liabilities: companies may be reluctant to be held liable for statements made in a P3P policy, particularly compact policies comprised of "tokens"[86]. Some sites have disclaimer statements informing users that the policies are not legally binding, which is of doubtful

---

[78] J Harvey and KM Sanzaro: *P3P and IE 6: Raising More Privacy Issues Than They Resolve?*, 2002.

[79] Electronic Privacy Information Center and Jukbusters: *Pretty Poor Privacy: An Assessment of P3P and Internet Privacy*, 2000.

[80] G Hogben, op cit., 2002.

[81] J Harvey and KM Sanzaro, op cit., 2002.

[82] W3C maintains a list at http://www.w3.org/P3P/implementations. E.g. P3PEdit, at http://p3pedit.com/ or the JRC Java P3P APPEL Privacy Preference Editor at http://cybersecurity.jrc.it/Privacy/p3p/JRCAppelRulesetEditor.htm.

[83] M Cutler: P3P's Arrival Raises Concerns That Tool May Create Liability, Drive Away Site Traffic

[84] L Cranor and D Weitzner: *Summary Report, W3C Workshop on the Future of P3P*, 2002

[85] L Cranor and D Weitzner, op cit. 2002.

[86] J Harvey and KM Sanzaro, op cit. 2002.

legal value. Liability could arise for differences between and among non-P3P policies, P3P policies and actual practices.

There have been other more general criticisms, key among them being the "Annoyance Factor": continuous requests for consent or notifications are bothering for users. Many larger sites with third-party content (e.g. provided by affiliates) may find out that their own cookies won't be accepted on their own site. And also as customers move through multiple site pages (with different policies for different pages), first-party cookies that are accepted in one area turn into third-party cookies that violate P3P rules in another. Some privacy advocates disagree with the entire premise of P3P: they do not believe that, by making it easier for consumers to access and understand web site privacy policies, the general state of data privacy will improve[87]. P3P could even have the opposite effect, because the existence of P3P may serve to stall proposed privacy legislation.

In summary, P3P in its current version is a partial solution that helps users understand privacy policies but does not actively protect personal data. As a first improvement, it should be completed by:
- Encryption tools to secure data in transit and storage, and guarantee authenticity of any policies
- Anonymity tools to reduce the amount of information revealed while browsing
- Seal programs and regulations to help ensure that sites comply with their policies
- Laws and codes of practice to provide a base line level for acceptable policies.

However, it may be enough for simple agent applications if one can assume good faith of all the intervening parties, including network providers, agent hosts and other intermediaries (which, seeing the current surge in spam, web-bugs, spy-ware and other invasive elements, does not seem likely).

4.3.3 Standards and automated privacy compliance processes

The conceptual model for P3P is interesting for us, in that it bears certain characteristics of agent-based computing. It aims for automated declaration and negotiation of technical aspects of privacy, with variable degrees of autonomy and interoperability for web-based applications in specific privacy related areas (e.g. cookie management). This form of negotiation may also be implemented through rule-based agent negotiation, on the basis of privacy ontologies and templates, personal preferences, processing

---

[87] J Catlett: *Open Letter to P3P Developers & Replies*, 1999; M Cutler: op cit, 2001.

permissions, and exception handling (privacy breaches)[88]. With artificial intelligence, it may be extended with learning capacities regarding acceptable web-site policies and user preferences (analysing accepted and rejected cookies, for example).

The technical standardisation approach is also close to the process modelling approach we suggest in our conclusions. Standardisation methodology in general involves the conceptual modelling of the certain guiding principles or business constraints, and creating an abstraction of transactions in order to create models and processes that are machine understandable and – by being standardised – interoperable. In the area of privacy, this involves modelling data protection principles. By doing so we believe we can create a technical architecture that is understandable by both managers and technologists. This "legalised" architecture leads to compliant process design and eventually automated implementation through agent technologies. In addition, the IT tools envisaged by both approaches are the same: knowledge representation and structuring through ontologies and rules (DAML is an example for agent technologies[89]), and workflow or rule engines (e.g. APPEL, in P3P) for executing policies and the related processes[90]. We comment some more on this in the conclusions to this Chapter and in Chapter 6.

5.   DEVELOPMENTS AND INITIAL CONCLUSIONS

In this section we comment on some recent developments and draw up some conclusions on the theme of privacy and agents in general and within the Research Scenario.

5.1   Developments

There have been some recent developments that affect the question of privacy within the Research Scenario. The first has been the adoption of the Privacy and Electronic Communications Directive in June 2002, to be implemented by October 2003. The provisions are already set out and discussed above. The USA is undertaking a legal fight against spam that may lead to some form of opt-in system, or a Robinson-type "do-not-spam" list. It will be interesting to see what form of transaction automation may be possible under any new legislation adopted by the US Congress.

---

[88] See an example in G Yee and L Korba: *The negotiation of privacy policies in distance education*, 2003.

[89] See at www.daml.org

[90] See Yee and Korba: *The negotiation of privacy policies in distance education*, 2003, for policy negotiation in the online education sector.

Another interesting development is IPv6[91]. This is a protocol for Internet addresses, conceived to cater for the increased number of computers and devices connected to the Internet. It will increase the number of bites from 4 to 16, with 6 of the 16 dedicated to a serial number of the Ethernet card on the computer or device. This will provide numeric identification of all devices connected to the Internet, without the user's ability to object (no number, no address, no connection) and for all purposes (browsing, emails, SMS, chats, etc.). It is yet to be seen how this protocol will interact with agent software, whether for example an agent could have an IPv6 address, providing greater levels of identification ... but destroying a great measure of privacy. While the IETF states that privacy can be maintained, there are interesting proposals to raise or maintain privacy in IPv6[92].

Other privacy initiatives include an extension of P3P (to version 2.0), which involves developing the possibilities of P3P as a distributed web service, as well as a client application. Investigation is being made into how P3P works as a proxy service and especially the commercial implications of this, in terms of consumer confidence in trusted third parties. Also, the possibilities for using the SOAP protocol[93] to create a highly distributed version of P3P are being considered. This may enable, for example, an APPEL evaluator class to be created as a web service.

– The Research Scenario contemplates shopping in a ubiquitous computing environment, using Radio Frequency Identity (RFID) tags or EPCs (Electronic Product Codes) for automated interactions between products and a user's mobile device, such as a mobile phone or a portable computer (notepad)[94]. While this chapter has focussed on agent-related privacy issues, it is important to note in relation to the Research Scenario that RFIDs raise legitimate privacy concerns, which may be increased in the event of autonomous agent-based computing[95]. While the current debate is probably exaggerated and one should not blame the technology but the way it is used (just like CCTV or cookies), as we noted in section 2.2 ubiquitous computing creates the potential for increased privacy invasion and breaches of data protection laws. The question is not to reject a potentially useful technology, however, but see how to address

---

[91] See the IPv6 website at http://www.ipv6tf.org/ and Table 1.3 in Chapter 1.

[92] See IETF: *RFC 3041, Privacy Extensions for Stateless Address Autoconfiguration in IPv6*, 2001. Also Escudero et al.: *Location Privacy in Mobile Internet - An extension to Freedom Network*, 2001.

[93] Specified in http://www.w3.org/TR/SOAP/

[94] For more details, see the work of the Auto-Id Center at www.autoidcenter.org/

[95] Commented in K Ashton: *Testimony before the California State Senate Subcommittee on New Technologies Hearing on RFID and Privacy*, 2003; B Givens: *RFID and the Public Policy Void*, 2003; K Albrecht: *Supermarket Cards: The Tip of the Retail Surveillance Iceberg*, 2002.

the legitimate concerns and design and implement IT architectures and applications that respect current laws and user's privacy.

5.2   Initial privacy-related conclusions

The issue of privacy will be fundamental to the success of agent development in any implementation of the Research Scenario. Not only do automated transactions take place between consumers and retail stores (online and off-line), but also many aspects of this automation are based on personal profiles and customer profiling, and other data mining processes that will involve personal data. It makes good sense – legal, technical and business-wise – to deal with privacy as something that matters: to deal with it in a positive and pro-active way and to develop good processes for privacy governance. This is essential not just for compliance with the legal framework but also for confidence in new technologies, especially ubiquitous and hidden technologies as those considered by the Research Scenario. Software agents within the Scenario should therefore reflect in an early stage of design on the implications of the use of intelligent agents for the privacy of individuals.

5.2.1   A preliminary legal framework for the Research Scenario

Certain important points need to be taken into account in establishing a legal framework for agents within the Research Scenario. First, a general comment is that for so long as these software agents operate in a closed network (e.g. the retail store's own information systems), most privacy issues are theoretically not too difficult to solve. This conclusion is drawn on the basis of the following principles which are outlined below.

Notification and consent: In relation to most personal data processing, including data collection in relation to RFID-enhanced products, shoppers can be notified and their consent obtained in advance through express notices and consent processes either on initial registration with the system, and on each log-on. Notifications and express consent provisions should be reflected not only in the system's general terms (unfortunately usually a "take it or leave it" agreement), but also explicitly set out in the registration and log-on process. This initial agreement and consent may eventually be achieved through the matching of computer understandable privacy policies, as we discussed above. We believe that for the sending of any commercial offers to shoppers (special offers, promotions, etc.) or transmitting customer data to third parties, the data subject's consent may be obtained through an explicit opt-in process. Eventually, this consent process may be automated via agent negotiation, through negotiated agreement or previously determined policies such as conceived for the next version of P3P[96].

Risk management: For so long as personal data remains within the store's systems there will be few external privacy risks such as those set out above. In all events, the store must respect the national provisions implementing the European Privacy Directives. This also includes guidelines for using surveillance or other systems for the prevention of crime[97]. In particular, however, we would argue that the store would have legitimate reasons for agent-based processing of personal data for the provision of customised services, and may be able to store this data for long periods in order to build up customer histories and profiles. It will however be important to implement high levels of security. Security is easier to guarantee within the store's private systems, given appropriate firewalls, passwords and other security management processes.

Profiling and anonymisation: Inference agents that process customer profiles and behaviours (for extrapolating rules of behaviour and general customer profiles and determining new goals for themselves) may do so working on anonymous or pseudonymous data. These could then be personalised for determining the goals and intentions of agents towards specific shoppers.

"Augmented reality" shopping: RFID based environments will need changes in both commercial infrastructure and processes. While retail organizations and supply chains are currently focusing on RFIDs for tracking and tracing supplies and inventory management, consumers are more concerned about what happens in and after leaving the store. In line with our comments above on the use of different forms of electronic product identification, a response to concerns about privacy threats would include the following privacy strategies:

- Clearly indicating the existence and location of electronically identified products.
- Notifying customers of the RFID- related data collection and processing, and obtaining their explicit consent prior to any personal data processing.
- Respecting other obligations imposed by the data protection legislation, including appropriateness and relevance of the data collection and storage, adequate security levels, automated processing obligations, and data transfer restrictions.
- Offering an easy option to disable RFIDs on leaving the store, to inhibit any possibility of further tracing and monitoring. Better still would be to disable the tags on leaving the store as a default setting, and if tracing

---

[96] L Cranor et al: *Summary Report, W3C Workshop on the Future of P3P*, 2002.
[97] See, for example the UK Information Commissioner's guidelines on the use of CCTV for the prevention of crime. See UK Information Commissioner: CCTV Code of Practice, 2000, online at http://www.informationcommissioner.gov.uk/.

were a commercial or safety objective (e.g. for pharmaceuticals), allow customers to maintain the RFID intact.

5.2.2   Some agent-specific protections that are worth considering

There are several advantages to using agents within the Research Scenario, not just for commercial reasons (user profiling, data-mining, shopping and advertising) but also for privacy protections. For example, agents should be able to verify the privacy policies of online merchants, and they are also capable of selective communication and filtering of personal information based on criteria established by users. They could also monitor the use of location and other data collected through EPC marked products in the store.

However, due to the higher privacy risks of agent computing outlined above, we suggest some technology design specifications for raising personal data protection and complying with the legal framework. These are:

– Certification of the agent's working method;
– Logging of all internal and external actions of the agent itself;
– Identification and authentication of all agents;
– Logging of all actions performed by other agents that collect personal data;
– Integrity mechanisms to control the integrity of stored or exchanged data and to control the integrity of working methods of agents or trusted components, like digital signatures;
– Using existing Privacy-Enhancing Technologies such as digital pseudonyms, blind digital signatures, and Trusted Third Parties (TTPs).
– The use of programs to render the user and/or the agent anonymous, or alternatively, the use of a "pseudo-identity" unless identification is specifically required for the performance of a transaction;
– The use of identification and authentication mechanisms such as digital signatures and digital certificates to prevent the "spoofing" of a user or their agent by a malicious third party intent on committing fraud or agent theft;
– The exclusive use of data encryption technology to prevent unauthorised "sniffing" or accessing of agent transaction details;
– Placing limitations on an agent's autonomy so it can only perform a certain range of activities. Limited activities will be permitted to be freely conducted without additional authorisation; any requests for unauthorised transactions will be flagged for the user to scrutinise.

These protections are illustrated in the following tables, which set out minimum processes that are required for the store-controlled advertising and selling Agent B and independent shopping Agent C (described in chapter 2) to comply with the privacy regulatory framework.

Table 5-4. Advertising and Selling Agent - Privacy processes

Principal Process	Legal issue (privacy related)	Additional processes for compliance and/or certainty
Consumer registration for in-store agent-based services	Collection of consumer personal data (identification, ID number, address, payment details, etc.)	Establish general framework for privacy notifications and consents, general terms of personal data processing and privacy codes of conduct
Consumer logs on to shopping assistant services	Identification of consumer; Activation of consumer personal profile DB	Provide anonymous or pseudonymous transaction options; Notify and obtain explicit consent for locating, advertising, automated processing, profiling.
Agent B becomes aware of customer within target area for its particular advert	Processing of consumer location data linked with consumer identification	Notify and obtain consent for processing of location data in each case.
Agent B considers rules for sending adverts	Unsolicited commercial communications	Check customer consent DB - obtain specific consent for in-store advertising if not already given (e.g. at log-on).
Agent B sends an advertisement to the customer device, without review by staff	Unsolicited commercial communications	Idem
Agent B provides a means for accepting the offered product (accept button, voice acceptance, etc)	Recording of transaction data linked with party identification	Full identity discloser processes; Security processes (SLL, SET, etc.) for transferring personal data (e.g. name, delivery address)
Agent B records and processes sale	Collection of transaction data for personal profile	Check extent of consent given for data processing (NB contractual relationship exemptions)
A payment agent contacts credit card or electronic payment service provider (PSP) and processes payment according to relevant system	Identification of parties to PSP; Processing of consumer financial data	Consent for transmitting personal data to third party (payment party): transaction identification and details; Security processes: digital signatures for payments (e.g. SET)
Agent B monitors and updates customer reaction to message and stores this for further processing	Retention of personal data files; Storing consumer behaviour; Processing / profiling of consumer	Delete or Anonymise if possible any unnecessary data; Register of processes to indicate logic of automated processing; Check extent of consent given for profiling; Security processes for stored data, e.g. encryption for integrity, authenticity and confidentiality

Table 5-5. Shopping Agent C - Privacy processes

Principal Process	Legal issues (consumer related)	Additional processes: compliance / consumer confidence
Agent C determines a need to purchase specific item	Processing of personal data and profile	Registration of original agent programming / parameters (trigger events, purchase conditions)
Agent C searches the network for various stores selling relevant products	Exchange of personal data contained in / accessed by Agent C; Provision of personal data to third parties ("browser" chatter); Registration of user agent actions on sites	Negotiation of privacy processes in relation to websites - incorporation of user privacy preference rules in website processing, e.g. via XML and rule/workflow language. ■ Receive/record with privacy policies ■ Receive notification and warn user in certain events (e.g. processing of sensitive data) ■ Provide consent (user defined conditions) ■ Security processes surrounding negotiation and results
Agent C negotiates with store(s) for the terms of sale, including treatment of personal data	Identification of parties: agent user identified as a consumer; Negotiation of use of personal data (financial data, transaction data)	Registration of contract negotiation results in relation to personal data
Agent C concludes purchase agreement	Recording of personal data in transaction	Tagging of personal data (if possible) to ensure proper use. Delete or anonymise transaction data if possible
Agent C provides delivery and payment details to website / transfer to Payment service provider (PSP	Identification of parties to PSP; Processing of user's financial data	Consent for transfer and processing of financial data to PSP. Security procedures: Digital signatures for payments (e.g. SET protocol), reference to user for PIN
Agent C records transaction	Storage of personal data and transaction data on seller's systems; Guaranteeing compliance with privacy policies and rules	Register of processes relating to recorded personal data. Security processes – e.g. encryption for integrity and confidentiality. Access and modification processes. Tagging of personal data (if possible) allowing tracing of actions applied to it)

Alternative techniques include the creation or inclusion of an intelligent privacy protection agent, which controls interfaces between sensitive data and external elements (main systems, third party agents, RFID tags, etc.). This agent can be placed anywhere in the system where personal data is exchanged and can incorporate features mentioned above: digital signatures, blind digital signatures, digital pseudonyms, and trusted third parties. This is the approach aimed at by the European research project PISA[98].

5.2.3   Security issues

As can be seen from the discussions above, security and security technologies play an important role in designing systems to maintain privacy. An important point is the close relationship (but also differences) between data protection and security. We have seen that data protection is wider principle, including control of the collection, use and disclosure of personal information, and is oriented by certain principles which are laid out in the Personal Data Directive as well as other public instruments (e.g. OCED principles of 1980). One of the implications of these principles is that data collected must be kept and transmitted safely. Security technologies and processes aim to guarantee this safety, or at least reduce the exposure and opportunity for abuse, in various ways, including preventing internal or external attacks on the access to and integrity of such data. These measures may be technical (encryption, access controls) or architectural (reducing the amount of data stored).

A brief example is presented next. One of the problems highlighted above is the question of privacy policies, and how they are used by online merchants. Two problems exist: first, there is currently no secure way of proving that a certain privacy policy was declared by a company. Second, there is no way to ensure that any privacy policy is actually carried out in relation to the data in question. The first problem may be solved by certain security mechanisms for maintaining data integrity and authenticity: policy declarations may be digitally signed so that a user may provide non-repudiatable evidence of its existence and contents on a certain date. But this security process cannot guarantee that the company will respect the policy in question. This will be more a matter of privacy auditing, until personal data is tagged in a manner allowing the data subject to monitor what is happening to the data in question.

Accordingly, security and privacy can be seen as complementary but not overlapping. However, the implementation of security may intrude on privacy and vice-versa. Those responsible for security tasks may have a legitimate need to control certain data and transmissions to know what is happening at all times: who has access to data, what is that person or agent

---

[98] JJ Borking: *Privacy incorporated software agents: a proposal for building a privacy guardian for the electronic age*, 2000; K. Cartrysse et al: *Privacy protection software design*, 2002; Paul Verhaar et al: *Handbook Privacy and PET for ISAT's*, 2002.

doing (electronically and physically). Resulting security and control structures for data processing may therefore prejudice certain aspects of privacy thorough such activities as employee email monitoring, controlling user logs, or making off-site backups of databases. On the contrary, access, correction and notification measures to comply with personal data protection may collide with security measures limiting access to these databases.

This debate between privacy and security is also heightened by potential legal obligations and liabilities that are imposed on Data Processors (ISPs, for example) for investigative or judicial purposes – all the more so in the current climate – which tend to favour retention of data for longer periods. The more data kept, the greater the risks of security breaches, and the greater the risks of violation of privacy.

5.2.4 Privacy processes, models and standardisation

We have identified here some of the privacy-related legal challenges of automated processing for retail systems, more specifically within the Research Scenario. Highlighted risks include agent-based "spamming" of customers within the Research Scenario, automated processing of personal data and problems of providing notifications and obtaining consent through agent interactions. Due to the onerous personal data obligations and the negative effect any breach would have on the activities, reputation and ultimately value of a retail store or online merchant[99], it is critical to identify the risk bearing processes of the system. Once these are identified, we can define the legal risks that are associated to those processes.

While this approach is tailored to the Research Scenario, it is fairly demanding, and many online commerce projects and even agent projects are not going to enter into this kind of analysis, even though they should. To resolve this problem, we suggest that data protection principles – along with other legal principles such as Intellectual Property Rights and Consumer protection principles – could be modelled and translated into computer understandable languages. This model can then be applied to the corporate business process model, independently of how the latter is implemented through technology – whether traditional computing, software agents or ubiquitous computing systems for RFID-enhanced environments. This may eventually enable autonomous agents to reason and negotiate their (commercial) behaviour in accordance with (legal) principles embedded in the corporate data model – a form of legalising agent processes. Particular instances of this need are in relation to two areas we have commented above: automated privacy policy declaration and negotiation (including notifications and consent), and ensuring that enterprise systems comply with corporate privacy policies and data subject preferences attached to certain

---

[99] Kenny and Borking: *The Value of Privacy Engineering*, 2002.

personal data. If the corporate privacy policy is modelled, the rules and constraints set out in the model and applicable to certain identified data (personal data) can be applied to the general corporate IT architecture and its processes.

Therefore we argue that if data protection principles are modelled and codified in computer systems in a standardised process-based manner, then not only should interoperability be increased between commerce applications (independent buying and selling agents, for example) and across jurisdictions, but also agent systems can achieve higher levels of privacy compliance without giving up the advantages of automation, autonomy and learning.

This approach, and the implications for research and technologies, is further discussed in Chapter 6.

Chapter 6

CONCLUSIONS
Approaching legal compliance through process models

As can be deduced from the analysis and discussions in the previous chapters, electronic agents pose several conceptual and practical legal problems in the area of electronic and mobile commerce. We have now described these issues in the context of the Research Scenario, agent-based "augmented reality" shopping, where the different parties and their agents also interact with an RFID-enhanced environment. Some of these problems may be easy to solve, others may require advances in technology or changes in the law. In this chapter, we aim to bring together our ideas for legally compliant ecommerce applications and the formalisation of the relevant issues.

We first synthesise the conclusions of the previous chapters, and provide a general outline of the legal implications of agent-based ecommerce. We then present our conclusions of the challenges that exist to build a framework for legally compliant agent-based ecommerce applications, as a subset of e-business IT infrastructures. Then, using the process-based approach to the question, we provide a more theoretical analysis of the problem. We show how a conceptual framework based on a new view of the firm, and organisations in general, provides useful insights that assist in our analysis. Finally, this conceptual framework also supports and illustrates potential solutions to the problem at hand. We contend that these issues have implications for establishing organisational models and technical architectures for e-business infrastructures that must respect what we call a *legal process model architecture.* This is a model of legal principles, entities, roles, concepts, data and processes that should be established by the current legal framework.

1.   REVIEW OF LEGAL ISSUES: STATEMENT OF THE PROBLEM

1.1   A brief summary of issues

The legal analysis in the previous chapters has outlined a series of problems that are and may be raised by agent-based e- and m-commerce applications. To summarise, the key issues are:
– Contract law: problems of legal personality, contractual capacity and intent, and respect for online contracting requirements.
– Intellectual Property Rights: problems regarding the automation of certain potentially infringing activities such as linking, copying and storing data on local networks, automatically accessing databases, as well as questions about ownership of agent-created works.
– Privacy: problems of intermediation by agents, reducing possibilities of notifications and informed consent from data subjects, and higher privacy risks through larger amounts of available data and higher levels of automated and invisible processing.
– Consumer Protection: problems of information of agent users and levels of transparency in agent-based consumer transactions, including liability regimes for both stores and consumers in their use of agents; difficulties with complying with advertising information obligations and certain procedural obligations, and questions of user awareness of potentially invalid contractual disclaimers.
– Digital Signatures: potential difficulties with authentication and digital signatures, concerns about the attribution of liability.
Common to most of these issues is the question of attribution of responsibility and liability for agent actions, whether in contract, IPR or privacy. Is there a direct chain of responsibility or causality between an agent's actions and its user? Should this responsibility be established and certified? Can users be deemed aware of their agent's "state" (e.g. regarding privacy or consumer notifications), and therefore the knowledge of the agent attributed to the user? Can or should the user be identified? Could shared or contributory liability be attributed to agent hosts, and would they benefit from any law that relieves them of responsibility for a breach committed by a software agent running on the host machines?
We find that there is little if any assistance towards answering these questions in the European legal framework that has been established for the Information Society reviewed in this monograph. While *electronic* transactions are often covered (e.g. en Art. 9 of the Ecommerce Directive, supporting contracts by "electronic means"), there is little consideration for *automated electronic* transactions. On the contrary, in the interest of protecting users and consumers there are increased notification, information

and consent obligations that may be difficult to satisfy with agent intermediation. Even the UNCITRAL Model Law on Ecommerce or the Draft Model Law on Electronic Contracts, while considering human mistake in electronic transactions, fail to contemplate machine made mistakes.

Today, automated information systems are liable to crash at any time, either locally or within the network, and there are growing security risks due to data and identity theft and illegal access to or interference with these data systems. Failure to provide for these system and machine errors – and other issues such as programming errors, transaction persistence and electronic records – within the legal framework for what are now commonplace digital transactions, is incomprehensible in these circumstances.

1.2   Abstraction: a general statement of the problem

On the basis of these comments, we contend more generally that the current approach to building and implementing ecommerce applications leads to illegality in several ways.

1.2.1   The law doesn't match technological processes and innovation

First, as suggested above, there is a problem with the current legal framework. Until recently, most laws and, more generally speaking, regulations have not truly taken into account technological concepts. This is partially natural, considering that legislation aims to provide a framework for existing interactions and finds it difficult to anticipate the next generation of technology. However, despite the rapid and indeed praiseworthy increase in Internet-related legislation, from the Data Protection Directive to the most recent Distance Marketing of Financial Services Directive,[1] there is still no clear legal framework for many online transactions. Concepts used by legislation do not necessarily correspond to what happens in a fast-moving reality. It took over a year to agree on how to describe Internet marketing for the purposes of the "Brussels Regulation": "directing activities to that Member State or to several countries including that Member State". This definition is still unclear, in the age of pop-ups and banner-ads, SMS advertising, wireless or GPS location, and more generally the borderless digital world. The definition of "Information Society" services and service providers themselves is still debated in several member states, notably Spain where the wide definition covers many private non-commercial activities. The EU's desire not to interfere with Member State contractual regimes has

---

[1] Directive 2002/65/EC of the European Parliament and of the Council concerning the distance marketing of consumer financial services and amending Council Directives 90/619/EEC, 97/7/EC and 98/27/EC (17 June 2002), OJ L 271/16, 9th Oct 2002.

left open the question of what constitutes an "offer" and "acceptance" in an online negotiation.

These laws also find it difficult to adapt to the speed of technological change. This is either from lack of awareness and foresight (e.g. the need for a second Privacy and Electronic Communications Directive in 2002) or from a desire not to upset national regimes (e.g. contracting processes, or the IPR debates about available exemptions or patenting software). We find that agent technologies are now upsetting even the most recent framework. We have commented how digital signature regulations potentially preclude software agents from providing legally valid advanced digital signatures, or how agent processing may blur the borders between Data Controller, Data Processor and Data Subject. In the realm of IPR, even the recent Copyright in the Information Society Directive fails to deal with the creation and protection of agent created databases and content, the liability of software agents as intermediaries, or the attribution of liability between agent programmer, agent provider, agent host and agent user.

It is true that more recently, certain legislation has been drafted in the aim to provide more abstract concepts. These include "commercial communications" and "communication networks" (Ecommerce Directive), data subject, controller and processors and "automated individual decisions" (Data Protection Directive), "making available" (Copyright in the Information Society Directive). They may and can withstand the change in technologies. The UNCITRAL Model Law on Ecommerce is helpful too, providing for "automated computer systems". This concept may overcome the problem of attributing intent to agents and of providing them with capacity to contract on behalf of users. But even this concept may be overtaken, for example if ever automated systems are not computer-based.

We believe that this failure stems in part from a lack of conceptual abstraction in legal drafting. Laws are made piecemeal to deal with current technologies and business transactions. We argue that this shortcoming could be overcome by creating norms that are conceived and drafted in terms of processes. More research needs to be undertaken to determine to what extent a process based approach is possible. The objective would be that, in relation to agent-based transactions, it is irrelevant whether a certain action is taken or initiated by a human person or a machine, as it is the process itself that is regulated. We contend that laws conceived in this way may be able to create a coherent legal model and framework for online transactions. Eventually, this legal model for processes could map directly onto technology processes through machine understandable modelling.

1.2.2   Technological development doesn't respect legal requirements

On the other had, the technologies involved in ecommerce take no account of the law, either at component level (access protocols, URIs, etc.)

or in ecommerce applications and application development, i.e. at software engineering levels. HTTP and other protocols, such as SMTP in relation to emails, enable breaches of privacy through traffic data collection, retention and analysis. Unless privacy protecting measures are taken, IPv6 should enable all devices connected to the network to be identified, allowing substantially more precise data to be collected about individuals (house contents, locations, etc.) and entailing further privacy breaches. Nor do localisation technologies, such as GPS or local positioning through Wi-Fi, telephone networks or Bluetooth, incorporate legal protections. Persistence in session management is also problematic, leaving online negotiators in doubt when systems partially or totally crash in the middle of a transaction (whether B2B or B2C).

Neither are current technological development methodologies – Object Oriented Programming, Rational Unified Process, etc. – designed to take into account legal issues from the start. Few ecommerce projects, or even research projects on advanced computing, focus on legal issues until after the main architecture and processes have been designed and programmed. This has been evident in the area of privacy, especially in the USA where there are few privacy rules, but also in the EU where there is specific regional and national legislation (albeit adopted fairly late, if at all). While privacy policies have been redrafted to take into account of – or often, pay lip service to – data subject rights and service provider obligations, often little is done to redesign websites and their underlying processes to comply with data protection laws. Ecommerce platforms are still using cookies, web-bugs and traffic data analysis in breach of privacy laws. Spam is still being sent massively, despite available technologies enabling the checking of "Robinson"-type lists (do not send / do not call lists) or verifying that the consent of the recipient has been obtained through opt-in or opt-out systems (many of the latter still being in place, despite their illegality under the Privacy and Electronic Communications Directive).

1.2.3 Retrofitting

The result is that ecommerce applications are being programmed on the basis of available technologies without fully considering the legal dimensions. This results in partially or fully illegal commerce systems. Conceptually speaking, we believe this situation derives from a mismatch or disparity between law and technology. While both fields are relevant to e-business, they are conceived and specified from different perspectives. The law does not integrate technological concepts, or deals with them at a level which is not always appropriate. Technology specifications do not take into account legal obligations – incorporated as specifications. To some extent, this is understandable given that technology is borderless, while laws are conceived, drafted and applied within national boundaries. The advantages of Uniform Laws in the international arena, such as those drafted by UNCITRAL, the EU or debated at the Hague Conference, are often outweighed by local political and legal considerations. Even if there is substantial national support (or obligation, in the case of EU Directives), these laws need to be drafted in a manner that respects national and regional cultures. This not only leads to disparities between national regimes, but also can detract from the desired goal of the law matching technology through abstraction, technological neutrality and even functional equivalency.

This disparity forces both law and technology to be retrofitted to fit or adapt to each other. The EU Data Protection Directive (1995), the Privacy in Telecoms Sector Directive (1997) and the Ecommerce Directive (2000), for example, have been updated in the Privacy and Electronic Communications Directive (2002) to take into account new forms of telecommunication networking and commercial practices such as spamming. To quote from the Recitals:

> (4) Directive 97/66/EC has to be adapted to developments in the markets and technologies for electronic communications services in order to provide an equal level of protection of personal data and privacy for users of publicly available electronic communications services, regardless of the technologies used. That Directive should therefore be repealed and replaced by this Directive.

And, on the technology side, many systems have had to be redesigned and reprogrammed to take into account lawyers' recommendations: higher levels of privacy protection, adequate contractual processes, new processes for data integrity, authentication and security to comply with relevant laws. Retrofitting may also lead to other legal problems, as the systems have to be updated every time there is a change in the laws, or if the organisation in question wishes to do business in another country... or it finds itself doing business abroad due to the international nature of the Internet. In addition, reprogramming systems to take account of current laws is counterproductive in the long term, as the rules are embedded at system level. When the law changes, the whole application has to be reviewed – reprogrammed – to be brought into line with the new laws. In our research, legal specifications were made at the time of the initial design of the data systems, on purpose to avoid this problem of reprogramming. The recommendations and specifications for ensuring legal compliance in relation to Consumer Protection, as an example within the research scenario, are set out below, based on our previous analysis.

On the basis of the analysis carried out here, there seems to be no way in traditional computing to square the circle so that ecommerce applications may be programmed safely from the start, but also adapt easily to a changing legal framework, whether public or private (i.e. contract based). Ecommerce applications always need external or internal legal auditing – usually subsequent to design, but in the best cases prior – and the law always follows technology.

1.3   What our analysis suggests: solving the law-technology mismatch

Our research suggests that several elements may be necessary to solve the law-technology mismatch. As the problem is situated on the conceptual level, we believe the solution may also reside here: there is a need to find an approach that shares a similar "conception". If both technology and law can "conceive" applications and transactions in the same way, the disparity should be reduced, if not removed. As we argue below, we believe that this can be achieved at the level of processes and within a more general conceptual model of the firm and business transactions.

This means a dual approach:

- A new form of laws to adapt the legal framework to technology. To be perfectly adaptable, laws would have to refer conceptually to technological terms and components such as cookies, email, web-forms, etc. Direct reference is not an answer, due to technological progress, as terms become rapidly outdated. To avoid this problem, laws could use terms and concepts that are conceptually one level "up" from the technology. Above, we suggested that "commercial communication" may be a prototype of this form of concept, as it describes conceptually all forms of emails, banner ads, pop-ups, SMS messages and even cold calling for commercial purposes. A similar methodology already exists in software engineering, in the process modelling approach. If the law refers to these processes or common constructs, then the computer models that are used to describe and design both a business model and the underlying ecommerce applications can incorporate matching legal process specifications. In a very preliminary way, process modelling and the extension to the legal framework is described and commented below.
- A new software engineering methodology and components ("environment"), to adapt technology to the law at design time. This environment will enable new technical platforms to be built that are consistent with this legal architecture and evolving laws and private norms. Again, an ingredient for this methodology and environment could be based on the process modelling approach. If legal specifications and constraints are embedded in the system design methodology (e.g. in business modelling or workflow languages), then any change in the laws may be made at the level of the business and process model.

These two components could form part of a larger "legal architecture", a system that incorporates different elements that can be used by information system designers to build compliant ecommerce applications. This architecture is more fully described below. We propose therefore another way to look at this problem, based on a process modelling and business modelling approach to IT development. We believe that this provides insights into the problems of legality in ecommerce, and may provide ideas and support why these elements may be essential ingredients of a solution to the mismatch.

Before developing this more theoretical proposal for a generic legal programming environment, we outline in the next section a more traditional means of determining legal specifications for an implementation of the Research Scenario. It illustrates a form of manual specification and even retrofitting, taking the view that existing commerce processes are already implemented.

2.   INITIAL TECHNOLOGY AND DESIGN RECOMMENDATIONS

In this section, we provide some technical design recommendations that develop a partial solution to the problems posed by the Research Scenario outlined in the previous chapters. We choose the area of Consumer Protection law, as one of the core elements of the shopping scenario. First we set out some general design recommendations, before suggesting a Process Monitor Agent as a way of applying agent technologies to solve some of the Consumer Protection issues raised.

2.1   General Design Recommendations

In our conclusions to Chapter 4, we certain outlined rules and principles necessary for consumer protection and confidence. Any application or agent implemented in the Research Scenario should comply or fulfil the identified needs of respect of fundamental consumer principles (transparency and fair trading); support consumer-oriented secure contracting requirements (authenticity, integrity, confidentiality and non-repudiation); and provide support services: Secure payments, Privacy and Protection against crime (e.g. fraud).

We believe that most of these issues can technically be dealt with by proper programming of the retail store's systems, online merchant sites and procedures, with supporting requirements dealt with by encryption and digital signature technology. This, however, is not currently widespread in consumer electronic commerce (except SSL, incorporated into browsers) and may only be available in mobile transactions on cell phones with emerging UMTS technology, or with shoppers using mobile devices such as computer terminals (notepads, etc.) communicating via Wi-Fi (e.g. with the Wi-Fi WEP security protocol).

Agents should be designed and eventually programmed to provide and interface with these features (supported by legal framework, e.g. on digital signatures, data protection, electronic commerce). The aim is that, even if total consumer protection is not possible at the start of a project (given the technological limitations of 2 or 2.5G and Wi-Fi), the agent platform progresses to provide the adequate level of protection, either through technology in the agent environment and infrastructure or through interaction of consumer protection / privacy enhancing agents (Process Monitoring Agents) that supervise the levels of policy determined by both merchant and consumer users.

2.2 A consumer oriented legal framework

A first step to legally specifying an implementation of the Research Scenario is to define an appropriate legal framework that will provide compliance with legal standards and adequate measures for consumer confidence. In the Chapter 4 we provided a preliminary outline of this framework, which should include:

- **A contractual framework** between merchants and users regarding use of the system's applications and agents;
- **A code of conduct** and guarantees, together with dispute resolution procedures over and above national protections.
- **A privacy policy:** for respecting legal requirements and user wishes, and express consents for automatic calling and other mobile communications with users and RFID tracking.
- **Document storage mechanisms:** for evidentiary and confidence building purposes.
- **Declared levels of consumer protection and procedures:** for eventual acceptance of third party interoperable agents within the research scenario framework.

2.3 Consumer oriented technical proposals

Underlying the legal framework, the technology architecture should be specified to meet the legal requirements. Several technical solutions have been put forward for increased consumer confidence and transaction security: cryptography (e.g. SSL, SET, and XML-based digital signatures), labels, smart cards, physical devices / tokens, biometrics and watermarks. Below, we set out the basic principles for a technology framework that incorporates higher levels of consumer protection for several process categories of the Research Scenario: advertising, contracting and post-contractual processing.

2.3.1   Consumer advertising

a) Messaging (SMS, Wi-Fi, etc.)
- To the extent that the message is automatic, the store's system (or an alternative sender) must obtain the consumer's consent (opt-in obligation). This should be expressly obtained when the consumer registers with the store (or other agent service provider) or on daily log-in. Non-automatic calling on the basis of an ongoing relationship should at least provide an opportunity for consumers to opt out.
- Any messages that are of commercial nature should comply with the information requirements set out in the national implementation of Art. 6 Ecommerce Directive: identification, details, sender, etc.
- If they are unsolicited, this should be identified as soon as it is received by the recipient (allowing filter services, for example). The communication agent provider may also have to contact national "opted-out" register (Robinson lists) for consumers that do not wish to be contacted.

b) Services
- All digital services should provide a link to the provider's (merchant, third party store) identity and address, description of the item, price, payment methods, and, depending on the goods purchased, the right to withdraw, the cost of the distance sales technique, the terms of the offer/price.
- Information that has to be available at all times includes: name, address, contact details, VAT registration, and trade registration.
- All agent-based communications regarding products offered by the store via the mobile device should contain the same details as the actual items in the store, and comply with the relevant indication rules as to selling price and the unit price, etc. (Price Indications Directive etc., rules for foods and non-foods).

2.3.2   Consumer contracting

a) Process for the conclusion of contracts through agents
Apart from standard contact formation processes (offer, acceptance) agent-based applications for concluding transactions with consumers may have to follow certain extra steps. These include:
- Merchant sites and their agents should establish clearly which party is making the offer / acceptance / acknowledgement.
- The supplier (agent) must acknowledge any order placed by the consumer.

- The system must allow the consumer (or consumer's agent) a means to verify and correct the order (input errors) prior to placing the order.

b) Form requirements for contracts through agents

Certain form requirements may be applicable, although generally the Ecommerce Directive requires member states to permit electronic contracts.

- For certain products only (not food or drink), written confirmation of the contract on a durable medium should be provided, e.g. email confirmation would be sufficient, a storable WAP page or SMS if the storage capacity and features of the mobile device allow it. This will include information on the right to withdraw, after-sales service and guarantees[2].
- The terms of the contract must be accessible, storable and reproducible by the consumer or his/her agent.
- The store or online merchant's General Terms and Conditions should be incorporated (by reference or factually) so it will be important to include a link or other technical means of retrieving or receiving such terms in the event of an agent-based contract.

In any event, even though such rules may not apply in all circumstances, it would be of good practice for the store and other agent providers to comply with these requirements, to avoid any doubt and in the interest of consumer confidence.

c) Invoicing

As regards invoices, the new VAT Invoicing Directive[3] will enable the acceptation of invoices sent by electronic means, but for this asymmetric encryption (digital signatures) may be required[4]. National regimes (e.g. Spain) already allow electronic invoicing on certain technical conditions such as auditing of the systems by national tax authorities, and are setting up procedures for recognising certificates for digitally signed invoices[5]. This is a jurisdiction specific issue that will have to be verified in the country of the store.

---

[2] These supplier obligations may also be avoided if the contract is for a single performance (delivery) and the order is invoiced by the communication service provider (not the store). This may arise if the payment method chosen is, for example, by adding the amount to a telephone bill.

[3] Council Directive 2001/115/EC, of 20 December 2001, amending Directive 77/388/EEC with a view to simplifying, modernising and harmonising the conditions laid down for invoicing in respect of value added tax (2001 VAT Invoicing Directive).

[4] Oddly enough, Member States may vary this requirement (paragraph 3(c) of Art 28 of the principal EU VAT Directive 77/388/EEC, as provided by Art 2 of the 2001 VAT Invoicing Directive).

[5] See, for example, at under "comercio electrónico" at www.aeat.es

2.3.3   Information: Recording of transaction

As regards the recording of electronic transactions, there are no extra rules for mobile or agent-based transactions than there are for traditional electronic commerce. Appropriate procedures should be programmed and established (in agents and the store's or web merchant's main systems) so that documentary evidence is kept of all transactions (both merchant-side and client-side) in such a way as to provide authenticity, integrity and non-repudiation. There are widely recognised standards relating to document management (BS7799 and ISO 17799, for example), although those are not guarantees of court admissibility. This level of protection is currently greater than consumers usually have capacity for (home computers or portable devices do not usually provide such features). The issue will be more relevant for merchants, especially in relation to fraud, electronic payments and tax/invoicing requirements

2.4   A Consumer Protection Process Monitor Agent

In addition to these practical design recommendations, we envisage that agent technologies should be able to deal with some if not many of the legal issues posed by both normal online commerce and agent-enhanced commerce. We suggest a Process Monitor Agent as an agent-based means for protection consumer interests.

This consumer protection oriented Process Monitor Agent (PMA) is conceived as a composite agent that could monitor relations between the store and the consumers, freeing off other applications from having consumer protection "coded" into the internal processes and architecture of the system. The principal applications will then consult the PMA (and the rules modelled in its programming) as regards content, timing, procedures, recording, etc, of processes so that they comply with local consumer protection laws.

This agent should incorporate flexibly the store and the consumer's preferences regarding consumer protection, mostly in relation to obligatory provisions of Consumer Protection law. It could also be extended to assist in providing more secure consumer contracting (trusted third party confirmations, digitally signed envelopes, encrypted storage, etc.).

a) Core PMA Functionalities:
- **Message Content control**: for compliance with advertising rules, ecommerce, marketing guidelines. This will incorporate rules for message content and may even evolve to ascertain transparency and fairness (e.g. with regard to timing of offers).

- **Overlapping Consumer and Data Protection functionalities**: negotiation and provision of consent to receive certain commercial messages.
- **Consumer Information control**: will handle information provided to consumer regarding any offer or other commercial process (e.g. notification of rights of return, guarantee obligations, product information, etc.).
- **Contract Process control**: for incorporation of terms, reasonableness of limitations and exemptions, negotiation, authentication and validation of transaction. This may have a user stated preference filter, in relation to applicable law, liability exemptions, returns policy, etc.
- **Data recording**: for non-repudiation, tax and other purposes. Includes for example sending copies to home email address, registering sale with manufacturer (for guarantees, etc.), and providing security layers.

b) Sub-agents or processes

The PMA may have the following subagents or processes:

- **Interface sub-agent**: deals with communications from and to the User.
- **Auditing and Data recording sub-agent**: monitors transactions with consumers and deals with e-records, etc. Includes interaction with certification subagent for supplier information (e.g. sending details to home email).
- **Negotiation sub-agent**: handles contract preferences and processes (checks contractual steps etc.).
- **Consumer knowledge status sub-agent**: monitors consumer status regarding information about the product / service, supplier, ecommerce merchant identification. Provides basis for accepting or refusing a message or a contract (e.g. consumer insufficiently informed about guarantees, rights to return, etc.).
- **Certification / Validation sub-agent:** Permits validation of merchant parties and may have log of rejected / prohibited suppliers.
- **Data Security sub-agent**: ensures security with regard to data transmission: it should determine whether a communication should be encrypted, authenticated, or otherwise protected. Includes digital signature processes, and secure registration of data flows.

In the table below, we describe a specific use-case of an implementation of the Research Scenario, incorporating the design recommendations with PMA. It is based partially on Agent B, described in more detail in Chapter 2.

Table 6-1. Example Use-Case with Consumer PMA

The global promoband

The store transmits promotional data to shoppers within the store, without user intervention. As soon as a new offer enters the data repository, the system (Agent B) finds out (with the aid of the User Profile Agent) which users are interested in that specific product. Agent B takes the initiative to broadcast a message to the user's mobile device (SMS, WAP, WiFi) or a screen on the store trolley if the user is logged in the system. Agent B waits for the user to react to the promotion (cancel, purchase, further information request) to update the shopper's profile. Consumer PMA intervenes to ensure legality of overall process.

Processes	Legal Qualification	Consumer PMA specification
...		
Agent B sends an advertisement to the customer device, without review by staff	Unsolicited commercial communication	**Consumer and Data Protection control**: intercepts message and checks if consent has been (or has to be) obtained before displaying message (prior agreement, express consent, negotiated consent). **Message Content control**: checks message is identified and that data in message complies with content rules (advertising rules, Ecommerce Dir. rules, Distance Sales rules). NB: PMA can check most parameters in User's general and session profile (e.g. accept adverts, acknowledge terms of sale, credit card details, home address, etc.). Also, consents for messages can be referred from a separate Privacy PMA.
Agent B provides a means for accepting the offered product (accept button, voice acceptance, etc)	Information requirements (consumer contracting) Identification of parties Incorporation of terms Secure contracting	**Consumer Information control**: check data supplied regarding consumer rights (guarantees, exclusions, etc.) **Contract Process:** Check: Full identity discloser. Ensure: process for access and storage of terms, error correction and confirmation in the event the transaction is outside certain parameters (price, guarantees, supplier reputation, exclusions, etc.) **Transaction data recording:** secure record of sale data and invoice (digital signature). Apply security processes (SLL, SET, etc.) for any open network digital transmission of this registration. Error procedure in the event of any rejection by the PMA – negotiation or correction by store system (Agent B and associates).
...		

As we can see, the PMA acts as a screen or filter for the consumer, ensuring the store or online promoter complies with mandatory information requirements and processes under Consumer Protection laws.

Note that this is one process in many within the Research Scenario. In this use-case alone there are previous and subsequent processes that may need monitoring to ensure the shopper's privacy and respect for other legal obligations such as IPR or contract processes. For example, the fact that the store system is monitoring the position and purchases of the shopper through RFIDs will require explicit consent from the shopper each time he or she enters the store. This could be negotiated (to the extent allowed by law) or at least monitored by a separate Data Protection PMA (e.g. negotiating a discount of 2% in exchange for allowing the shop to store the shopper's consumer behaviour).

There are several limitations or constraints on this design process. First, the shopper is in a certain country and benefits from local consumer protection laws. Both Agents in the scenario, Agent B and the Consumer PMA, must be programmed or parameterised to comply with these laws, which introduces a high degree of inflexibility and non-interoperability across borders. In addition these laws change, so there must be a definite agent version control process (e.g. agent compliant with laws on 01/01/2004). Also, the programming will require a high level of expressivity and granularity (of shop and user policies) in order to get anywhere near to mapping the real preferences of the shopper. This may be built up by agents that learn. In addition, these processes have to integrate with other processes, for example as we have suggested, a data protection or an IPR PMA on the consumer side, and the store's own back-office and principal technology architecture on the server side, not to mention third party systems and architectures. Finally, the system will need reprogramming when the store changes its advertising, selling or consumer relationship processes, or wants to export the software to another jurisdiction. In other words, it is not very interoperable, it is not very flexible and it is not necessarily persistent.

We have in fact just used the traditional specification method to specify the PMA and show how our ideas can be integrated into mainstream software engineering. We contend that this specification methodology is, in the end, just an elaborate patch: it covers over the more basic issue that law and technology are currently mismatched and does not take advantage of the alternative technological concepts that may overcome these issues. To achieve the advantages of digitisation and new commercial innovations of the digital economy, we believe a more conceptual – higher level – approach is needed, and the whole business process should be modelled. This approach is presented next.

3.   BUSINESS PROCESS MODELLING AND THE MIT VIEW OF THE FIRM

3.1   Process View and Business Constraints

In the first chapter we briefly introduced business processes and, in previous chapters, we have tried to define certain commercial activities of the agents under study from a process view, breaking down each agent into a series of interdependent and coordinated steps (simpler processes). This has enabled us to consider specific legal problems raised by specific processes (sending SMSs, identifying users) and determine some form of solution for that problem. In this section we want to analyse the contribution that this approach makes to finding a more conceptual or general solution to the legal issues raised by ecommerce oriented agent technologies.

We described in Chapter 1 how business process modelling starts with a picture of what the process looks like as a whole. It is decomposed in terms of the specific activities to be completed, and the order in which they must be carried out. A complete model includes the dependencies (or conditions) between those activities, and a definition of who is responsible for making sure those activities are completed. A business process model therefore describes the chain of events that must occur rather than the specific details about how those events will occur – as we have argued here, by human or machine "operator".

Proponents of this process modelling approach maintain that the rigour of this exercise allows systematic organisational management and control[6]. Once clear processes are identified and modelled within a common framework it is easier to act with regard to planning, control, organisation and even leadership. Using various simulation tools, managers can vary or "play around" with different process alternatives to determine which chain or structure is both optimum for the business. Moreover, once a complete model is in place, the ability to change business processes in response to market variations or legal evolution is also enhanced.

In addition, a process-based approach is interesting in our agent-oriented scenario, as the legal analysis and understanding of the issues raised by generic or specific processes (including their characteristics and procedures) should be valid for both human and automated actors.

We also argue that this process modelling can apply to a wider organisational form, the business network[7]. The agent-based transactions we have contemplated within the Research Scenario occur not just within the

---

[6] T Malone et al: *Tools for inventing organizations: Toward a handbook of organizational processes,* 1993-1999

[7] Giglio et al: *An Analytical Framework and a Development Method for Inter-Organisational Business Process Modelling,* 2002.

store, but also between retail supply chain participants and between customers, the store and other web-merchants. In this environment, the legal risks are multiplied. "Networked business" process modelling which minimises these risks can multiply the benefits of single company modelling.

One approach in particular to business process design and knowledge management is of interest: the MIT Process Handbook[8]. This initiative aims to provide a systematic theoretical and empirical foundation for understanding business processes, by collecting and organising examples of how different businesses perform similar processes. The general objective is to recognise and represent organisational processes at varying levels of abstraction, collected in an online "handbook". This handbook allows users who want to improve their business to consider optimal or alternative processes, and invent new processes. Ideally, the creators hope to be able to use the handbook to create software to support or analyse business processes through component based software development, automatically (or semi-automatically) generating software that implements the process in question. As we discuss below, we believe that tools of this kind may be enhanced by embedding legal obligations and processes within process collection or repository.

A key concept of the process view of organisations involves the idea that processes may be governed by "business constraints" or "business rules" (or "dependencies", in coordination theory language)[9]. Each business process is an activity that must be done by a person or equipment (technology). Flows from one process to the next may be conditional or unconditional. This means that there are rules or constraints that establish the conditions that must be satisfied in order for the next activity in the process to be executed. There may also be rules that specify when a particular activity has been completed or what to do in the event of an error. A constraint is therefore a restriction on the degree of freedom an enterprise has on carrying out a process, and ultimately providing a solution. These rules or constraints constitute the knowledge and business logic of an enterprise, as they determine how one company differentiates from others: from manufacturing processes such as how products are created, to sales and marketing processes including pricing systems, discounts and offers.

The advantage of this approach is that there are methods for graphically modelling processes and their constraints and dependencies, formalising business or legal policies, processes and constraints in diagrammatical and even machine-understandable form. We elaborate on this next.

---

[8] Malone et al: op cit., 1999.
[9] Ross: *The Business Rule Book,* 1997; see also Business Rules Group: *Final Report,* 2000.

3.2   Business Modelling

There is no generally accepted definition or classification of business models. According to OMG group a business model is an abstraction of how a business functions (the method of doing business). According to Timmers, for example, a business model refers to the architecture of products, services and the information flows, including a description of the various business actors involved and their roles[10]. As explained by Petrovic et al., a business model can also describe the logic of a "business system" for creating value, that lies behind the actual processes.[11] A business model should therefore provide an understanding of how the business mission and objective within the model is realised in practice, and what are the constraints on the enterprise processes. A market or industry models widens this process to cover various actors, roles and relationships within the specified market, for example in relation to a supply chain or other market mechanism (auctions, licences, customer management, etc.).

Modelling involves clarifying within the firm's overall "system" the different actors that are involved in these processes, and establishing their roles and relationships. In the case of the Research Scenario, internal actors are the store, its staff and consumers. External actors include suppliers, partner companies, service providers, and intermediaries such as IT system hosts, servers, even down to the level of routers. Once these actors are identified, their roles and the related processes that constitute what the organisation is offering can be defined: purchasing materials from suppliers, offering consumers certain discounts, or creating a database of products and catalogues that is hosted online.

This model of the processes assists in designing and building a business and technical architecture and workflow. This workflow is a graphic representation of the "flow" of the business processes and the constraints or conditions applicable to each. Typically the logic of a business, its policies and knowledge structure, have been buried in enterprise "traditions" (the "ways things are done") and, in the enterprise IT systems, the program code or in database structures. This is reinforced by the third generation computing languages which tended to be sequential in nature, lending themselves to rigid codification of business activity, within a procedural and structured software engineering methodology.

As a modern alternative, design methods based on process modelling develop explicit models and rules or workflow making these policies and constraints explicit. In the process model, activities are linked together with indications of the flow from one activity to the next. These indications

---

[10] P Timmers: *Electronic Commerce: Strategies and models for business-to-business trading*, 1999.

[11] Petrovic et al.: *Developing Business Models for eBusiness*, 2001.

specify the conditions and constraints on carrying out the process and executing the next. Examples include action constraints that define the dynamic aspects of the model, structural constraints which determine the static aspects, and derivation constraints define the way in which information can be derived from the model. Within this model, business constraints can be modelled in a variety of ways, for example through formal logic, static process constraints embedded within the business model or more dynamically in explicit rules (such as workflow in XPLD or other workflow language, or business rules expressed in emerging technical languages such as RuleML). This can then be represented and formalised in machine understandable language (e.g. "executable" UML) and used as the basis for developing compliant automated processes.

This shift in thinking from lower level code to higher level models enables relationships and processes to be automated in a manner that more closely resembles natural workflow, where implicit and explicit constraints or norms govern relationships between the different elements of a business.

And, as we argue in section 3, there is little difference between business constraints and legal constraints. The concept of business rule or constraint – a restriction on the degree of freedom an enterprise has on carrying out a process – is a close definition to legal rules discussed here, such as personal data processing restrictions or IPR prohibitions on exploitation acts in relation to protected works. These same modelling methods should therefore be adaptable, to create conceptual models for the legal principles discussed here – privacy, contract, consumer protection and intellectual property rights. This implies "codifying" the law in a more structured and standardised way for interpretation by both human participants (managers, computer engineers) and machines (software agents, in particular). By extension, we argue below that if the model of the firm and its processes is standardised, we have the advantage of being able to create a generic legal architecture or model for online activities.

3.3 The MIT View of the firm

Based on this discussion, a key objective is to develop an industry or business framework and an architecture abstraction stack that supports an approach that aims to incorporate legal enhancements into electronic commerce. Grounded in process modelling theory, this framework would be based on an abstract design or model of the firm as a whole, including its internal and external processes. The model lays down the roles of the different actors – organisations, machines, humans and software – and relationships involved in a transaction or business process. This model could standardise a representation of the firm architecture and its relationship with the environment. As we argue below, this model could then integrate the legal dimensions.

In Figure 6.1 we present one possible conceptual framework that includes a novel view of the firm. We believe that this model may usefully be used as a first step towards creating legally compliant architectures, in the manner explained above: by creating a standard view of the firm, we may be able to create a standard legal model that applies to it. This framework is interpreted as follows.

First of all, we consider organisations and their interactions with third parties as systems whose elements are people, technology, information, materials and processes. The active parties are either people or technology (automated equipment). These operate within the organisational structure applying various processes to information and materials (or resources). For example, our Research Scenario grocery store is a system combining staff, suppliers, consumers, on the one hand, and computer equipment on the other. These parties carry out various operations in relation to supermarket and organisational products and advertising materials, among other components.

All the organisation's transactions are therefore considered processes that are carried out by people or technology in relation to information and materials. These processes, for instance, include buying and selling products, collecting data, sending advertisements. Processes are therefore at the centre of the model, whether manual or automated. Thus the company's fundamental architecture is built by people and machines, and their corresponding activities.

These processes create the organisation's value proposition, i.e. what it offers clients and users. Retail value, for example, is generated and offered not just through available products but also electronic payments and financial services, interactive product information and recommendations, consumer shopping behaviour and feedback data, and analysis of sales and stocks data (providing value for suppliers). Conceptually, we break this value down into material value (goods), information value and process value (combined for example, in a service). Whereas information value in the form of leaflets for special offers may be offered through leaving a pile of leaflets at the door, this may be enhanced by an alternative process such as having staff specifically hand out the leaflets – or, in our Research Scenario, have the equivalent information made available to consumers through their mobile shopping device. The process, however, is basically the same, while the value proposition can change radically – the information value is enhanced by process value.

Increasingly these processes are being automated today through Information Technologies such as software agents and workflow tools, as computers gain in terms of "intelligence" and can substitute human involvement. Formerly manual processes (handing out brochures or leaflets, providing product information, checking shelf contents, reading bar codes) are carried out by more or less intelligent software applications – – as we have suggested here, through agents analysing the consumer's shopping list or personal profile, the store's product catalogue and advertising database or interacting with electronic product codes embedded in RFIDs.

Finally, to achieve a more precise and therefore more adequate model of the organisation, it and the value it produces should be understood in the context in which the firm's processes are "executed" or operate. The environment, for example the retail sector, can be highly relevant to the firm's activities. Significant elements for the retail store are the firm's position in the retail supply chain, its size, its location, its country, etc. This environment also determines many legal compliance issues for the firm's processes. For example in our Research Scenario, the central firm is the retail store, who interacts with consumers: consumer protection and advertising issues are fundamental. If we were considering a player further up the supply chain, legal rules such as product liability and guarantees would be more relevant.

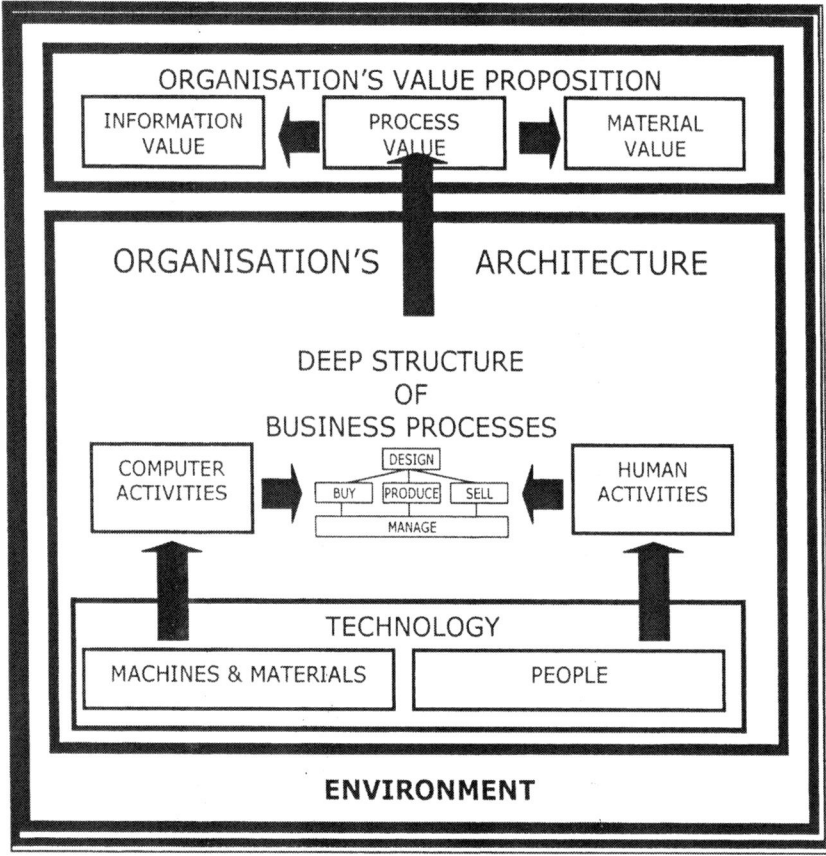

Figure 6-1. MIT Process view of the Firm[12]

As we commented above, eventually this formal model may be incorporated into IT designs via a series of modelling languages and transformation of the model into machine understandable code. Any change in the processes is reflected in the overall model (allowing the value proposition to be evaluated) and once approved, translated into new or modified applications for the firm.

We believe that one of the advantages of this process view and conceptual model is that once it is applied to enterprises, it allows them to determine with ease the legal issues – or in fact any issues – corresponding to the chosen business processes and model. As we illustrated in the previous legal analysis, each process may be associated with a certain legal specification or constraint. Once these are determined, the firm can embed the compliance constraints and procedures (either regulatory or contractual)

---

[12] B. Subirana and T. Malone: Unpublished diagram resulting from joint work between Prof. Brian Subirana and Prof. Thomas Malone at the Center for Coordination Science, MIT Sloan School of Management, 2002.

into the business processes, whether human/manual or automated through technology. If they are automated, the computer systems that are developed should therefore already incorporate the required levels of compliance.

Accordingly, we hold that these high-level computational abstractions and process models are suitable to integrate the legal aspects studied here. These legal aspects can be represented through "legal processes" and through constraints or "dependencies" which act like rules. In addition, as the model is abstract, it would also be flexible enough to incorporate new concepts derived from laws as they evolve in the future. When laws change, the model can be reviewed and appropriate modifications made to both the legal model that is applied to the business model, and the resulting business processes.

Finally, these abstractions could be referred to in legislation, regulations and case law or administrative rulings for ease of integration of the legal framework with the business and technological environment. This is also briefly outlined next.

We submit therefore that the process view of organisations offered here enhances the possibilities for creating legally compliant business networks. It enables models to be developed that may incorporate legal processes, constraints and dependencies at design and development time, within a coherent industry and organisational technological framework. The fact that these systems are thus legalised enhances the value proposition of organisations, supporting sustainability and growth in the medium and long term.

4.   A LEGAL PROCESS MODEL OR ARCHITECTURE

The MIT view of the firm supports our suggestion that a solution to the problem of the legality of ecommerce transactions may usefully consider an architecture base on **business processes** and a more **general computational model** as a methodology and conceptual framework, to help legalise technology-based business transactions. We argue that the MIT view of the firm develops a model that integrates the business technical and legal aspects and that can be incorporated into IT designs, using business process models and higher level computational designs.

4.1   New insights and new architecture

The MIT view of the firm provides a conceptual abstraction of both the business and technical environments for ecommerce transactions. This may be used effectively as a tool to analyse the legal difficulties, allowing us to see the legal problems in a different manner. This provides some insights into how to conceive of a potential legal solution for the business and technical environment. It provides a systematic way to analyse any situation or planned application (whether it is known that there are legal problems or not), as part of the business and technical analysts' and system designers' tool kits. Integrating the two aspects, it is an interdisciplinary way to address the issues.

4.1.1   New insights

On the basis of the process oriented approach, we can define the problem at hand in a new way and gain some new insights. On the one hand, law is being created without taking into account business and technology processes, i.e. without a process oriented analysis. It then uses terms and concepts that are not abstract enough to apply to all business activities and apply with difficulty to a moving technological background. While original privacy controls were envisaged for "automated calling systems" in the 1997 Privacy in the Telecommunications Sector Directive, it is doubtful whether the definition is sufficient to cover many forms of personalised or general advertisements such as emails, location sensitive SMSs, pop-ups and banners, etc., which in the end fulfil a function similar to a telephone calling system. A more process oriented approach such as the new criteria of "commercial communication" seems more adaptable and durable, and also something that can be modelled in a computer environment.

On the other hand, technology is being used and ecommerce applications programmed in deterministic ways that are centred on code: carefully customised applications, databases, middleware, protocols. Most companies implement piecemeal solutions to expose, integrate, transform, and connect disjointed applications and information. Specifications are taken from business units, and only in few cases are legal obligations incorporated at design time. There is no model created to represent the business processes and constraints or dependencies. When a business activity is modified, for example from offline to online delivery of information, books or software, new specific IT extensions are developed to cater for the new circumstances. In the event of any change in legislation, for example obliging opt-in procedures for obtaining consent to commercial emails (rather than opt-out), further changes would have to be made. In this manner, IT systems get more and more complex. As an alternative, process modelling may enable IT systems to be designed at a higher level of abstraction, and while in the end similar applications are developed, the effect of new regulations or the new legal issues raised by a new process can be considered and incorporated at this higher level, leading to appropriate computer engineering specifications.

For instance, while CD-based software is often sold under shrink wrap licenses, digital downloading requires click-wrap contracts. Companies that sell software could just paste the text of their standard license into the appropriate screen. This, however, may leave them open to questions of the valid incorporation of the terms. Alternatively, they could incorporate in their process models the effects of legal decisions on the validity of certain click-wrap clauses – e.g. new processes for bringing arbitration clauses to the express notice of clients, to mention a recent US decision. This new "legalized" process would then provide new specifications for the download process, which can then be implemented in the corporate IT systems either manually or, ideally, automatically using component based computing[13]. While more complex modelling will be required for ensuring privacy protections (for obtaining user consent, encrypting data storage and transmission, ensuring access to personal data), we believe a similar approach could be used.

4.1.2 New architecture

The MIT view is not just a tool for providing insights and analysis: conceptually, it also suggests that any legally compliant methodology to improve the legality of ecommerce transactions and overcome the identified technology-legal mismatch will need to include a "legalized" business process handbook and legal engineering environment (or equivalent pieces) within what we call a "legal architecture".

This architecture should be able to deal with both the legal and the technical failures outlined above. As regards the former, by using the process based approach we should be able to model legal obligations, rights and regulations. We can create abstract concepts (e.g. commercial communications, automatic processing, etc.) and legal processes (provide consent, notify, certify) that can map onto businesses and business processes, regardless of the speed of technology change. This would create a Legal Process Handbook, a description of processes that reflect and comply with the law.

As regards the latter, we contend that to build a legally compliant technical architecture, a novel language needs to be developed that can formalise business and legal constraints and dependencies. Currently modelling and programming languages do not take account of the law. A "Legal Engineering Environment" would create a framework for legalising these processes within the technical architecture at design level, formalised in the above-mentioned Legal Process Handbook and implemented in practice via technology components and a programming methodology:

   a) Specific technology processes may be combined to form a single core technology component such as an access protocol (e.g. Legal Access Protocol);

---

[13] GT Leavens and M Sitaraman: *Foundations of Component-Based Systems*, 2000.

b) The modelling and the technology together form a legal programming environment that determines how to develop applications that are consistent with the law. This is an approach more than a tool, a means to ensure that applications can be programmed taking into account the legal aspects that we have discussed here, for example on the basis of the legal process handbook, implementing abstract models for particular cases.

This architecture is further explained below.

4.2   Legal Processes

While the identification of business processes, constraints or dependencies is important in its own right, we argue that it can be matched or paired with legal processes and constraints or dependencies. Laws are forms of constraints and govern how a business carries out certain actions. They therefore underlie business constraints. We argue that it should be possible therefore to enhance business process models by incorporating these legal constraints and dependencies. In addition, while we have been considering up to now the "external" or public legality of business processes so that they comply with applicable laws, these constraints could also capture what we might call internal or private legality, i.e. compliance with negotiated and agreed contracts. It should be possible therefore to incorporate both laws and contractual obligations (including, for example, privacy policies) into business process models.

Using this process oriented approach, an understanding of the legal implications of the processes could enable us to create an abstract legal model or architecture of the transactions and, more generally speaking, organisations as a whole. This architecture could be represented through a language that combines constraints and dependencies, relevant ontologies (for describing in a standard and hierarchical manner legal concepts and knowledge) and processes. This legal architecture can be mapped onto, or extend, the business process description of the organisation and its model. This would "legalise" the model. As a result, when business processes are automated by technology, either partially as in today's ecommerce environment or fully through agent technologies, the resulting transactions would be more legally compliant.

Therefore, once actors, roles and relationships are defined and combined into processes, it is critical to identify the risk bearing processes of the system. This is due to the onerous legal obligations that we have outlined in previous chapters, and any breach would have a negative effect on the firm's activities, reputation and ultimately value[14]. Once these are identified, we can define the associated legal risks as we have done here, and develop a

---

[14] Kenny and Borking: *The Value of Privacy Engineering,* 2002.

legal model or architecture for the organisation's processes. These may be modelled in accordance with the law, incorporating for example negotiating and contracting process for purchasing supplies, privacy and consumer protection safeguards for offering consumers certain discounts, or IPR protections and respect in creating a database of products and catalogues that is hosted online.

The resulting technical architecture and workflow would integrate legal compliance and also contractual requirements, enabling compliant automated transactions and activities within the system. This conceptual framework and consequent technological implementation (e.g. through agents) could be "legal domain" specific (e.g. P3P and Privacy, XRML and Digital Rights) or more generic. In the latter case, this would allow developers to determine models and applications that are applicable in a variety of domains, taking advantage of universal or similar processes such as identification, discovery and description, negotiation, repositories, invocation, monitoring, and auditing and logging. One area where this should apply is in negotiation and providing consent, a process that is common to many domains such as commercial contracts, IPR licences and data processing consents – albeit with different specific requirements and rules.

Combining this idea with the MIT Process Handbook, for example, leads us to consider how to enhance the Process Handbook with concepts of binding constraints and legality, so the tool can be used not only for analysing and optimising business processes, but also legalising them.

4.3 Capturing public and private legal norms

We should also consider legal compliance from a double perspective: regulatory compliance with obligatory norms and contractual compliance with binding agreements. While the first refers to top down legislated obligations such as those related to personal data processing, consumer protection, taxation and administrative tasks, the latter refers to the mutually agreed – and flexible – contractual relationships and commitments that underlie most commercial transactions, and form the basis for most e-business networks today. Both affect enterprise business processes and even the overall business model.

Future work should aim to incorporate these external and internal commitments and obligations – constraints on transactions and interactions in formal language, or dependencies (in coordination theory) – into the business processes and technical infrastructure of these networks. Contract terms involve conditional relationships, which are the basis for formalizing constraints and dependencies. This can be expressed, for example, with IF-THEN syntax: IF there is a contract conflict, THEN English law will apply (applicable law clause); or IF delivery is not made by Friday THEN you are in breach of contract (contract performance); IF the data subject's informed consent has been obtained THEN his/her personal data may be processed (privacy protection). These conditions may also be expressed in terms of dependencies: proper interpretation of the contract depends on applying English law. Valid performance of the contract is dependant on delivering by Friday. Personal data processing is dependant on obtaining (having obtained) the data subject's informed consent. It will be important to identify the types of dependencies that may exist in order to determine the mechanisms for coordinating and executing (in a computer environment) the different business activities: sending an email, downloading a file, providing a name and/or credit card number. While coordination theory aims to understand how to manage dependencies among activities, work in the legal area should be aimed at understanding how to model and enforce dependencies between or among activities.

Negotiation of contracts also responds to business policies (for price discounting, price and quantity, delivery, etc.), which means that the negotiation protocols may also be modelled, just as P3P has made the first steps in modelling privacy negotiations. The resulting contracts can then be described by formal logic or some other type of formalized rules, which apply constraints to the business processes ("200 units must be delivered by a certain date"). Other contract elements, such as service provisions (e.g. rules for refunds, lead time to place an order) can also be integrated into the model.

For this, it will be necessary to investigate how these public and private constraints and dependencies may be captured in a formal model and transformed into a form which is understandable at design and development time. While public regulation is a given (though evolving over time) and may be modelled asynchronously, capturing contractual commitments means identifying and understanding the procedures that define how private norms are created and discharged, under which circumstances they can be avoided or cancelled, and what happens if they are breached. Once apprehended in this way, it will be easier to develop a means for incorporating such constraints and dependencies into business processes and models and the underlying ICTs. In this way, enterprises may integrate or align organisational policies with regulatory and contract policies. At the same time, flexibility must ensure that the evolutionary nature of businesses and business networks is translated into the legal dimension taking into account regulatory changes, technologies and evolving participant agreements, requirements and needs.

We argue that laws framed in a process-oriented manner can be embedded in the software engineering process: in the components such as business constraints or rules and protocols, and in the methodology, just as building regulations force buildings to be built according to the law. For this, the law must also be "technology friendly", i.e. conceived and drafted in a way that can be modelled and eventually machine interpreted. New technologies and languages, including XML-based modelling languages, are being developed that change the way applications are being built and reduce the role of the simple programmer while highlighting the role of business analyst and the understanding of business constraints.

For our suggested approach to work, business requirements, constraints and dependencies should be modelled through processes and rules or workflow, so that eventually the organisation's process and rule repository may be automatically deployed and updated through a series of CASE-like systems. In a similar fashion, laws – which are also constraints on businesses and create dependencies – that are conceived on the basis of processes may be modelled and automatically integrated into business models, directly affecting the resulting IT systems and ensuring their compliance.

This embedding however poses the challenge of incorporating different legal cultures and frameworks across national boundaries, and creating a system that evolves as the legal landscape evolves. Self-regulation is one alternative, taking advantage of business party autonomy. But legally compliant process models and coding is another: each service and functionality is modelled together with the corresponding relationship governance and monitoring, automatically building trust into the network framework. In addition, adaptable and adaptive (e.g. agent-based) contractual frameworks responding to modelled business processes are conceivable, where individual relationships are legally structured as and when systems interact, in line with the "ecosystem" view of networks.

One alternative, perhaps an idealised view and the simplest one, would be for technology standardisation bodies and legislators to work hand in hand to create legally compliant architectural "components" (for the technical and legal architecture) that evolve one version at a time, through carefully synchronised version control.

4.4   A new type of laws?

This conceptual framework is in fact part of a two-way dialogue between law and technology. Our research also suggests that future laws and regulations should be developed so that they can be incorporated into future legally compliant architectures, and be conceptually extendable to networked organisations such as the retail chain in the Research Scenario. Our work suggests therefore that a new legal macro-framework is needed: a new type of law that can match, map or fit onto at least one (if not many) generation of technology, focusing on universal processes and models that are not limited by the current technological paradigm. This is by analogy to its application in the business world, where the process handbook abstracts business processes (get, send, receive, exchange) and allows them to be specialised in any business structure.

This would require laws to be written in the language of process modelling, that can map bi-directionally onto the business process model and technology, through formalisation and modelling. Recent European legislation may align with this, in the attempt to create more abstract (and sometimes process-oriented) concepts such as commercial communications or automated processing systems, and defining roles such as Data Subject, Controller and Processor. This abstract legal framework would enable the practical design and programming of models that can capture, for every program instance, the relevant jurisdictions, the attribution of responsibility and the extent of liability.

We are suggesting that a potential solution to the problems outlined here are laws written as a function of a standard organisational model. Laws are generally drafted to deal with a specific situation. We argue that this is insufficient, that if we can create a standard model of commerce and organisations, that adapts to ALL organisations and business transactions, then we can legislate for the standard model, using similar models and abstractions. We contend that the MIT view may be a step towards such a universal model, applying to all organisations. If it represents companies so that they fall within the model, it will be a useful legal tool (for process legalisation) as well as business tool (for process modelling and optimisation).

4.5   Examples of applications of process view to agent processing

Below, we provide a brief outline of some examples of how this approach may be used.

4.5.1   Agent negotiation

An agent based contracting scenario was used by the SweetDeal project, a rule-based approach to representing business contracts.[15] It enables software agents to create, evaluate, negotiate, and execute contracts with substantial automation and modularity. The negotiation and contract performance processes are first modelled and implemented through situated courteous logic programs for knowledge representation in RuleML (an emerging standard for Semantic Web XML rules). This research project extends previous versions of the SweetDeal approach by also incorporating process knowledge descriptions whose ontologies are represented in DAML+OIL (emerging standard for Semantic Web ontologies). This

---

[15] B Grosof and T Poon: *Representing Agent Contracts with Exceptions using XML Rules,* 2002. Extended with a Situated Courteous Logic Program to represent contracts dynamically, as in a real world negotiation process.

representation of negotiating stances through policy declarations and business process rules enables more complex contracts with behavioural provisions to be automatically concluded. In the SweetDeal case, specific processes were created for handling exception conditions that might arise during the execution of the contract (e.g., late delivery or non-payment).

From a legal point of view, we have seen that these automated contracts may fail as regards consent to specific terms and being considered unilateral adherence contracts (e.g. in a consumer transaction). The automated negotiation and contracting based on previously modelled preferences and processes may assist with these issues, personalising contracts and thus avoiding unilateralism. Specific consent could be obtained for certain clauses that are required to be negotiated (e.g. excluding liability, for data collection, or the reproduction of a work). Subsequent online performance could also be monitored and controlled through automated forms of Service Level Agreements, that compare actual performance with obligations that are captured by a modelling and representational language. The (contracting) processes established by businesses using such representation acquire greater external legal validity as there is less of a risk of the contract being declared invalid. Thus we argue that agent-supported negotiation of this type, modelled through the knowledge representation language, can be considered a first step towards designing more compliant business processes.

4.5.2 Privacy standardisation solutions

Standardisation efforts with regard to privacy protection, such as the afore-mentioned P3P, are also close to the process modelling approach discussed above. Both approaches involve an abstraction of transactions, processes and policies or personal rules (such as user registration, data collection and privacy preferences). These are called policies or preferences. These are then declared in computer understandable language. IT tools envisaged by both approaches are similar: the hierarchical representation of knowledge through ontologies and constraints or rules, and workflow or rule engines (e.g. APPEL in P3P) for executing policies and the related processes[16]. We argue that by modelling the legal requirements for privacy, we can create a legal architecture that is understandable from both a business and technological perspective. This will allow compliant processes to be designed and eventually implemented.

---

[16] Yee and Korba: *The negotiation of privacy policies in distance education,* 2003, for education related policy negotiation.

4.5.3   Digital Rights Management Systems

A firm can model the different processes that are applied to data in automated transactions. It should also be able to verify whether certain processes such as reproduction or distribution affect the IPR attached to the data. These processes can then be allowed or forbidden, in accordance with a previously negotiated DRM contract (see above, on agent negotiating) or with Rights Management Information embedded in digital materials. We should also consider how to model the various exemptions that allow different exploitation uses to be carried out by different categories of persons (end-users, education establishments, etc.). This would improve IPR management for both content providers and users. Therefore there would also be less of a need for personal supervision of data processing, as agents can carry out this verification and compare the content providers and content users' objectives and constraints, as well as applicable laws, for processing with embedded or negotiated rules.

4.5.4   Jurisdictional specificity

Differences in legal regimes complicate any standardised modelling of legal processes and this concept of a legal architecture. Models and related automated processes may only be valid in specified jurisdictions. This may mean that different modelling tools and systems will have to be adapted to the legal frameworks where the business in question operates – multiplying the complexity of subsequent automation. Implemented through agents, one may have to consider contracting agents that can operate in all EU jurisdictions, complying with variable processes and regulations governing invoicing requirements, e-record and data retention obligations, and privacy controls.

5.   AGENT AND MULTI-AGENT ARCHITECTURES

5.1   Agent programming

It has been argued that the mainstream ideas in software engineering have been driven by the problem of dealing with larger and larger systems, and handling this complexity mainly through distributed computing.[17] For several years, computer engineering has taken up the challenge of constructing flexible independent systems that can evolve with changing requirements over time. Just as we seem to be able to cope with this complexity, the world is moving towards networked applications, thus

---

[17] Parnas: *On the Criteria To Be Used in Decomposing Systems into Modules*, 1972.

adding a whole new layer of complexity to the already existing one. The concept and development of web-services are one result of this, with the promise of offering modular and supposedly combinable or interoperable services over the network. However, in this "system of systems" there are no centralised institutions coordinating the distributed development effort, resulting in a number of integration and interoperability problems.

More recently, as we have described, agent-based computing is being considered. The agent paradigm is being given considerable impetus in relation to self-configuring evolving network environments, and is also a useful tool for approaching legal compliance from a process perspective. As with process modelling, it offers a range of high-level abstractions that facilitate the conceptual and technical integration of communications and interactions. This approach is highly significant for networked business systems since business processes are driven by and directed towards entities (actors, agents), and hence have to comply with the physical, social and regulatory dynamics of interacting individuals and organisations. While in most large or distributed organisations, ICTs are currently based on data management and data flow, agent-based computing emphasises the important role of entities and their priorities, policies, local constraints and (mental) state, and of communication and interaction between them – the key systemic elements from a legal point of view – for analysing and designing organisations and their information systems. This seems ideal for representing and implementing processes.

This agent paradigm, providing a mindset and techniques involving decomposition, abstraction and organisation of the complex problem at hand, is also the approach that may be required by lawyers for specifying the legal dimensions of (agent mediated) networked e-commerce. For example, in view of the increasing complexity of automated networked e-business transactions, it is worth considering a framework that provides numerous agents that are both technically and legally interoperable, breaking down the complex business, technical, legal (and social) processes, functions and requirements into component parts which may be modelled. As we argued above, these decomposed interaction processes among business entities and their representative agents are defined and constrained by process constraints or rules (declarations of policy or conditions that must be satisfied) which can be modelled and expressed in a technologically meaningful way. This becomes the legal equivalent or specification for the business model and technical interoperability, interaction and integrity in multi-agent systems.

We also noted that agents can be seen as mediators – i.e. they simply automate certain non-intentional processes such as data mining or archiving, or support interactions initiated by humans. Gradually, however, agents may evolve to become transaction initiators. As mentioned above, the MIT view of the firm adapts to this evolution, as it the model could provide an answer whether a transaction is automated or not: it is the very process that is being carried out that is "legalised" by the legal architecture. To a great extent, the legal issues of the process should have been solved beforehand, within the model.

What becomes a challenge, however, is to model the process of agents gaining intelligence: how to model this agent intelligence? Can we define ways of modelling the autonomy, adaptive reasoning, learning capacity of an agent, so that a more complete model can be created to anticipate agent evolution?

5.2   Agent commerce models

We have seen that in agent mediated electronic commerce (AMEC), agents can be used in many ways, representing buyers, sellers and intermediaries, and participating in many electronic markets throughout the stages of need identification, matchmaking, negotiation, contracting, contract fulfilment and service provision. Conceptually speaking, commercial transactions within these markets can be either hierarchical (within an established framework) or market-based (open participants, open parameters), and the appropriateness of one or the other may depend on the products in question.[18]

This means that there are two types of systems to model when developing an agent-based commerce application or system. On the one hand, a hierarchical model, which is more static and where processes are confined to known variables and actors. The laws and regulations governing these relationships are known and can be incorporated into the model, for example under a framework contract which establishes the particular ground rules. The rights and obligations of this framework can be modelled and embedded into the processes permitted by the hierarchy.

On the other hand, there is the open-ended model which needs to map not the particular participants and their roles, but the flexible relationships between market participants. These may have to be categorised to fulfil one or more specific roles: "buyer", "seller", "Trusted third party", "contract repository". Policies for agent behaviour would therefore be designed to cater for an evolving set of partners or parties, and deal with many more unknown variables and process – such as new agents interacting with the system and maybe new service offerings. This would require standardisation of interaction protocols, e.g. for access, resource negotiation, contract negotiation, repositories. From our legal perspective, we believe there may be a need to incorporate legality at this level of interaction, for example in the form of a legal access protocol. Examples include incorporating privacy and confidentiality in the agent exchanged data, and ensuring the electronic recording of interactions. The process view leads us to consider conditions

---

[18] F Dignum: *Agents, Markets, Institutions and Protocols,* 2000.

and processes for legalising the interactions between agents rather than in ensuring the legality of the negotiated content between agents.

This general conceptual breakdown between hierarchies and markets is reflected in the AMEC Science and Technology Roadmap[19]. Current perspectives of AMEC view agent systems as part of an electronic brokerage service, mediating between suppliers and customers, with strict protocols and (central) institutional control. This is a hierarchical model – which allows itself to be modelled on the basis of the approach suggested by the MIT View of the firm.

We conceive that trust mechanisms for inter-agent transactions (the raison d'être of these electronic institutions) will get more robust. They will gradually include processes to guarantee the four requirements for secure electronic contracting: confidentiality, integrity, authentication and non-repudiation. As this happens, contacts and contracts among agents may be more automatic and direct, and MAS will become contract-based rather than protocol-based. This is the market model, and involves more complex interaction in dynamic open networks. The processes for interaction in this context will have to be standardised to a high degree, and we argue that it is in this process and interface standardisation that the required elements for legal compliance could be embedded.

A scenario based on this model, for instance, could envisage breaking down tasks between mediating and initiating agents in MAS in this open model. User interface agents – specialised maybe in user preferences – could delegate the negotiation and contracting tasks to specialised trading agents – experts in different trading procedures (auctions, requests for quotes, etc). Whereupon, contract monitoring and fulfilment agents step in to control performance[20]. What will be important from a legal perspective is to model the relations and transactions between the agents to ensure compliance at all levels. This level of complexity may be necessary as ubiquitous computing systems and devices, combined with mobile communications, provide more and more data and opportunities for user overload, and more need for distributed autonomous computing to deal with each situation.[21] The legal complexity will rise correspondingly, as we comment next.

5.3 Multi Agent Systems and the MIT View of organisations

In multi-agent systems, agents can interact either within a closed framework (closer to hierarchies and closed process models) or on the open network. We mentioned above that in closed models, the legal issues may be

[19] C. Sierra: *AMEC S&T Road-map,* 2001.
[20] Grosof and Poon: *Representing Agent Contracts with Exceptions using XML Rules,* 2002.
[21] C. Sierra: op cit., 2001.

restricted and modelled fairly clearly. The trouble lies with open MAS, especially with open and negotiated relationships and complex transactions. One of the key issues for open MAS are the need for creating and building trust, how laws contribute to this, and how this trust can be modelled at a conceptual level[22].

This issue of trust between agents and between agents and users is fundamental.[23] Castelfranchi describes trust as both a mental state and a social attitude and relation. It is related to attributes such as reliability, dependability, security, honesty and competence. Another approach considers it *an attitude an agent has with respect to the dependability/capabilities of other agents*[24]. This trust exists at two levels, in task delegation to agents on the one hand, and interaction between agents in MAS on the other. In the first case, trust is an essential ingredient leading to acceptance and development of open market ecommerce, whether B2B or B2C, and to overcoming resistance in commercial actors to the delegation to or cooperation with software agents. This delegation of initiative to agents lies in direct contrast to traditional systems (the direct manipulation of IT systems by humans), where the power of decision to "trust the system" and to proceed lies with the human actors. In the second case, if agents cannot trust other agents, or trust a MAS supervisory system to guarantee the reputation or capabilities and processes other agents, the essential interactions between agents in MAS will not take place.

At both levels, law and legal compliance (normative compliance, in a wider sense) is one of the main ingredients. Obedience to the law is one of the basic elements of any normative behaviour, and therefore has a fundamental role in establishing this trust. Humans will trust agents more if they know these will comply with applicable laws, agents will trust each other more if their compliance with norms (whether external / legal or internal / contractual) is also guaranteed or vouched for. Frameworks considered for open MAS, such as electronic institutions or contract frameworks, aim to provide levels of trust found offline that are provided by the legal, social and institutional systems of the real world.

The question is then how to model this trust in formal terms – how to create machine equivalents of knowledge relating to security, honesty, reliability, etc. Within cooperative agent systems, this includes modelling permissions and delegations. This leads to designing a business model and framework for agent systems that includes processes to allow "trust-bound" agents – i.e. those that will only interact with trusted counterparts – to

---

[22] Castelfranchi: *Principles of Trust,* 1998; and Castelfranchi et al (Eds): *Trust in Agents,* 2000.

[23] Castelfranchi et al: op cit, 2000; and M. Child: *Trust Issues and user reaction to e-services and electronic marketplaces,* 2001 for trust between agents; also see A. Kini, and J. Choobinch: *Trust in electronic commerce,* 1998.

[24] T. Tang et al.: *Who can I trust?,* 2002.

proceed. Commonly, these processes include authorisation, certification, access controls, security policies and reputation mechanisms.[25] The legal dimension of these processes (excluding, for example, the purely security aspects), should try to model rights and obligations, permissions and prohibitions, between agents, and determine actions to be carried out if an agent fails to fulfil its obligations. Reputation mechanisms include associating levels of trust with agents, and which can be modified on the basis of fulfilment or not of the obligations. This indicates a need to formulate a language and logic that can represent basic notions such as commitments, constraints, reliability and other legal concepts particularly found in, or in relation to, contracts.

For this, some authors have suggested creating a trusted third party (TTP), similar to those certification authorities that are being set up to guarantee the validity of digital certificates, through external verification of authenticity. For MAS projects, this TTP has included a supervising authority or sentinel[26] or a contract manager[27] to monitor the behaviour of agents and provide trust services such as security and auditing (identification and logging) as well as norm enforcement within the system. These norms include legal rules determined externally by the applicable legal system or internally by contractual negotiation or agent system ownership[28]. Other suggestions aim to incorporate trust mechanisms into agent interactions through a (decentralised) reputation system[29]. In design terms, for example, Zambonelli, Omicini et al suggest a coordination model[30], whereby social tasks (such as law enforcement) are modelled separately and entrusted to (embedded in) the MAS, as opposed to being incorporated in the agents themselves. Taken to the extreme, this means modelling and embedding a virtual "jurisdiction" within which agents interact and evolve, with its own laws, enforcement procedures and sanctions, which ideally should

---

[25] Castelfranchi et al: op cit. 2000.

[26] C Dellarocas: *Contractual agent societies: Negotiated shared context and social control in open multi- agent systems,* 2000.

[27] Kollingbaum and Norman: *Supervised Interaction,* 2002.

[28] See for example, the MAGNET project: "the existence of an independent market infrastructure can add value and practicality to contracting protocols, by providing protection against fraud and misrepresentation, and by curtailing unproductive value-based or time-based counterspeculation by participating agents. Furthermore, we have introduced a flexible contracting protocol which can take full advantage of the proposed market architecture to facilitate agent interactions." See Collins J et al: *A multi-agent negotiation testbed for contracting tasks with temporal and precedence constraints,* 2002 and project at <http://www.cs.umn.edu/magnet/>

[29] L Kagal, T. Finin and Y Peng: *A delegation model for distributed trust,* 2001.

[30] Zambonelli et al.: *Agent oriented software engineering,* 2001. The authors suggest coordination models are composed of three elements: the subjects of coordination (coordinables - i.e. software agents), the coordination media (spaces and tools for agent interaction) and the coordination laws (behaviour definition).

incorporate real world laws to establish neutrality between online and offline commerce.[31]

In order for a stable society to emerge, a common language, a common ontology, and common norms and rules are needed[32]. The fundamental issue for developing agent-based ecommerce will be to determine these common norms, at both technical and legal levels. This is where standardisation enters: at language and ontology levels, there are many efforts to provide uniform vocabularies and syntax[33]. At the normative level, however, research is still at the pre-modelling stage. There is a need to progress towards either common laws or protocols for agent interactions (comparable to real world legal harmonisation), or common rules for negotiating between agents and distributing normative determination (comparable to real world contractual autonomy and conflict of law rules). This commonality is not unique to agents in MAS, but should also apply to single agents that will need to be able to interact with third party systems. A part-way example in the non-agent world could see in the standards incorporated in P3P enabled browsers that can communicate with P3P compliant web-sites. One of the major criticisms of P3P is that it does not enable compliance with the European legal framework for personal data protection. Yet it creates a model for interactions (a series of predefined processes and ontologies) that should enable jurisdiction specific rules or norms to be embedded, as "content".

This is where the MIT view of the firm can assist, as it can provide a standard framework for determining the constraints and policies, and subsequent processes, which underlie business transactions. In the extreme, if every organisation were modelled along the lines of the MIT view, the resulting processes should be fully interoperable. As we argued above, a legal architecture applied to the model would then apply to all processes (human and automated) within the system. Either interactions would occur within an agreed jurisdictional framework and applicable law, or there would be processes for resolving conflict of law issues.

A good example of this relates to the concept of an MAS "agent coordinating institution" for ecommerce. This has several implications from a legal perspective. First, the processes of the institution will themselves be subject to a certain law, and will subject agents within the environment to the norms applied and enforced by it. In transborder ecommerce, agents potentially "originate from" several countries and are themselves either

---

[31] One could envisage (agent assisted) online dispute resolution between agents, along the lines of the ODR efforts for B2C ecommerce. (e.g. the EU sponsored E-confidence forum).

[32] Alfabiite Project, *D1 Emergence of societies*. See also Castelfranchi and Falcone: *Current issues on Trust in Multi Agent Systems and Artificial Societies* (Alfabiite D5, 2001).

[33] Standards contributing to legal ontologies and languages include RDF, DAML-S, OWL, XML based schemes such as Legal-XML.

subject to different laws or at least designed to deal on the basis of the law of the user/owner. This gives rise to conflicts over how such laws are reconciled and applied within the MAS[34]. In B2B ecommerce, general acceptation of party autonomy allows users – potentially agents – to negotiate terms as to applicable law and jurisdiction. However, in B2C ecommerce, an agent organising institution that wishes to apply its own terms may enter into conflict with mandatory consumer and privacy protections (e.g. as to applicable law, unreasonable terms, the provision of information, the obtaining of consents and certain rights to cancel). More complex computing may eventually take this consideration into account, and permit mixed B2B and B2C agent commerce platforms.

The MIT view of the firm may assist in this respect, forcing system designers to decompose the MAS into separate processes. The overall model would incorporate constraints and procedures for making the different processes compatible, despite the fact that different laws may apply to different elements: for example, a transaction made on a US website by an EU customer, with delivery from a third jurisdiction. Each of these could be entrusted to separate coordinated or cooperative agents: commercial product and merchant discovery and brokering, negotiation of terms (price, quantity, delivery, etc.), and communication, negotiation and agreement on the legal aspects (consents, notifications, applicable laws, dispute resolution, etc.). Each one subject to their own (declared) applicable laws and contractual agreements.

A model designed for such an "agent institution" would have to take into account (and therefore, implement adequate processes to deal with) not only the legal issues that have been set out here, particularly in relation to contract validity and data protection, but also such other issues as[35]:

– Rights to limit access or remove a "visiting" agent
– Distributed authentication and trust mechanisms
– Rights to retain essential services or require service levels (security, communications, etc.)
– Obligations to provide such support tasks
– Conflicting goals relating to itself and other agents that may not be reconcilable or prioritised

These however, could be viewed as separate aspects of the general legal issues raised by agents commented above, as in fact they may consist in a more generalised version of agent-agent interactions. The operating / coordinating system or institution itself could be considered an agent.

---

[34] See Øren J: *Electronic Agents and the Notion Of Establishment*, 2001, for more details of this issue.
[35] Brazier, et al: *Are law abiding agents realistic?*, 2002.

5.4   Agents, Web-service models and the Semantic Web

Two principal areas of research and development in ICTs today are also
of relevance to the concept of legalising agent processing: web-services and
the Semantic Web.

Web-services can be considered web sites and other applications linked
to the network that do not just provide information but allow interlocutors to
cause some action or process to be carried out, such as the sale of a product
or the control of a physical device. Their operation is based on seven main
processes[36]: Discovery (finding the service you want); Invocation (activating
the service); Deal formation (negotiation: concluding a contract for the
services); Composition and Inter-operation (putting various services together
to form a whole); Monitoring (seeing what processes occur); and
Verification (checking that the services are those described and contracted
for). This analysis or breakdown already falls within the process view of
organisations and transactions. The MIT view of the firm suggests that
within this conceptual framework, organisations can be conceived as a
combination of different services (whether on the web or not). These
services can be broken down into a series of processes, which may be
"legalised" as outlined above.

While there may have been theoretical struggle between the web-services
models and agents, we believe that agents can be considered as services and
integrated into the web-service model framework described above.[37] This is
all the more so as agent technology may be important for aspects of
interoperability between applications and services. Software agents can
perform delegated tasks or processes such as service discovery and contract
negotiation, representing the agent user and defending his or her interests,
and monitoring of service performance. Agent-based applications can offer
different services over the Internet as business applications are decomposed
into processes, each one represented by an agent – combining together to
provide a complete service. This could include services for e-contracting and
reputation control, as conceived for electronic institutions and secure
contracting.

From our legal point of view, currently this means putting agents into a
technology framework that already includes a legal dimension. Web-service
frameworks such as UDDI[38], RosettaNet[39] and ebXML[40] include pre-

---

[36] The DAML Services Coalition: *DAML-S: A Semantic Markup For Web Services,* 2001,
online at http://www.daml.org/services/daml-s/2001/10/daml-s.pdf.

[37] DAML-S is an ontology of web-services based on an agent description language,
DAML+OIL. See also B. Burg: *Agents in the World of Web Services* (2002). DAML-S
provides Web services with a core set of markup language concepts to describe properties
and capabilities in computer-readable form. The automation of web service tasks comprise
web service discovery, execution, interoperation, composition and execution monitoring.

[38] At http://www.uddi.org/

established protocols and template documents, somewhat like an enhanced version of EDI. The XML nature of service specification allows agents to negotiate automatically the terms of supply of the services, within controlled parameters which (potentially) provide higher levels of legal certainty. Though at the moment standard terms mainly prevail,) in the future more flexible contracts for web-services could be formed. This would reduce legal certainty as these contracts may fall outside pre-established standards. In line with our argument, demands for legal certainty will require legality to be incorporated at higher levels of abstraction, at process or service modelling stage.

The logical extension of a network of machine intelligible documents is the Semantic Web[41]: this network encodes knowledge using a structured, logically connected representation (ontology -dictionaries of meanings and relations between sets of vocabulary). It determines inference rules that can be used to conduct automated reasoning – i.e. an environment that seems perfect for agent oriented computing. One drawback is that there is no single language or reference guide to meaning over the web: each domain is developing and extending its ontologies and inference rules. Accordingly applications without access to the same or partially shared ontology cannot talk or reason together (like not having a dictionary in a foreign country). Shared or discovered ontologies on the contrary enable interoperability and communication / composition among applications. An ontology language for agents, DAML[42], has been drafted and many advanced agent research is now using it.

This environment is favourable for automated transactions, as applications – agents – will "understand" commercial, technical and legal content on the web. This includes comprehending not only the products or services on offer or searched, but also the technical requirements for interacting with parties and, one day, the legal restrictions and terms for any transaction. As we have seen, one of the most advanced initiatives in the legal domain so far is P3P[43], whereby browsers can automatically understand XML declared web-site privacy policies and match these (using APPEL) with user declared privacy preferences set out in the browser configuration. Forms of automated consent are given to the recording of cookies. So one area – maybe the most important – for the law to get involved in to promote compliant agent transactions is the determination of law-related ontologies. We have already mentioned Legal-XML, but also there are initiatives such as XrML[44] for IPR, and P3P for privacy.

---

[39] At http://www.rosettanet.org

[40] At http://www.ebxml.org

[41] www.semanticweb.org and see Hendler, J: *Agents and the Semantic Web,* 2001.

[42] www.daml.org

[43] www.w3c.org/p3p/

[44] www.xrml.org/ and see also the work at http://:dmag.upf.es

In this environment, interoperable agents may offer web-based services (semantic web services) on the basis of negotiated contracts that refer to shared knowledge (e.g. a legal ontology) represented in standardised languages (XML, RDF-schemes, XPDL (XML Process Definition Language[45]), RuleML, XRML, and DAML-S[46] are some that are currently being developed). They will be bound by externally imposed regulation embedded in the processes. Agent-based processes will also infer and learn from interactions and external events, for example a change in law that will be reflected in dynamic RDF-schemes, and update their rule sets. Agents will respect internal contractual constraints or rules and external regulation through embedded coding.

In addition, if legal knowledge can be represented and understood by automatic processes on the semantic web, technology platforms will move away from contract templates. The legal knowledge representation will permit policy-based negotiation and the determination of context or person specific clauses and terms.

6.   AREAS FOR FUTURE WORK

Our conclusions so far in this chapter point to some directions where further research could be undertaken. We believe our approach leads to various suggestions for creating legally compliant ecommerce applications. As we note below, there are several additional research areas that may contribute to this.

6.1   From designing complex applications to modelling processes

We mentioned above that recent schools of thought on IT system design are considering modelling as the ideal approach to dealing with increasingly complex and flexible systems. This modelling is based on overall design models and architectures, within which specific processes are then coded. One advantage of this is that business constraints, dependencies or rules are no longer hidden within technical processes, but conceived and coded separately in rule or workflow engines.

We have envisaged that on the basis of a standard model of the firm, a new element, a legal architecture (or legal process model) can be added or overlaid. This is a framework of constraints and dependencies that maps onto the technology and business architectures and models. The legal architecture could tell you for example that there are actors (people and

---

[45] Described at http://www.wfmc.org/ of the Workflow Management Coalition
[46] See DARPA Agent Markup Language initiative at www.daml.org.

computers), there are internal processes, and there are interchange processes. It will set out the constraints for this model. Using this architecture as a lense or design tool will enable developers to look at their processes and their process model and to create a legal specification and requirements for compliance (constraints and dependencies, processes, objects, etc.). This can be incorporated into or mapped onto the technological and business architectures. For instance, an ecommerce application rule engine can be enhanced by legal constraints as well as business constraints:

– Business constraint: "if the client is regular, the discount is 5%". "Buy if the prices is less than 10".
– Community constraint: "If the subscriber is registered, it may access this data".
– Legal constraint: "If the data is personal data, it must be encrypted" or "Data identified as protected may not be redistributed".

This may result in new elements in the corporate data model and architecture. For instance, the legal architecture should indicate that sending SMS to private individuals requires obtaining their consent first. The result for technical architecture is a new object (consent), a new process (obtain), governed by new constraints or rules (e.g. "no SMS without prior consent"). This process can be broken down into elements: consent can be (1) explicit or (2) part of contractual relationship. The technical result would be another new process (check if consent obtained) related to a new constraint (no need to obtain prior consent if already in cases 1 or 2). In coordination theory, this would be phrased as "task T2 (sending SMS) is dependant on a resource R (the recipient's consent) which itself is the result of another task T1 (obtain consent).

This approach suggests developing technology languages and tools for modelling processes that incorporate the legal dimension. These could for example be extensions in Business Process Languages and Suites (see table below) or a complete legal process handbook with automatically programmable and compilable modules as outlined above.

Table 6-2. Business Process Modelling Technologies

Existing tools that belong to the area of business process modelling and associated domains such as automated software generation are organisational workflow management, Business Process Management, Enterprise Resource Planning, Supply Chain Management and collaborative planning and forecasting (the latter only within very specific fields or large enterprises that have the sufficient resources). Models and software components developed to support compliant execution of business processes are based on several emerging languages and standards for both workflows and Business Process Modelling (BPML, BPQL, XPDL, etc.) service composition (WSFL, WSCL, WSCI, XLANG, DAML-S, etc) and rule description (BRML, Jess, and RuleML, for rule interoperation between industry standards[47]), whereas top layer B2B protocols are developed by such initiatives as ebXML or RosettaNet. The most common tool for modelling software programmes, as opposed to business processes, is Unified Modelling Language (UML, sponsored by OMG.org) and associated standards (MOF, MDA, XMI, etc[48].).

---

[47] See the Rule Markup Initiative online at http://www.dfki.uni-kl.de/ruleml/

6.2   From policies to constraints: the need for languages

While modelling languages can represent business and process models, another form of language is needed to incorporate, represent and express legal and business constraints and dependencies.

Certain attempts have been made to standardise data formats and labelling, for example HTML which aims to provide a standard language for descriptive structures. This standardisation can never be complete (witness the complexity of today's web pages) and focuses on presentation and not the underlying meaning, which is what we are interested in.

To overcome structural differences in order to directly access content, new languages such as those of the XML family have been developed. These languages standardise notations for content, either locally (in DTDs) or more generally (using web-based namespaces). This ensures that the flexibility and innovation of notation systems is supportable and universally understandable, leading to application interoperability. From our legal perspective, one of the research objectives has been to design an agent architecture so that a standard language and structure can express content and value not just in commercial terms (price, volume, dates) but also in legal terms (privacy, applicable law, guarantees, etc.). These metadata exchange structures, providing the context and substance of transactions, should enable agent-based automatic or semi-automatic intelligent commercial transactions to be legally more valid. Now, new generations of the XML family are being created for different areas of legal content, such as XRML for IPR notations and digital rights management, and more recently Legal-XML for more general legal document content[49].

Within a process, any interaction can be considered the exchange of views or positions in relation to an object and its properties – including elements of intent. Accordingly, the general trend in research projects has been to model those views and positions into policy expressions in a standard form. In this way, a smart organisation (and users of smart technology) can specify what their policies are regarding the whole range of information transactions in which they participate. When ecommerce applications interrelate, they negotiate and compare their policy preferences, and attempt to come to an agreement. These policies can be expressed in XML-based mark-up languages: RuleML has been suggested for business (and wider) process preferences[50], but other XML languages are being proposed (XRML or P3P and APPEL, for example, as mentioned above). We believe that these policies should include all aspects discussed here such

---

[48] For more details, consult online at http://www.omg.org

[49] See Legal XML pages at Oasis, at http://www.oasis-open.org

[50] Grosof and Poon: *Representing Agent Contracts with Exceptions using XML Rules,* 2002.

as privacy preferences, consumer protection processes (information, notice, etc.), contracting and payment terms, etc.

More generally, these policy expressions can be considered local or organisational constraints and articulate organisational dependencies. Each "policy" is a set of terms and conditions under which a resource or user may participate in one or more classes of transactions (tasks) – a form of business or organisational constraint or dependency. Within the more general business model, formal constraints or rules can therefore be used to describe the business's service process models. For instance, they can represent:
– preconditions and post-conditions, and their contingent relationships
– contingent behaviour/features of the service more generally, e.g., exceptions/problems
– agreements about contracted services.

The legal risk assessment included in the general structural analysis such as that presented in this work should aim to raise points of legal concern and provide the relevant rules or policies. This creates an opportunity to design technical processes and architectures that will minimise liability for all parties. In the Research Scenario, for instance, the grocer merchant's policies can be associated with particular objects and properties or combinations of these, which determine the flow and content of communications with shoppers and suppliers. The legal model will enhance these to ensure the communications comply with the relevant legal framework. Once policies are established, organisations and users can plan, monitor and regulate their transactions through preference setting on the basis of these rules. In addition, the information architectures should also establish those decisions – expressions of intent and value – (and data structures which maintain them) as a potential source of "law" for any dispute arising out of any transaction conducted on such a system.

Accordingly, we argue that a design objective is to develop a representation language that integrates constraints or rules, ontologies and processes for the more general conceptual framework. Such a representation language should enable inheritance and reasoning across jurisdictions and standard practices.

A typical example of this creation of process or behavioural constraints through policy or preference setting is the P3P project commented in Chapter 5. Another could be related to the use of digital signatures: a web merchant may determine that only agents incorporating such technology may be "accepted" by its commercial platform. The merchant's policy being that of only contracting with identifiable parties. Finally, another instance could evolve around the issue of the origin or the nature of parties. A web merchant may wish to restrict its clients to business organisations and not deal with consumers. This would be implemented through notations concerning the nature of the visiting "agent", and rules governing specific responses to such visitors: prohibitions of access, requirements to provide

VAT numbers, etc. On the contrary, a more open website (including B2C), on recognising consumer agents, could fulfil obligations to provide relevant information under the Consumer Protection legislation and make other required notifications to users.

Such structured forms of interaction assist in complying with contracting, consumer protection and privacy requirements, as parties can have notice of, define and negotiate certain terms established within the transaction model. Accordingly this may help solve some basic issues for agent transactions, increasing trust and security from both commercial and legal points of view (e.g. improving legal certainty through contractual validity, documentary evidence, respect of consumer protections and privacy).

Considering the basic conditions for agent-based interactions, we believe that greater levels of trust will be achieved through the transparency of the policy expressions and knowledge that parties have access to and record of such policies. Confirmable policies provide confirmable transactions. As we argue below, once a trust model is determined – e.g. based on processes for authorisation, authentication, access control, policy declarations and record-keeping –, efforts will then focus on technical processes for implementing these policies. This dimension of trust, especially in the context of multi-agent systems, is further commented below.

The discussions above lead to several areas already mentioned where future research could usefully be undertaken in the overall aim of achieving legally compliant ecommerce platforms, and in particular agent-based ecommerce systems. Two areas are covered here: modelling and computer science (focused on agent technologies).

6.3   Legal and Business Modelling research

Since companies determine their own enterprise business model, it is very important in networked commerce for the descriptions of these models and their elements to be interoperable. Enterprises must therefore have a common understanding over the values that the various parameters of the business model may take. To enable this kind of interoperability, shared ontologies must be developed for each of the business model parameters (activities, roles, constraints) and for legal parameters. In particular ontologies are needed for the core elements described in the model, including services, competencies and assets or resources on the one hand, and legal principles and rules on the other.

First, therefore, there is a need to investigate further areas in the field of business and legal modelling within the context of a process view of organisations, such as the MIT view of the firm. This should aim to satisfy certain identified needs:

– Modelling tasks and processes that are carried out independently of geographical or organisational constraints. This will enable a more complete model of businesses and organisations to be created, and allow the conceptual framework to integrate the international dimension of the Internet. It will also incorporate the elements of networked business, or the "virtual organisation".

- Modelling of ecommerce participants' behaviour as a bottom up approach. We suggest this as an alternative approach, focusing on the specific business elements and related processes of a single company: contributed assets, accepted responsibilities, acquired rights, individual commitments and other legal obligations
- Modelling contractual (private law) frameworks in constraints and compliant processes. This should create a model establishing a general framework for contractual obligations, and devising means for representing these formally in the form of constraints and norms.
- Devising the processes for regulatory compliance to be embedded in enterprise and inter-organisational systems

6.4 Computer science research

Perhaps the single most important technical area of future research outlined in this work is the need for a new programming language, a legal programming language, that addresses two simultaneous and seemingly incompatible needs: the need for a working networked infrastructure and the need for legal compliance. These two needs, as we have seen, are yet to be reconciled. There are three fertile areas of research that may be undertaken with an interdisciplinary approach (including law, management science and computer science) to develop such a legal programming language that is truly compliant. These areas are:

- Ontologies, content languages and shared vocabulary. Ontologies define and describe the meanings, properties and relations of concepts in a specific domain, a form of hierarchical knowledge. Agents that use the same ontology have the same understanding of terms. If heterogeneous agents are to interact in a legal manner, or legal MAS evolve, there is a need to develop ontologies for legal domains that not only are open to access for all applications (shared), but may also be interpretable across jurisdictions. For example, this could be "applicable law", "jurisdiction", "notification", "exploitation right", etc. Content level description and preference modelling are also important in this area. These are languages that allow agents to express the user's preference and therefore the content of an outgoing message. Most are XML based, for example the P3P specification for expressing privacy preferences. This work could be extended for expressing other dimensions of legal preferences and evaluation, such as for contract matters (jurisdiction and applicable law, guarantees, licence rights, force majeur, etc.)

- Logic languages for agent reasoning rules, constraints and dependencies. These are languages that allow agents to reason about their own beliefs and input from other sources (e.g. other agents declaration of preferences). They also determine the compliance of the agent with norms of agent society institutions. Some initiatives are aiming for languages that can reason about legal issues, for example RuleML[51] is a suggestion for an XML based language for representing rules, while APPEL[52] is a language for evaluating privacy preferences.
- Dialogue and interaction protocols. These are required for the automated and interoperable flow of an interaction (e.g. English or Dutch auction model, matching of preferences, or simple offer and acceptance without negotiation). To negotiate validly, agents share an interaction protocol – or could "import" one from a third party source / agent society institution – so that two counterparts (e.g. web site / selling agent and purchase agent) may interact and negotiate terms[53].

7.   CONCLUDING COMMENTS

In the current European legal environment there are several conceptual risks in agent-based trading that we cannot solve until judicial or legislative "pronouncement" on the matter: for example, on the validity of purely agent-based transactions (and specifically contractual consent), or on the automated provision of consent for personal data processing or IPR licensing purposes. In the meantime, to provide greater legal certainty in automated contracting and reduce the legal risks reviewed above, it is necessary to establish technical measures that make agent processes more legally compliant. We have taken a process oriented analysis of commercial transactions and use-cases within the Research Scenario, and suggested "legally engineering" the software code: this means inputting legal specifications and criteria at design time.

Thus we have set out the preliminary legal specification for an example use-case within the Research Scenario, to be implemented through both traditional and agent-based computing. Other examples include the identification of parties (or at least identification of their nature as consumers), exception handling in the contract negotiation process, and incorporating reasonableness tests relating to particular outcomes (checks against the sale of certain quantities of products, or over a certain financial

---

[51]See online at http://www.dfki.uni-kl.de/ruleml/

[52] See W3C Working Draft APPEL specification at http://www.w3.org/TR/P3P-preferences/

[53] E.g. a template contract management described by Kollingbaum and Norman: *Supervised Interaction,* 2002.

limit). This is just a first step, while agent-oriented projects are still within research laboratories and controlled environments.

However, we have a long term vision of legally compliant agent mediated electronic commerce over global public networks. This may involve web-services models, the semantic web, or multi-agent systems where agents representing different participants and services interact to create legally binding agreements, enforceable both on and offline. All legal aspects of a commercial relationship (privacy, intellectual property, contract, consumer protection, tax, etc.) will be included in the negotiation processes. Various agents will provide the appropriate processes and take on the functions of privacy protector, consumer protection monitor, contracting assistants, security protocol management (e.g. digital signature mechanism), trust, auditing and evidence recording.

We have presented here a suggestion for how this vision may be enabled, through a standardised model of enterprises, markets and the law. The key for compliant applications for e-business in general – not just ecommerce – is to create clear and interoperable conceptual models for the enterprise processes and shared definitions of legal principles that can be applied to them. We believe that a key implication for research and development is that these legal principles and relationships will require modelling and codification, to create a legal architecture that can be easily applied to technology. The gap between legal and technical worlds can therefore be bridged at a common conceptual level.

REFERENCES

Ajmani, S., Morris R., Liskov, B.: A Trusted Third-Party Computation Service, MIT LCS Technical Report 847, 2001, online at http://www.lcs.mit.edu/publications/pubs/pdf/MIT-LCS-TR-847.pdf (visited 10/09/2003)

Albrecht, K.: Supermarket Cards: The Tip of the Retail Surveillance Iceberg. Denver University Law Review, Summer 2002, Volume 79, Issue 4, pp. 534-539 and 558-565.

Allen T and Widdison R: Can Computers Make Contracts?, *(1996) 9 Harvard Journal of Law & Technology*

American Bar Association's Cyberspace Law Committee: Software "Agents" Project, Electronic Contracts Work Group online at http://civics.com/content/agents/ (visited 20/05/2002)

Anthes, GH: *Agents of Change - Software agents tame supply chain complexity and optimize performance*. Computerworld.com, January 27, 2003

Aparicio, M., Chiariglione, L Mamdani E.; MacCabe, F.; Nicol, R.; Steiner, D.; Suguri, H. FIPA - Intelligent agents from theory to practice, Telecom 99, Geneva, October 1999

Apistola M, Brazier FMT, Kubbe O, Oskamp A, Schellekens MHM and Voulon MB: Legal aspects of agent technology, 17th BILETA conference, 2002

ARETE: On-line services and data protection and the protection of privacy, Study for DG XV, available online at http://europa.eu.int/comm/internal_market/en/dataprot/studies/serven.pdf (visited 25/08/2003)

Armstrong J: The legal issues surrounding SMS, Internet world at <http://www.internetworld.co.uk/mcomm/vRoot/articles/article.cfm/69730349-6054-4862-9CD96345ACF52AF6> (visited 25/08/2003)

Ashton, K.: Testimony before the California State Senate Subcommittee on New Technologies, Hearing on RFID and Privacy, August 18, 2003, online at www.autoidcenter.org/privacy_hearing.asp (visited 10/10/2003)

Australian National Office of Information Economy (NOIE): Final Report: Review Of The Spam Problem And How It Can Be Countered, 16 April 2003, online at www.privacy.gov.au

Barbuceanu M, Gray T, Mankovski S.: The role of Obligations in Multi-agent Coordination. *Applied Artificial Intelligence 13 (1-2)* Jan -March 1999.

Bing J: Legal aspects of electronic agents, with and emphasis on Intellectual Property Law, Alfebiite (2002) Deliverable D5, on file with author

Blanchard C W: Wireless security, BT Technol J Vol 19 No 3 July 2001

Blocher, K., and Turpeinen, M., "Survey on Commercially Available Agents", online at http://web.media.mit.edu/~mtu/agents.html

Bohlman E: Privacy in the Age of Information, *The Journal of Information, Law and Technology (JILT)* 2002 (2) <http://elj.warwick.ac.uk/jilt/02-2/bohlman.html>(visited 15/12/2002)

Boman: Norms in Artificial Decision Making, DECIDE Research Group, http://wwwdsv.su.se/DECIDE

Borking J.J., van Eck B.M.A and Siepel P. Intelligent Software Agents and Privacy Achtergrondstudies en verkenningen 13, Den Haag, Registratiekamer, 1999

Borking JJ: On PET and other privacy supporting technologies, online at <http://www.privacyservice.org/files/what_is_pet.htm> (visited 15/04/2003)

Borking JJ: Privacy incorporated software agents: a proposal for building a privacy guardian for the electronic age, (2000) 7 *Privacy Law & Policy Reporter*, pp. 91–96.

Brazier, F.M.T. , Kubbe, O. , Oskamp, A. , Wijngaards, N.J.E. Are Law-Abiding Agents Realistic?, In: *Proceedings of the workshop on the Law of Electronic Agents (LEA02)*, (ed. Sartor, G., Cevenini, C.), pp. 151-155, July 2002

Burg B: "Agents in the World of Web Services" Springer lecture notes in Computer Science, March 2002

Burk D: The Trouble With Trespass, 4 J. Small & Emerging Bus. L. 27 (2000)

Business Rules Group, Final Report 2000, at http://www.businessrulesgroup.org/brgactv.htm (visited 15/05/2003)

Bygrave L: Electronic Agents and Privacy - A Cyberspace Odyssey 2001 – *International Journal of Law and Information Technology*, Volume 9, Issue 3, Autumn 2001

Bygrave L: Privacy-Enhancing Technologies – Caught between a Rock and a Hard Place", *Privacy Law & Policy Reporter*, 2002, vol. 9, pp. 135–137.

Bygrave LA: Minding the Machine: Article 15 of the EC Data Protection Directive and Automated Profiling (2000) 7 *Privacy Law & Policy Reporter*, pp. 67–76.

Caglayan A and Harrison C: Agent Sourcebook, Wiley & Sons 1997.

Cartrysse K., van der Lubbe J. C. A., Youssouf A.: Privacy protection software design, PISA Project Report, September 2002 online at http://www.pet-pisa.nl/pisa_org/pisa/index.html (visited 02/06/2003)

Castelfranchi C, Dignum F, Jonker C.M., Treur J: Deliberative Normative Agents: principles and architecture. Proceedings of the Sixth International Workshop on Agent Theories, Architectures and Languages (ATAL-99) July 1999

Castelfranchi C, Falcone R: Current issues on Trust in Multi Agent Systems and Artificial Societies - Alfebiite D5

Castelfranchi C., Falcone R., (1998) Principles of trust for MAS: cognitive anatomy, social importance, and quantification, *Proceedings of the International Conference of Multi-Agent Systems (ICMAS'98)*, pp. 72-79, Paris, July.

Castelfranchi C., Falcone R., Firozabadi B., Tan Y. (Editors), Taylor and Francis 14 (8), *Applied Artificial Intelligence* journal, Special Issue on "Trust in Agents" Part1, (2000).

Catlett J: Open Letter to P3P Developers & Replies, Junkbusters Corp, 1999, http://www.junkbusters.com (visited 15/12/2001)

Cavoukian A and Gurski M: Privacy in a Wireless World, Ontario Information and Privacy Commission

Centeno C: Building Security and Consumer Trust in Internet Payments, Background Paper No. 7 Electronic Payment Systems Observatory (ePSO) April 2002 online at http://epso.jrc.es/ (visited 08/11/2002).

Child M: *Trust Issues and user reaction to e-services and electronic marketplaces*. HP laboratories February 2001

Chissik, M., Kelman, A.: Electronic Commerce: Law and Practice , Sweet and Maxwell (1999) London.

Clarke, R: Platform for privacy preferences: A critique, 1998. Online at http://www.anu.edu.au/people/Roger.Clarke/DV/P3PCrit.html (visited 20/11/2002)

Collins J, Ketter W, Gini M and Mobasher B: *A multi-agent negotiation testbed for contracting tasks with temporal and precedence constraints*. Int'l Journal of Electronic Commerce, 2002.

Colombetti M, Fornara N, and Verdicchio M: *The Role of Institutions in Multiagent Systems* Workshop su agenti per la rappresentazione della conoscenza ed il ragionamento AIIA 2002 available at www-dii.ing.unisi.it/aiia2002/paper/AGENTI/colombetti-aiia02.pdf

Conan V, Dinant J-M, Louveaux S.: Privacy protection and Internet agents, at - www.aimedia.org (visited 15/04/2003)

Connolly, Ch.: An International Standard for Privacy (1997) 4 Privacy Law & Policy Reporter 90, available online at http://www2.austlii.edu.au/itlaw/articles/ConnollyISO.html (visited 10/09/2003)

Consumers International: Consumers@shopping, An international comparative study of electronic commerce. Available at: http://www.consumersinternational.org/document_store/Doc28.pdf (visited 12/07/2003)

Consumers International: *Privacy@net: an international comparative study of consumer privacy on the internet*, 2001, Consumers International, London, available at http://www.consumersinternational.org/news/pressreleases/fprivreport.pdf (visited 10/09/2003)

Conte R, Falcone R, Sartor G: *Agents and Norms: How to fill the gap?* Artificial Intelligence and Law 7(1) March 1999.

Cranor L, Langheinrich M, Marchiori M, and ReagleJ: The platform for privacy preferences 1.0 (p3p1.0) specification. W3C Candidate Recommendation, www.w3.org/TR/P3P/, (visited 15/04/2003)

Cranor L, Langheinrich M, Marchiori M: APPEL: A P3P Preference Exchange Language, W3C Working Draft 15 April 2002, online at http://www.w3.org/TR/P3P-preferences/ (visited 15/04/2003)

Cranor L., Weitzner D: Summary Report, W3C Workshop on the Future of P3P, Dulles, USA, 2002. Online at http://www.w3.org/2002/p3p-ws/ (visited 20/05/2003)

Cranor L: The P3P Protocol Standardizes Online Privacy Statements. E-*commerce Law & Strategy*. January 2002, p.1, 8-9.

Crowston, K. (1997). A coordination theory approach to organizational process design. *Organization Science, 8* (2), 157-175.

Cruquenaire A: Electronic Agents as Search Engines: Copyright related aspects, *International Journal of Law and Information Technology*, Volume 9, Issue 3, Autumn 2001

Curtis W. Kellner M.I. and Over J. 1992, "Process Modelling",. *Communications of the ACM, 35, 9*, pp. 75-90.

Cutler M: P3P's Arrival Raises Concerns That Tool May Create Liability, Drive Away Site Traffic, Electronic Commerce & Law Report Volume 6 Number 38, October 3, 2001 (visited 20/11/2002)

DAML Services Coalition (A. Ankolekar, M. Burstein, J. Hobbs, O. Lassila, D. Martin, S. McIlraith, S. Narayanan, M. Paolucci, T. Payne, K. Sycara, H. Zeng), DAML-S: Semantic Markup for Web Services, in *Proceedings of the International Semantic Web Working Symposium* (SWWS), July 2001.

Dastani, M, Jacobs, N., Jonker, C.M., Treur, J: Modelling user preferences and mediating agents in electronic commerce, in F. Dignum and C. Sierra (Eds.) *Agent-mediated Electronic commerce (The European AgentLink Perspective)*, LNAI 1991, 2000

Davidsson, P: Emergent Societies of Information Agents, Fourth International Workshop CIA-2000 on Cooperative Information Agents, July 7 - 9, 2000, Boston, USA

Davis J.R: On self-enforcing contracts, the right to hack, and willfully ignorant agents, *13 Berkeley Technology Law Journal 1148*, 1998

de Cock Buning, M, Hondius E, Prins C, and de Vries, M: Consumer@Protection.EU. An Analysis of European Consumer Legislation in the Information Society, Journal of Consumer Policy 24: 287–338, 2001, Kluwer Academic Publishers.

De Miglio F, Onida T, Romano F, Santoro S: Electronic Agents and the Law of Agency, Papers of the LEA 2002 Workshop on Law of Electronic Agents

Dellarocas, C Negotiated shared context and social control in open multi-agent systems. In Conte, R. and Dellarocas, C., editors, Social Order in MAS. Kluwer 2001.

Dellarocas, C., Contractual agent societies: Negotiated shared context and social control in open multi- agent systems, Proceedings of the Workshop on Norms and Institutions in Multi-Agent Systems (Autonomous Agents 2000), Barcelona (2000).

Dignum V et al: Agent Societies: Towards frameworks-based design, in M.J. Wooldridge, G. Weiß, P. Ciancarini (Eds.): Agent-Oriented Software Engineering II Second International Workshop, AOSE 2001

Dignum, F. Autonomous agents and social norms. In ICMAS'96 Workshop on Norms, Obligations and Conventions. (1996).

Dignum, F.: Agents, Markets, Institutions and Protocols, in F. Dignum and C. Sierra (Eds.) *Agent-mediated Electronic commerce (The European AgentLink Perspective)*, LNAI 1991, 2000

Dinant, J-M., Platform for Privacy Preferences (P3P) :How Far can P3P Guarantee the Respect of the Data Protection Directive Requirements?, Centre de Recherches Informatique et Droit, 1999

Dusollier, S, Poullet, Y, and Buydens, M: Copyright and access to information in the digital environment, Third UNESCO congress on ethical legal and societal challenges of cyberspace, Infoethics, 2000

Electronic Privacy Information Center: Pretty Poor Privacy: An Assessment of P3P and Internet Privacy, (with Jukbusters), June 2000, online at www.epic.org (visited 20/11/2002)

Escudero A., Hedenfalk M., Heselius P. *"Location Privacy in Mobile Internet - An extension to Freedom Network".* INET2001. Stockholm. June 2001

Esteva, M., Rodriguez JA, Sierra C, Garcia P, and. Arcos JL: On the formal specifications of electronic institutions, in F. Dignum and C. Sierra, eds., Agent mediated electronic commerce (The European AgentLink Perspective), Springer, (2001) 126-147.

European Commission: A possible legal framework for the single payment area in the internal market, Working Document, MARKT/208/2001 - Rev. 1, 07/05/02, online at http://europa.eu.int/comm/internal_market/ (visited 112/06/2003)

European Commission Art 29 Data Protection Working Party: Opinions and Working Papers online at http://europa.eu.int/comm/internal_market/privacy/workingroup/wp2003/wpdocs03_en.ht m (visited 10/09/2003)

European Commission: Art 29 Data Protection Working Party: Working Document on on-line authentication services, 10054/03/EN, Working Paper 68, 29 January 2003. Online at http://europa.eu.int/comm/internal_market/privacy/docs/wpdocs/2003/wp68_en.pdf (visited 20/09/2003)

European Commission: Communication from the Commission to the Council, the European Parliament, the Economic and Social Committee and the Committee of the Regions: Towards the Full Roll-Out of Third Generation Mobile Communications, COM(2002) 301 final, 11.6.2002

European Commission: Communication from the Commission to the Council and the European Parliament on European Contract Law issued by the CEC on 11 July 2001, COM(2001) 398 final

European Commission: First report on the implementation of the Data Protection Directive (95/46/EC), COM(2003) 265 final, 15 March 2003

European Commission: Green Paper on European Union Consumer Protection - Brussels, 2.10.2001 COM(2001) 531 final

European Commission: Open Consultation Report, *Trust barriers for B2B e-marketplaces,* 2002.

European Commission: Report on Consumer complaints in respect of distance selling and comparative advertising (10 March 2000)

European Commission: Study on the implementation of Recommendation 97/489/EC concerning transactions carried out by electronic payment instruments and in particular the relationship between holder and issuer, 21 May 2001, online at http://europa.eu.int/comm/internal_market/payments/payment-instruments/study_en.htm

Fayat, J.R., Nevejan, F., Nordquist, F.: Consumer confidence in E-commerce - 16th BILETA Annual Conference 2001

Federal Trade Commission: Consumer Protection in the Global Electronic Marketplace: Looking Ahead, September 6, 2000, online at http://www.ftc.gov/opa/2000/09/globalecommfin.htm (visited 22/08/2002).

Federal Trade Commission: Privacy online: fair information practices in the electronic marketplace:a Federal Trade Commission report to Congress, Federal Trade Commission, May 2000, Washington DC, available at http://www.ftc.gov/reports/privacy2000/privacy2000text.pdf (visited 10/09/2003)

Feigenbaum, J., Freedman, M.J., Sander, T. and Shostack, A. (2002) Privacy Engineering for Digital Rights Management Systems, in Tomas Sander (Ed.): Security and Privacy in Digital Rights Management, ACM CCS-8 Workshop DRM 2001, Lecture Notes in Computer Science 2320 Springer 2002

Feliu, S.: Intelligent Agents and Consumer Protection, *International Journal of Law and Information Technology*, Volume 9, Issue 3, Autumn 2001

Fingar, P.: CEO Guide to eCommerce Using Object-Oriented Intelligent Agent Technology - http://home1.gte.net/pfingar/eba.htm (visited 10.10.2002)

Fitzgerald, A., Fitzgerald, B., Cook, P., Cifuentes, C. (eds); Going Digital 2000: Legal Issues for Electronic Commerce, Multimedia and the Internet, Prospect Media Pty Ltd, Aust, 2000

Foss, M. and Bygrave, L.A.: International Consumer Purchases through the Internet: Jurisdictional Issues pursuant to European Law, *International Journal of Law and Information Technology*, Volume 8, Issue 2: Summer 2000

Garcia, R. and Delgado, J.: Brokerage of Intellectual Property Rights in the Semantic Web, International Semantic Web Working Symposium Proceedings (2001)

Gauthronet, S., Drouard, E.: Communications Commerciales Non-Sollicitées et Protection des Données, For European Commission, 2001 online at europa.eu.int/comm/internal_market/privacy/ docs/studies/spamsum_fr.pdf (visited 02/10/2002)

Geist, M.: Is there a there there? Toward greater certainty for internet jurisdiction, 16 Berkeley Technology Law Journal 1345-1406 (2001)

Giaglis, G.M.: A Taxonomy of Business Process Modelling and Information Systems Modelling Techniques, *International Journal of Flexible Manufacturing Systems, 13, 2*, pp. 209-228, 2001

Giaglis, G.M., Papakiriakopoulos, D.A. and Doukidis, G.J.: An Analytical Framework and a Development Method for Inter-Organisational Business Process Modelling, International Journal of Simulation, 2,2,pp.5-15, 2002

Gillies L.: A Review of the New Jurisdiction Rules for Electronic Consumer Contracts within the European Union, Commentary, 2001 (1) The Journal of Information, Law and Technology (JILT) <http://elj.warwick.ac.uk/jilt/01-1/gillies.html> (visited 20.07/2002).

Gini, M.: Agents and other 'Intelligent Software' for e-commerce, 1999, Departement of Computer Science and Engineering, University of Minnesota http://www-users.cs.umn.edu/~gini/csom.html (visited 10.09.2002)

Givens, B.: RFID and the Public Policy Void, Testimony, Joint Committee on Preparing California for the 21st Century California Legislature, August 18, 2003, online at www.privacyrights.org/ar/RFIDHearing.htm (visited 10/10/2003)

Gonzalo, S.: A business outlook regarding Electronic Agents, *International Journal of Law and Information Technology*, Volume 9, Issue 3, Autumn 2001

Gratton, E.: The legality of online Privacy-Enhancing Technologies, *Lex Electronica, vol. 7, n°2, printemps 2002, <http://www.lex-electronica.org/articles/v7-2/gratton.htm>* (visited 10.05.2003)

Grijpink, J.H.A.M. and Prins, J.E.J.: New Rules for Anonymous Electronic Transactions? An Exploration of the Private Law Implications of Digital Anonymity, 2001 (2) *The Journal of Information, Law and Technology (JILT)* <http://elj.warwick.ac.uk/jilt/01-2/grijpink.html> (visited 20/02/2003)

Grosof, B., Poon, T.: Representing Agent Contracts with Exceptions using XML Rules, Ontologies and Process Description, *International Workshop on Rule Markup Languages for Business Rules on the Semantic Web*, June 2002

Grosse Ruse, H.: Electronic Agents and the Legal Protection of Non-creative Databases, *International Journal of Law and Information Technology*, Volume 9, Issue 3, Autumn 2001

Guttman, R.H., Moukas A.G. and Maes P.: "Agent mediated Electronic Commerce: A Survey", *Knowledge Engineering Review*. June 1998.

Haines, A.: The Impact of the Internet on the Judgments Project: Thoughts for the Future, Preliminary Document No 17 of February 2002 for the attention of the Special Commission of April 2002 on general affairs and policy of the Conference, Hague Conference on Private International Law

Harvey, J.A., Sanzaro, K.M.: P3P and IE 6: Raising More Privacy Issues Than They Resolve? GigaLaw.com in February 2002, online at http://www.gigalaw.com/articles/2002-all/harvey-2002-02-all.html (visited 10/09/2003)

He, Q., Sycara, K., Finin, T.: Personal Security Agent: KQML-based Public Key Infrastructure', Proceedings of the ACM Conference on Autonomous Agents (Agents'98), May, 1998.

Hendler, J.: Agents and the Semantic Web, *Intelligent Systems Journal, IEEE*, March/April 2001 (Vol. 16, No. 2)

Hermans, B., "Intelligent Software Agents On The Internet: An Inventory of Currently Offered Functionality in the Information Society and a Prediction of (Near) Future Developments", *First Monday Peer-Reviewed Journal On The Internet*, 1997. Online at <http://www.firstmonday.dk/issues/issue2_3/ch_123/index.html> (visited 28/03/2003)

Higgins, C.: Legal Issues of Electronic Commerce: Activity Policies, Intelligent Agents and Ethical Transactions - Conference Proceedings of SGML/XML Europe 1998

Hindelang, S.: No Remedy for Disappointed Trust – The Liability Regime for Certification Authorities Towards Third Parties Outwith the EC Directive in England and Germany Compared, Refereed article, *The Journal of Information, Law and Technology (JILT)*, 2002 (1) <http://elj.warwick.ac.uk/jilt/02-1/hindelang.html>. (visited 10.05.2003)

Hogben, G.: Technical analysis of problems with P3P v1.0 and possible solutions, Joint Research Centre Position paper for "Future of P3P" workshop, Virginia, USA, 12-13 November 2002.

Hustinx, P., Cavoukian, A.: Intelligent Software Agents: Turning a Privacy Threat into a Privacy Protector. Toronto, On; The Hague: Information and Privacy Commissioner / OntarioRegistratiekamer, The Hague, 1999

IETF: RFC 3041, *Privacy Extensions for Stateless Address Autoconfiguration in IPv6, http://www.ietf.org/rfc/rfc3041.txt* (visited 10/09/2003)

Initiative on Privacy Standardization in Europe: Final Report, CEN/ISSS, February 13, 2001,

Institut für Europäisches Wirtschafts- und Verbraucherrecht e.V - Study on the Feasibility of a General Legislative Framework on Fair Trading - November 2000.

International Working Group on Data Protection in Telecommunications, Common Position on Intelligent Software Agents, 25th Meeting of the Working Group, 29 April 1999 in Norway http://ig.cs.tu-berlin.de/~dsb/doc/int/iwgdpt/agent_en.htm (visited 10/09/2003)

Istituto per lo Studio della Vulnerabilità delle Società Tecnologicamente Evolute: Legal Issues of Evidence and Liability in the Provision of Trusted Services, *Final Report,* October 1998, report for the European Commission

Jalali, M., Hachez, G., Vasserot, C.: FILIGRANE (FlexIbLe IPR for Software AGent ReliANcE): A security framework for trading of mobile code in Internet.. In *Autonomous Agents 2000 Workshop: Agents in Industry*. June 2000

Jennings, N.R., Wooldridge, M.J.: Applications Of Intelligent Agents, in. Jennings and Wooldridge (Eds.), *Agent Technology Foundations, Applications, and Markets* , Springer-Verlag, 1998

Jennings, N.: Building Complex Software Systems, Comm. of the ACM, April 2001/Vol 44, No.4

Jennings, N. Faratin, P. Lomuscio, A.R., Parsons, S., Sierra, C., Wooldridge, M.: Automated Negotiation: Prospects, Methods and Challenges, Group Decision and Negotiation 10(2): 199-215; March 2001

Kagal L., Finin T. and Joshi, A.: Trust based security in Pervasive Computing Environments, Computer Magazine, December 2001

Kagal L., Finin T. and Peng Y.: A delegation model for distributed trust - *Proceedings of the IJCAI-01 Workshop on Autonomy Delegation and Control*, 2001

Karnow A.: Liability for Distributed Artificial Intelligences (1996) *11 Berkerley Technology Law Journal*

Karygiannis, T., Owens, L.: Wireless Network Security, Draft NIST Special Publication 800-48, December

Kenny S. and Borking J., 'The Value of Privacy Engineering', Refereed Article, *The Journal of Information, Law and Technology (JILT)*. 2002 (1) <http://elj.warwick.ac.uk/jilt/02-1/kenny.html>

Kerr I.R.: Providing for Autonomous Electronic Devices in the Uniform Electronic Commerce Act", in Annual Proceedings of the Uniform Law Conference of Canada (Ottawa, 2000)

Kerr. I.R.: Ensuring the Success of Contract Formation in Agent-Mediated Electronic Commerce" (2001) 1 Electronic Commerce Research Journal 183-202

Kini A., and Choobinch J.: Trust in electronic commerce: definitions and theoretical considerations, in: *Proceedings of the 31st Hawaii Int'l Conf. System Sciences*, Hawaii, 1998.

Koelman, K.J. (2001) The protection of technological measures vs. the copyright limitations", ALAI 2001 (Association Littéraire et Artistique Internationale) Congress "Adjuncts and Alternatives for Copyright", at <http://www.ivir.nl/publications/koelman/alaiNY.htm>. (visited 05/04/2003)

Kollingbaum M. and Norman J.: Supervised Interaction - creating a web of trust for contracting agents in electronic environments, *Proceedings of the first international joint conference on Autonomous agents and multiagent systems*: AAMAS 2002

Korba, L. and Kenny, S. (2002) Applying Digital Rights Management Systems to Privacy Rights Management, Computers & Security, 21 (7) (2002) pp. 648-664

Korff D.: Study on the protection of the rights and interests of legal persons with regard to the processing of personal data relating to such persons, for the CEC, October 1998, online at http://europa.eu.int/comm/internal_market/privacy/studies/legal_en.htm (visited 10/09/2003)

Koster, M.: Robots in the Web: Threat or Treat?" (available at http://info.webcrawler.com/mak/projects/robots/threat-or-treat.html) (visited 15.06.2003)

Krisch, Andreas: RFIDs in Euro banknotes, October 2003, online at http://www.unwatched.org/article4.html, (visited 10.11.2003)

Krogh, Ch: The Rights of Agents; in Wooldridge M, Muller J and Tambe M (Eds); *Intelligent Agents II -- Proceedings of the 1995 Workshop on Agent Theories, Architectures and Languages* (ATAL-95), Lecture Notes in Computer Science, Springer-Verlag, 1996.

Langheinrich, M.: Privacy by Design - Principles of Privacy-Aware Ubiquitous Systems - Proc. Ubicomp 2001, Springer-Verlag, at www.inf.ethz.ch

Leavens, G.T., Sitaraman, M.(eds): *Foundations of Component-Based Systems*, Cambridge University Press, 2000

Lerouge, J.F.: The use of electronic agents questioned under contractual law: suggested solutions on a European and American Level, *The John Marshall Journal of Computer & Information Law, Vol. XVIII No. 2, Winter 2000*

Lessig, L: Code and Other Laws of Cyberspace, Basic Books, New York, 1999

Likkannen, E.: *Going Digital: Meeting the E-Business Challenge for Europe in the New Economy* European Days of Commerce Conference Brussels, 4 December 2000

Lin, E.: *Prioritizing Privacy: A Constitutional Response To The Internet* 17:3 Berkeley Technology Law Journal (2003)

Lloyd, I.: Information Technology Law (3rd ed.), Butterworths, 2000

Lomuscio, A., Wooldridge, M., Jennings, N. R.: A classification scheme for negotiation in electronic commerce, in (F. Dignum and C. Sierra eds.) *Agent-mediated Electronic commerce (The European AgentLink Perspective)*, LNAI 1991, 2000

Loney, M.: Kodak snaps under customer pressure, ZDNet UK, 31.012002 online at <http://news.zdnet.co.uk/business/0,39020645,2103494,00.htm> (visited 05/04/2003)

Louveaux, S.: Privacy Issues, ECLIP Project Deliverable, October 1999, online at http://www.jura.uni-muenster.de/eclip/documentsII/sum/research.htm (last visited 20/02/2003)

Lu, S., Dong, M. and Fotouhi, F.: The Semantic Web: opportunities and challenges for next-generation Web applications, *Information Research* 7(4), (2002), available at: http://InformationR.net/ir/7-4/paper134..html (visited 09/12/2002)

Macdonald, E. and Poyton, D.: A particular problem for e-commerce: Section 3 of the Unfair Contract Terms Act 1977. - Web Journal of Current Legal Issues http://webjcli.ncl.ac.uk/2000/issue3/macdonald3.html

Maes, P., Guttman, R.H. and Moukas, A.G: Agents that Buy and Sell, *Communications of the ACM*, Vol. 42, No.3, 1999

Malone, T.W., Crowston, K., Lee, J., Pentland, B., Dellarocas, C., Wyner, G., Quimby, J., Osborn, C.S.., Bernstein, A., Herman, G., Klein, M., and O'Donnell, E. (1999) Tools for Inventing Organizations: Toward a Handbook of Organizational Processes. Management Science, 45(3): p. 425-443

Davara Rodríguez, M. A.: *Manual de Derecho informático*. Pamplona, Aranzadi, 3.ª edición, 2001

Mateo Hernández J.L. y Iglesias Portela, M.J.: Mcommerce Contract Law, Electronic Payment and Consumer Protection, ECLIP Research Report, online at http://www.eclip.org/documentsII/sum/research.htm (visited 10.07.2003)

McCullagh A et al, 'Signature Stripping: A Digital Dilemma', Refereed article, 2001 (1) *The Journal of Information, Law and Technology (JILT)*. <http://elj.warwick.ac.uk/jilt/01-1/mccullagh.html> (visited 10.05.2003)

Morciniec M., Salle M., Monahan B.: Towards Regulating Electronic communities with contracts, *Second Workshop on Norms and Institutions in Multiagent Systems*, June 2001.

Mulligan, D., Schwartz, A., Caoukian, A., Gurski, M.: P3P and Privacy: An Update for the Privacy Community, Center for Democracy and Technology, March, 2000, online at http://www.cdt.org/privacy/pet/p3pprivacy.shtml (visited 20/11/2002)

National Office for the Information Economy (NOIE- Australia): Final report of the NOIE review of the spam problem and how it can be countered, online at http://www.noie.gov.au/publications/NOIE/spam/final_report/index.htm (visited 20/08/2003).

Nwana, H. and Ndumu, D.: Perspective on Software Agents Research, *The Knowledge Engineering Review*, January 1999.

Nwana, H., Lee, L., Jennings, N.: Coordination in Software Agent Systems. *Applied Research and Technology*, BT Labs, 1996

Object Management Group, Agent Technology Green Paper, September 2000 at <http://www.obs.com/agent/index.html> (visited 29/11/2002)

Opinions and Working Papers of the Art 29 Data Protection Working Party online at http://europa.eu.int/comm/internal_market/privacy/workingroup/wp2003/wpdocs03_en.html

Øren, J.: Electronic Agents and the Notion Of Establishment, *International Journal of Law and Information Technology*, Volume 9, Issue 3, Autumn 2001

Organization for Economic Cooperation and Development: OECD Guidelines for Consumer Protection in the context of Electronic Commerce, OECD, 1999

Organization for Economic Cooperation and Development: ICCP, A Proposal for work on codes of conduct for electronic commerce, DSTI/ICCP/RD(2001)1 (7 March 2001) and Codes of Conduct: Data DSTI/ICCP(2001)8, (06 February 2001)

Organization for Economic Cooperation and Development. *OECD Guidelines on the Protection of Privacy and Transborder Flows of Personal Data*. 1980. Available from http://www.oecd.org//dsti/sti/it/secur/prod/PRIV-EN.HTM. (visited 10/09/2003)

Organization for Economic Cooperation and Development: Report On The OECD Forum Session On Privacy-Enhancing Technologies (PETs), DSTI/ICCP/REG(2001)6/FINAL, December 2001.

Parnas, D.L.: On the Criteria To Be Used in Decomposing Systems into Modules Communications of the ACM, Vol. 15, No. 12, December 1972 pp. 1053 - 1058

Pelino, E.: Autonomous Software Agents as Legal Persons, Alfebiite Project, on file,

Peterovic, O., Kittl, C., Teksten, R.D.: Developing Business Models for eBusiness, *International Conference on Electronic Commerce 2001*, Vienna, October 31 – November 4, 2001

Phillips, J. (Ed): Butterworths e-Commerce and Information Technology Law Handbook 1st edition, 2000

Pitt, V, Mamdani, A., Charlton, P.: The Open Agent Society and Its Enemies. In K. Stathis (ed.): *Local Nets; Proceedings International Workshop on Community-Based Interactive Systems*, Siena, pp89–104, 1999.

PricewaterhouseCoopers - Final Report Study on Consumer Law and the Information Society, 17 August 2000, at <http://europa.eu.int/comm/dgs/health_consumer/library/surveys/sur20_study_en.pdf> (visited 10.05.2003)

Priest, C.: Agent Mediated Electronic Commerce, Presentation at AgentLink AMEC SIG Meeting, Prague 2001

Reed, C.: What is a Signature?, 2000 (3) *The Journal of Information, Law and Technology (JILT)*. <http://elj.warwick.ac.uk/jilt/00-3/reed.html/> (visited 10.05.2003)

Reed, C.: Copyright in www pages, Computer Law and Security Report. Volume 13, Issue 3, 1997

Reidenberg, J.R., Schwartz, P.M..: Online Services and Data Protection Law: Regulatory Responses. Published by European Commission's Office of Official Publications, Euro-Op, (1998).

Ross, R.G.: The Business Rule Book. Classifying, Defining and Modeling Rules, 2nd edition, Boston, 1997.

Russell, S.J. and Norvig, P.: Artificial Intelligence: A modern approach, Prentice Hall, 1995

Sableman, M.: Link Law Revisited: Internet Linking Law at Five Years, Berkeley TLJ, Vol 16.3 (fall 2001)

Samuelson P and Reichman JH: Intellectual Property Rights in Data? 50 V and. L. Rev. 51 (1997)

Samuelson, P.: Digital Rights Management {and, or, vs.} the Law, Communications of the ACM April 2003/Vol. 46, No. 4

Samuelson P.: The Constitutional Law of Intellectual Property After Eldred v. Ashcroft, 50 J. Cop. Soc'y (forthcoming 2003) , online at http://www.sims.berkeley.edu/~pam/papers.html (visited 10.07.2003)

Samuelson, P.: Intellectual Property and Contract Law for the Information Age: Foreword to a Symposium, 87 Calif. L. Rev. 1 (1999)

Sapherstein, M.: Intelligent Agents and Copyright: Internet Technology Outpaces the Law . . . Again 1997 *B.C. Intell. Prop. & Tech. F.* 102801

Sartor, G.: Agents in Cyberlaw, Papers of the LEA 2002 Workshop on Law of Electronic Agents

Sartor, G.: Why agents comply with norms and why they should. In Conte, R. and Dellarocas, C., editors, Social order in MAS. Kluwer 2001

Schultz, T; Kaufmann-Kohler, G; Langer, D; and Bonnet, V: Online Dispute Resolution: The State of the Art and the Issues, E-Com Research Project of the University of Geneva, Geneva, 2001

Schwartz, E: RFID ripples through software industry, September 2003, online at http://www.infoworld.com/article/03/09/26/38NNrfid_1.html (visited 10/12/2003)

Sieber, U.: COMCRIME-Study on Legal Aspects of Computer-Related Crime in the Information Society, prepared for the European Commission, Version 1.0 of 1 January 1998.

Sierra, C., Dignum, F. (2001), Agent-Mediated Electronic Commerce: Scientific and Technological Roadmap, in F. Dignum and C. Sierra (Eds.) *Agent-mediated Electronic commerce (The European AgentLink Perspective)*, LNAI 1991, 2000

Sorkin, D.: Technical and Legal Approaches to Unsolicited Electronic Mail, 35 U.S.F. L. REV. 325 (2001)

Strowel,A. Triaille, J-P., Sirinelli, P.,: Le droit d'auteur, du logiciel au multimedia, Cahiers du Crid, No. 11, Bruylant, 1997

Study Group on a European Civil Code: EU Study on Property Law and Non-contractual Liability Law; at http://www.sgecc.net (visited 10.05.2003)

Stuurman, K. and Wijnands, H.: Software law: intelligent agents: a curse or a blessing? A survey of the legal aspects of the application of intelligent software systems, *Computer Law & Security Report Vol. 17 no. 2 2001.*

Subirana, B.: J & J Internet Book Shopping Robot. *IESE Publishing Case Series.* Case SI-91. 1996. Last Edition 10/97

Subirana, B. and Carvajal, P.: Transaction streams: theory and examples related to confidence in Internet-based electronic commerce. *Journal of Information Technology.* Vol. 15. No. 1, pp: 3 – 16. 2000

Subirana, B.: Transactions streams and value added: sustainable business models on the Internet. New managerial mindsets: organizational and strategy implementation, 1998. Edited by M.A.Hitt, J.E.Ricart and R.D.Nixon. John Wiley & Sons. Pp. 129-148

Subirana, B.: Transaction streams: sustainable business models on the Internet. Fifth European Research Workshop on Electronic Markets, Brunel University, Uxbridge, London, England, September 14-15, 1998

Subirana, B.: Zero Entry Barriers in Computationally Complex World: Transaction Streams and the Complexity of the Digital Trade of Intangible Goods, Journal of End User Computing, Special Issue on Digital trade of intangible goods: technologies, applications and business models

Swindells, C. et al: Legal Regulation of Electronic Commerce, 1998 (3) The Journal of Information, Law and Technology (JILT). <http://elj.warwick.ac.uk/jilt/98-3/swindells.html> (visited 10.05.2003)

Sycara, K.: Multi-agent infrastructure for Agent Interoperability in Open Computational Environments -Carnegie Mellon University 2002

Szabo, N.: Trusted Third Parties Are Security Holes, 2001, online at http://szabo.best.vwh.net/ttps.html (visited 10/09/2003)

Tang, T., Winoto, P. and Niu, X.L.: Who can I trust? Investigating Trust between users and agents in a mult-agent portfolio management system. AAA-I 2002 Workshop on Autonomy , Delegation and Control

The Information and Privacy Commissioner, Ontario: Privacy and Digital Rights Management (DRM): An Oxymoron, 2002. Online at <www.ipc.on.ca/english/pubpres/papers/drm.pdf> (visited 06/05/2003)

Thoumyre, P.L.: L'échange des consentements dans le commerce électronique, *Lex-Electronica, Vol. 5 no. 1,* University of Montréal, http://www.lex-electronica.org/articles/v5-1/thoumfr.htm, (visited 10.05.2003)

Timmers, P., 1999, Electronic Commerce: Strategies and models for business-to-business trading, John Wiley.

US Department of Commerce: Safe Harbor Privacy Principles 21.7.2000, online at http://europa.eu.int/comm/internal_market/en/media/dataprot/news/shprinciples.pdf (visited 10/09/2003)

UK Information Commissioner: CCTV Code of Practice, 2000, online at http://www.informationcommissioner.gov.uk (visited 12/09/2003)

van Haentjens, O.: Shopping Agents and Their legal Implications Regarding Austrian Law, Papers of the LEA 2002 Workshop on Law of Electronic Agents

Verhaar, P., van Blarkom G., Borking J., Kenny S.: Handbook Privacy and PET for ISAT's, PISA Project Report (draft), September 2002 online at http://www.pet-pisa.nl/pisa_org/pisa/index.html (visited 02/06/2003)

Wagemans, T,: An introduction to the labelling of websites, Programme for Comparative Media Law and Policy, Centre for Socio- Legal Studies, Oxford University for DG Information Society conference 'Quality labels for websites-alternative approaches to content rating' 27 February 2003, Luxembourg. Online at www.selfregulation.info/iapcoda/ qual_lab_bkgd-030225.pdf (visited 12/07/2003)

Walker, K.: Where Everybody Knows Your Name: A Pragmatic Look at the Costs of Privacy and the Benefits of Information Exchange, 2000 STAN. TECH. L. REV. 2, http://stlr.stanford.edu/STLR/Articles/00_STLR_2/index.htm (visited 10/09/2003)

Weitzenböck, E.M., Electronic Agents and Contract Performance: Good Faith and fair Dealing, Papers of the LEA 2002 Workshop on Law of Electronic Agents

Weitzenböck, E.M.: Electronic Agents and the formation of contracts, *International Journal of Law and Information Technology*, Volume 9, Issue 3, Autumn 2001

Weitzenböck, E.M.: Good Faith and Fair Dealing in the Context of Contract Formation by Electronic Agents, *Proceedings of the AISB 2002 Symposium on Intelligent Agents in Virtual Markets*, April 2002.

WIPO: Intellectual property on the Internet: a survey of Issues, WIPO/INT/02, December 2002.

WIPO: Primer on Electronic Commerce and Intellectual Property Issues, WIPO/OLOA/EC/PRIMER, May 2000.

Wireless Ethernet Compatibility Alliance: WEP Security Statement, September 7, 2001

Wong, C. and Sycara, K.: Adding security and trust to agent systems, *Proceedings of Autonomous Agents '99 Workshop on Deception, Fraud, and Trust in Agent Societies*, May, 1999

Wooldridge, M., Jennings, N.: Intelligent Agents: theory and Practice, *The Knowledge Engineering Review*, 10(2), 1995

Wooldridge, M., Jennings, N.R., Kinny, D.: The Gaia Methodology for Agent-Oriented Analysis and Design. In Int Journal of Autonomous Agents and Multi-Agent Systems, 3 (3), 2000.

Xu, Y. and Korba, L.: A Trust Model for Distributed E-Learning Service Control, World Conference on E-Learning in Corporate, Government, Healthcare and Higher Education (E-Learn 2002) Montreal, Canada, October 2002

Yee, G. and Korba, L.: The negotiation of privacy policies in distance education, National Research Council of Canada, Report NRC 44985, 2003

Yip, A. and Cunningham, J.: Some Issues on Agent Ownership, Papers of the LEA 2002 Workshop on Law of Electronic Agents

York, S., Tunkel D. (Hammond Suddards Edge): E-Commerce: A Guide to the Law of Electronic Business, Thrid edition, Butterworths, London, 2003.

Yoshida, Yunko: Euro bank notes to embed RFID chips by 2005, EETimes, 2001, online at http://www.eetimes.com/story/OEG20011219S0016 (visited 10/12/2003)

Zadrazil, M.: Rôle et travaux au sein de l'Union européenne et de l'Allemagne en matière de la protection des consommateurs en Commerce Électronique - *Lex Electronica, vol. 7, n°1, été 2001, <http://www.lex-electronica.org/articles/v7-1/zadrazil.htm>* (visited 10.05.2003)

Zambonelli, F., Jennings, N., Omicini, A., Wooldridge, M.: Agent-oriented Software Engineering for Internet Applications, *Coordination of Internet Agents: Models, Technologies and Applications*, Omicini et al. (Eds) Springer, March 2001

Zekos, G.: EDI: Electronic Techniques of EDI, Legal Problems and European Union Law, Web Journal of Current Legal Issues, [1999] 2 Web JCLI

Zhu, H., Madnick, S., Siegel M.: The Interplay of Web Aggregation and Regulations, Proceedings of the IASTED International Conference on Law and Technology (LAWTECH 2002), Cambridge, MA, November 6-8, 2002, SWP #4397-02, CISL #2002-17, <http://papers.ssrn.com/sol3/papers.cfm?abstract_id=365061> (visited 10.05.2003)

Zittrain, J,: Be Careful What You Ask For: Reconciling a Global Internet and Local Law, Harvard Law School Public Law Research Paper No. 60, Social Science Research Network Electronic Paper Collection at: http://ssrn.com/abstract_id=395300 (visited 10/09/2003)

Legislation and other formal instruments

EU legislation

All legislation is available online at

http://europa.eu.int/information_society/topics/ebusiness/ecommerce/8epolicy_elaw/law_eco mmerce/index_en.htm

Ecommerce

Directive 2000/31/EC of the European Parliament and of the Council of 8 June 2000 on certain legal aspects of information society services, in particular electronic commerce, in the Internal Market (OJ L178/1, 17.7.2000)

Directive 2001/115/EC of 20 December 2001 amending Directive 77/388/EEC with a view to simplifying, modernising and harmonising the conditions laid down for invoicing in respect of value added tax (OJ L 015, 17/01/2002 p. 0024 – 0028)

Directive 99/93/EC of the European Parliament and of the Council of 13 December 1999 on a Community framework for electronic signatures (OJ L 013 , 19/01/2000 p. 0012 – 0020)

Commission Recommendation of 30 July 1997 concerning transactions by electronic payment instruments and in particular the relationship between issuer and holder, 97/489/EC - 30 July 1997, (OJ L208, 02/08/1997)

Council Regulation (EC) No 44/2001 of 22 December 2000 on jurisdiction and the recognition and enforcement of judgments in civil and commercial matters (OJ L 12, 16.01.2001).

Commission Recommendation 2001/310/EC on Principles for out-of-court bodies involved in the consensual resolution of consumer disputes, 4 April 2001 (OJ L 109/56, 19.04.2001)

Intellectual Property Rights

Directive 91/250/EEC of 14 May 1991 on the Legal Protection of Computer Programs (OJ L 122 of 17/05/91)

Directive 93/98/EEC of 29 October 1993 Harmonising the Term of Protection of Copyright and Certain Related Rights (OJ L 290 of 24/11/93)

Directive 96/9/EC of 11 March 1996 of the European Parliament and of the Council on the Legal Protection of Databases (OJ L 077 of 27/03/96 (396L0009))

Directive 2001/29/EC of the European Parliament and of the Council of 22 May 2001 on the harmonisation of certain aspects of copyright and related rights in the information society, (OJ L 167 22.06.2001 p.10)

Consumer Protection

Directive 76/768/EEC of 27.7.1976 on the approximation of laws of the Member States relating to cosmetic products (OJ L262 of 27.9.1976, p.169), amended by Directive 79/661/EEC (OJ L192 of 31.7.1979, p.35), Directive 82/368/EEC (OJ L167 of 15.6.1982, p.1), Directive 83/574/EEC (OJ L332 of 28.11.1983, p.38), Directive 88/667/EEC (OJ L382 of 31.12.1988, 46), Directive 89/679/EEC (OJ L398 of 30.12.89, p.25), Directive 93/35/EEC (OJ L151 of 23.6.1993 p.32) and Directive 97/18/EC (OJ L114 of 1.5.1997).

Directive 84/450/EC of 10 September 1984 relating to the approximations of laws, regulations and administrative provisions of the Member States concerning misleading advertisements (OJ L250, 19.09.1984)

Directive 85/374/EEC Council Directive of 25 July 1985 on the approximation of the laws, regulations and administrative provisions of the Member States concerning liability for defective products (OJ L 210 , 07/08/1985 p. 0029).

Directive 87/102/EEC of 22.12.1986 for the approximation of the laws, regulations and administrative provisions of the Member States concerning consumer credit (OJ L 42 of 12.02.1987, pp. 48-53). Amended by: Council Directive 90/88/EEC of 22.02.1990 (OJ L 61 of 10.03.1990, pp. 14-18) Council and European Parliament Directive 98/7/EC of 16.02.1998 (OJ L 101 of 01.04.1998, pp. 17-23)

Directive 92/28/EEC of 31 March 1992 on the advertising of medicinal products for human use (OJ L113, 30.04.1992)

Directive 93/13/EEC of 5 April 1993 on unfair terms in consumer contracts (OJ L95 21.04.1993, pp. 29-34)

Directive 95/58/EC European Parliament and of the Council of 29.11.95 amending 79/581/EEC on consumer protection in the indication of prices of foodstuffs and Directive 88/314/EEC on consumer protection of prices of non-food products (JO L 299 du 12.12.1995,pp.11-12)

Directive 96/74/EC of the European Parliament and of the Council of 16.12.1996 on textile names (OJ L32 of 3.2.1997, p.38), amended by Directive 97/37/EC (OJ L169 of 27.6.1997, p.74)

Directive 97/55/EC of European Parliament and of the Council of 6 October 1997 amending Directive 84/450/EEC concerning misleading advertising so as to include comparative advertising (OJ L290 23.10.1997)

Directive 97/7/EC of the European Parliament and of the Council, of 20.05.97, on the protection of consumers in respect of distance contracts. (JO L 144 of 04.06.1997, pp. 19-28)

Directive 98/27/EC of the European Parliament and of the Council of 19.05.1998 on injunctions for the protection of consumers' interests. (OJ L 166 of 11.06.1998, pp. 51-56)

Directive 1999/44/EC of the European Parliament and of the Council of 25 May 1999 on certain aspects of the sale of consumer goods and associated guarantees (OJ L 171 of 07.07.1999, pp. 12-15)

Recommendation on on the principles for out-of-court bodies involved in the consensual resolution of consumer disputes (2001/310/EC), 4 April 2001– OJ L 109/56

Directive 2002/65/EC of the European Parliament and of the Council concerning the distance marketing of consumer financial services and amending Council Directives 90/619/EEC, 97/7/EC and 98/27/EC (17 June 2002) (OJ L 271/16, 09.11.2002)

Proposal for a Regulation of the European Parliament and the Council concerning sales promotions in the Internal Market, COM(2001) 546 final, (2/10/2001)

Proposal for a Directive of the European Parliament and of the Council concerning unfair business-to-consumer commercial practices in the Internal Market and amending directives 84/450/EEC, 97/7/EC and 98/27/EC (the Unfair Commercial Practices Directive), 18 June 2003, (2003) 356 final

Privacy

Directive 95/46/EC of the European Parliament and of the Council of 24.10.1995 on the protection of individuals with regard to the processing of personal data and on the free movement of such data (O.J. L 281, 23.11.1995)

Directive 97/66/EC on the processing of personal data and the protection of privacy in the telecommunications sector (OJ L 024 , 30/01/1998 p. 0001 – 0008)

Directive 2002/58/EC on the processing of personal data and the protection of privacy in the electronic communications sector (OJ L 201 of 31.07.2002, p37-47)

Decision 520/2000/EC recognising the Safe Harbour international privacy principles issued by the US Department of Commerce, 26.7.2000. (OJ 215 of 28.08.2000, p 7)

Certain National laws

Australia: The Australian Copyright Amendment (Digital Agenda) Act 2000

France: Code de la Propriété Intellectuelle (1992)

Spain: Ley 34/2002 de de 11 de julio, de Servicios de la Sociedad de la Información y de Comercio Electrónico

Spain: Ley Orgánica 5/1992, de 29 de octubre, de Regulación del Tratamiento Automatizado de Datos de carácter personal

Spain: REAL DECRETO 994/1999, de 11 de junio, por el que se aprueba el Reglamento de medidas de seguridad de los ficheros automatizados que contengan datos de carácter personal

Spain: Texto Refundido de la Ley de la Propiedad Intelectual, Real Decreto Legislativo 1/1996, de 12 de abril.

UK: Data Protection Act 1998

UK: The Electronic Commerce (EC Directive) Regulations 2002 (UK)

UK: Copyright, Designs and Patents Act, 1988

USA: Digital Millennium Copyright Act, H.R.2281, October 28, 1998

USA: The Uniform Electronic Transactions Act (1999) (UETA, USA), online at http://www.law.upenn.edu/bll/ulc/fnact99/1990s/ueta99.html

USA: Uniform Electronic Commerce Act 1999, (UECA - Canada) online at http://www.law.ualberta.ca/alri/ulc/current/euecafin.html

Other documents

Berne Convention for the Protection of Literary and Artistic Works, Paris Act of July 24, 1971, as amended on September 28, 1979

UNCITRAL Model Law on Ecommerce - UN General Assembly Resolution 51/162 of 16 December 1996, UN publication V.97-22269-May 1997- 5,100,

UNCITRAL Model Law on Digital Signatures, UN General Assembly Resolution 56/80 of 12 December 2001, online at http://www.uncitral.org/english/texts/electcom/ml-elecsig-e.pdf

UNCITRAL: Electronic contracting: provisions for draft convention on electronic contracting - A/CN.9/WG.IV/WP.95 –

http://www.uncitral.org/english/workinggroups/wg_ec/index.htm

WIPO Copyright Treaty, Geneva, December 20, 1996

WIPO Performances and Phonograms Treaty, Geneva, December 20, 1996

310

Case citations

Europe

Ajoderse.com, DP 827/02-C (Spain)

Danske Dagblades Forening v. Newsbooster.com, Copenhagen Bailiff's Court, July 5, 2002, *unreported, (Denmark)*

PCM v. Eureka Internetdiensten, (Kranten.com) August 22, 2000, Mediaforum 2000 *(Holland)*

Pop-up LG Duesseldorf, March 26, 2003, O 186/02 *(Germany)*

Road Tech Computer Systems v. Mandata (Management & Data Services) Limited, [2000] ETMR 970 *(England)*

Shetland Times Ltd. v. Wills, 1997 S.L.T. 669, (Sess. Cas. 1996) or *F. S. R. 604* (OH) *(Scotland)*

St Albans City and District Council v. International Computers Limited [1997] FSR 251 *(England)*

Stepstone v. OFir, LG Köln, February 28, 2001 – 28 O 692/00 (Germany)

UEJF and LICRA v. Yahoo! Inc., November 20, 2000, TGI de Paris, référé, *(France)*

Verlagsruppe Holtzbrinck v. Paperboy.de, July 17, 2003, Case No. I ZR 259/00, unpublished to date *(Germany)*.

USA:

A&M Records, Inc. v. Napster, Inc., 239 F.3d 1004 (9th Cir. 2001).

Barcelona.com Inc. v. Excelentísimo Ayuntamiento de Barcelona, E.D. Va., No. 00-1412-A, 2/22/02

Bruce G. Forrest v. Verizon Communications Inc., No. 01-CV-1101. (Washington DC)

Comb v. PayPal Inc., N.D. Cal., No. C-02-1227 JF (PVT), 8/30/02

DeJohn v. .TV Corporation International, *ND Ill., No. 02 C 4497, 1/16/03*

E-bay v. Bidder's Edge, 100 F. Supp. 2d 1058 (N.D. Cal. 2000)

Kanitz v. Rogers Cable Inc., [2002] O.J. No. 665

Kelly v. Arriba Soft Corp., 77 F. Supp. 2d 1116 (C.D. Cal. 1999).

M-G-M v. Grokster, CV 01-8541, April 2003

Playboy Enterprises Inc. v. Welles, 7 F. Supp. 2d 1098 (S.D. Cal.) (preliminary injunction), aff'd, 162 F.3d 1169 (9th Cir. 1998), and 78 F. Supp. 2d 1066 (S.D. Cal. 1999) (summary judgment)

Specht v. Netscape Communications Corp., 150 F. Supp. 2d 585 (S.D.N.Y., July 5, 2001), aff'd. 306 F.3d 17 (2nd Cir. 2002)

Ticketmaster Corp.'s Complaint, Ticketmaster Corp. v. Microsoft Corp., No. 97-3055 DDP (C.D. Cal., filed Apr. 28, 1997),

Ticketmaster Corp. v. Tickets.com, Inc. 2000 US Dist. Lexis 4553 (CD Ca., March 27, 2000), 2000 U.S. Dist. Lexis 12987 (C.D. Ca., August 10, 2000), U.S. Dist. LEXIS 6483 (C.D. Ca., March 7, 2003)

Washington Post Co. v. Total News, Inc. 97 Civ. 1190 (SDNY Feb 20, 1997)

Other jurisdictions

Gutnick v Dow Jones & Co Inc., [2001] VSC 305 (28 August 2001) (Australia)

INDEX

Lightning Source UK Ltd.
Milton Keynes UK
178587UK00007B/64/P

9 780387 234144